Encounters with the Self

Fourth Edition

DON HAMACHEK

Michigan State University

Harcourt Brace Jovanovich College Publishers

Fort Worth   Philadelphia   San Diego   New York   Orlando   Austin   San Antonio
Toronto   Montreal   London   Sydney   Tokyo

Publisher	Ted Buchholz
Acquisitions Editor	Eve Howard
Project Editor	Angela Williams
Production Manager	Kathleen Ferguson
Manager of Art and Design	Guy Jacobs
Text Designer	Guy Jacobs
Cover Designer	Pat Sloan

Library of Congress Cataloging-in-Publication Data
Hamachek, Don E.
   Encounters with the self / Don Hamachek. — 4th ed.
     p.   cm.
   Includes bibliographical references and indexes.
   ISBN 0-03-055744-5
   1. Self-perception. 2. Self. I. Title.
BF697.5.S43H36   1991   91-12734
155.2—dc20   CIP

Cover image: CLOWN by Paul Klee (1929). Oil on canvas, 26 3/8 × 19 5/8 inches. Private collection, St. Louis. Copyright © 1992 by COSMOPRESS, Geneva. Photograph by Bob Kolbrener, St. Louis.

Address for editorial correspondence: 301 Commerce Street, Suite 3700, Fort Worth, TX 76102.

Address for orders: 6277 Sea Harbor Drive, Orlando, Florida 32887.
1-800-782-4479, or 1-800-433-0001 (in Florida)

PRINTED IN THE UNITED STATES OF AMERICA

6 7 8 9 0 1 2 3 4 5 016 13 12 11 10 9 8 7 6 5 4

Just go to the mirror and look at yourself
And see what the reflection has to say;
For it isn't your father, or mother, or spouse, or friend
Whose judgment you must pass.
The person whose verdict counts most in your life
Is the one staring back from the glass.

Author unknown

PREFACE

This is a book about the self, self-concept, and self-esteem. It is a volume directed to how the self, the central core of our identity, grows, changes, and is expressed in behavior. It focuses on that very private picture each of us has that reflects our feelings about who we think we are and why and how those feelings have evolved the way they have. As in the previous three editions, there are discussions related to various approaches to understanding oneself, a consideration of some of the perceptual processes and theoretical perspectives associated with a self-concept point of view, a look at the dynamics of self-consistency, and an overview of how and why self-concept is an important aspect of mental health. In addition, there is an examination of how self-concept is linked to physical growth, appearance, and developmental changes and how it is related to parent-child relationships, family dynamics, and genetic possibilities. Further, there is an overview of how self-concept both affects and is affected by academic achievement and teachers' expectations and of the implications for teaching practices. Last, there are some reflections related to developing and maintaining healthy self-esteem and a positive self-concept.

The content I have chosen to study and include in this volume reflects intra- and interpersonal themes about which I have always been curious. My own search for an identity that fit, for some modicum of self-understanding that would enable me to know the deeper person within; my curiosities about the impact that my own family dynamics had on my behavior and self-attitudes as I grew up; my questions about the possible relationships and interactions between my academic performance and my self-concept of ability during my formal schooling—indeed, my need to have some kind of unifying theme or framework that could help me develop a deeper understanding of my own and others' behavior—these questions and many related ones have helped to make the writing of this book feel like an adventure filled with exciting new discoveries.

The scope of this volume is broad, including as it does ideas about understanding one's self, self-consistency, self-concept as related to developmental changes, child-rearing practices, school performance, and so on; but all the ideas fit under the same theoretical umbrella, which, for me at least, provides a sort of unifying framework and "tying together" that helps to give sense and meaning to the many diverse life happenings that we humans experience as we move along a developmental continuum. This theoretical undercurrent evolves from a frame of reference that is basically psychodynamic, in the sense that human behavior is seen as an interactive process that involves the person, perceptions, and environment, each component interacting with the others in a self-perpetuating cycle of action and reaction. In a less abstract way, it is a point of view that looks at human behavior not only through the eyes of an outsider, but also through the eyes of the person doing the behaving. It is a psychology searching to understand not only *what* is going on inside us, but *why* it is happening in the first place. In an everyday sense, it is the psychology that concerned friends use when they wonder why we "seem so unhappy today;" in a clinical sense, it is what mental health workers use when probing for the deeper implications behind what personal experiences mean to those they counsel.

The underlying philosophy of this book resides on a simple assumption, namely, the greater our knowledge and awareness of who we are and of how we became the person we are, the more choices we have in our lives. Choosing our life course is more possible, I think, when self-knowledge is expanded to the point where we are able to see that we can be the master of our ship and not merely its mechanic. With this view from the helm in mind, I have attempted to write in a descriptive and explanatory manner as opposed to a style that might be viewed as prescriptive and theoretical. More specifically, I have made a deliberate effort to present the content of this book in a manner that could be understood by readers who come to it from a variety of backgrounds. (Whether or not that has been accomplished is better left for you to decide.) Thus, a goal I had in mind as I organized and wrote this book was to reach a diverse audience with diverse interests, who, among other things, are curious about how personality develops, how self-concept forms as an expression of personality, and how the blend of these two components contribute to the form and substance of their personal lives and interpersonal relationships.

This book has an extensive research base drawn from both empirical and clinical sources. Many exciting advances in thinking and research have occurred since the first edition of this volume appeared, and I have made every effort with each new edition to revise this book to reflect current knowledge. From time to time, I found it helpful to illustrate certain ideas with examples drawn from my own and others' professional experiences, which I hope you will find clarifying and interesting.

It is my hope that this volume can be a useful source of information for students and practicing professionals in teaching, counseling, school psychology, social work, and educational psychology who are interested in understanding humans both as they see themselves and as they react to forces outside themselves. If you have questions about who you are and how you arrived at being the sort of person you are at this point in time, I hope this book will be helpful in answering those questions and in stimulating you to read more widely and deeply in order to develop insights into yourself and others.

ACKNOWLEDGMENTS

Many people contribute to the making of a book, and I feel extremely fortunate to have had the capable talents of Holt, Rinehart and Winston editors John Haley, Eve Howard, Shelia Odak, and Angela Williams handle the production aspects of this volume. And I would like to extend a sincere thank you to Professors Gerald Adams (Utah State University), Katharine E. Cummings (North Dakota State University), Glenance Edwall (Baylor University), Robert Leonetti (Trinidad State Junior College), James R. Nevitt (Mid-Plains Community College), Frank Vitro (Texas Woman's University), and John M. Watkins (Ferris State University) for their thoughtful, critical reviews and feedback, which I found invaluable as I worked on this fourth edition. And, finally, a big thank you to Lisa Payne and Joni Smith, whose secretarial skills helped me in more ways than I can count.

D.H.

BRIEF CONTENTS

TABLE OF CONTENTS

Chapter 1

Toward Understanding Oneself

PROLOGUE

Can there be anything more complex and paradoxical than human behavior? Think about it. We tend to protest loudly about those matters in life that offend us but remain silent and unthankful about those things that please us. It is sometimes easier for us to act in a warm and tolerant manner to a person we don't like than to behave in a loving and forgiving way to a person we care for deeply. We are quick to spot and even criticize minor flaws in someone else but remain relatively myopic to possible chinks in our own psychic armor. We can easily enough detail what we are against but tend to have considerably more difficulty specifying what we are for. We can have a clear realization that certain behaviors are self-defeating and/or self-destructive, but we go ahead and do them anyway. We can see where we are, but we're not always sure how we got there. We can see clearly to where it is that we want to go but yet invent endless excuses for not getting started. We find it easier to explain what we do than to characterize who we are.

Given the deep intricacies of human nature, it is not difficult to understand why the ancient injunction of Socrates to "know thyself" has met with results that are a mixed bag of satisfactions and disappointments. Actually, "knowing" ourselves totally and completely is probably not possible, nor for that matter is it even necessary. But knowing ourselves better is possible. (Whether it is necessary is probably best left for you to decide.) In the final analysis, each of us is inescapably confronted with the problem of meaning—with the question of what life is all about and how to make it as happy and worthwhile as possible in the time that we have. To find that meaning, each of us is faced with at least four questions that must be addressed and answered before we can give our lives a sense of direction and purpose.

1

Who am I?

Where am I going?

Where do I want to go?

What route shall I take?

These are important questions, concerned as they are with personal identity, real and imagined strengths and weaknesses, personal goals, and life-style preferences. They are, in a larger sense, existential questions, reflecting, as they do, our opportunities for personal choice and for exercising our freedom and responsibility; these questions also point to the infinite number of options we have for living productive, useful lives and for giving meaning to our existence. They are questions that reflect this personal inner etching that we call our sense of self.

THE SELF: AN IDEA WITH PHILOSOPHICAL ROOTS

Interest in the self, what it is and how it develops, goes back deep in time. As a theoretical concept, the self has ebbed and flowed with the currents of philosophical pondering since the seventeenth century when the French mathematician and philosopher René Descartes first discussed the "cognition," or self, as a thinking substance. With Descartes leading the way, the concept of the self was subjected to the vigorous philosophical remunerations of such thinkers as Leibnitz, Locke, Hume, and Berkeley. As psychology evolved from philosophy as a distinct discipline, the self, as a related idea, evolved along with it. However, as the tides of behaviorism swept the shores of psychological thinking during the first 40 years of the twentieth century, the self almost disappeared as an idea of any stature. Because the self was not something that could be easily investigated under rigidly controlled laboratory conditions—a format favored by behaviorism—the self as a subject for study was not considered appropriate for scientific pursuit. Nonetheless, it was kept from being swept entirely out to sea during the early part of this century by Charles H. Cooley (1902), John Dewey (1916), William James (1890), and George Herman Mead (1934). Since the 1940s, the concept of self has been resuscitated fully back to life and has exhibited remarkable vitality ever since. For example, Allport (1955) noted:

> . . . the tide has turned. Perhaps without being fully aware of the historical situation, many psychologists have commenced to embrace what two decades ago would have been considered a heresy. They have re-introduced self and ego unashamedly and, as if to make up for lost time, have employed ancillary concepts such as self-image, self-actualization, self-affirmation, phenomenal ego, ego-involvement, ego-striving, and many other hyphenated elaborations which to experimental positivism still have a slight flavor of scientific obscenity. (pp. 104–105)

Although William James had written a brilliant, insightful chapter on "The Consciousness of Self" in his book *Principles of Psychology,* published in 1890, 60 years passed before systematic empirical research was used to investigate questions and problems related to the self. In just the two decades after Raimy's (1948) initial research, which was related to self-references in counseling interviews, almost 2,000 studies were conducted on self and self-concept problems (Gergen, 1971).

An enormous amount of research and writing related to the self and its related components—self-concept, self-image, self-actualization, and the like—has been generated in the past 40 years or so, and such work continues to this day. This work has provided the intellectual nutrients that stimulated growth of the self from a purely metaphysical idea in its infancy to its current status as a legitimate psychological construct. In terms of where the self is on a growth continuum, it can probably best be described as being in its adolescence. Born from philosophy's womb, nurtured by psychophilosophical thinking, directed by psychological theory, and disciplined by empirical research, it is now going through the inevitable, lengthy period of refinement and alteration so characteristic of people and ideas as they progress through their own particular "adolescence" toward greater maturity and acceptance—which leads us to an important question.

WHAT IS THE SELF?

Anthropologists and philosophers have long sought to delineate those characteristics that make us humans clearly distinguishable from all other animal forms. Some theorists have pointed to our superior use of tools; others have pointed to our advanced form of language. But probably the most basic distinction between us and other creatures is our unique capacity for self-consciousness. Although other animal forms may have consciousness, *self*-consciousness requires a far more advanced and complex level of functioning. Not only can we think, but we can think about our thinking. Not only can we feel, but we can have feelings about our feelings. How many times have you heard yourself say, after a bit of reflection, "How could I have thought that way?" or "How could I have felt that way?"

As the concept of self has evolved in psychological research literature, it has come to have two distinct meanings. One meaning grows from what has been called the *self-as-object* definition, referring to our capacity to stand outside of ourselves and evaluate our attitudes, feelings, and behavior from a more or less detached point of view. Statements we may make like "I'm the sort of person who is . . ." or "I would describe myself as . . ." reflect that capacity. The other meaning stems from what is referred to as the *self-as-process* definition. In this case, the self is a doer, in the sense that it includes an active group of processes such as thinking, remembering, perceiving, performing, and so forth. Statements such as "I am going to study hard for the exam tomorrow" or "I recall thinking that way once, but my ideas have since changed" reflect the idea that the self is not just what we have and what we are, as suggested in the self-as-object definition, but also what we *do*. Indeed, a very strong case can be made (and will be made, in the pages ahead) for the idea that what we do is enormously instrumental in determining for ourselves and others who we are.

What, then, is the self? Broadly defined, the self is that component of our consciousness that gives us a sense of personal existence. Defined more specifically, the self is the sum total of all we refer to as "mine." As a central aspect of our existence, the self houses our total subjective and intrapersonal world; it is the distinctive center of our experience and significance. It includes, among other things, our basic system beliefs, attitudes, and values. The self is what constitutes our inner world as distinguished from the outer world consisting of all other people and things.

The self is not just a physical entity surrounded by skin; it is a psychological construct in which the concept of *me* and *my* are blended into a unique identity.

HOW DOES THE SELF GROW AND DEVELOP?

You and I have become the persons we are as the self that characterizes each of us evolved slowly from an undifferentiated five to seven pound (in most cases) mass of vulnerable potential at birth to our current highly differentiated and tightly defended sense of personal identity. The evolution of that self continues throughout life, although, for most of us, it proceeds more slowly and with fewer dramatic changes. It is a long and complex process that involves an ongoing interaction between our genetic potentials and environmental experiences.

Figure 1-1 is a schematic overview of the self's development. Basically, it is an effort to reduce an enormously long and complex process to its simplest and most basic components. I have taken some of the most frequently mentioned and commonly discussed aspects of the self and endeavored to show how they may relate and interconnect along a developmental continuum.

As depicted in Figure 1-1, the beginnings of the self occur with the aid of four primary input channels: auditory cues, physical sensations, body image cues, and personal memories. Each of these experiential channels is an important source of information to young children about how they are faring in their personal and interpersonal worlds. Achieving a sense of self is an accomplishment that develops by degrees and is shaped over time by more and complex understandings. There are indications from contemporary research that infants' personality development and educational potential begin at a tender age. For example, after 17 years of research on the behavior and development of infants between birth and three years of age, White (1975) concluded, ". . . our studies show that the period that starts at eight months and ends at three years is a period of primary importance in the development of a human being" (p. 4).

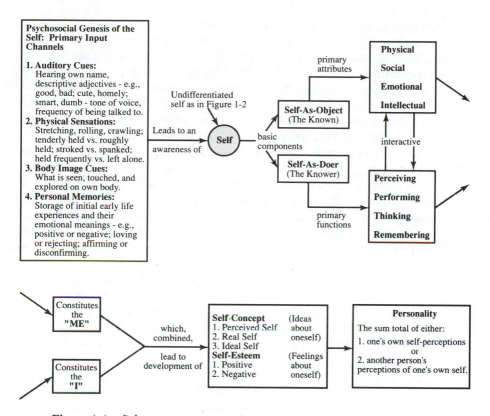

Figure 1-1 *Schematic overview of the self's development.*

Adapted from: Don Hamachek, "The Self's Development and Ego Growth: Conceptual Analysis and Implications for Counselors," *Journal of Counseling and Development,* 1985, *64:* 136–142. Used by permission.

The Beginnings of Self-Awareness

Since we cannot directly assess the nature of children's growing awareness, we must appraise the stages through which children become aware of themselves largely through an inferential process. The first stage of children's self-awareness occurs when they begin to learn that they are separate from others, that the caregiver's body is not part of their own. This is what Lewis and Brooks-Gunn (1979) have called the *existential self,* the fundamental sense of being separate from others. Until this happens, we can't really talk about a child having a self-concept at all.

The awareness of this separation appears to develop during the first eight to 12 months, during which time the understanding of *object permanence* occurs. Basically, infants learn that objects continue to exist even when the infants can't see or feel them any longer. This is an enormous cognitive step toward developing a sense of self. Just as infants come to see the mother as a "continuing event," a "permanent object" who continues to exist even when not seen, so, too, do they gradually develop an awareness of themselves as existing continuously in time and space. This is followed by infants learning that individual objects remain the same from one encounter to another. When the mother goes away and then comes back again, it is the same mother both times; the rattle is the same, the crib is the same object each time the infant is placed in it, and so on. This understanding is called *object identity.*

Together, object permanence (things continue to exist when not seen) and object identity (things continue to exist in the same form when not seen) are prerequisite understandings to developing a sense of self—the existential self mentioned earlier. For example, think of several of the most important people in your life. Now try to imagine them not existing when you're apart from them. Imagine them appearing as different people the next time you see them. Disconcerting, isn't it? The point is, knowing that the important people in our lives do exist even when we're not with them, and that they very likely will be the same as we remember them the next time we meet, frees us to be our own separate, individual selves because there is a certain reassurance and reduction in anxiety when we know that the people we love (and who, we presume, love us) are alive and well and the same as ever. In a much more complex and unconscious way, a somewhat similar process may constitute the undercurrent of an infant's newly developing sense of self.

The next step in the beginning of self-awareness is the development of the *categorical self,* another term of Lewis and Brooks-Gunn. This happens as young children come to define themselves in terms of a set of categories, such as gender, age, size, color, and specific skills or knowledge. One sign that children have achieved this understanding is that they begin to recognize themselves and to use their own names. Research has shown that by the time children are between 18 and 24 months of age, they recognize themselves in mirrors, name themselves in pictures, and look more at their own pictures than at the pictures of other children (Gallup, 1979; Dickie and Strader, 1974). In addition, they are able to categorize themselves and others in terms of correct gender identity by about two and one-half years of age (Thompson, 1975), and between three and five years of age, they are able to make distinctions on the basis of age (Edwards and Lewis, 1979); for example, they are able to sort photographs into groups such as "little children," "big children," "parents," and "grandparents." They are also able to identify themselves as "little children" or "big children."

By the time children are about five years of age, the basic foundation has been laid for how the self will grow and for the way that self-concept will develop. The vast array of categories into which children place themselves (or are placed into by others)—sex, height, weight, age, intelligence, athletic ability, and so on—are merely descriptive labels. It is important to remember that each label carries with it a certain positive and negative charge, which is what affects self-concept for better or worse. For example, it is one thing to be called a "girl" (if that is what one is), but it is quite another to be labeled "*just* a girl" or a "dumb girl." It is one thing for a five-year-old child to know that he weighs 70 pounds but quite another to know that others see him as a "fat kid."

As children move through their school years, learning more and more about themselves and the world they live in, their self-concept grows increasingly more complex. This was nicely shown in a study by Montemayor and Eisen (1977), who asked a group of fourth-, sixth-, eighth-, tenth-, and 12th-grade students each to write 20 different answers to the question "Who am I?" Younger children's answers focused on externally visible categories, such as their age, size, home address, or favorite activities. Older children, on the other hand, focused more on internal matters, such as their beliefs, relationships to people, and their personality characteristics. You can understand these sorts of differences in the following two examples. Notice the differences in complexity and level of sophistication between them.

Nine-year-old, fourth-grade boy:

My name is Bruce C. I have brown eyes. I have brown hair. I have seven people in my family. I have great! eye site. I have lots! of friends. I live on 1923 Pinecrest Dr. I'm going on 10 in September. I'm a boy. I have an uncle that is almost 7 feet tall. My school is Pinecrest. My teacher is Mrs. V. I play Hockey! I'm almost the smartest boy in the class. I LOVE! food. I love fresh air. I LOVE school.

Seventeen-year-old, 12th-grade girl:

I am a human being. I am a girl. I am an individual. I don't know who I am. I am a Pisces. I am a moody person. I am an indecisive person. I am an ambitious person. I am a very curious person. I am not an individual. I am a loner. I am an American (God help me). I am a Democrat. I am a liberal person. I am a radical. I am a conservative. I am a pseudo-liberal. I am an atheist. I am not a classifiable person (i.e., I don't want to be).

As personal experience widens and intellectual functioning deepens, the self differentiates further; children gain in their abilities to understand their world more fully (to be the "knower" or "doer") and to see themselves as objects in the outside world (to be the "known"). As seen in Figure 1-1, the self-as-object involves attributes that are physical (how one looks), social (how one relates), emotional (how one feels), and intellectual (how one thinks). These attributes interact with that aspect of the self that comes to know through its perceiving, performing, thinking, and remembering functions. The component of the self that is the knower constitutes the "I" or the "agent of experience," and that dimension of the self that is the known constitutes the "me" or "the content of experience."

As delineated further in Figure 1-1, the interactive combination of these attributes and functions leads to the development of two core ingredients of the self, namely, self-concept (ideas about oneself) and self-esteem (feelings and evaluations about oneself). Self-concept can be more specifically differentiated into the perceived self (the way people see themselves) and into what can be referred to as the "real" self (the way a person really is, as measured more objectively through tests or clinical assessments) and the "ideal" self (the way a person would like to be). Out of all of this emerges what might be called personality, which, depending on who is describing it, can be either the sum total of (1) one's own internal self-perceptions, or (2) of another person's external perceptions of that individual.

THE SELF'S DEVELOPMENT WITHIN THE FRAMEWORK OF PSYCHOSOCIAL STAGES

According to Erikson (1963, 1980, 1982), each individual passes through a succession of eight psychosocial stages, beginning at birth and ending in the retirement years. Five of those stages are experienced during the first 20 years of life and the remaining three during adulthood. The eight psychosocial stages and the approximate time span usually associated with each are as follows:

1. Trust versus mistrust (birth to 18 months)
2. Autonomy versus shame and doubt (18 months to 3 years)
3. Initiative versus guilt (3 to 6 years)
4. Industry versus inferiority (6 to 12 years)
5. Identity versus identity confusion (12 to 20 years)
6. Intimacy versus isolation (20 to 35 years)
7. Generativity versus self-absorption (35 years to retirement)
8. Integrity versus despair (retirement years)

Erikson's first five stages are emphasized in this chapter because (1) each is critical as a building block for subsequent stages (Erikson gave more painstaking attention to Stages 1 and 5 than to the other six stages combined) and (2) there are considerable data (Brim and Kagan, 1980; Mischel, 1984) suggesting that development continues in the direction it starts; hence, understanding the early years is important. Thus, our focus will be on the first five stages so as to identify ego qualities that seem most prominently associated with the self's development during those times.

In Erikson's view, each stage represents a "psychosocial crisis" or turning point when both potential and vulnerability are greatly increased, a time when things may go either well or not well depending on one's life experiences. In all of us, there is probably a certain ratio between the positive and negative qualities associated with each stage. A more positive ratio will help us in coping with later crises.

The idea of acquiring a healthy ratio between positive and negative ego qualities is an important one; sometimes, however, the focus is almost entirely on the positive outcomes of each psychosocial stage, which misses the point. According to Erikson (Evans, 1981):

> When these stages are quoted, people often take away mistrust and doubt and shame and all of these not so nice, "negative" things and try to make an Eriksonian achievement scale out of it all, according to which in the first stage trust is "achieved." Actually, a certain ratio of trust and mistrust in our basic social attitude is the critical factor. When we enter a situation, we must be able to differentiate how much we can trust and how much we must mistrust, and I use mistrust in the sense of a readiness for danger and an anticipation of discomfort. (p. 15)

It is desirable that there be more positive ego qualities than negative ego qualities. However, if positive ego qualities are all that are considered when assessing the overall health of the self's development, we could easily overlook the possible value to be found in the negative ego qualities associated with each stage. For example, a certain amount of mistrust helps people to be less gullible and more cautious; a certain readiness to feel shame and doubt helps people behave appropriately and pursue assertively goals that are important to them; the capacity to feel guilt helps people make correct moral judgments and behave responsibly toward others; knowing what it is like to feel inferior helps people stay motivated to do their best; and a certain degree of identity confusion helps people sharpen their self-perceptions and make new adjustments in light of new experiences and changing life circumstances.

Each stage builds on the psychological outcomes of the previous stage(s), although not according to a rigid timetable. For example, when development proceeds normally, with no outstanding traumatic events to derail its progress, the attitude of basic trust that develops during Stage 1 helps children feel safe enough to expand the range and diversity of their experiences and, in the process, develop an attitude of autonomy in Stage 2. Trusting their environment and feeling the necessary autonomy to move freely in it, children reinforce the attitude of initiative associated with Stage 3. This freedom encourages the industry of Stage 4, an attitude that emerges as children learn to control their lively imaginations and apply themselves to formal education. With the basic groundwork laid (basic trust, autonomy, initiative, industry), young people are ready for the monumental challenge of Stage 5—establishing an identity, a sense of who they are as individuals. The result is an overall personality structure, which, when things go well, houses an essentially positive self-concept.

Of course, there may be breakdowns during any of the five psychosocial stages that predispose individuals to a greater likelihood of acquiring a higher ratio of any one or more negative ego qualities, such as mistrust, shame and doubt, guilt, and inferiority. This higher ratio of negative ego qualities increases the probability of a greater degree of identity confusion and subsequent problems down the road.

Self's Development Marked by Rings of Ego Growth

Figure 1-2 represents an attempt to deepen our understanding of the self's development within Erikson's psychosocial framework. If you will imagine that the undifferentiated self described in the upper part of Figure 1-1 has grown and expanded through a series of growth rings, as in Figure 1-2, this may provide a visual concept of the various experiential components of the self's development.

As depicted in Figure 1-2, each state of the self's development is rimmed by what can be called a "ring of ego growth." The ego is that part of the self that is in touch with the outside world. Each hypothetical "ring of ego growth" is, thus, an expression of how well the ego qualities associated with each of the psychosocial stages have developed. For the sake of illustration, the rings of ego growth in Example A of Figure 1-2 have been drawn equidistant from each other to illustrate what the self's growth might look like when each aspect of its development has had a chance to develop under the best of conditions. In this case, a sense of trust, autonomy, initiative, industry, and personal identity have developed fully, leading to a positive and clear delineation of self-concept and self-esteem.

The idea of the self having rings of ego growth is somewhat analogous to a tree having rings of growth, a phenomenon that can be observed in a cross-sectional slice of its trunk. Not only is it possible to assess the age of the tree by counting the number of rings it has, but biologists are also able to infer some information about the ecological conditions that the tree lived through during any particular ring of its growth. For example, when there is a good balance of rain and sunshine and when temperature ranges are about normal, the tree will grow quickly and its rings will be wide. In other words, it grows to its potential in a particular growth year because the ecological conditions are such that nutrient needs are fully satisfied. On the other hand, when ecological conditions are too dry, too hot, or too cold, as the case may be, the tree will grow more slowly and its rings will be narrower. It fails to reach its growth potential.

With the tree model in mind, it may be somewhat easier to mentally conceptualize the self's development by visualizing it as surrounded by a series of ego rings, similar to tree rings, wide or narrow, that spread out from the center. Just as a tree's rings grow quickly and become wider when its nutrient needs are satisfied by the right ecological conditions, it is possible to reason analogically that the self's ego rings tend to grow quickly and

Figure 1-2 *Conceptual illustrations of healthy and unhealthy self-development and ego growth during the first five psychosocial stages.*

Adapted from: Don Hamachek, "The Self's Development and Ego Growth: Conceptual Analysis and Implications for Counselors," *Journal of Counseling and Development,* 1985, *64*: 136–142. Used by permission.

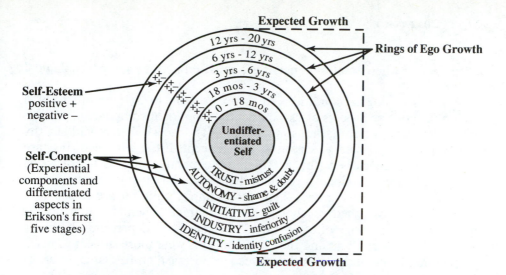

A. Healthy Self-Development - Experiential components of self-concept are growth promoting and well differentiated; as a consequence, self-esteem is essentially positive; ego boundaries are intact, wide, flexible; psychological growth is about where expected.

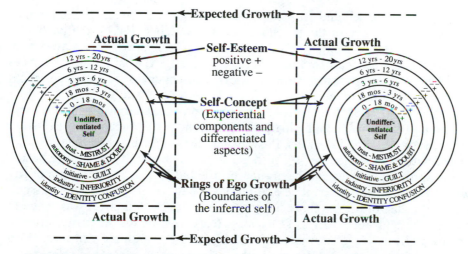

B. Restricted Self-Development
Experiential components of self-concept are growth inhibiting and negatively defined; as a consequence, self-esteem is essentially low; ego boundaries are intact but narrow, leaving them less flexible; psychological growth is below expected limits.

C. Restricted, Uneven Self-Development
Experiential components of self-concept are growth inhibiting and negatively defined; as a result, self-esteem is low, particularly in relation to trust and autonomy issues; ego boundaries are uneven, narrow, and likely more rigid; psychological growth is below expected limits.

become wider when emotional needs are satisfied by the right psychological conditions.

When psychological conditions are favorable, then, the self is more likely to develop the positive aspects of its experiential emotional components, such as trust, autonomy, initiative, industry, and identity, into a coherent and healthy sense of personal existence, a positive self-concept. If the self's ego rings are wide and fully developed, the self that subsequently emerges is apt to be stronger and more emotionally resilient than would be expected in the case of Examples B and C in Figure 1-2. If, for example, children are raised in a chronically impoverished psychological environment, then it would not be surprising if their "rings of ego growth" reflected this deprivation by being narrower and less resilient and their self-concepts were more subject to nega-tive experiential emotional outcomes, such as mistrust, guilt, shame, inferior-ity feelings, and identity confusion.

Healthy and Unhealthy Behaviors Associated with Each Psychosocial Stage

It is clear that our self and self-concept development can be either enhanced or inhibited during any of the psychosocial stages, depending on the particular constellation of life events that we experience. Although we do not always re-member (in our own case) or know (in the case of others) what those experiences have been, we can see some of the behavioral consequences of those experiences once we know what to look for.

Tables 1-1 through 1-5 depict some of the characteristic behaviors and implicit attitudes that can be logically and clinically deduced from Erikson's (1963, 1968, 1980, 1982; Evans, 1981) discussions of the psychodynamics asso-ciated with each of the five psychosocial stages. The validity of the five behav-ioral expressions tables can be argued on the basis of their "closeness of fit" with Erikson's own descriptive and clinical analyses of the behaviors associ-ated with each of the psychosocial stages. A concentrated effort was made to express the central polarities of each stage (e.g., trust versus mistrust, initiative versus guilt) as ten observable behaviors and three implicit attitudes. With Erikson's discussions and descriptions of each stage as a frame of reference, I addressed two basic questions: (1) What behaviors would one likely see among people with high trust or low trust, or with a sense of autonomy or shame and guilt, and so on through the next three stages? (2) What implicit undercurrent attitudes would one likely see reflected in people in each polarity of each stage? Although I do not believe that these are the only polarities of behaviors and attitudes that could be associated with each stage, I do believe that they are representative of and consistent with the basic psychodynamic themes Erikson had in mind (Hamachek, 1988).

No single statement on any of the five behavioral expressions tables can be considered a reliable index of the overall psychological growth or specific self-concept development of particular individuals. However, when a person

Table 1–1   BEHAVIORAL EXPRESSIONS OF A SENSE OF TRUST AND MISTRUST—STAGE 1

Characteristic Behaviors of People Who Have a High Sense of Basic Trust			Characteristic Behaviors of People Who Have a Low Sense of Basic Trust		
Like me	Unlike me	They:	Like me	Unlike me	They:
——	——	1. are able to ask others for help or emotional support without overdoing it.	——	——	1. tend to have trouble asking others for help or emotional support.
——	——	2. are inclined to believe that others will come through for them, unless there is good reason not to believe that.	——	——	2. are inclined to believe that others will not come through for them, even when there is no reason to believe that.
——	——	3. start with the assumption that people are generally good.	——	——	3. start with the assumption that people are generally bad or evil.
——	——	4. tend to focus on the positive aspects of others' behavior.	——	——	4. tend to focus on the negative aspects of others' behavior.
——	——	5. tend to behave in a relatively disclosing and open manner when around others.	——	——	5. tend to behave in a relatively guarded and closed manner when around others.
——	——	6. find it relatively easy to receive (favors, compliments, gifts, etc.) from other people, but prefer a balance of giving and receiving.	——	——	6. find it rather difficult to receive (favors, compliments, gifts, etc.) from other people, and find it easier to be the giver than the taker.
——	——	7. have no trouble sharing their possessions, the "things" in their lives with other people.	——	——	7. have problems sharing their possessions, the "things" in their lives with other people.
——	——	8. are not particularly fearful of disclosing themselves, even their more negative qualities, to other people.	——	——	8. are very hesitant about disclosing themselves, particularly their negative qualities, to other people.
——	——	9. tend to have a generally optimistic worldview without being Pollyannaish or unrealistic about it.	——	——	9. tend to have a generally pessimistic worldview even when things are going well and sometimes *particularly* when things are going well.
——	——	10. are inclined to believe that other people know what is best for themselves, even though they may privately feel differently about others' choices.	——	——	10. are inclined to believe that other people usually do not know what is best for themselves, and prefer to tell others what to do.
		Implicit Attitude			**Implicit Attitude**
——	——	1. You're O.K.	——	——	1. You're not O.K.
——	——	2. Life is generally fair and good to me.	——	——	2. Life is generally unfair and unkind to me.
——	——	3. I'm willing to share what I have.	——	——	3. I'm not willing to share what I have.

Adapted from: Don Hamachek, "Evaluating Self-Concept and Ego Development Within Erikson's Psychosocial Framework." *Journal of Counseling and Development*, 1988, 66: 354-360. Used by permission.

Table 1–2   BEHAVIORAL EXPRESSIONS OF A SENSE OF AUTONOMY AND SHAME AND DOUBT—STAGE 2

Characteristic Behaviors of People Who Have a Sense of Autonomy			Characteristic Behaviors of People Who Have a Sense of Shame and Doubt		
Like me	Unlike me	They:	Like me	Unlike me	They:
___	___	1. like to make their own decisions, particularly about matters important to them.	___	___	1. prefer being told what to do rather than make their own decisions.
___	___	2. are able to say no to requests made of them without feeling guilty.	___	___	2. have problems saying no to requests made of them.
___	___	3. are inclined to express themselves in terms of what they "will" do or "want" to do.	___	___	3. are inclined to express themselves in terms of what they "should" do or "ought" to do.
___	___	4. tent to resist being dominated by people wanting to control them.	___	___	4. tend to allow themselves to be dominated by others, even though they may not like it.
___	___	5. are able to work well by themselves or with others, depending on the situation.	___	___	5. are not comfortable working by themselves, particularly when they know work will be judged or evaluated.
___	___	6. are inclined to get on with what needs to be done and remain task-persistent until finished.	___	___	6. have trouble getting started with what needs to be done; procrastination may be a key feature of personality.
___	___	7. can work easily with either open-ended or structured work assignments, although they may prefer more open-endedness.	___	___	7. have problems working with open-ended work assignments, preferring more structure and direction.
___	___	8. are able to listen to their own inner feelings when deciding what is right or wrong, appropriate or inappropriate.	___	___	8. have difficulty listening to their own inner feelings when deciding what is right or wrong, appropriate or inappropriate.
___	___	9. tend to feel relatively un-self-conscious and at ease when in group situations.	___	___	9. tend to feel uneasy and self-conscious, even embarrassed, when in group situations.
___	___	10. tend to want a certain amount of order and organization in their lives to reinforce feelings of personal control and self-approval.	___	___	10. tend to want things "just so" as one way of avoiding others' disapproval and criticism.
		Implicit Attitude			**Implicit Attitude**
___	___	1 . I think I can do it.	___	___	1. I don't think I can do it.
___	___	2. This is what needs to be done.	___	___	2. Tell me what needs to be done.
___	___	3. I have something of value to offer.	___	___	3. I have little of value to offer.

Adapted from: Don Hamachek, "Evaluating Self-Concept and Ego Development Within Erikson's Psychosocial Framework." *Journal of Counseling and Development*, 1988, *66*: 354-360. Used by permission.

Table 1–3   BEHAVIORAL EXPRESSIONS OF A SENSE OF INITIATIVE AND GUILT—STAGE 3

Characteristic Behaviors of People Who Have a Sense of Initiative			Characteristic Behaviors of People Who Have a Sense of Guilt		
Like me	**Unlike me**	**They:**	**Like me**	**Unlike me**	**They:**
—	—	1. prefer to get on with what needs to be done to complete the task at hand.	—	—	1. tend to postpone, put off, put aside, and generally procrastinate starting.
—	—	2. like accepting new challenges now and then.	—	—	2. are inclined to resist new challenges.
—	—	3. tend to be fast self-starters.	—	—	3. tend to be slow self-starters.
—	—	4. tend to be effective leaders when in that position.	—	—	4. tend to be ineffective leaders when in that position.
—	—	5. tend to set goals and then set out to accomplish them.	—	—	5. may set goals but have problems getting them accomplished.
—	—	6. tend to have high energy levels.	—	—	6. tend to have low energy levels.
—	—	7. have a strong sense of personal adequacy.	—	—	7. have a weak sense of personal adequacy.
—	—	8. seem to enjoy "making things happen."	—	—	8. prefer to remain in the background, preferring not to stir things up.
—	—	9. are able to emotionally appreciate the idea that initiative begins and ends with the person, not the production it generates.	—	—	9. may try to outrun their guilt with a tireless show of accomplishment, believing that efficient production may compensate for being a deficient person.
—	—	10. have a balanced sense of right and wrong without being overly moralistic.	—	—	10. tend to focus moralistically on those things in life that are "wrong."
		Implicit Attitude			**Implicit Attitude**
—	—	1. I will start now.	—	—	1. I will start tomorrow.
—	—	2. I enjoy new challenges.	—	—	2. I prefer sticking with what I know.
—	—	3. This is what needs to be done, and I will do it.	—	—	3. This is what needs to be done. but who will do it?

Adapted from: Don Hamachek, "Evaluating Self-Concept and Ego Development Within Erikson's Psychosocial Framework." *Journal of Counseling and Development*, 1988, *66*: 354-360. Used by permission.

Table 1–4 BEHAVIORAL EXPRESSIONS OF A SENSE OF INDUSTRY AND INFERIORITY—STAGE 4

Like me	Unlike me	Characteristic Behaviors of People Who Have a Sense of Industry — They:	Like me	Unlike me	Characteristic Behaviors of People Who Have a Sense of Inferiority — They:
___	___	1. enjoy learning about new things and ideas.	___	___	1. do not particularly enjoy learning about new things and ideas.
___	___	2. reflect a healthy balance between doing what they *have* to do and what they *like* to do.	___	___	2. tend to concentrate mostly on what they believe they *have* to do, neglecting what they would *like* to do.
___	___	3. reflect strong curiosities about how and why things work the way they do.	___	___	3. are not terribly curious about why and how things work.
___	___	4. enjoy experimenting with new combinations, new ideas, and arriving at new syntheses.	___	___	4. prefer staying with what is known; new ways do not attract them so much as do proven ways.
___	___	5. are excited by the idea of being producers.	___	___	5. tend to be threatened, even guilty, about the idea of being producers.
___	___	6. like the recognition that producing things brings, which reinforces sense of industry.	___	___	6. would like the recognition that production brings, but sense of inferiority stands in the way.
___	___	7. develop a habit of work completion through steady attention and persevering diligence.	___	___	7. develop a habit of work delay by ongoing procrastinations.
___	___	8. have a sense of pride in doing at least one thing well.	___	___	8. have problems taking pride in their work, believing it is not worth it.
___	___	9. take criticism well and use it to improve their performance.	___	___	9. take criticism poorly and use it as a reason to stop trying.
___	___	10. tend to have a strong sense of persistence.	___	___	10. tend to have a weak sense of persistence.

		Implicit Attitude			**Implicit Attitude**
___	___	1. I'm a pretty good learner.	___	___	1. I'm not a very good learner.
___	___	2. Being a producer excites me.	___	___	2. Being a producer frightens me.
___	___	3. I'll work hard to succeed.	___	___	3. I'll work hard to avoid failing.

Adapted from: Don Hamachek, "Evaluating Self-Concept and Ego Development Within Erikson's Psychosocial Framework." *Journal of Counseling and Development*, 1988, *66*: 354-360. Used by permission.

Table 1–5 BEHAVIORAL EXPRESSIONS OF A SENSE OF IDENTITY AND IDENTITY CONFUSION—STAGE 5

Characteristic Behaviors of People Who Have a Sense of Identity			Characteristic Behaviors of People Who Have a Sense of Identity Confusion		
Like me	Unlike me	They:	Like me	Unlike me	They:
___	___	1. have a stable self-concept that does not easily change.	___	___	1. tend to have an unstable self-concept marked by ups and downs.
___	___	2. are able to combine short-term goals with long range plans.	___	___	2. tend to set short-term goals, but have trouble establishing long-range plans.
___	___	3. are less susceptible to the shifting whims of peer pressure influences.	___	___	3. are more susceptible to the shifting whims of peer pressure influences.
___	___	4. tend to have reasonably high levels of self-acceptance.	___	___	4. tend to have rather low levels of self-acceptance.
___	___	5. are able to make decisions without undue wavering and indecisiveness.	___	___	5. are apt to have trouble making decisions, fearing that they will be wrong.
___	___	6. tend to be optimistic about themselves, others, and life generally.	___	___	6. tend to have a somewhat cynical attitude about themselves, others, and life generally.
___	___	7. tend to believe that they are responsible for what happens to them, good or bad.	___	___	7. tend to believe that what happens to them is largely out of their hands, a matter of fate or breaks.
___	___	8. are able to seek self-acceptance directly by being their own person.	___	___	8. are inclined to seek self-acceptance indirectly by being what they believe others want them to be.
___	___	9. are able to be physically and emotionally close to another person without fearing a loss of self.	___	___	9. are inclined to have trouble being physically and emotionally close to another person without being either too dependent or too separate.
___	___	10. tend to be cognitively flexible; their sense of self does not depend on being "right."	___	___	10. tend to be cognitively inflexible; their sense of self resides heavily on being "right."
		Implicit Attitude			**Implicit Attitude**
___	___	1. I am this kind of person . . .	___	___	1. I am not sure who I am as a person.
___	___	2. I'm not perfect, but I'm still O.K.	___	___	2. I should be much better/more than I am.
___	___	3. I can accept your shortcomings because I can accept my own.	___	___	3. I have trouble accepting your shortcomings just as I have trouble accepting my own.

Adapted from: Don Hamachek, "Evaluating Self-Concept and Ego Development Within Erikson's Psychosocial Framework." *Journal of Counseling and Development*, 1988, 66: 354–360. Used by permission.

reflects three, four, or more behaviors resembling those suggested on a given table, then there may be reason to suspect that he or she is displaying expressions of healthy or unhealthy self-concept development, as the case may be.

The tables are presented in such a manner that you can make a general assessment of your own self-concept development over the first five stages of your psychological growth. As you go through each of the behavioral expressions tables, consider what you know about yourself, and, for each statement, check the blank that seems to most closely reflect your behavior in most instances. Notice I said "most instances." Try to avoid thinking about yourself in specific situations. Go for the bigger picture of yourself. Consider how you tend to behave more generally.

A word of caution about the behavioral expressions tables: In interpreting Erikson's descriptions of psychosocial stages, particularly as they are reflected in Tables 1-1 through 1-5, it would seem prudent to keep in mind that these tables are highlighting expressions of behavior that are *likely* to be associated with healthy and unhealthy self-concept development. The behaviors and attitudes that are emphasized in Tables 1-1 through 1-5 may *not* be crucial in the development of all people in the same way, and types of behavior may be more or less significant, depending on the person and circumstances.

The behaviors that are associated with healthy and unhealthy growth during each of these five stages are meant to be illustrative and suggestive, not exhaustive and exclusive. Responded to honestly, the self-assessment feedback you obtain from Tables 1-1 through 1-5 may help you to have a clearer view of your particular areas of self-concept strengths and weaknesses and their genesis in your psychosocial development.

THE IMPORTANCE OF SOCIAL INTERACTION ON THE SELF'S DEVELOPMENT

The self grows in a social framework. If, for example, you were to make a list of as many personality characteristics as you could think of, you would find that each is influenced in some way by social interaction. Some, like cooperative or friendly, are social by definition; that is, one cannot be cooperative or friendly except in relation to other people. Other characteristics, like intellectual or emotional, are less social by definition; that is, one can be intellectual or emotional in solitude. Still, it is difficult to imagine how one could have learned those traits in the absence of social interaction.

As children grow up, they learn to conceive of themselves as having characteristics that are responded to and encouraged by others. For example, they learn that words such as *cute, good, bad, intelligent, dumb, fat, lazy, shy,* and so on are attributed to them as persons; it is through a long immersion in an interpersonal stream of continual reflected appraisals from other people (particularly people who are emotionally important to them) that they gradually develop a picture of themselves that they then strive to maintain. The feedback they receive in their ongoing social interactions becomes the foundation of an evolving personality.

Perhaps we can appreciate the importance of social interaction by looking at an example in which there was virtually no interaction at all. Davis (1974) reported the case of Anna, a five-year-old child who was found tied to a chair in a secluded room. She had apparently been kept there for several years by her grandfather, who found her unbearable because she was a second illegitimate child. When found, she was unable to move or talk. Her leg muscles had atrophied to the point that her flaccid feet fell forward. She was malnourished and showed no response to sound and sight. Within three days of being taken out of this isolated environment, she was able to sit up if placed in a sitting position and could move her arms and hands. She was massaged, placed on a high vitamin diet, and given lots of attention. At first, she neither smiled nor cried and was almost expressionless, although later she began to smile if coaxed and showed signs of temper if physically restrained. Ten days after the first visit, the examiners found the child more alert and able to fix her attention. She showed taste and visual discrimination, smiled more often, and began to display ritualistic motions with her hands and a series of tricks that any infant performs. Two months after being found, Anna ceased to improve. In nine months, she had learned little. She could not chew or drink from a glass or control her bodily processes, and she could barely stand, even when holding on to some support.

At this time, Anna was placed in a foster home with a warm, supporting foster mother. Within a month of this placement, she had learned to eat, hold a glass, and feed herself. Improvement continued until she understood many instructions and babbled, although she could not use words. Motor ability increased, but her initiative was low. Again, her progress seemed to plateau, and she was placed in a home for retarded children. In several years, she was speaking at about the level of a two-year-old child. She showed signs of being socialized, used a spoon, conformed to toilet habits, loved her dolls, and spoke a few simple sentences. She died shortly thereafter at an estimated age of ten and one-half years.

Records revealed that as a baby she had appeared normal, indeed attractive. The matter of hereditary endowment in this case is open to speculation, for the mother was dull mentally, and her father's identity was doubted. Nonetheless, Anna's lack of social interaction and environmental stimulation undoubtedly contributed heavily to her retarded growth as a total human being.

Then, there is the record of the Holy Roman Emperor of the thirteenth century, Frederick II, who sought to learn the innate language of orphaned babies. He ordered them to be raised by nursemaids who would not show the babies any form of love, either in words or touch. What language would they speak? Hebrew? Latin? Greek? He never received an answer. Every baby died (Arnstein, 1975).

THE SHAPING POWER OF SOCIAL ROLES AND OTHERS' EXPECTATIONS

To some extent, our sense of identity is influenced by other people's responses to the roles that (1) we put ourselves in by virtue of the way we behave or (2) that others put us in by virtue of their *perceptions* of our behavior. For example, if the group we're with regards us as a leader or a relaxed person or a comedian or a social clod, we are likely to regard ourselves in somewhat the same way. In other words, we tend to adopt the behaviors and attitudes expected of a person in any of those various roles. In so doing, we begin to get a certain kind of feedback; this in turn reinforces how we feel about ourselves.

Social psychology research has demonstrated convincingly that our pre-conceptions and stereotypes play an enormous part in shaping our attitudes and behaviors in relation to certain individuals and groups (Miller, 1982; Miller, 1986; Snyder, 1982). Consider, for example, the various attitudes and feelings that are aroused in you when you think about or encounter people associated with any of the following groups: Catholics, Jews, fundamentalists, blacks, whites, feminists, gays, body builders, Rhodes Scholars, communists, prochoicers, prolifers, democrats, republicans, libertarians, and so on. Some groups arouse little, if any, feeling in you; some trigger a positive response; and others elicit a negative reaction. That is, certain stereotyped preconceptions can put you in a state of emotional readiness to react in a particular way. Once a stereotype is established, there is a strong tendency on the part of most people to react to the stereotype rather than to the person. Stereotyping people and then responding to the stereotype can have a powerful shaping effect. The shaping power of expectations is illustrated in the following excerpt by Haimowitz (1968), who speculates about how others' expectations may contribute to the "making" of a criminal:

> Gradually, over the years, if he (the Criminal) comes to expect of himself what his neighbors expect of him, he becomes a professional criminal. . . . As a professional criminal, he has standards to live up to, friends who will help him when in trouble . . . tell him where the police are lax and where strict. . . . At twelve, fourteen, sixteen, or eighteen he has come to a conclusion about his career that ordinary boys may not make until they are twenty or even forty. And he could not have drifted into his career without the help of his family and neighbors who sought a scapegoat and unwittingly suggested to him that he become an outlaw. (p. 473)

Haimowitz's account is not merely an isolated example of how expecta-tions can influence behavior. There is a growing and convincing body of re-search literature to suggest that expectations, or "self-fulfilling prophecies," as they are called, work with significant potency both in schools and in homes (Braun, 1976; Brophy, 1983; Jussim, 1989). Research indicates strongly that variables such as name, ethnic background, sex, cumulative folder, physical characteristics, and intelligence test results all tend to influence a teacher's expectations for better or worse (more about this in Chapter 6).

In keeping with the idea of how expectations can shape behavior, I remember an interview I had with a 17-year-old delinquent boy who had just been returned to the reformatory. I asked him why he had gotten into so much trouble while he was back home for three weeks. He screwed up his face and replied, "Man, I wanted to do good—I tried, but even my grandfather wouldn't hardly talk to me. Some of the parents in the neighborhood—some with kids in more trouble than me—wouldn't even let their kids talk to me. They would say something like 'There goes that kid from the vocational school; watch out for him.' They had their minds made up before they even looked to see if I had changed. Hell with them. They want me to be bad—I'll *be* bad." In other words, it was clear to this boy that people in his neighborhood *expected* him to play the role of the delinquent, and he ended up doing so. True, his delinquency history determined their expectations, but their expectations facilitated the very behavior they were opposed to in the first place. Thus began a mutually reinforcing cycle of behavior, each side living up to the other side's original beliefs. The delinquent boy may have changed the neighborhood's expectations and beliefs about him if he had kept his act clean for a long enough time, but once a belief is established, it does not change easily.

IS THERE ONE SELF OR MANY?

You may recall the advice of Polonius to his son, Laertes, in Shakespeare's *Hamlet* (Scene I, Act III):

> To Thine own self be true, and it must follow, as the night the day, thou canst not then be false to any man.

Polonius no doubt was filled with true and noble intentions; his counsel to Laertes seems both reasonable and uncommonly wise. It has a ring of validity and seems to coincide with our ideas about playing straight, being who we are openly, and behaving in a way that is consistent with the self we want to be. But in the non-Shakespearian world of real life and real people, it seems not to work out in quite that way.

If someone were to follow you for one week and record all your behavior on camera, how do you think the film record would look? Would we see one self consistently behaving in the same way at all times? Or would we see slightly different versions of that self, depending on the circumstances and the people involved? Consider, for example, how you typically behave when in the company of your very best friend or loved one. Contrast that with how you usually behave when you're with someone you've just met for the first time.

If you are like most people, you can quickly see that it is difficult to find a single, basic self to which you can be true. It is not so much that your basic self changes, but rather your *presentation* of that basic self changes to fit the situation. James (1890) no doubt had this possibility in mind when he observed:

> Properly speaking, a man has as many social selves as there are individuals who recognize him and carry an image of him in their mind. . . . We may practically say that he has as many different social selves as there are distinct groups of persons about whose opinion he cares. He generally shows a different side of himself to each of these groups. . . . We do not show ourselves to our children as to our club-companions, to our customers and to the laborers we employ . . . as to our intimate friends. (p. 294)

James was saying here that we have a variety of social selves because we act differently with different types of people. We do not become a different person (after all, we cannot change who we are), but we do have the capacity *to show different aspects of the person we are to different people*. In his insightful book, *The Presentation of Self in Everyday Life* (1959), Goffman suggested that the way we do this is through alterations in the manner of presentations or "face" we show others, which is a kind of staged performance or "front" that we put up in hopes that it will satisfy the expectations we feel others have for us at the moment. When it is done primarily for the purpose of behaving the way we feel others expect us to, it is rightly called *impression management*. Some people engage in impression management more often—and with greater skill—than others. Public relations people, lobbyists, professional actors, and many trial lawyers are no doubt among the best. So are successful salespeople, con artists, and certainly, politicians. Indeed, politicians' political survival depends largely on their skills in "managing" an impression that is acceptable to diverse groups and organizations at different times. (You may have noted that politicians go through their most difficult moments when they have to talk to diverse groups representing different points of view at the *same* time.)

If you have ever been interviewed for a job, you probably know how important impression management is from having to present what you had hoped would be your "best self" during that interview. The very expression "presenting one's best self" suggests that we have an assortment of "selves" in our psychological closet, which further suggests that there are choices we can make for the "self" we wear at any given time. Please note that the self we have been examining is the self we present to others, or our "public self," which involves how we want *others* to see us. There is another, more private aspect of the self called *self-concept,* which involves how we see ourselves, an idea that we will be turning to shortly. However, before we do, there is an important question that needs to be addressed.

WHY DO WE PRESENT DIFFERENT SELVES?

Most people in our social world see only an edited version of our behavior, which is usually staged to present a certain image. Goffman (1959, 1971) described those stagings as theatrical performances in which each of us acts out a "line," which is basically a set of carefully chosen verbal and nonverbal acts that expresses the self we feel we have to be at a particular moment. In Goffman's view, each of us seems to be merely the sum of our various performances.

The question remains: Why do we behave in this way? Essentially, it's a matter of necessity. Goffman, for example, argued that societal norms are such that we expect to present ourselves in certain ways when interacting with our superiors, parents, peers, co-workers, subordinates, and so forth. Goffman also pointed out that social norms for what is appropriate or inappropriate behavior also support other people's acceptance of our efforts to present ourselves in certain ways. Although people may be skeptical and even wary of another person's self-presentation, they rarely challenge it. For example, if a salesperson approaches you with gushing enthusiasm for his or her product, are you apt to question that person's honesty, even when you have doubts about it? If an acquaintance, in passing, hopes you have a "nice day," are you inclined to question his sincerity, even when you strongly suspect it missing? Maybe you, as an individual, would raise those questions, but it is likely that most people would not. Most of the time, we respond to each other's presentations of the public self in predictable, ritualistic ways. Unless our self-presentation is so blatantly out of line with what could be considered normal behavior, we tend to keep our suspicions to ourselves. We politely listen to the gushy salesperson; we express the hope that our acquaintance also has a pleasant day.

To sum up: We tend to present different aspects of the self at different times to different people as part of an overall impression management effort. It appears that we engage in impression management for essentially two reasons: (1) We have learned that it is *expected* of us. (How many times have you heard parents admonish their children to behave in a certain way or *not* to behave *like that,* heaven forbid, depending on the circumstances and situation?) (2) We have learned that it is *necessary* if we want people to love us, like us, listen to us, respect us, hire us, buy wares from us, and so forth. (How often have you heard parents tell their children, "Nobody will like you if you act that way"?)

The idea of turning on a particular aspect of the public self depending on the situation is perfectly normal behavior and all of us do it. The fact that we don't tell the boss what we really feel about him or her, that we don't behave at a dignified social function the way we might at a raucous party, or that we don't confront John's efforts to be sincere when we think he's being the opposite has obvious social advantages. It helps us avoid needless, endless interpersonal conflicts (think about anyone you happen to know who seems to enjoy telling people what he or she *really* thinks about them and you'll have an idea of what I mean here). It also helps us behave appropriately and in a manner that fits the situation. You may, for example, really want to give that so-and-so boss of yours a piece of your mind, but to do so now, in this particular situation at this time, may not be timely or appropriate, so you are patient, even friendly—you put on a "face," as Goffman would say—and wait for a better moment.

Each of us, then, has a certain number of "selves" from which to choose for a particular self-presentation. Although we all engage in *some* impression management behavior, we differ greatly in *how much*.

Differences in Self-Presentation: High Versus Low Self-Monitors

You no doubt have seen that some people are particularly sensitive to the ways they present and express themselves in social situations—at meetings, parties, job interviews, encounters of all kinds in which an individual might choose to create and maintain a certain kind of appearance. On the other hand, there are people who seem to present a "self" that is basically the same from one situation to another.

Before reading further, you may find it interesting to answer the ten questions in the Self-Monitoring Inventory in Table 1-6.

Your responses to the inventory will give you a general idea of whether you are what Snyder (1974, 1979) has called a "high self-monitor" or a "low self-monitor" or whether you are somewhere in between. (This is a shorter version of Snyder's original 25-item inventory, so it may not be as accurate.) According

Table 1–6   SELF-MONITORING INVENTORY

These statements concern personal reactions to a number of different situations. No two statements are exactly alike, so consider each statement carefully before answering. If a statement is true, or mostly true, as applied to you, circle the T. If a statement is false, or not usually true, as applied to you, circle the F.

1. I find it hard to imitate the behavior of other people.   T   F
2. I guess I put on a show to impress or entertain people.   T   F
3. I would probably make a good actor.   T   F
4. I sometimes appear to others to be experiencing deeper emotions
    than I actually am.   T   F
5. In a group of people I am rarely the center of attention.   T   F
6. In different situations and with different people, I often act like very
    different persons.   T   F
7. I can only argue for ideas I already believe.   T   F
8. In order to get along and be liked, I tend to be what people expect me
    to be rather than anything else.   T   F
9. I may deceive people by being friendly when I really dislike them.   T   F
10. I'm not always the person I appear to be.   T   F

SCORING: Give yourself one point for each of questions 1, 5, and 7 that you answered F. Give yourself one point for each of the remaining questions that you answered T. Add up your points. If you are a good judge of yourself and scored 7 or above, you are propbably a high self-monitoring individual; 3 or below, you are probably a low self-monitoring individual.

Source: Mark Snyder, "The Many Me's of the Self-Monitor," *Psychology Today.* March, 1983. p. 34. Reprinted with permission.

to the theory, high self-monitors are good "people-readers"; they are people who have developed the ability to monitor carefully their own behavior and to adjust skillfully the self they are presenting when signals from others tell them that they are not having the desired effect. They tend to be good impression managers (Gabrenya and Arkin, 1980). Low self-monitors, on the other hand, seem not so concerned about the social cues that surround them; instead, they tend to express what they feel rather than tailor their presentation of self to fit the situation. This is quite different from the behavior of high self-monitors who, as Lippa's (1976, 1978) studies have shown, may be such polished actors that they can successfully adopt the mannerisms of a friendly, outgoing, extraverted personality and then do an about-face and convey, just as convincingly, a somewhat shy, withdrawn, and introverted individual.

Although high self-monitors are skilled practitioners of impression management, it would not be accurate to say that they necessarily use these skills for deceptive or manipulative purposes. Indeed, in their ongoing relationships with friends and acquaintances, they seem eager to use their self-monitoring abilities to facilitate smooth social interactions. We find some evidence for this in an interesting study by Ickes and Barnes (1977), who arranged for pairs of strangers to spend time together in a waiting room, ostensibly to wait their turn to participate in an experiment. All possible pairings of same-sex high, moderate, and low self-monitors were represented. Using videotapes and audiotapes, the researchers recorded the behavior of each pair (unknown to them) over a five-minute period and then analyzed the interactions. Not surprisingly, high self-monitors took an active and controlling role in the conversation soon after meeting the other person. They were the ones who usually talked first and who kept the conversation going. They not only talked more but also were viewed by themselves and their partners as having a greater need to talk more. It was as if high self-monitoring persons were somewhat more concerned about managing themselves in such a way as to create, facilitate, and maintain smooth interactions. Interestingly, the longest silences occurred among high and low self-monitors paired together, and the ones who felt most self-conscious were the high self-monitors within the high-low pairs. This is not surprising. Because high self-monitors depend on as many social cues as possible to present themselves in ways they hope will be appropriate, they may indeed become self-conscious and uneasy in the company of someone who is not easy to read.

All in all, high and low self-monitors have quite different ideas about what constitutes a self, and their views are quite well suited to how they live. High self-monitoring people see themselves as flexible and adaptive and capable of presenting a social self designed to fit the situation at hand. They believe that a person is whomever he or she appears to be at any particular moment. In effect, they say, "The me I am is the me I am right now." This view of self fits well with how high self-monitoring people present themselves to the world, a view that allows them to behave in ways that are consistent with how they believe they should act.

Low self-monitors, in contrast, have a firmer, more focused idea of what a self should be. They are more likely to view the self as a single identity that should not be compromised for the sake of situational demands. Thus, they value and strive for congruence between how they see themselves and how they behave, and they see their actions as honest reflections of how they feel and think. It is this particular view of the self that accounts for the low self-monitoring individual's relatively consistent and stable self-presentation.

High self-monitoring individuals tend to be flexible and adaptive—behavior on the plus side—but their efforts to become what they feel situations and people want them to be may make them emotionally and psychologically elusive and evasive—behavior on the negative side. Low self-monitoring individuals tend to be relatively stable and consistent—behavior on the positive side—but their firm and unchanging demeanor may cause them to be unresponsive and insensitive—behavior on the more negative side. There are strengths and weaknesses associated with both high and low self-monitoring behaviors. The more extreme either behavior is in a person, the more likely that person will suffer its shortcomings. In day-to-day living, not many of us qualify for *always* being high or low self-monitors, as the case may be; rather, we lean by degrees in one direction or the other. Still, chances are that each of us tends to lean one way or the other more often than not, and having an *awareness* of our own emotional tilting is the first step toward creating a self that is consciously chosen, as opposed to being molded largely by unconscious determinants.

What is important in understanding oneself and others, then, is not the elusive question of whether there is necessarily one self or many, but rather how different people express those components of their experience and behavior that they privately regard as "me." It is to this more private sense of self to which we now turn.

SELF-CONCEPT: THE VIEW WE HAVE OF OURSELVES

The aspect of self that we have focused on to this point has been what is properly called the "public self," which, as mentioned earlier, is how we want *others* to see us. We are talking now about the more private aspects of the self, known as our self-concept, which involves how *we* see ourselves. In this sense, *self-concept* refers to that particular cluster of ideas and attitudes we have about ourselves at any given moment. Another way of understanding self-concept is to view it as the organized cognitive structure of ourselves as individuals derived from the sum of all our experiences. From these experiences grow the ideas (concepts) of the kind of person we see ourselves as being. Self-concept, then, is our own private mental image of ourselves, a collection of beliefs about the kind of person we are.

Components of Self-Concept

One person sees himself as too short; another sees himself as very friendly; still another views herself as an emotional person; yet another describes herself as having above-average intelligence. You can quickly see that self-concept involves at least four separate but interrelated components, a physical self-concept, a social self-concept, an emotional self-concept, and an intellectual self-concept. They are separate because each has a uniqueness of its own, but they are interrelated insofar as our self-concept in one area may influence our self-concept in other areas. For example, if, for whatever reason, my physical self-concept is somewhat shaky, it may inhibit the risks I am willing to take with my social self, and it may stand in the way of expressing my emotional self more fully. On the other hand, if I have a positive physical self-concept, it may help me to feel more confident about my social self, and it may enable me to express my emotional self more frequently. The various components of the self that contribute to our overall feelings about ourselves as individuals do not exist as watertight compartments, each protected from the other. What is felt in one area spills over to some extent to other areas. If, for example, you receive a warm, affirming note from a loved one (positive input to your emotional self-concept), your social self may feel more expressive, your physical self may feel more buoyant, and your intellectual self may even feel a bit sharper. I do not have to remind you of how you have felt after a serious argument with a loved one or after a lower grade than was expected on a test. Whether we feel elation or depression, it is not just our emotional self that is involved but a feeling that cuts across all aspects of our being.

The interconnectedness of our emotional circuitry is important to understand and appreciate if for no other reason than to help us see that, whether in ourselves or others, a short circuit in one part of the system can affect all other parts. Sometimes the short-circuited part of the self can be fixed directly. For example, a student in one of my graduate courses, painfully shy, mustered up the courage to take several classes in public speaking and even attended a weekend assertiveness training workshop. It almost frightened her to death, but she did it. As a consequence, she emerged with a new image of herself as a social person (this didn't happen overnight; about 20 weeks were involved here), which not only enabled her to interact with greater confidence in social situations but also enabled her to try out for a women's intramural basketball team (she made it) and to take a tough math course she had been avoiding. As her social self-concept grew stronger from a direct focus on ways to strengthen it, so too did her willingness to risk her physical and intellectual self, positive steps in the right direction because without risk there is little chance for gain.

In other instances, a short-circuited aspect of the self has to be repaired more indirectly. We see illustrations of this in various compensatory behaviors. For example, Donna may not be as attractive as she would like to be (low physical self-concept), but she works very hard at her studies (enhances her intellectual self-concept) and makes an effort to be a friendly, pleasant person, ready and willing to help others (develops a positive social concept). David may feel that he is not as smart as he would like to be (low intellectual self-concept), but he puts extra time into his studies and works on projects for extra credit whenever possible (does what he can to enhance the intellectual image), and he exercises every day so he can look good, feel good, and keep his weight down (maintains a high physical self-image). Both Donna and David compensate for what they see as shortcomings in themselves by strengthening other aspects of the self they present to others or by working extra hard on the perceived shortcoming.

Generally, when a chronic low self-concept is experienced in relation to any one of the four major aspects of the self—physical, emotional, social, intellectual—it may be triggered and sustained by any one or more of the following three causes: (1) We have established expectations that are unreachable and unreasonable; (2) we have chosen goals that are incompatible with our abilities or interests (or both); or (3) we have not put as much effort and time into achieving our goals as we could.

Domains of Self-Concept

The self we perceive ourselves as being may or may not be similar to the self we ideally would like to be, and it may or may not be similar to the self we really are. Our perception of who we are, how we look, how well we do, and so forth is only one domain of our overall concept of self. It is necessary to consider our "ideal" self—the self we would like to be—and our "real" self—the self that can be assessed and measured by more objective appraisals than our own subjective estimates.

For example, let's assume that Jim rates himself rather low on a physical attractiveness scale. Let's further assume that ideally he would like to be a handsome man. Go one step further and assume that by objective measures— e.g., impartial judgments by many people—Jim's "real" physical self is considered rather nice looking. If we could sketch this idea diagrammatically, the three aspects related to Jim's attractiveness might look like Figure 1-3. There is a fair amount of discrepancy between the three domains of Jim's concept of himself. Actually, Jim's ideal self and his real self greatly overlap, but his perceived self, the way he sees himself (and the one that really counts), overlaps very little with the other two domains.

Consider another example. Imagine that Jane perceives herself as having above-average social skills, but ideally she would like to have exceptional social skills. Imagine, further, that her "real" social skills as determined by her actual interactions are perceived by others as above average. As Jane's situation is depicted in Figure 1-3, you can see that there is considerably more overlapping, or *congruency,* among her three domains of self. When considered in light of psychological research (Rogers, 1963; Seeman, 1989) that suggests that high levels of self-congruence are associated with psychological health, Jane's overlapping selves bode well for her emotional well being. Jim, on the other hand, may have more trouble feeling like an integrated person precisely because of the lack of congruency among the three domains of his self-concept. Generally speaking, the greater the gap between the way we perceive ourselves and the way we really want to be, the more dissatisfied with ourselves we tend to be.

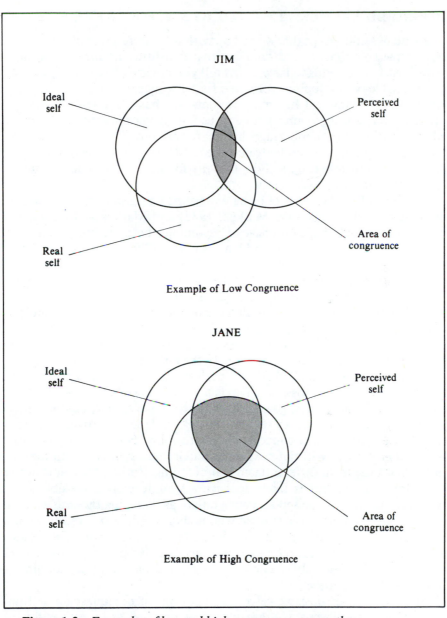

Figure 1-3 *Examples of low and high congruence among three domains of self-concept.*

POSSIBLE SELVES: THE IDEALS WE STRIVE FOR

The kind of self-concept that we end up with is the outgrowth of the interactive mix of the components and domains that constitute its inner workings. Although each of us tends to have an overall global view of ourselves, we are also quite capable of developing more specific self-concepts related to our particular ideals. For example, I am amazed at how very busy I suddenly become when invited to join a bridge game, knowing, as I do, the problems I have in deciding what to bid or in remembering which cards are out. I am equally amazed at how unimportant work suddenly becomes and how *un*busy I am when asked to play tennis, remembering, as I do, that my forehand is not bad and my backhand has improved considerably.

Although I am far short of being a polished tennis player, my ideal is to be much improved in this area. Markus (1983) and Markus and Nurius (1986) would suggest that this ideal I have of becoming a better tennis player is one of my *possible selves*. As Markus and Nurius (1986) described this idea, "Possible selves are the ideal selves that we would very much like to become. They are also the selves we could become and the selves we are afraid of becoming" (p. 954).

This suggests that our possible selves can be either positive or negative. Possible selves we might hope for that are on the positive side might include the creative self, the successful self, the thin self, the loved and admired self, or even the good tennis player self. Possible selves we may wish to avoid on the negative side could be the depressed self, the failure self, the alcoholic self, the loveless self, the unemployed self, or, perhaps, the lousy tennis player self.

The idea of having possible selves is an intriguing one because it is a way of clarifying how our hopes, goals, aspirations, motives, fear, and anxieties are linked to behaviors driven by self-concept. Possible selves provide the essential connection between self-concept and motivation. For example, the student who fears he or she will not pass a particular course carries with him or her more than a vague, undifferentiated fear of failing. Rather, the fear is personalized, and that student is likely to have a well-developed possible self that represents this fear—the self as having failed, as repeating the course, as angry and disappointed, or as the student who is short graduation credits. Similarly, the person who diets and exercises to lose 30 pounds does not see this outcome as a vague possibility, but rather sees a clearly defined possible self—the self as thinner, more comfortable, more attractive, and happier, with an altogether more accepting attitude.

The concept of possible selves is important in our quest for self-understanding for two reasons: (1) Possible selves function as incentives for future behavior, in the sense that they help us clarify the selves to strive for or to avoid, and (2) they provide us with a way to interpret and evaluate our current view of self, in the sense that we can assess our current status against what *could* or *might* happen if we changed or remained the same.

I am, at this moment, a quite average tennis player. My current tennis self-concept reflects that reality; it is average. I am becoming more aware of a strong desire to be a bit better than average, which explains to me (and others) why there is a willingness to purchase a tennis membership and practice more in order to achieve that goal. It is one of my positive possible selves. My current bridge-playing self-concept is low (realistically so), and I have no desire to improve it. In that sense, it is one of my negative possible selves and one that I will avoid by choice.

By developing an awareness of our positive possible selves (not just the things we already do well in, but those things we want to learn about or to improve in), we are in a better position to channel our energies and direct our motivations toward goals that are both reasonable and reachable, thus improving self-concept outcomes. In our search for understanding ourselves and others better, perhaps a question worth asking more often is, "What do I (you) see as possible to accomplish in my (your) life?"

SELF-ESTEEM: HOW WE FEEL ABOUT OURSELVES

Whereas self-concept is the *cognitive* part of self-perception, a way to understand self-esteem is to view it as the *affective* dimension of self-perception. That is, not only do we have certain *ideas* about who we are, but also we have certain *feelings* about who we are. Self-concept is the purely descriptive aspect of our self-perceptions; for example, we might say, "I am a student" or "I weigh 170 pounds" or "I have many friends." These are descriptive statements that can be easily enough verified. Self-esteem, on the other hand, is the evaluative component of our self-perceptions and is reflected in statements such as "I am an excellent (or average or poor) student" or "My weight is ideal" or "I am a friendly person." The descriptive statement "I am a student" is part of self-concept but is not necessarily relevant to self-esteem; the statement "I am an excellent student," on the other hand, clearly is. Self-esteem, then, is constructed out of our evaluations of the things we do, of who we are, and of what we achieve in terms of our private assessments of the goodness, worthiness, or significance of those things.

Important questions need answering: How do people decide what is "good" or "worthwhile" or "significant?" What are the intrapersonal factors and interpersonal experiences that seem most likely to influence, for better or worse, one's feelings of self-esteem? Let's turn our attention to these questions.

Social Comparisons and Self-Esteem

How we feel about ourselves depends heavily on how we believe we compare to others whose skills, abilities, and talents are similar to our own.

Mettee and Riskin (1974) found some interesting experimental evidence for this statement by pitting pairs of college women against each other in written tests. After revealing the results of the tests, they asked each woman whether she liked her partner. To Mettee and Riskin's surprise, the woman who was decisively outscored by her partner tended to like that partner. The probable reason for this outcome is that the woman who was outscored by a wide margin saw her competitor as being so different from herself that any comparison with her would have been meaningless. But the woman who was outscored by only a slight margin did compare herself and perceived herself as inferior to her competitor. This threatened her self-esteem, and, in defense, she developed a strong dislike for her competitor. Mettee and Riskin speculated that the most accurate and, hence, most potent comparison information is derived from people who are similar. When we perceive others as greatly dissimilar, they are perceived as incomparable. This comparable-incomparable distinction allows people to screen out much negative information about themselves because the only information that really "counts" comes from comparable people, an idea that has also been supported by the findings of Tesser and Campbell (1980) and Tesser and Paulhus (1983). Thus, C students tend to compare themselves with other C students, and A students compare themselves with other A students. The point is, most of us "back" ourselves to be at least as good as most others in one or two areas, and the reference group we use for comparison will tend to be more like us than unlike us. I might add, too, that this same comparable-incomparable defense system is used to protect us from the achievements of persons we may regard as inferior. For example, if we are outperformed by somebody we perceive as far inferior to ourselves, the performance can be dismissed as an isolated incident. Self-esteem is not apt to suffer much because of the tendency to consider the inferior person too far below us for comparison.

The comparisons we've looked at are comparisons of performance and ability. What happens when people compare themselves with others in appearance?

In a cleverly designed study by Morse and Gergen (1970), male applicants were recruited for interesting summer work that paid well. As each applicant arrived for an interview, he was seated alone in a room with a long table and given a long battery of forms to fill out, among which was a self-esteem test. The applicant was told that his responses on this test had nothing to do with being hired but that his honest answers were needed to construct a good test. When the applicant had completed half the self-esteem test, an accomplice of the investigators was sent in—supposedly another applicant for the job. In half of the cases, the accomplice was an impressive figure, one who wore a nice-looking suit, polished shoes, and had a smart attaché case, from which he took a sharpened pencil, a slide rule, and a book by Plato. Morse and Gergen privately referred to him as Mr. Clean. In the other half of the cases, the accomplice was a different collaborator, one who wore a smelly sweatshirt, torn pants, and had several days' worth of whiskers. He looked a bit dazed, had no pencils and, as he slumped into his chair, tossed a dog-eared copy of Harold Robbins' *The Carpetbaggers* on the table. He was labeled, appropriately enough, Mr. Dirty. There was no verbal exchange between the accomplice and the applicant. After the accomplice was seated, the applicant completed the second half of the self-esteem test.

When the self-esteem scores were analyzed, a striking difference was noted. In the presence of Mr. Clean, applicants showed a marked *decline* in good feelings about themselves. They suddenly felt sloppy, stupid, and generally inferior by comparison. Ratings were significantly more negative than they had been before Mr. Clean arrived. Mr. Dirty, on the other hand, gave everyone a psychological lift. After his entrance, applicants showed a marked *increase* in self-esteem; they felt more handsome, confident, and optimistic. It appears that we may feel terrific or awful about our physical self, depending, at least in part, on how those around us look. If you've ever gone to a party where everyone was dressed up and you were in a pair of jeans, you will understand.

All in all, the groups we compare ourselves with play an important part in helping us sort through how we feel and think about ourselves. Because high self-esteem usually comes from being able to do one or two things at least as well as, if not a trifle better than, most other people, it would be difficult to maintain, not to mention enhance, self-esteem if we compared ourselves with persons who were obviously either too superior or too inferior to ourselves in accomplishment. In the first case, it's a losing battle, whereas in the second case, it's a hollow victory.

Personal Aspirations and Self-Esteem

What we set as our personal levels of aspiration are also important to our feelings of self-esteem because they help establish what we regard as either success or failure. What is a success or an enhancing experience for one can be a failure or deflating experience for another. For example, I remember I received a C in an undergraduate economics course that I regarded as particularly difficult. That C, however, was quite consistent with my expectations and level of aspiration for performance, and I felt it was a minor, if not a major, success. On the other hand, a friend of mine who also received a C in that course viewed it as a total failure because his expectations and level of aspiration were not lower than a B. (Political science was his major, a fact that raised his level of aspiration for performing well in economics. My own major was psychology, and in that course of study, my aspirations were much higher than those for economics.) In other words, by getting that C, I maintained my self-esteem because it was an even-money return on my personal investment in the course. My friend lost a measure of self-esteem *because the return was less than his personal investment.* By starting out with different amounts of personal investment, we had different expectations for a personal return to maintain our original investments. In a similar view, both of us could have enhanced our self-esteem if we had received a grade that *exceeded* our original levels of aspiration.

Although our levels of aspiration determine to a large extent what we interpret as failure or success and, hence, what either adds to or subtracts from our self-esteem, another factor worth considering is our history of successes and failures. For example, to fail at something is more tolerable and less apt to threaten our self-esteem if we have had a history of success in that particular endeavor. A girl who has had many boyfriends is not likely to sour on boys if she loses one, but a girl with few boyfriends could; a team with a 10-0 record is not apt to give up after losing the 11th game, but a 0-10 team might; a .350 baseball player is not particularly discouraged when he or she strikes out, but a .150 player is; a student with a long string of above-average grades is not likely to quit school if he gets a low grade now and then, but a below-average student who continually gets low grades might. In other words, the impact of falling short of our personal aspirations stands to be a less self-deflating experience if our list of successes in that endeavor exceeds our tally of failures.

When it comes to determining what is a success or failure, Coopersmith (1967) showed that people usually assess their success in terms of one or more of the following categories:

1. *Power:* the ability to influence and control others.
2. *Significance:* the acceptance, attention, and affection of others.
3. *Virtue:* adherence to certain moral and ethical standards.
4. *Competence:* successful performance in meeting demands for achievement.

There are many individual differences among us when it comes to assessing our successes, either within or between categories. One person may derive a sense of competence and positive self-esteem from being intellectually capable; another, from being good athletically, and still another from being in positions of leadership and authority. There are many avenues to positive self-esteem.

Feedback from Others and Self-Esteem

Have you ever begun a day feeling reasonably good about yourself and then either (1) someone said to you something like "Gee, what's wrong with you today? You don't look well at all" or (2) you received a lower grade than you expected on a test? If doing well on that test was important to you, your self-esteem probably took a dip because performance fell below expectations. If the feedback (appraisals, evaluations) about how bad you looked came from a highly credible source—someone who knew you and was an emotionally important person in your life—your self-esteem would sink further than if it came from someone who didn't know you and wasn't important to you. Bergin (1962), for example, found that we tend to dismiss or discount the feedback we receive from those we dislike or consider incompetent. We do, however, tend to give more weight to feedback received from individuals perceived as important, attractive, competent, or powerful (Backman, Secord, and Pierce, 1963).

Generally speaking, research has shown that how we feel about ourselves in terms of self-worth and self-esteem is related to the sort of reflected

It probably helps to be careful about how we word our feedback to others.

Reprinted by permission of UFS, INC.

appraisals we get from those in our social world (Baumgardner and Arkin, 1987; Schlenker, 1980).

As an example of how this process works, Gergen (1972) described an experiment in which a clinical psychology trainee interviewed 18 women undergraduates. He asked each student a variety of questions, some related to background information and many related to how each woman saw herself. Every time the student said something positive about herself, the trainee smiled, nodded approvingly, and occasionally spoke in agreement. Conversely, the trainee would disapprove of the student's negative self-evaluations: she might shake her head, frown, or say something in disagreement. By agreeing with the positive and disagreeing with the negative, it was made clear to the student that she was viewed very positively. As a result of this sort of selective feedback, the students' self-evaluations grew progressively more positive. This increase was decidedly greater than the minimal change that was observed in a control group, in which students received no feedback from the trainee.

All in all, research related to the effects of feedback suggests that sometimes the feedback we receive from others, especially those who are credible and in some way significant to us, is so powerful and so related to our self-image that it may trigger either a heightened or reduced sense of self-esteem. However, as Shrauger and Schoeneman (1979) pointed out in a critical review of self-appraisal literature, it would be erroneous to conclude that feedback is always responsible for causing corresponding changes in feelings of self-esteem. In some cases, people's actual abilities are most responsible for producing both their self-evaluations and the evaluations they receive from others, in which case reflected appraisals may have only minimal impact. For example, if you are already a fine student or a superb tennis player, your high self-esteem is likely to be nurtured more by your excellent performance than by others' feedback about it. In other cases, it may be that people form their own self-evaluations first and behave in such a way as to elicit the positive feedback. For example, assume that you are just an average student and just a so-so tennis player, but you talk in a self-assured way about your studies and play your so-so tennis with confidence and no apologies. Although the excellent performance is missing, the positive "I'm O.K." attitude is not, which may elicit positive feedback from others based more on your attitude than your scores. Of course, it can work the other way, too. That is, you could be a fine student or an excellent tennis player but so successfully degrade your own abilities that others end up agreeing with you and you with them in a self-perpetuating cycle.

To summarize, positive feedback tends to raise self-esteem, and negative feedback tends to lower it. We are usually more vulnerable to feedback that comes from people who are important to us in some way and who are credible. If we begin by projecting positive self-esteem (e.g., confidence in our own abilities), this is more likely to elicit positive feedback in return (but not if we are perceived as self-centered braggarts, which may bring us scorn rather than praise). Even though it is not possible to specify exactly which comes first, positive self-esteem or positive feedback, it seems reasonable to suggest that each is mutually reinforcing to the other to the extent that a positive expression of one facilitates a positive expression in the other.

You may get a more personal glimpse of the power of positive feedback on self-esteem by making a deliberate effort to give liberal doses of it to someone you know whose ego may need a boost. It has to be real—you have to mean it—and it works best when it is specific rather than general. For example, to say to a somewhat timid friend who just asserted him- or herself, however waveringly, "I like it when you stand up for yourself" is much more potent than saying, "I like it when people stand up for themselves." See for yourself how personal, behavior-specific positive feedback can make a difference to the people in your life.

TOWARD ENHANCING SELF-ESTEEM: SELF-ATTRIBUTION PROCESSES

There are probably no personal attributes more important to us than our feelings of self-worth, competency, and personal pride. We all have a need—with large individual differences as to how this need is expressed—to present our best self to others, to show ourselves off to the best advantage. We do this so we can be liked and accepted by others. When (or if) this happens, we tend to feel good about ourselves; self-esteem is boosted. People with positive self-esteem tend to be happier, healthier, and more productive than people with low self-esteem, each a good reason for trying to enhance self-esteem whenever it is possible.

There are at least four behaviors that most of us engage in from time to time that reflect our strong need to present and protect a positive self-image: (1) a self-serving bias, (2) egocentricity, (3) cognitive conservatism, and (4) self-handicapping. Each falls under the heading of a self-attribution process because each refers to a particular way that can be used literally to "attribute" certain reasons and explanations for our behavior, each designed to help us present ourselves in the best light possible. We seldom do these things consciously, which is a good reason for knowing how and under what conditions self-attributions work so that we are aware of the possible underlying meaning of our behavior, specifically, and the behavior of others, generally.

Let's begin with the attributional process that is probably used most frequently.

The Self-Serving Bias: The Tendency to Assume That We Can Do No Wrong

Are the following scenarios familiar? Michael and his girlfriend go out for the evening and soon argue over where to eat and what movie to see. The next day, a friend asks Michael how his date went and Michael replies, "Lousy; Susan is so rigid about where she goes and what she does—she can never give up her fixed ideas." Michael seems to forget that the restaurant he suggested is one they've been to twice in a row or that the last movie they saw was one *he* particularly wanted to see.

Marcia gets her midterm exam back and notes that she earned an A –, which is considerably better than she hoped for. A friend asks her how she did so well, and Marcia replies, "Well, for one thing I studied very hard and put more time into preparing than I usually do. I also took many good notes in class." Previously, Marcia had explained her mediocre performance on a quiz in that same course by the fact that the quiz was unfair and too long for the time allotted, conveniently forgetting to mention that the test was particularly easy.

Michael and Marcia reflect what social psychology literature and research refer to as a *self-serving bias* in the way we perceive events (Miller and Ross, 1975; Russell, McAuley, and Tarico, 1987). We seem inclined to attribute the negative things that happen to us to external factors (according to Michael, it was Susan's fault they had the argument, not his) and the positive outcomes to dispositional factors (according to Marcia, she received a high grade because of her brains and preparation, not because the test may have been easy). This bias enables us to take credit for our good acts and find scapegoats for the bad. Research shows that this sort of self-serving perception serves two basic purposes: (1) It helps us to protect and enhance self-esteem, and (2) it serves as a means of enhancing our public image, of "looking good" in the eyes of others (Greenberg, Pyszczynski, and Solomon, 1982; Weary and Arkin, 1981).

We find illustrations of the self-serving bias in many different arenas of life. For example, when a team loses, players and coaches are much more likely to attribute the loss to poor playing conditions, bad refereeing, or key injuries than to lack of skill or ability. When they win, however, then victory is more likely to be attributed to heroic effort, determined play, or great ability than to lucky breaks or their opponent's poor play (Lau and Russell, 1980). When students do poorly, teachers are inclined to blame the students' lack of ability or effort; however, when students do well, teachers are much more likely to take credit themselves (Johnson, Feigenbaum, and Weiby, 1964). And, from the students' point of view, when they do well, they see this as emanating from their own ability and effort, rather than the teachers' skills, but when they do poorly, they are inclined to attribute it to circumstances or poor teaching (Berstein, Stephan, and Davis, 1979). This self-serving bias has also been observed among psychotherapists, who seem willing to claim credit for their therapeutic cures but not for their therapeutic failures (Weary, 1980).

The list goes on, but the conclusion is generally the same. We are ready to take credit for our good performances and equally ready to blame our failures on bad luck or other outside factors. Bradley's (1978) analysis of research suggests that we are most likely to behave as though we can do no wrong during any one or more of the following conditions: (1) when we are highly *involved* in an activity, (2) when we have *chosen* to be involved, and (3) when the results of our involvement are public.

All in all, it appears that we have a considerable stake in protecting both our public and private images from interpretations that may suggest we are not so infallible as we seem, perhaps because we learned at a very young age that to be "good" and in the right was to be lovable and to be "bad" and that to be in the wrong was to be unlovable.

The inclination to highlight our accomplishments and downplay our shortcomings is natural and normal. It helps us to accentuate the positive and to reduce the power of the negative. However, it seems important to remember that it *is* a self-serving process, which means that unless we're aware of this tendency (1) we may fail to see shortcomings in ourselves that if recognized and admitted could be strengthened and (2) we may merrily and wrongly persist in the myopic belief that where wrong *does* exist, it must of course be in the other person, a line of reasoning that through the ages has provoked fights between friends, breakups between spouses, and, on a larger scale, wars between nations.

Egocentricity: The Inclination to Hype Our Own Importance

Another method we use for protecting and enhancing self-esteem is a process that Greenwald (1980) called *egocentricity,* a label for the tendency to exaggerate the importance of our role in shaping events in which we've participated.

Ross (1981) pointed to numerous illustrations of how this process works. For example, people who have worked together on a newspaper story or a research project or a musical composition may try to reconstruct the magnitude of their contributions to determine whose name goes where in the order of authorship. Since this ordering from first to last author implies level of contribution, many collaborators sit in disbelief as they hear their partners wax eloquently about why they should be the first author. None of the participants may be lying when they speak of their significant contributions because each recalls with a sort of selective, egocentric memory what he or she has done and remembers less well what others have accomplished.

This tendency to hype one's own performance is found even in marriages. For example, when Ross and Sicoly (1979) asked married couples how much each contributed to cleaning, caring for the children, making important decisions, and causing conflicts, they found that both partners claimed to have made the major contribution about 70% of the time. Of course, it is not statistically possible for a husband and a wife to each bear 70% of the responsibility for the same activity at the same time. It is not that the partners were lying about their contributions; rather, their perceptions of responsibility for everyday activities were self-centered.

All in all, social psychology research indicates that most of us see our neighbors, friends, co-workers, and classmates, compared with ourselves, as a sorry lot. Some examples you may recognize: "I was shocked to hear that Carol would do something like . . ." (others are morally and ethically weaker); "I'm no Einstein, that's for sure, but even a moron would look ahead and . . ." (others are less intelligent); "I have a few prejudices of my own, I'll admit, but I couldn't believe it when Frank refused to . . ." (others are more intolerant); "I've probably stepped on a few toes in my time, but when I heard her tell Stan that he could . . ." (others are less sensitive); "Sure I've seen reports that relate smoking to cancer, but not everyone . . ." (other smokers are more likely to get cancer). In fact, we are even inclined to think that our peers are more likely to die sooner than we are. Snyder (1980), for example, reported that college students view themselves as likely to outlive their peers by some 10 to 20 years more than predicted by actuarial tables. (Along this line, you may recall the joke about the man who said to his wife, "If one of us should die first, I think I would go live in Paris.")

It would appear that, in a subdued and controlled sort of way, an air of superiority pervades most of our self-perceptions, although it may in many instances be merely a facade for deeper insecurities. We can see such behavior most clearly in the self-centered monologues of braggarts, who, in the process of carrying on about their latest achievements, unconsciously transmit their doubts about whether or not their achievements really amounted to anything. When carried to extremes, this tendency to hype our own importance can lead to serious distortions in judgment.

The capacity to recognize our own ability and to take credit where credit is due are healthy ways to enhance our feelings of self-esteem. However, when carried to extremes this same capacity can lead to serious distortions in how we see the world around us, distortions typically caused by giving ourselves too much credit and others too little.

Cognitive Conservatism: The Tendency to Resist Change

Research on this topic points consistently to a central conclusion: people tend to selectively remember their past and choose current experiences in such a way so as to preserve and protect their views both of themselves and their world (Greenwald, 1980; Swann and Read, 1981).

The tendency to resist change fosters a common delusion, one that leads individuals, organizations, and even nations to assume that others, not they, will have to change when change is necessary. At the individual level, examples can be seen in the spouse who proclaims that if this marriage is to last, the spouse had better change his or her act, and in the students who say that if they are to learn anything, their instructors had better do something different. At the organizational level, during the mid-1970s, auto executives who had thought that their big cars would always be in demand regardless of escalating gas prices and foreign small-car competition found themselves swimming in the red ink of a dying large-car market. Chrysler, of course, did go down. Only when it changed completely, by building quality small cars, was it able to float in solvent waters (with the help of a large government loan). We have seen, indeed, continue to see, this "I don't have to change" attitude among many college administrators who, although they know that the pool of college-aged Americans will decrease by nearly 25% in the next 15 years, are slow in making concrete plans to deal with the probable decline in admissions. They figure, rightly, that even in lean years, not all colleges will shrink. And since they all tend to see their own colleges as better than average, they have little doubt that their institutions will be among the few that do not suffer.

At an international level, this "I'm O.K. as I am" posture is reflected time and again between nations in conflict. Janis (1972), for example, noted that one source of international conflict is the tendency of each side to believe in the moral superiority of its acts, which of course leads each side to conclude that it is right and need not change. Naturally, with each side sitting on the same self-righteous assumption, the dominant undercurrent will be competition rather than cooperation. Whether between two nations or two individuals, the dynamics and outcomes are similar, and the dangers are painfully evident.

Self-Handicapping: A Way to Discount Possible Failures

It is easy enough to take credit for our victories and accomplishments when we feel that our successes are basically due to our skills and competence, but what happens when we feel that our success in a particular endeavor is due more to luck than ability? Enter self-handicapping, a tactic that a person may unconsciously use in order to sabotage or avoid later performances so that a clear evaluation of ability cannot be made, thus protecting the initial favorable impression.

Imagine the following scenarios: David gets back a chemistry test and discovers, to his surprise, that he received a B +, a grade considerably higher than the C he had been hoping for. Diane, to her amazement, scores 21 points for her basketball team, a far cry from her 6.8 points-per-game average. How will David and Diane handle their unexpected successes? One way would be to bask in them, feel rewarded for their efforts, and vow publicly and privately to do equally as well if not better next time. This is a possibility if both have reasonably high self-esteem and believe that their successes are due to ability rather than luck. However, if self-esteem is low ("I'm really not that good"), or if they suspect that luck was the major factor in their successes, they may feel more threatened by the possibility of not doing as well than excited by the prospect of excelling the next time around.

To cover themselves in the event that they do not do so well in the future, David and Diane may unconsciously "handicap" themselves by placing certain obstacles in their paths so that possible future failure could be attributed to some external cause rather than to their abilities. For example, David could hardly be blamed for a poor performance on the next chemistry exam if he had been at a party the night before and was somewhat hungover. People may be more inclined to question his lack of good judgment than lack of knowledge in chemistry. Diane could hardly be expected to have a good shooting game the next time out if, during the week, she had to miss two days of practice because she did not "feel well."

In David's case, there is evidence to indicate that some people do indeed use alcohol as a self-handicapping tactic. For example, in an interesting study that illustrates this behavior, recruited students were told that they would be participating in a study designed to investigate the effects of self-determined quantities of alcohol on their intellectual performance. They took what they believed to be a high-level test of their intelligence, after which they knew they could have as much alcohol beverages as they wished (including none if they so wished) and then would take a second test. For half the subjects, the first test consisted of unsolvable problems; for the other half, the first test had straightforward answerable problems. Half the subjects in both groups were told that they were quite successful on the first test; the other half received no feedback. Two major findings emerged: (1) those subjects who received no feedback and those who were told that they were successful on the answerable problems, did not have different drinking behaviors; (2) those subjects who were told that they were successful on the unsolvable problems drank more frequently, presumably because they did well but did not know why and, thus, were anxious about their ability to do as well on the second test. Hence, they drank more, not so much to celebrate their good fortune but, presumably, to create a kind of "handicap" to which they could point an accusing finger in the event luck abandoned them in the second test (Tucker, Vuchinish, and Sobell, 1981).

In Diane's case, she could, of course, point to the fact that she had been ill, something that many people do as an expression of self-handicapping behavior (Smith, Snyder, and Perkins, 1983). Or, she could emphasize the fact that she had not been able to prepare as thoroughly as her teammates. This is, in fact, a real possibility, as was found by Rhodewalt, Saltzman, and Wittmer's (1982) investigation of swimmers. After administering a self-handicap inventory to identify high and low self-handicappers, the researchers predicted that the tendency to engage in self-handicapping behavior would be greatest before a big important meet, thinking that the swimmers might want an excuse for failure. Interestingly, there were no important differences between high and low self-handicappers in their behavior during practice before the smaller, less-important meets. However, before the *important* meets, the low self-handicappers increased their workouts and practice times, whereas high self-handicappers did not.

It is interesting to speculate about how often behavior of a similar sort occurs among students at all levels of schooling. Have you ever noted yourself backing off a bit from putting a 100 percent effort into preparation for an important event or test in which there was a great deal at stake? Could it be that you were handicapping yourself, preparing an excuse if needed? Of course, on the other side of self-handicapping behavior, if we succeed *in spite* of the obstacles we've set before us, the success looks even more impressive.

To put it in perspective, the four attribution processes we've examined are behaviors designed to help us present ourselves as positively as possible to others and to ourselves. Unwittingly, we go through our daily lives with an inclination to believe that we can do no wrong (other people are the wrongdoers), a tendency to hype our own importance (other people contribute less), a penchant for thinking that we don't need to change (others probably should, however), and an affinity for finding convenient excuses for our failures (illnesses, heavy drinking the night before, etc.). We are inclined to credit our success and achievements to personal dispositions, such as hard work, ability, and determination and to blame our failures and shortcomings on external factors, such as bad luck, unfairness, or impossible conditions (or sometimes fate when nothing else seems to fit).

Our self-serving biases would be less troubling if we were equally generous in our perception of others. However, as Ross (1977) pointed out, we are inclined to make the "fundamental attribution error" by assuming that others' failures and shortcomings are due largely to their personal qualities. By failing to give others the same benefit of the doubt that we give ourselves, the wheels of blame and accusation are set in motion, thus reducing our chances to be empathetic and understanding, responses that are more productive in the long run.

Being aware of our penchant for using these attributional processes is a big step in seeing ourselves and others more honestly. Although it is important to build a positive self-concept, it is equally important to build an accurate one so that we can know where our real strengths reside.

One of the ways we can assist ourselves in building an accurate self-concept is by being aware of the various defense mechanisms we use to protect our self-pictures, an idea we turn to next.

DEFENSE MECHANISMS
FOR PROTECTING THE SELF

The use of defense mechanisms is a normal human reaction, unless they are used to such an extreme that they begin to interfere with our ability to cope realistically with problems. For example, people who continually rationalize away their blunders are not likely to profit on subsequent occasions from their mistakes. Defense mechanisms involve a fair degree of self-deception and reality distortion. Furthermore, they function on relatively unconscious levels and, therefore, are not subject to the usual checks and balances of more conscious processes. In fact, we usually resent having someone call our attention to them because once we are conscious of them they do not serve their purposes as well.

Defense mechanisms can be best understood in view of the *objective* they serve, which is to safeguard the integrity and worth of the self. Thus, these make sense only as we conceive of an active, dynamic self that struggles to maintain a certain stability. Once we view the "self" in this framework, we may be better able to understand our ability to protect it by utilizing defense mechanisms to change the so-called "facts" so that they fit our personal needs. Knowledge about what these defense mechanisms are and how they work may help us to be aware of when we are using them in self-defeating ways and, thus, help us to stop the process before it goes too far.

With this small introduction, let us now turn to a consideration of the more important of these defense mechanisms along with a brief discussion of how each functions.

Compensation (Making Up for Perceived Deficiencies)

Compensation is an attempt to disguise or overcome the existence of what is perceived as a weak or undesirable characteristic by emphasizing a particular strength or by becoming unusually adept in one or two other areas. This defensive reaction takes many forms. For example, physically handicapped individuals may attempt to overcome their handicaps directly through increased effort and persistence. Tom Dempsey, who with a genetically deformed foot set a National Football League field goal record of 63 yards, and Jerry Taylor, crippled at birth by cerebral palsy, who completed a 12-mile marathon in little over seven hours on special arm crutches, are specific examples of how it is possible to compensate for a shortcoming through extra effort and hard work.

Usually, however, compensatory reactions are more indirect. That is, there is an effort either to substitute for the defect or to draw attention away from it: the girl who regards herself as unattractive may develop an exceptionally winning personality; the uncoordinated boy may turn from athletics to scholastics. Indeed, a whole science of cosmetics and dress has developed that has as its major objectives the modification of the human anatomy—its features, expressions, and protrusions. The short man is made to look tall, the fat woman thin, the colorless one glamorous, the flat one curvaceous, and so on, each modified to compensate for having too much or too little, as the case may be.

Not all compensatory behaviors are desirable or useful. For example, a person who feels unloved may become sexually promiscuous; the boy who feels inferior may become the neighborhood bully; the person who feels insecure may eat or drink too much; the individual who feels inadequate may brag endlessly.

We constantly compare ourselves with others and frequently gauge our worth by how we see ourselves in relation to other people's status, achievements, and possessions. This can lead to strong motivation toward at least average and, if possible, superior achievement. In meeting these conditions, compensating behaviors may help, but when they become exaggerated or take antisocial forms, they hinder rather than assist people who are trying to express their potential.

Denial (Ignoring the Unpleasant)

Sometimes we manage to avoid disagreeable realities by ignoring or refusing to acknowledge them. This inclination is exemplified in a great many of our everyday behaviors. We turn away from unpleasant sights; we refuse to discuss unpleasant topics; we ignore or disclaim criticism; and sometimes we refuse to face our real problems. A vain woman may deny a vision problem to avoid wearing glasses; an insecure middle-aged man may deny his years by pursuing younger women; or a student with low self-esteem may deny his competency by attributing a high grade on a test to "luck." Parents, for example, are notoriously blind when it comes to the defects of their offspring. I recall one mother, whose ten-year-old boy had been diagnosed as brain damaged by a team of experts, who asserted that his "head was just developing slower than the rest of him, that's all."

The common adages "None is so blind as he who will not see" and "Love is blind" perhaps illustrate even more clearly our tendency to look away from those things that are incompatible with our desires and needs. This mechanism does, indeed, guard us from painful experiences. However, like the proverbial ostrich who buries his head in the sand, denial may also get in the way of our "seeing" things that might otherwise facilitate progress toward more effective living and greater maturity.

Displacement (Shifting Negative Feelings to Someone Safer)

Displacement refers to the shift of emotion or fantasy away from the person or object toward which it was originally directed to a more neutral or less-dangerous person or object. For example, the man upbraided by his boss may suppress the anger he feels toward the boss because he knows he would be in deep trouble if he expressed his feelings. So he comes home and yells at his wife for not having dinner ready and at the children for being too noisy. Not infrequently, the smallest incident may serve as a trigger that releases pent-up emotional feelings in a torrent of displaced anger and abuse. A young house-wife had been admonished by her husband for not being more efficient and later in the same day lost her purse while shopping. On her way home she was halted by a police officer for speeding. That was the final straw. She exploded with a volley of abuse on the startled officer, ranging from "Haven't you anything better to do than chase women?" to blaming him generally for the city's traffic condition, which he should have been working on rather than harassing busy, civic-minded citizens for barely exceeding the speed limit.

Displacement is a valuable mechanism because it enables us to vent dangerous emotional impulses without risking loss of love and possible retaliation and without the necessity of even recognizing the person for whom such feelings were originally intended. By displacing his bottled-up anger on his wife and children, the man maintains his feelings of respect and cordiality toward his domineering boss. The wife who released her rage on the police officer can more easily avoid ambivalent feelings toward a husband who demands that she be more tidy.

Unfortunately, displacements can become too deviant and can result in continual avoidance of situations that could be more efficiently handled by a more direct approach. Usually, we are psychologically better off when we learn to express and discuss our feelings with the person for whom the feelings are intended in the first place.

Emotional Insulation (Putting Up a Wall of Armor)

An emotionally insulated person is basically an individual who has put up a wall between himself or herself and the outside world and stands passively behind it. It is usually a person who has been hurt, or disappointed, or disillusioned and who, as a consequence, pulls back from further risks. For example, it is not uncommon to see this behavior in people coming away from broken relationships. If there has been deep hurt, they may have difficulty letting themselves go in the sense of entering fully into other close relationships. Living in the wraps of emotional insulation may be a safe mode of living, but it can also be a lonely one.

Getting emotionally involved in the business of living does, indeed, involve certain "calculated risks." For example, there is always the possibility that the person we give our affection to may reject us or be taken from us by death. Healthy people operate on the assumption that the rewards of emotional involvement are worth the risks, even though they also know that they shall inevitably feel pain and disappointment in life, too.

Used in mild dosages, emotional insulation is an important defense against too much hurt and disappointment. However, when used to the extent that one becomes "an island unto oneself," it can curtail a person's healthy and active participation in life and can lead to eventual shallowness and blunting of emotional involvement. When we dare not hope, we cease to grow. When there is no risk, there is no loss; but there is no gain either.

Fantasy (Imagining Something Better)

Not only do we frequently deny unpleasant reality, but we are also inclined to "embellish" our perceptions so that the world is seen more as we would like it to be. Fantasy is stimulated by frustrated desires and grows primarily out of mental images associated with need gratification. It can be productive or nonproductive. Productive fantasy, as in creative imagination, can be used constructively in solving problems or it can be a kind of nonproductive wish-fulfilling activity that compensates for a *lack* of achievement rather than stimulating or promoting it. Albert Einstein, for example, used mental pictures, or "fantasies," that led to productive hypotheses, formulas, and solutions. On the other hand, James Thurber's *The Secret Life of Walter Mitty* is a classic example of how we can achieve wished-for status by imagining that we are rich, powerful, and respected.

The capacity to remove ourselves temporarily from unpleasant reality into a more affable world of fantasy has considerable therapeutic value. Fantasy may, for example, add the dash of excitement and interest we need to motivate us to greater efforts toward our goals in real life. However, the individual who *consistently* turns to fantasy as a solution to a troublesome reality is in danger psychologically. It is particularly under conditions of extreme frustration and deprivation that our fantasies are likely to get out of hand. During times of this sort, we would be well advised to be wary of solutions conjured up by fantasies. For example, Bettelheim (1943) found that at the concentration camps of Dachau and Buchenwald, "the longer the time a prisoner had spent in camp, the less true to reality were his daydreams; so much so that the hopes and expectations of the old prisoners often took the form of eschatological and messianic hopes."

Nonetheless, there is good evidence to suggest that fantasizing and daydreaming are not only normal but also an almost universal activity among people of both sexes. It is when we use these processes as a permanent and not a temporary escape that we are apt to get ourselves into trouble. It is one thing to build a castle in the sky; it is quite another to try to live in it.

Humor (Looking at the Lighter Side)

A nonhostile sense of humor is one of the truly elegant defenses in the human repertoire. Humor, like hope, can be one of our most potent antidotes in dealing with the inevitable hurts and disappointments of everyday living. It is the capacity to see something lighter in the darker moments. In a longitudinal study designed to follow the lives of 268 men over a 35-year period, Vaillant (1977) noted that the psychologically healthiest, those best at coping with life's ups and downs, were most apt to have a well-developed sense of humor.

Through humor and wit, emotional effect is momentarily displaced or concealed. Unlike repression, which buries problems, or denial, which overlooks them, humor provides temporary relief by restructuring the problem into something less threatening. For example, a couple of years ago I was flying home from a conference when suddenly, at 30,000 feet, the aircraft began to vibrate and shake and lose altitude quickly, emergency lights went on, seat belt signs flashed, there were gasps, a few screams, and a subdued wave of panic among the passengers. My eyes met those of the man next to me, who looked as frightened as I felt. Smiling weakly, he said, "You know, if the worst happens, I'm in deep trouble with my wife. I told her I'd mow the lawn *after* I got home." In spite of our circumstances, we both chuckled. (And, I presume, his lawn did get mowed.)

There is an old saying, more true than we may have suspected: He who laughs, lasts.

Projection (Blaming the Other Person)

Projection is a means by which people (1) relegate the blame for their own shortcomings, mistakes, and transgressions to others, and (2) attribute to others their own unacceptable impulses, feelings, thoughts, and desires. Projection is a form of blame (Hamachek, 1987). It enables people to look outward at others' behaviors rather than inward at their own. For example, who among us has not taken refuge in the comforting conclusion that it is the other person—certainly not oneself—who is untrustworthy, stupid, phony, unfriendly, or the cause of one's latest problem? Who has not felt at one time or another that life's difficulties would diminish significantly if it were not for that other person's manner, temperament, or personality?

When something is projected, whether it is a beam of light cast on a screen or one's own personal characteristics attributed to another person, it is taken from the inside and put on the outside where it can be seen more clearly. Even though we may not be aware of it, those characteristics that we see so vividly in others may simply be reflected images of certain aspects of our own self-concept about which we prefer not to think.

One way to keep a disturbing feeling at a distance is to act as if it were not one's own; this is when projection enters the picture. Denial, as one of the featured cogs in the mechanism of projection, begins the process by blocking an anxiety-provoking feeling or impulse from awareness. The next step is the displacement of those feelings onto someone else. Thus, it is not my anger at Robert that is the issue, it is Robert's anger at me; it is not my lack of good judgment that got us into this mess, it is Sally's lack of common sense; it is not me who is a phony, it is my boss and his or her manipulative behavior. Once cast out onto someone else, the projected aspect of the self is encountered as though it were a complete stranger—though one that reflects a remarkable similarity to the denied and displaced original. Thus, projection has performed its ultimate function: a personally threatening thought was alienated from the self, denied access to awareness, suppressed into the unconscious, and then passed on to someone outside oneself, where one then sees the thought or a flaw in another person. More often than we may recognize, the windows through which we claim to see so clearly the behavior of others may really be a mirror reflecting our own.

Rationalization (Inventing Excuses)

Rationalization has two primary defensive objectives: (1) It helps us invent excuses for doing what we don't think we should do but want to do anyway, and (2) it helps us soften the disappointment connected to not reaching a goal we had set for ourselves. Typically, it involves thinking up logical, socially acceptable reasons for our past, present, or future behavior. With not too much effort, we can soon think of a reason for not getting up for an eight o'clock class ("It'll probably be a dull lecture anyway"), for going to a movie instead of studying ("There really isn't *that* much to do"), for eating too much ("*Tomorrow* I'll start my diet"), and on and on.

There are endless ways for justifying our behavior and protecting our self-concept. Some examples are: Marty, who feels he may have a drinking problem, vows to have only one beer at the party, but he ends up drinking five after telling himself that, since it was a lite beer, it wasn't as harmful; Mandy, who is opposed to cheating, ends up getting answers from the exam of two of her classmates after she convinces herself that, since everyone cheats, this is her only chance. If Marty had to face the seriousness of his drinking problem or if Mandy had to acknowledge that she was really not well prepared, each would probably feel ashamed and guilty—hence, the rationalizations, the excuses.

Sometimes, of course, it is difficult to know where an objective consideration of facts leaves off and rationalization begins. Two behavioral symptoms of excessive rationalization are (1) hunting for reasons to justify behavior and beliefs and (2) getting emotional (angry, reactive) when someone questions the reasons we offer. Should these reactions occur, it is usually a good time to pause and examine how factual our reasons really are. The price of excessive rationalization, of course, is self-deception, for if we accept reasons for our behavior that are not true, we are less likely to profit from our errors. Carried to extremes, this could lead eventually to the development of false beliefs or delusions sustained in the face of contradictory evidence.

Reaction Formation (Feeling One Way, Behaving in Another)

Whereas denial is the reluctance to see things as they are, reaction formation (sometimes called "reversal") carries denial one step further. A fact or feeling is denied, then transformed into its opposite: "I detest you" becomes "I love you"; "I am depressed and sad" changes to "I am happy and joyful." Thus, reaction formation is a handy way to sanitize impulses and feelings that reflect the darker side of one's nature. For example, it is not uncommon to find that certain people interested in serving as self-appointed guardians of the public's morals, who voluntarily devote time to reading "dirty" books and magazines and investigating burlesque shows and who are generally obsessed with censoring all things with implicit or explicit sexual content, are frequently found to have unusually high impulses in that direction themselves. Sometimes, the most aggressive crusaders are fighting their own suppressed impulses as well as condemning them in others.

Reaction formation has adjustive value insofar as it helps us to maintain socially approved behavior and to control unacceptable impulses. On the other hand, this mechanism, too, is self-deceptive and can lead to exaggerated and rigid fears or beliefs, which could lead to excessive harshness or severity in dealing with the values of others and ourselves.

Regression (Returning to Younger Behaviors)

Regression involves a retreat, in the face of stress, to the use of behavioral patterns appropriate at earlier levels of development. It usually involves modification of behavior in the direction of more primitive, infantile expressions. For example, when a new addition to the family is brought home from the hospital, it is not uncommon for the older child, who may feel that her status is threatened, to regress, or "go back," to bedwetting, baby talk, thumb sucking, demands for her mother's attention, and other infantile behaviors. We may, when frustrated, return to the temper tantrums or sulking that got us our way when growing up; we may pout when we don't get our own way; or we may "cry like a baby" when feeling great emotional pain.

Regression can perhaps be better understood if we remember a child's gradual shift from helplessness and dependency on parents to increasingly independent behavior and responsibility. This developmental process from dependency to independency is an arduous task, and it is common for all of us, confronting a harsher and more demanding adult world, to yearn now and then for the carefree and sheltered days of infancy and childhood. Consequently, it is not surprising that in the face of severe stress we may retreat periodically from our adult status to an earlier level of growth and adjustment.

Regression is, however, more comprehensive than merely resorting to earlier behavior patterns when new ones have failed. In regression, a person retreats to a less-demanding personal status—one that involves lower personal goals and expectations and more readily accomplished satisfaction. For example, watching hours of television when feeling heavily burdened would be a milder expression of regressive behavior.

Regression may help us find some temporary relief from the demands and responsibilities of our adult worlds, but as with other defense mechanisms, when used as a primary mode of adjustment, it can serve as a giant roadblock to more mature behavior.

Repression (Forgetting the Unpleasant)

Repression is a defensive reaction through which painful or dangerous thoughts and desires are excluded from consciousness. It has often been labeled as "selective forgetting," but it is more in the nature of selective remembering. It is a way of protecting one's personal equilibrium by forgetting experiences that are upsetting. Repression is by no means always complete. Vague feelings of unworthiness, insecurity, and guilt often are signs of incomplete repression. Along this line, I recall a client of mine who struggled for several months working through the nagging guilt feelings he always had whenever he felt sexually attracted to a woman. He knew it was in some way related to his childhood and his mother's attitudes, but he didn't know exactly how. During one of our sessions, as he was sorting through his buried file of memories, he recalled a time when he was eight years old and his mother caught him and a seven-year-old girl in the basement, both with pants down, exploring each other. He was spanked, admonished for being a bad, nasty boy, and sent directly to bed. So painful was that experience that, with time, he "forgot" it, but it served nonetheless as an unconscious hatchery from which guilt was spawned whenever he had any kind of sexual feeling about a woman. It was the key to insight, and once he had unlocked that memory and was able to look at it in connection with a mother who had neurotic fears about sex, he was in a better position to examine his own fears, which, with this new understanding, he was able to overcome.

The repression of undesirable impulses and experiences not only demands considerable energy but also hinders healthy personality integration. A realistic confrontation of problems is always more conducive to good mental health and positive self-development.

Sublimation (Substituting One Goal for Another)

Sublimation involves the acceptance of a socially approved substitute goal for a drive whose normal channel of expression is blocked. There are many ways in which motives can be sublimated. As an illustration, curiosity about people, which can express itself in undesirable ways (voyeurism, sexual conversation, gossip, nosiness about the affairs of others) and which may lead to feelings of guilt, can be sublimated into art and medicine, in which the human body can be viewed without conflict or reprisal, or it can be sublimated into counseling or psychology, in which behavior and motives can be discussed at will. Individuals with strong aggressive impulses may find suitable expression for those impulses in competitive sports or vigorous physical outlets, which range from karate to judo to aerobic dancing.

The defensive functions of sublimation are somewhat different from those of compensation because the motivation is different. Whereas compensation is founded on some kind of inadequacy, sublimation is directed more toward the reduction of guilt associated with such motives as aggression, sex, curiosity, cruelty, and the paternal or maternal drive. A classic illustration of sublimation is the redirection of the maternal or paternal drive of the childless woman or man through teaching, social work, recreation work, or pediatric medicine, all of which provide opportunities for a wholesome expression of the desire for and love of children.

Suppression (Conscious Exclusion of Unpleasant Thoughts)

Suppression differs from repression in that it is largely a conscious process of deliberately excluding certain thoughts from immediate awareness because they are disturbing or painful. For example, to be thinking constantly about the assignment due in one week, or the serious talk that has to happen with a loved one, or the pile of bills that need to be paid in the near future are upsetting thoughts, and we might easily conclude, "I will think about that tomorrow." We allow ourselves a temporary respite. However, when tomorrow arrives we *do* remember to think about it.

Undoing (Counteracting Unacceptable Desires or Acts)

Undoing involves behavior that is designed to negate or atone for some disapproved act or thought. It is as if a person has misspelled a word and wants to erase it and start again. An apology is an act of undoing. If sincere, it is an effort to "undo" the damage and start fresh. Frequently, however, the undoing is more indirect. For example, one unfaithful spouse may suddenly shower the other with especially loving attention; an unethical business executive may give a large sum of money to the church; or the busy and much-absent parent may pamper and spoil the children when he or she is not working.

Undoing can be a healthy and normal response when we realize we have hurt someone, and when we would like to make amends in a way that might help patch the relationship. It is unhealthy and self-defeating when it becomes a substitute for the kind of forethought that would have prevented the need for amends in the first place.

Defense Mechanisms in Perspective

The very name, "defense mechanisms," suggests the basic function of these psychic guardians. Each plays a part in helping to preserve the identity and integrity of the self. We would be in serious trouble if, from time to time, we couldn't compensate for a weakness or rationalize a failure or repress a hurtful experience or fantasize a more pleasant reality when the one we live in is too upsetting. On the other hand, we would be in equally serious trouble if we compensated so often and so quickly for our weaknesses that we failed to see if the weaknesses themselves could be repaired, if we so consistently rationalized our failures that we blinded ourselves to why they happened in the first place, or if we so quickly repressed hurtful experiences (by refusing to think about them) that we didn't allow ourselves to learn why they happened so we could be wiser in the future.

Defense mechanisms, then, help us to keep our self-concept intact and reasonably stable. They constitute a kind of psychological buffer zone through which our assorted failures, shames, shortcomings, and embarrassments must first pass. When we are too heavily defended, we may never see those qualities in our behavior or performance that may need correcting. For example, if you are so busy claiming it is *my* fault, you are not likely to see where your own fault lies. On the other hand, if all our defenses were to break down, the slightest criticism or the smallest failure could cause our self-concept to crumble for lack of support.

Usually, you can tell if your defense mechanisms are operating at about the right level of efficiency when you feel unhappy about a blunder but not destroyed or when you feel personally disappointed about a flawed performance but not emotionally decimated or when on the heels of failing, you are able to conclude, "I *have* failed and I don't like it" rather than "I *am* a failure and I don't like *myself.*"

SELF-PERCEPTION THEORY: A WAY TO GROW IN SELF-KNOWLEDGE

Not long ago, I asked a friend and colleague—a graduate of a nearby university, which happens to be a fierce athletic rival—who he was going to root for at an important basketball game. Torn as ever between his old ties and his new allegiance, he said, "You know, I just haven't decided yet. I'll have to wait and see which side I yell for." In this candid response lies the central idea behind Bem's (1972) interesting theory of self-perception, which is, basically, that we come to know our own attitudes or feelings partly by inferring them from observations of our own behavior.

One way, for example, that we come to know others is by watching and listening to their nonverbal and verbal behavior and then making inferences based on those observations. We can use this same technique for knowing ourselves, at least in some instances. The qualifier "in some instances" is added because this process is most likely to work in situations in which our own internal feelings are weak or ambiguous or, as in the case of my friend, conflicted. For example, if we very much like another person and know it, we wouldn't have to infer those positive feelings from the fact that we may look for excuses to be in his or her company. Similarly, we are only inclined to use our overt behavior as a guide to our inner feelings in situations in which this behavior is freely chosen. In conditions in which we feel somehow forced to behave in one way or the other, we will not be likely to use that behavior (e.g., reading the book) as a sign (that we really like the book).

There are any number of illustrations of how self-perception theory works in our everyday lives without us even knowing it. For example, have you ever found, once you sat down to the table and started eating, that you were hungrier than you thought? Have you ever, once you started to say goodbye to someone, found you were going to miss that person more than you had realized? Or once the exam was in front of you, did you feel more fearful and uncertain than you imagined? Or once you lost your temper, did you discover you were much angrier than you believed? Or have you ever found yourself, as did my friend, in a conflict, not knowing your real feelings until you had to make a choice? (Couples, married and unmarried, frequently discover their *real* feelings for each other, for better or worse, when confronted with the decision—choice, actually—of staying together or not.) My friend, should you be interested, yelled himself hoarse for his alma mater, which told both him and me something about his true feelings on that matter.

Just as we learn about the nature of others by observing their behavior, self-perception theory suggests that we can also keep a watchful eye on our own behavior to learn more about ourselves. Thus, if you want to assess what kind of self-concept you have under certain conditions, observe how you behave in those conditions.

SPECULATIONS ABOUT WHY SELF-GROWTH MAY BE RESISTED

The self is a growing, expanding, dynamic phenomenon—more so for some than for others. For some, personal growth and movement toward higher levels of achievement and self-expression seem more scary than exciting. Let us turn to some speculations about why this may be so.

Fear of Maturity

Some individuals avoid finding out more about themselves for fear of having to give up a self with which they have grown comfortable or "satisfied." Most people have an initial inclination to resist personal change anyway, but this resistance is even stronger for those who refuse to insert new or changed behavior into their current concept of self. For example, a shy, timid, submissive person may not want to know his strengths and assets for fear that he might have to be more assertive and socially aggressive. If shyness has become a way of life designed to protect him from the risks of social disapproval (in this case, nothing ventured, nothing lost in terms of self-esteem), it may be difficult, indeed, for him to give up being timid. Other individuals are reluctant to find out more about themselves because of the threat of having to become more personally mature. Maturity implies many things, among which are certain degrees of independence and autonomy, capacity for self-discipline, certainty about goals and values, and motivation toward some level of personal achievement. Most of all, greater maturity means greater responsibility, and for some, this may be a frightening possibility.

Fear of Success

Success has many meanings: it may mean getting an A in a particular course, winning a tennis match, changing a psychological "tape," getting married, losing weight, making a million dollars, and so on. What is a success for one person may not be for another, and in this sense, success is a highly individual matter. The fears and penalties associated with achieving success, however we define it, appear to be an age-old phenomenon that few entirely escape.

Why should some people fear success more than others? One possible reason is that success establishes a precedent, a standard to be lived up to, or a performance level to be maintained, and this may be frightening to individuals who have basic doubts about their ability to sustain a high level of personal performance. For example, I have known students who will invest only a given amount of time to preparing for an exam. One student explained, "You see, if I study too hard—I mean really study—I might get a high grade; it would be because I studied so hard. Other students in the class might think I was smarter than I really was, and what would they think of me the first time I *didn't* do real well?" This particular student persisted in getting C's and an occasional B here and there and, in so doing, avoided both the stigma of failure and the risk of success.

Success may also mean "I am my brother's keeper." That is, success could be interpreted as having to take care of those less successful, which could be felt as something of a burden. I recall a salesperson client of mine who deliberately made less money (and in that sense was less successful) than he was capable of making to avoid the possibility of taking care of his parents in their later years. As he said, "Look, I've never felt too close to my parents anyway, and if I made more money, I'd feel guilty if I didn't look out for them. This way I made enough but not so much that I have to worry about that."

Some persons are fearful of success, fearful of moving on to higher levels of personal realization and personal performance primarily because they doubt their ability to maintain a high standard of performance if they do achieve it. In this sense, fear of success and fear of greater maturity are very much related. The more successful one is in, let's say, performance, skills, knowledge, sense of perspective, or leadership, the more people expect of that person. And the more people expect of a person, the more opportunities or possibilities there are for failing. For some individuals, there seems to be just too great a risk in establishing a reputation for competency; too much is then expected. Some persons find refuge and safety in being neither too far behind the pack nor too far ahead of it.

Fear of One's Best

Although most of us have a need to improve ourselves, to actualize more of our potentialities, and to move toward greater human fulfillment, Maslow (1967) noted that many of us stop short of becoming what we could become because of what he called a "fear of one's own greatness" or the "invasion of one's destiny" or the "running away from one's best talent."

> Not only are we ambivalent about our own highest possibilities, we are also in perpetual . . . conflict and ambivalence over these same possibilities in other people, and in human nature in general. Certainly we love and admire good men, saints—honest, virtuous, clean men. But could anybody who has looked into the depths of human nature fail to be aware of our mixed and often hostile feelings toward saintly men? Or toward our intellectual geniuses? . . . We surely love and admire all the persons who have incarnated the true, the good, the beautiful, and just, the perfect, the ultimately successful. And yet they also make us uneasy, anxious, confused, perhaps a little jealous or envious, a little inferior, clumsy. They usually make us lose our aplomb, our self-possession and self-regard. (p. 164)

Why should this be? Why is it that our self-composure frequently leaves in the face of another person's eminence, greatness, intellect, beauty, or whatever? One reason may be that people who are superior in one way or other make us momentarily more aware of our lesser abilities or skills, without even intending to do so. We may not be conscious of why we feel stupid or unattractive or inferior, and we sometimes end up being defensive and resentful. That is, we respond as if the person we regard as superior were deliberately trying to make us feel inferior. Resentment, jealousy, or envy are then undesirable consequences.

Understandable as they may be, feelings of this sort are ultimately self-defeating. In the process of being resentful or envious of another person's accomplishments, we sometimes deny that that person attained them in any honorable way. And what we may unwittingly do is invent excuses for why people who are superior to us happen to be more important or successful or skilled than we see ourselves. For example, how many times have you heard comments like "If I brownnosed like he did, I'd get A's, too"; "Sure she dates lots of men, but look at how aggressive she is"; "Big deal—I'd have high grades too, if all I did was study"; "Well, who wouldn't be beautiful if they could afford to have their hair done once a week like she does!" And so it goes. These are self-defeating feelings because in the process of denying that another person is bright or skilled or accomplished or good-looking, we are also denying the possibility of having these qualities ourselves. For example, the student who says, "I'd have high grades, too, if all I did was study" could be making an assertion that is, in fact, true, or he could be insinuating that anyone (including himself, of course) was capable of getting high grades if he studied hard. In either case, the net effect is an effort to make nonattainment of high grades seem less important and less threatening than what actually may be the case. (If high grades were really *not* important to a person, he wouldn't have to *act* as if they were unimportant by reducing another individual's accomplishments.)

When we stop responding to people who are in some way superior to us as if they were trying to make us feel inferior, we are closer to appreciating not only what they have but also what we could be. We may also find that as we learn to accept more completely the highest values and qualities in others, we may be able to accept our own high qualities and values in a less-frightened way. Of course, it can work the other way, too. As we learn to accept our own accomplishments or talents without embarrassment, discomfort, defensiveness, or false humility, we may be better able to accept them in others as well.

Fear of Knowing

Fear of knowing is a tricky phenomenon. Although "knowing" or having knowledge can be one of the quickest ways to enhance self-esteem and to feel personally competent, it can also be felt as a high-risk means for achieving those ends. An observation by Maslow (1968) may help us understand this idea better:

> . . . we can seek knowledge in order to reduce anxiety and we can also avoid knowing in order to reduce anxiety. Knowledge and action are very closely bound together [and] this close relation between knowing and doing can help us to interpret one cause of the fear of knowing as deeply a fear of doing, a fear of the consequences that flow from knowing, a fear of its dangerous responsibilities. Often it is better not to know, because if you *did* know, then you would have to stick your neck out. (p. 66)

What Maslow is talking about is not unlike the wife who fears her husband is being unfaithful but prefers not to know it. If she did, she would have to do something about it and perhaps lose him in the process. It is better not to know. Or consider the pedestrians who continue hurriedly by a fallen man clutching his chest and asking for help as if they were suddenly deaf and blind to the sights and sounds around them. It is safer not to know. If they knew, they would either have to do something or else feel guilty about being cowards.

"Knowing" more or having more knowledge may cause three separate but related events, any one of which may intensify the fear of knowing. First, it heightens expectations from others for what we can do. Second, knowing makes it more difficult to remain in a safe, subordinate position to those we may regard as superior to ourselves. When we think of the number of times that children are taught that "knowing" more than their parents is wrong ("Who do you think you are, young lady!" "You're acting pretty big for your britches, aren't you fella!"), it is not difficult to understand why knowing more than someone in authority can be risky. Third, knowing makes us more personally responsible for our own behavior; we cannot as easily claim either innocence or ignorance as our excuse. An acquaintance of mine, an avid heavy smoker, deliberately goes out of his way to avoid either discussions or reading material regarding possible causal ties between cancer and smoking. As he says with his usual candor, "I don't *want* to know, dammit. I want to smoke!"

IN PERSPECTIVE

This chapter is devoted to the idea that the self is both an intellectual construct with roots as far back as the seventeenth century and a personal construct that helps each of us know who we are as individuals. We have examined its development within the framework of Erikson's first five psychosocial stages in an effort to identify some of the particular behaviors that might be associated with healthy or unhealthy self-concept and ego development within each stage. In addition, we have reviewed how social intervention, social roles, and others' expectations can shape both the content and expression of a person's concept of self. We have also explored the possibility that, although each of us has just one self, we may choose to show different versions of that self at different times depending on the situation and the people around us. Further, we have examined how the four major components of self-concept—physical, social, emotional, and intellectual—interact to influence each other in reciprocal ways. In turn, we have seen how these components of the self interact with the three major domains of the self—perceived self, ideal self, and real self—to affect the final shape of one's current concept of self.

Whereas self-concept reflects the cognitive part of our self-perceptions, self-esteem is the evaluative component of self-perceptions. Our level of self-esteem is a barometer of how we *feel* about ourselves—good or bad, high worth, or low worth. Self-esteem is influenced significantly by the comparisons we make of ourselves to others, by our personal aspirations, and by feedback we receive from others. It is greatly affected by both interpersonal and intrapsychic factors. People will go to great lengths to protect their self-esteem, since it is the foundation on which an entire personality superstructure resides. Ordinarily, we tend to use four rather common self-attributional processes to preserve and protect self-esteem, which include the tendency to assume that we can do no wrong, the inclination to hype our own importance, the tendency to resist change (the other person will have to), and a propensity for figuring out ways to discount failures. In addition, we have at our disposal a vast array of defense mechanisms, each specifically geared to helping us see ourselves and our circumstances in the most favorable way possible. We do not easily cave in to the stresses and demands of everyday living.

Our concept of ourselves is a very personal possession. How we view ourselves is determined partially by how we perceive ourselves as really being, how we view ourselves as we ideally want to be, and how we perceive the expectations that others have for us. These are complex, interrelated perceptual processes, no one of which is more important than the other. Depending on the individual, each of these perceptions contributes more or less to our feelings of selfhood. For some, expressing their real self, whatever it may be, is most important, and they struggle to stay as close as possible in tune with the harmony of that inner self. For others, striving to become that ideal self is the guiding star that gives them their sense of purpose and direction. For still others, looking to and obeying the expectations of the world around them is their most satisfying mode of self-expression.

Although complete knowledge about oneself is probably neither necessary nor possible, it is, nonetheless, possible to come closer to an understanding of our upper and lower limits, our private fears and guarded hopes, our secret dreams and wildest ambitions if we remain open to who we think we are, where we would like to go, and why we are headed in that direction to begin with.

QUESTIONS FOR STUDY, REVIEW, AND REFLECTION

1. The self contains both self-as-object and self-as-doer components. What are some differences between them, and how does each contribute to a person's overall self-concept?

2. How do the concepts, *object permanence* and *object identity* help us explain the development of self-awareness?

3. A parent asks you, "Is any one of Erikson's first five psychosocial stages more important than the rest?" How would you respond?

4. Based on your knowledge about yourself, which of those five stages is/are most positively developed in you? Which is/are least well developed? To which life experiences would you attribute your responses?

5. The discussion about stereotypes suggested that, where they exist, we tend to respond to the stereotype we have rather than to the person. Think about your own stereotypes for a moment. Do you have any in particular that shape your attitudes toward certain others? How is your behavior influenced by those stereotypes?

6. What are the basic differences between high and low self-monitors? Which are you most like? Who, in your family, are you most like in that regard? Why do you suppose you were so influenced by that person?

7. How does one's self-concept differ from one's self-esteem?

8. How would you explain the idea of *possible selves* to someone interested in greater personal awareness?

9. Suppose you were asked to explain how self-attribution processes are used to enhance self-esteem. How would you reply?

10. Of the four attribution processes described, which one(s) do you recognize in your own behavior?

11. How would you explain the basic purpose and objective of defense mechanisms to someone who was naive about them?

12. The point was made that if you want to know yourself better, observe how you behave. How would you explain this idea to someone who wanted to know how that worked?

13. Why do some people resist growing in self-knowledge?

REFERENCES

Allport, G. *Becoming.* New Haven: Yale University Press, 1955, pp. 104–105.

Arnstein, H. S. *The Roots of Love.* Indianapolis: Bobbs-Merrill, 1975.

Backman, C., Secord, P., and Pierce, J. "Resistance to Change in Self-Concept as a Function of Consensus Among Significant Others." *Sociometry,* 1963, *26:* 102–111.

Baumgardner, A. H., and Arkin, R. M. "Coping With the Prospect of Social Disapproval: Strategies and Sequelae," in C. R. Snyder and C. Ford (Eds.), *Clinical and Social Psychological Perspectives on Negative Life Events.* New York: Plenum, 1987.

Bem, D. J. "Self-Perception Theory," in L. Berkowitz (Ed.), *Advances in Experimental and Social Psychology,* Vol. 6. New York: Academic Press, 1972.

Bergin, A. E. "The Effect of Dissonant Persuasive Communications Upon Changes in Self-referring Attitudes." *Journal of Personality,* 1962, *30:* 423–438.

Berstein, A. M., Stephan, G., and Davis, M. H. "Explaining Attribution for Achievement: A Path Analytic Approach." *Journal of Personality and Social Psychology,* 1979, *37:* 1810–1821.

Bettelheim, B. "Individual and More Behavior in Extreme Situations." *Journal of Abnormal and Social Psychology,* 1943, *38:* 443.

Bradley, G. W. "Self-serving Biases in the Attribution Process: A Re-examination of the Fact or Fiction Question." *Journal of Personality and Social Psychology,* 1978, *35:* 56–71.

Braun, C. "Teacher Expectations: Socio-psychological Dynamics." *Review of Educational Research,* 1976, *46:* 185–213.

Brim, O. G., and Kagan, J. (Eds.). *Constancy and Change in Human Development.* Cambridge, Mass.: Harvard University Press, 1980.

Brophy, J. "Research on the Self-fulfilling Prophesy and Teacher Expectations." *Journal of Educational Psychology,* 1983, *75:* 631–661.

Cooley, C. H. *Human Nature and Social Order.* New York: Charles Scribner's Sons, 1902.

Coopersmith, S. *The Antecedents of Self-Esteem.* San Francisco: W. H. Freeman, 1967.

Davis, K. "Final Note on a Case of Extreme Isolation." *American Journal of Sociology,* 1974, *52:* 8.

Dewey, J. *Democracy and Education.* New York: Macmillan, 1916.

Dickie, J. R., and Strader, W. H. "Development of Mirror Image Responses in Infancy." *The Journal of Psychology,* 1974, *88:* 333–337.

Edwards, C. P., and Lewis, M. "Young Children's Concepts of Social Relations: Social Functions and Social Objects," in M. Lewis and L. Rosenblum (Eds.), *The Child and His Family.* New York: Plenum, 1979.

Erikson, E. H. *Childhood and Society,* 2nd ed. New York: Norton, 1963.

Erikson, E. H. *Identity, Youth, and Crises.* New York: Norton, 1968.

Erikson, E. H. *Identity and the Life Cycle.* New York: Norton, 1980.

Erikson, E. H. *The Life Cycle Completed.* New York: Norton, 1982.

Evans, R. I. *Dialogue With Erik Erikson.* New York: Praeger, 1981.

Gabrenya, W. R., and Arkin, R. M. "Self-Monitoring Scale: Factor Structure and Correlates." *Personality and Social Psychology Bulletin,* 1980, *6:* 12–22.

Gallup, G. G. "Self-recognition in Chimpanzees and Man: A Developmental and Comparative Perspective," in M. Lewis and L. Rosenbaum (Eds.), *The Child and His Family.* New York: Plenum, 1979.

Gergen, K. J. *The Concept of Self.* New York: Holt, Rinehart and Winston, 1971.

Gergen, K. J. "The Healthy, Happy Human Being Wears Many Masks." *Psychology Today,* May, 1972, pp. 31–35, 64, 66.

Goffman, E. *The Presentation of Self in Everyday Life.* Garden City, N.Y.: Doubleday Anchor, 1959.

Goffman, E. *Relations in Public.* New York: Basic Books, 1971.

Greenberg, J., Pyszczynski, T., and Solomon, S. "The Self-Serving Attributional Bias: Beyond Self-Presentation." *Journal of Experimental Social Psychology,* 1982, *18:* 56–67.

Greenwald, A. G. "The Totalitarian Ego: Fabrication and Revision of Personal History." *American Psychologist,* 1980, *35:* 603–613.

Haimowitz, M. L. "Criminals Are Made, Not Born," in D. E. Hamachek (Ed.), *Human Dynamics in Psychology and Education,* 3rd ed. Boston: Allyn S. Bacon, 1968.

Hamachek, D. "The Dynamics of Projection: It's Use in Expanding Self-knowledge." *Journal of Humanistic Education and Development,* 1987, *26:* 2–11.

Hamachek, D. "Evaluating Self-Concept and Ego Development Within Erikson's Psychosocial Framework." *Journal of Counseling and Development,* 1988, *66:* 354–360.

Ickes, W., and Barnes, R. D. "The Role of Sex and Self-monitoring in Unstructured Dyadic Interactions." *Journal of Personality and Social Psychology,* 1977, *35:* 315–330.

James, W. *Principles of Psychology.* New York: Henry Holt & Co., 1890.

Janis, I. L. *Victims of Groupthink: A Psychological Study of Foreign Policy Decisions and Fiascos.* Boston: Houghton Mifflin, 1972.

Johnson, T. J., Feigenbaum, R., and Weiby, M. "Some Determinants and Consequences of the Teacher's Perception of Causality." *Journal of Educational Psychology,* 1964, *55:* 237–246.

Jussim, L. "Teacher Expectations: Self-fulfilling Prophecies, Perceptual Biases, and Accuracy." *Journal of Personality and Social Psychology,* 1989, *57:* 469–480.

Lau, R. R., and Russell, D. "Attributions in the Sports Pages." *Journal of Personality and Social Psychology,* 1980, *39:* 29–38.

Lewis, M., and Brooks-Gunn, J. "Toward a Theory of Social Cognition: The Development of the Self," in I. C. Uzgiris (Ed.), *Social Interaction and Communication During Infancy.* San Francisco: Jossey-Bass, 1979.

Lippa, R. "Expressive Control and the Leakage of Introversion-Extraversion During Role-played Teaching." *Journal of Personality,* 1976, *44:* 541–559.

Lippa, R. "Expressive Control, Expressive Consistency and the Correspondence Between Expressive Behavior and Personality." *Journal of Personality,* 1978, *46:* 438–461.

Markus, H. "Self-knowledge: An Expanded View." *Journal of Personality,* 1983, *51:* 543–565.

Markus, H., and Nurius, P. "Possible Selves." *American Psychologist,* 1986, *41:* 954–969.

Maslow, A. H. "Neurosis as a Failure of Personal Growth." *Humanities,* 1967, *2:* 163–166.

Maslow, A. H. *Toward a Psychology of Being.* New York: Van Nostrand Reinhold, 1968.

Mettee, D., and Riskin, J. R. "Size of Defeat and Liking for Superior Ability Competitors." *Journal of Experimental Social Psychology,* 1974, *10:* 333–351.

Mead, G. H. *Mind, Self, and Society.* Chicago: University of Chicago Press, 1934.

Miller, A. G. (Ed.). *In the Eye of the Beholder: Contemporary Issues in Stereotyping.* New York: Praeger, 1982.

Miller, C. T. "Categorization and Stereotypes About Men and Women." *Personality and Social Psychology Bulletin,* 1986, *12:* 502–512.

Miller, D. T., and Ross, M. "Self-serving Biases in the Attribution of Causality: Fact or Fiction?" *Psychological Bulletin,* 1975, *82:* 213–225.

Mischel, W. "Convergences and Challenges in Search of Consistency." *American Psychologist,* 1984, *39:* 351–364.

Montemayor, R., and Eisen, M. "The Development of Self-Conceptions from Childhood to Adolescence." *Developmental Psychology,* 1977, *13:* 314–319.

Morse, S. J., and Gergen, K. J. "Social Comparison, Self-consistency and the Concept of Self." *Journal of Personality and Social Psychology,* 1970, *16:* 149–156.

Raimy, V. C. "Self-reference in Counseling Interviews." *Journal of Consulting Psychology,* 1948, *12:* 153–163.

Rhodewalt, F., Saltzman, A. T., and Wittmer, J. *Self-handicapping Among Competitive Athletes: The Role of Practice in Self-Esteem Protection.* Unpublished manuscript, University of Utah, Salt Lake City, 1982.

Rogers, C. R. *On Becoming a Person.* Boston: Houghton Mifflin, 1961.

Rogers, C. R. "The Concept of the Fully Functioning Person." *Psychotherapy: Theory, Research, and Practice,* 1963, *1:* 17–26.

Ross, L. "The Intuitive Psychologist and His Shortcomings: Distortions in the Attribution Process," in L. Berkowitz (Ed.), *Advances in Experimental Social Psychology,* Vol. 10. New York: Academic Press, 1977.

Ross, M. "Self-centered Biases in Attribution of Responsibility-Antecedents and Consequences," in E. T. Higgens, C. P. Herman, and M. P. Zanna (Eds.), *Social Cognition: The Ontario Symposium,* Vol. I. N.J.: Erlbaum, 1981.

Ross, M., and Sicoly, F. "Egocentric Biases in Availability and Attribution." *Journal of Personality and Social Psychology,* 1979, *37:* 322–336.

Russell, D. W., McAuley, E., and Tarico, V. "Measuring Causal Attributions for Success and Failure: A Comparison of Methodologies for Assessing Causal Dimensions." *Journal of Personality and Social Psychology,* 1987, *52:* 1248–1257.

Seeman, J. "Toward a Model of Positive Mental Health." *American Psychologist,* 1989, *44:* 1099–1109.

Schlenker, B. R. *Impression Management: The Self-Concept, Social Identity, and Interpersonal Relations.* Monterey, Calif.: Wadsworth, 1980, pp. 61–65.

Shrauger, J. S., and Schoeneman, T. J. "Symbolic Interactionist View of Self-Concept: Through the Looking Glass Darkly." *Psychological Bulletin,* 1979, *86:* 549–573.

Smith, T. W., Snyder, C. R., and Perkins, S. C. "The Self-Serving Function of Hypochondrial Complaints: Physical Symptoms as Self-handicapping Strategies." *Journal of Personality and Social Psychology,* 1983, *44:* 787–797.

Snyder, C. R. "The Uniqueness Mystique." *Psychology Today,* March, 1980, pp. 86–89.

Snyder, M. "The Self Monitoring of Expressive Behavior." *Journal of Personality and Social Psychology,* 1974, *30:* 526–537.

Snyder, M. "Self-Monitoring Processes," in L. Berkowitz (Ed.), *Advances in Experimental Social Psychology,* Vol. 2. New York: Academic Press, 1979.

Snyder, M. "Self-fulfilling Stereotypes." *Psychology Today,* July, 1982.

Swann, W. B., and Read, S. J. "Self-verification Processes: How We Sustain Our Self-Conceptions." *Journal of Experimental Social Psychology,* 1981, *17:* 351–372.

Tesser, A., and Campbell, J. "Self Definition: The Impact of Relative Performance and Similarity of Others." *Social Psychology Quarterly,* 1980, *43:* 341–347.

Tesser, A., and Paulhus, D. "The Definition of Self: Private and Public Self-Evaluation Management Strategies." *Journal of Personality and Social Psychology,* 1983, *44:* 672–682.

Thompson, S. K. "Gender Labels and Early Sex Role Development." *Child Development,* 1975, *46:* 339–347.

Tucker, J. A., Vuchinish, R. E., and Sobell, M. B. "Alcohol Consumption as a Self-handicapping Strategy." *Journal of Abnormal Psychology,* 1981, *90:* 220–230.

Vaillant, G. *Adaptation to Life.* Boston: Little, Brown, 1977.

Weary, G. "Examination of Affect and Egotism as Mediators of Bias in Causal Attributions." *Journal of Personality and Social Psychology,* 1980, *38:* 348–357.

Weary, G., and Arkin, R. M. "Attributional Self-presentation," in J. H. Harvey, W. J. Ickes, and R. F. Kidd (Eds.), *New Directions in Attribution Research,* Vol. 3. Hillsdale, N.J.: Erlbaum, 1981.

White, B. *The First Three Years of Life.* Englewood Cliffs, N.J.: Prentice-Hall, 1975.

Chapter 2

Perceptions and the Self: Processes and Theoretical Perspectives

PROLOGUE

On the surface, perception seems a simple term embodying a simple enough process. We see what is to be seen; we hear what is to be heard; we touch what is to be felt. And yet, if you and I were to see the same movie, or hear the same song, or touch the same object, we might have quite different interpretations of those similar experiences. A person listening to our separate descriptions of those sensory experiences might never suspect that they were the same.

The differences were not in the events themselves, but in our interpretations of those events. Thus, what may be an entertaining movie for me because I see it as providing a pleasant fantasy break from the reality of everyday life may be a depressing movie for you because it is too much like a reality you are trying to forget.

An idea that flows as an undercurrent throughout this book is the view that behavior is influenced not only by the accumulation of our past and current experiences but, importantly, by the personal meaning we attach to our perceptions of those experiences. A broad array of theoretical literature plus a rich body of empirical and clinical research data suggest that how we behave is more than simply a consequence of what happens to us on the outside; our behavior is also a function of how we feel about it on the inside, that is, how we perceive and interpret it.

The idea that perceptions play such an important role in shaping and molding behavior grows from a frame of reference in psychology that has been variously called the "phenomenological," "perceptual," *"existential," "interactional," or "humanistic" approach. Although each of these is a particular point of view, with its own slant and emphasis about the nature of human behavior, all share the idea that one way to understand people —but not the only way—is in terms of how people see themselves. This is a frame of reference that seeks to understand behavior from the point of view of the person doing the behaving. It is a psychology that probes and explores how needs, values, beliefs, and self-concepts cause people to have such different perceptions of similar experiences. In a personal sense, it is the psychology a concerned friend uses as he or she wonders why we're "feeling so down"; in a clinical sense, it is what a therapist uses while probing for the deeper meanings behind a client's depression. Self psychology is the generic label I am giving this frame of reference.*

There is little question that our experiences can have a vast influence on our current behavior. Although we cannot change what happened to us yesterday, we can change how we feel about it today. We cannot change the event, but we can modify our perceptions about the event. Therapy, for example, does not "cure" a person in the sense of removing problems, but it does assist an individual toward new perceptions of the problems so that new options for coping can be seen more clearly.

In this chapter, we will look at the nature of perception, what it is, how it works, and why it works the way it does. In addition, we will briefly discuss some of the major theorists who have contributed to our understanding of human behavior within a self psychology framework. Perception refers to a process by which we select, organize, and interpret sensory stimulation to obtain a meaningful and coherent picture of the world. Which brings us logically to our first topic of discussion.

HOW PERCEPTIONS INFLUENCE BEHAVIOR

A central concept among self psychologists is the idea suggested by Combs and Snygg (1976) that each person behaves in a manner consistent with his or her "perceptual field," which is a more or less fluid organization of personal meanings existing for every individual at any given time. The idea of perceptual field has also been called one's "private" or "personal world," one's "life space," and one's "phenomenal field." The last term, which appears often in literature related to perceptual processes, is derived from the word, *phenomenon,* which refers to the idea that knowledge is acquired through our senses and immediate experience rather than through deductions. Thus, from this point of view, reality lies not in the event but in the phenomenon, which is to say, in our *perception* of the event. The way we "see" things can dramatically influence the way we behave, an idea nicely illustrated in the following example cited by Combs, Richards and Richards (1988):

Several years ago a friend of mine was driving in a car at dusk along a Western road. A globular mass, about two feet in diameter, suddenly appeared directly in the path of the car. A passenger screamed and grasped the wheel attempting to steer the car around the object. The driver, however, tightened his grip on the wheel and drove directly into the object. The behavior of both the driver and the passenger was determined by his own *perceptions*. The passenger, an Easterner, saw the object in the highway as a boulder and fought desperately to steer the car around it. The driver, a native Westerner, saw it as a tumbleweed and devoted his efforts to keeping his passenger from overturning the car. (p. 17)

Each person in the car behaved according to what he "saw." Behavior was not determined by "objective" facts but by "subjective" interpretations of the facts. It turned out that the driver was correct: it wasn't a boulder. The passenger, however, at the instant of behaving, responded in terms of what he *thought* the facts were and not what they *actually* were. When the passenger grabbed the wheel, *he* was right, and he behaved as any reasonable person might have under the circumstances. Our perceptions of the world about us usually give us the feeling of "being right" at the instant of behaving. This may not be so true when we look back over the things we did yesterday or last week or three years ago, but at the time we acted, it very likely seemed to us that the things we did, the thoughts we had, and the feelings we felt were legitimate, valid, and rational. The basic principle here is that we behave in terms of what we believe to be true, which is, of course, determined by our particular interpretation of the facts. The deep truth of this principle is clearly reflected in the following true and humorous incident reported by Schlien (1963) about a 28-year-old graduate student in sociology who was wearily making his way home by bus after midterm examinations. In the graduate student's own words, this is what happened:

After an hour or so, the bus stopped in a small town, and a few passengers got on. One of them was a blonde girl, very good looking in a fresh but sort of sleazy way. I thought that she was probably a farm girl, and I wished she'd sit by me. By God, she did. She was really comely, if you know what I mean, and she smiled a bit so I felt sure she'd be approachable. Oh boy, what luck. I didn't want to be too eager, and I was still exhausted, so we just smiled. Then I sort of dozed off for a little while, hoping to recuperate by the time the driver turned out the lights and meanwhile enjoying my fantasies about the prospects for the rest of the trip. The last thing I remember was smiling at her and noticing that when her skirt slipped up on her knee as she reached up to the back of the seat, she didn't pull it down. Wow! About four hours later we were pounding along the road in complete darkness when I opened my eyes. Her leg, the outside of it, was against mine, and the way it pressed and moved with the motion of the bus woke me up. This was more than I'd dreamed of. I was terribly excited, and when I stirred a little the steady pressure of leg didn't move away. By this time, I was really aroused, and the more I thought about this cute little babe pressing against me, the more aroused I felt. I was just about to reach out and touch her when we pulled into a gas station for a stop, and when the light came through the window, *she* wasn't there at all! She must have left while I was asleep. A fat man with a growth of beard and a dead cigar dropping ash on his vest was sprawled next to me, sound asleep. It was *his* leg pressing against me, and he was so fat and slovenly that even when I drew myself away, his sloppy flesh stayed against me. I was so dumbfounded—disappointed too, and the funny thing—I lost those feelings of arousal almost immediately, got up and moved to another seat. What a letdown. (p. 295)

We organize, that is, we "see" our environment in such a way that it has personal meaning for us. Our perceptions do not always square with the "facts" because our views of the world are shaped by the beliefs, needs, values, stereotypes, and self-concepts, that each of us brings to the way we perceive "reality." Let's turn our attention to how these variables can influence perceptions.

One person's perceptions of reality may be quite different from someone else's.
Reprinted by permission of Universal Press Syndicate.

BELIEVING IS SEEING

Although there is an old maxim that proclaims, "seeing is believing," I think it might be more accurate to say, "believing is seeing," precisely because what we "see" is so often shaped by our assumptions, prior convictions, and early conditioning. By and large, we tend to behave in a manner that is consistent with what we believe to be true. In this sense, believing is not only seeing, seeing is behaving. A fact is not necessarily what a fact is; a fact is what one believes it to be. For example, if you tell a person that to get to Canada from Detroit you have to travel south or that Jacksonville, Florida, is further west than Cleveland, Ohio, or that the southernmost tip of Illinois is further south than the city of Richmond, Virginia, that person may wonder if you have lost not just your directions but your senses. Most people do not believe those geographical oddities until shown a map. In their own minds, they already have a map, one that says, "Canada is north of the United States," so how could anyone travel south from an American city and get to Canada? Florida is "south," so how can a Florida city be "more west" than one in Ohio? Illinois is in the "Midwest," so how can any part of Illinois be "more south" than the southern city of Richmond?

As far as geography is concerned, all of this is trivial. What is important is what these mistaken beliefs disclose about our ways of viewing more crucial subjects. Once a "map" has been etched in our minds, it is extremely difficult to draw a new one. Once a particular mental "fix" or belief is established about a certain person, group of people, a certain idea, or way of viewing the world, it is nearly impossible to dislodge it. Beliefs become "facts," right or wrong, which can have an enormous influence on how we behave.

For example, when people believed the earth was flat, they lived in terror that they might fall off its edges and be lost forever; when the belief flourished that bloodletting would drain out the evil spirits and effect miraculous cures, people persisted in this practice despite the fact that countless numbers died before their very eyes; when Galileo offered evidence to show that the earth was *not* the center of the universe as was commonly believed, the Inquisition of 1633 found him guilty of heresy and forced him to recant his assertion. Facts and beliefs collided and beliefs won out. The behavior of entire cultures can be affected by prevailing beliefs. For example, in India, cows are worshipped; in the United States, they are eaten. In China, roast dog is considered a delicacy; in America, it is considered an outrage.

Even the work of scientific researchers, who tend to be viewed as paragons of cold objectivity, can be influenced by their beliefs. Rosenthal (1966), for example, found that when researchers believe that their hypothesis is true, they are more apt to "see" evidence supporting that hypothesis than if they think it is not true. In a later investigation, Rosenthal (1978) reported that in 21 studies, which summarized the data from over 300 observers making about 140,000 observations, about 1% of all observations were probably in error. Although 1% seems a small enough error rate, given our fallible human ways, the interesting and revealing aspect of this figure is that two-thirds of all the errors favored the hypothesis of the researchers!

The impact that beliefs can have on perceptions—in this case perceptions of another person—was dramatically illustrated in a study by Kelley (1950). Before the appearance of a guest lecturer in Kelley's psychology class, students were given a brief biographical sketch of the lecturer, which, among other items, included the statement: "People who know him consider him to be a rather (cold/warm) person, industrious, critical, practical, and determined." Without the students knowing it, half of them received a description with the word *cold* in it, and half received a description with the word *warm* in it.

After hearing his lecture, the students who had received the "warm" description rated the lecturer as more considerate of others, more sociable, more popular, better natured, more humorous, and more humane than did students who had received the "cold" description. The findings directly reflect how implicit beliefs regarding which traits go with warmth and coldness influence what one "sees" in another person.

Kelley also found that the warm-cold variable affected the amount of interaction that the students engaged in with the lecturer. Fifty-six percent of the students who received the "warm" description participated in class discussion, but only 32% of the students who received the "cold" description did so—even though the students were sitting in the same room hearing the same lecture. Thus do our beliefs about people sway our reactions to them and influence the course of interpersonal behavior.

Our beliefs can even affect our perceptions of taste. For example, in an interesting wrinkle on the much touted Pepsi challenge, Pierce and Belke (Science Digest, 1988) set up a rigged test in a shopping mall and served colas in cups emblazoned with either Coke or Pepsi logos. Some of the coke cups actually contained Classic Coke; others were filled with Pepsi. Similarly, some of the Pepsi cups held Coke.

The researchers reported that, in fact, it didn't matter what was in the cups. People who preferred Coke over Pepsi before taking the test consistently favored whatever was in the cups with the Coke label, even when it was Pepsi. Pepsi fans followed suit, choosing Coke over their favored Pepsi when Coke was in cups with a Pepsi label. Taste buds, it appears, are located not only in our mouths but in our heads. Our experience of taste is affected by how we believe something *should* taste.

Beliefs can also influence what we think we see. This point was illustrated several years ago when one of the Minneapolis papers ran a photograph of a pair of beautiful breasts with the caption "Can you identify this famous movie star?" For three days, letters were printed from indignant citizens who felt that rampant free sex had taken over a formerly responsible "family" newspaper. Then, on the fourth day, they showed a picture of the entire head and torso, and it turned out to be none other than the late Johnny Weismuller of Tarzan fame (and an Olympic swimmer; hence, the well-developed pectoral muscles).

Reflect for a moment about your beliefs concerning how alcohol affects behavior. Do you believe that it makes people more social and extraverted or more quiet and withdrawn? Do you believe it makes people feel more relaxed? More easy to be sexually aroused? More prone to angry outbursts?

Marlatt and Rohsenhow's (1981) report of their own and others' research on the effects of alcohol on behavior suggests that people tend to act in certain stereotypic ways when they drink, even when they're drinking only tonic water that they have been led to believe is vodka and tonic. The results strongly suggest that cognitive processes—people's beliefs about how they are "supposed" to act when drinking alcohol—cause people to behave as if they really were drinking alcohol when in fact they weren't. Some of the major findings: (1) Men who believe they have been drinking alcohol become less anxious. In both cases, responses are determined by expectations (beliefs, hopes, fears) about what happens when people drink. (2) Alcoholics have a craving for more after one or two placebo drinks, a surprising finding because many experts believe alcoholics develop this craving when a small amount of alcohol triggers a physiologically based addictive mechanism. Even more surprising, alcoholics report almost no craving at all when they are given drinks containing alcohol that they *believe* are nonalcoholic. (3) Men become more aggressive in laboratory situations when they drink a placebo that they believe is vodka; and they become relatively less aggressive when drinking vodka that they believe is tonic water. (4) Men tend to become more sexually aroused when they believe they are drinking alcohol, even when they're not. Women, too, report feeling more aroused when drinking tonic water that they believe is vodka, although, curiously, a measure of their vaginal blood flow indicates, that, if anything, they have become *less* aroused.

This discussion, by the way, should not be construed to suggest that what happens as a result of imbibing a certain amount of alcohol is "all in one's head." Alcohol has very real effects on one's mind and body. The things that people sometimes do after drinking, particularly too much drinking, are sometimes humorous and frequently tragic and are by no means explainable in terms of a "belief" people have about how alcohol is supposed to affect behavior. However, when you combine a person's belief about how alcohol affects behavior with its actual effects, it can be a lethal combination.

What Happens When Facts Differ from Beliefs?

Our beliefs influence our perceptions, nurture our assumptions, and to a large extent determine our behavior. People do not easily give up that which they believe to be true, even in the face of facts suggesting those beliefs are in error.

For example, in an investigation to see how exposure to new information affected existing beliefs, Lord, Ross, and Lepper (1979) presented two groups of people with information regarding the deterrent effect of capital punishment on potential murderers. The subjects in one group believed strongly that capital punishment was an effective deterrent, while those in the second group had equally firm beliefs that it was not an effective deterrent. Both groups were shown two purportedly authentic studies on the effectiveness of capital punishment as a deterrent. One study supported the idea of capital punishment being an effective deterrent; the other did not. The results were interesting and revealing.

The people who believed in the deterrent value of capital punishment rated the study that supported this position as more convincing and better designed than the one that did not support their view. At the same time, however, the people who did *not* believe in capital punishment's deterrent value rated the study that supported *their* stance as the one that was more convincing and better designed than the one that offered opposing evidence. In addition, subjects, having been exposed to both a study supporting their point of view and one that did not, became *more* polarized and *more* confident in their view than they had been before reading the reports. It was as if the challenge to what they believed to be true motivated them to take an even firmer stand. We do not like our beliefs to be shaken, and when they are, our reaction is to hang on tenaciously and defensively to our version of the truth. In part, perhaps this is because it is only human nature to resist the idea of being wrong about something in which we have an emotional investment. And perhaps, too, it is related to our need for a stable belief system that makes the world, as we perceive it, a reasonably predictable, safe place in which to live.

Studies by Lord, Ross, and Lepper (1979), Lichtenberg (1984), and Ross and Lepper (1980) indicate that our beliefs not only survive powerful logical

One's beliefs can affect behavior in strange ways.
Reprinted by permission of UFS, INC.

and factual challenges, but they may also be bolstered by evidence that more objective observers would say should at least lead to some weakening of them.

Beliefs are difficult to change. Research (Allport, 1954; Skrypnek and Snyder, 1982) has shown that this is especially true for persons who have strong prejudices, which, after all, are nothing more than beliefs that have become so fixed as to become permanent props in one's mental processing. The idea about how difficult it is to change beliefs once they are formed is illustrated by the yarn about the man who believed he was dead. His psychiatrist, after hearing his story, suggested that during the next week he repeat thrice daily, "Dead men don't bleed." When the man returned the next week, the psychiatrist asked the man if he had followed his advice. Assured that he had, the psychiatrist took a needle and pricked the man's finger and squeezed out a drop of blood. "Well," said the psychiatrist, "What do you think about that?" The man regarded his finger with some care, looked up at the psychiatrist with a puzzled expression and answered, "I'll be darned. Dead men *do* bleed!"

EFFECT OF NEEDS AND VALUES ON PERCEPTIONS

To have a need is to lack something requisite, desirable, or useful; it is a personal state that demands some relief. What we value are those things in our lives that we rate highly, that we prize and esteem. Our many needs and values ebb and flow in and out of consciousness according to the circumstances of the moment and our own inner states. *What* we perceive in any given instance of our lives is determined by those needs that cry out for our most immediate attention; *how* we perceive, in terms of whether it is intense or casual, is affected by whatever valuing process is activated. For example, an acquaintance of mine frequently laments the fact that he is too inactive and that he needs to exercise to shed pounds, strengthen his heart, and so forth. However, he frequently makes disparaging remarks about people who exercise on a regular basis, claiming that there are "better things to do than run around and get sore muscles." Although he feels a certain need for exercise, it is clearly low on his list of values. He will, therefore, continue to complain periodically about his lack of exercise (this may satisfy his need to at least *say* something about it), but since the idea is held in such low esteem, it is not likely that he will *do* anything about it, unless he suffers a heart attack or some other physical ailment—which has been known to suddenly change people's ideas about the need for, and value of, regular exercise.

Needs and values, along with beliefs, constitute the hidden machinery of selective perception, a process that helps us stay focused on those aspects of our existence most central for coping successfully with the tasks at hand. Not every tree in the forest comes into focus, only the one we are chopping. Not every object on the dinner table is clearly perceived, only the morsel we are about to consume. In the babble of vague background chatter, how clearly *your* name stands out when it is mentioned.

Innumerable experiments have clearly established the fact that the words we hear or the sights we see—at least when they are not compellingly clear and well structured—are influenced by subjective conditions, shaped in part by needs and values. What this suggests is that, out of all the phenomena we might perceive, we usually select what is meaningful to us and consistent with our needs at the moment. For example, as lunch or dinner approaches, have you noted how your thoughts turn more and more to food? In food deprivation research, which involves keeping participants away from food for varying periods of time, it has been shown that as hunger increases, so, too, do erroneous perceptions of food. For example, Levine, Chein, and Murphy (1948) presented food-deprived subjects with pictures of various objects distorted behind a ground-glass screen and found that those who had gone three to nine hours without eating saw more food objects than those who had eaten 45 minutes to two hours before the experiment. McClelland and Atkinson (1948) deprived Navy men of food for periods ranging from one to 16 hours. The investigators then pretended to flash food pictures on a screen (but actually projected nothing at all) and asked the men to report what they saw. All the subjects were unaware of the relation between their hunger and the perceptual test they were taking. The hungrier men "saw" a greater number of food items than the less hungry ones. The differences in the number of food responses were particularly large between the one-hour and 16-hour groups. The experimenters also found that as the hours of food deprivation increased, so, too, did the apparent *size* of the perceived food objects.

Similarly, values also affect our perceptions. In our perceptual worlds, we more readily perceive those things, experiences, and people we value, prize, and esteem. How quick we are to spot a loved one in a group of people. Or have you noticed how much more willing you are to give time or money to an organization whose work is important to you than to one that you hold in lower esteem? We more quickly "see" the value in those organizations that we support.

Postman, Bruner, and McGinnus (1948) constructed an interesting study that demonstrates nicely the relationship between personal values and perceptual selectivity. First, they measured the value orientation of 25 subjects with a value scale. Then, they flashed words representing the six values one at a time on a screen with increasingly longer exposures until the words were recognized by each subject. Their general finding was that the more closely a given word reflected a value already held by subjects, the more rapidly they were able to recognize it. For example, subjects with dominant religious values would recognize on very brief exposure such words as *priest* or *minister* but take longer to perceive words relating to economics such as *cost, price,* or *bonds.* In other words, there seemed to be a predisposition, or readiness, to see more quickly words reflecting one's personal values.

In another study, Bruner and Goodman (1947) found that values exert other kinds of influence on perception. They asked 10- and 11-year-old boys from wealthy and poor families to guess the size of various denominations of coins (1, 5, 10, 25, 50 cents) by having them vary the diameter of a circle of light to the size of a remembered nickel or dime or half dollar; all the children tended to overestimate the size of the coins, the overestimation increasing with the increased value of the coin. The poorer boys, however, overestimated to a greater extent than did boys from more prosperous families. Dawson (1975) found this same tendency among a group of Chinese boys in Hong Kong. The hunch here is that perhaps because perceived size is related to perceived value, the personal value of the coins was greater for the poorer boys. (This brings back personal memories from my undergraduate and graduate college days. Although I didn't estimate the size of coins, I can remember times when a 5-dollar or even a 1-dollar bill seemed enormously large to me. If you are on a limited budget, you will know what I mean.)

It may be no surprise to you to learn that Majasan's (1972) research, which was designed to examine the similarity and differences between college students' and their professors' values, found that students who get higher grades tend to have values similar to those of their instructors. Students whose values were different from their instructors tended to get lower grades. These grades, by the way, were derived solely from textbook-based objective exams. Could it be that the closer your values are to your instructor's, the more you are likely to believe that that person has something important to teach you, which positively affects your motivation to learn?

A very lifelike example of how social values influence perception was reported by Hastorf and Cantril (1954) and dealt with the perceptions of Princeton and Dartmouth students of a rough and tense football game between the two schools. Each group of students was asked questions about which side was responsible for the "roughness" or "dirtiness" of the game. When asked which team "started it," 64% of the Dartmouth students said Princeton did, whereas 86% of the Princeton students blamed Dartmouth. When later shown the complete movie for the game, Princeton players "saw," on the average, about ten rule infractions by Dartmouth players. On the other hand, Dartmouth players "saw" less than half that much foul play on the part of their own team. (Alas, the report failed to mention who won.)

STEREOTYPES: PERCEPTIONS THAT ARE PREFORMED

Stereotypes are pictures in our heads. They are preconditioned perceptions. They are boxes into which we fit people based on ethnic origin, socio-economic group, religious affiliation, sexual orientation, gender, and even such specific categories as body build, first name, height, weight, hair color, clothing style, and on and on. Take clothes, for instance. On an everyday street corner, a conventionally dressed person is likely to collect more signatures for a cause than will an individual who is dressed in some offbeat or Bohemian way (Keasey and Tomlinson-Keasey, 1973). Yet at a rally for a liberal cause, such as at a promotion of peace or pro-choice rights, exactly the reverse may be true (Suedfeld, Bochner, and Matas, 1971). Apparently, many have a stereotyped view of individuals in off beat clothing, which allows us to assume that they are committed to liberal or radical causes.

Stereotypes affect our perceptions of others in at least three important ways. First, stereotypes may cause us to overgeneralize and to do so unfairly. Quattrone and Jones (1980), for example, have shown that when dealing with out-groups rather than in-groups, people seem to be generally more willing to generalize from the behavior of a single individual to a whole group. Thus, if a Spanish visitor behaves in a loud and boisterous manner, an American might be willing to conclude that all Spanish people behave in this way. However, if the same behavior were displayed by an American here in the United States, chances are good that no conclusion would be made about Americans in general.

Second, stereotypes may also create a *negative memory bias*. As research has shown, we tend to remember better those facts that support our stereotypes (Howard and Rothbart, 1980; Miller, 1986). Suppose someone asks you, "How have sororities, fraternities, unions, and religion contributed to the betterment of humankind?" If, for whatever reasons, you are opposed to any one or more of these organizations, it would probably be difficult for you to remember much about them in the way of noteworthy contributions but a good deal easier to cite their shortcomings. If, on the other hand, you are favorably predisposed to any one of them, you will have no difficulty at all in listing some of their noble contributions.

The actual existence of a negative memory bias was cleverly demonstrated in a study by Snyder and Uranowitz (1978), who had a group of students read a biography of a fictitious woman named Betty K. They constructed her biography so that it would fit stereotyped ideas about both lesbians and heterosexuals.

They wrote that Betty had never had steady boyfriends in high school but that she did go out on dates. Although they did write that she had a steady boyfriend in college, they were careful to note that he was more of a close friend than anything else. A week after the students had read the biography, they were given new information about Betty. Half the students were told that she was living with another woman in a lesbian relationship, and half were told that she was living with her husband. The students were then asked to answer a series of questions about Betty's life history. Their responses were very revealing. By and large, students reconstructed the events of Betty's past in ways that supported their particular stereotypes about her sexual orientation. Those who had been led to believe that Betty was a lesbian remembered that she had never had a steady boyfriend in high school but tended to forget that she had gone out on many dates in college. On the other hand, those who had been led to believe that Betty was heterosexual tended to remember that she formed a steady relationship with a man in college but were inclined to ignore the fact that this relationship was more of a friendship than a romance. Not only did the students tend to remember selectively those facts that supported their stereotypes, but also many showed a creative facility for interpreting what they remembered in such a way as to more firmly support those stereotypes. For instance, one student, who correctly remembered that a supposedly lesbian Betty never had a steady boyfriend in high school, suggested that this was an early sign of her lack of sexual interest in men. Another student, who remembered that a purportedly lesbian Betty frequently went on dates in college, was sure that these dates were attempts by Betty to camouflage her lesbian interests.

Without being aware of it, the students allowed their preconceptions about lesbians and heterosexuals to influence the way they perceived and interpreted the details of Betty's life. Thus, stereotypes make it easy to recall evidence that supports them and difficult to remember evidence that undermines them, a process guaranteed to distort one's perceptions of what the world is really like.

Third, stereotypes may *polarize our judgments* about others, especially if they are members of out-groups. This was illustrated in a study by Linville and Jones (1980), who had two groups of white subjects rate applications to a law school. One group was told that a particularly impressive application was from a black person, whereas the other group was told that it was from a white person. In this condition, the black applicant was judged far more positively than the white applicant. In the second condition of the study, subjects were asked to judge an unimpressive application, one group being told that the applicant was black, the other group, white. This time, the subjects judged the black applicant far more harshly than the white applicant. In effect, judgments of out-group members were polarized—the black applicants were either very good or very bad, something that also happened when males judged female applicants.

Stereotypes are by no means always bad. If there were no shared perceptions about individuals or groups, our interactions would be filled with chaos and conflict. For example, most of us believe the stereotype that other people are not dangerous. This frees us from having to be in a constant state of perceptual vigilance, always looking for the worst in others. Shared stereotypes about the positive aspects of other individuals and groups allow us to carry on reasonably smooth and cooperative interactions.

THE INFLUENCE OF SELF-CONCEPT ON PERCEPTIONS

Perception is a selective process, and the picture we have of ourselves is a vital factor in determining the richness and variety of the perceptions selected. It makes a great deal of difference how one perceives, let's say, the Pope, if one sees oneself as a Jew, Protestant, or Catholic. Depending on one's concept of self, an exam is perceived as either something to avoid failing or something to pass with as high a grade as possible; a class discussion is viewed as either something to engage in actively or something to sit quietly through for fear of saying the wrong thing; front seats of classrooms are seen as vantage points for better seeing and hearing or as potentially dangerous spots where one could be more easily seen and called on. It all depends on how we perceive ourselves.

Another consideration related to the impact of self-concept on perception is connected to its possible boomerang effect. For example, students who view themselves as poor in math not only internalize that perception but also are likely to *project* in their behavior. That is, they "project" the "I can't do math" perception outside of themselves by (1) avoiding math courses or by (2) being so tense in the math courses they take that they trip over their own anxiety while trying to work out problems they don't think they can solve in the first place. Through either course of action, it is possible to perpetuate a negative self-image. By avoiding math, the students are, in effect, saying, "I'm too dumb to take math," which serves to reinforce the negative attitude with which they started. By taking math with the "I can't do it" feeling, they are apt to increase the likelihood of overstimulating their anxiety to the point of not being able to think clearly when necessary. Naturally enough, this usually leads to poor performance and ultimately to further evidence to support their negative self-concept. That is what is meant by the boomerang effect. The very process of *beginning* with a negative attitude usually guarantees that it will be projected in behavior in such a way as to "bring back" to its owners evidence that they really cannot do what they thought they couldn't do in the first place. It ends up being a self-fulfilling prophecy. Of course, the boomerang effect can also work in the other direction. It is possible to start with a more positive attitude and accumulate evidence to support and maintain a more favorable self-perception.

I am not for a moment suggesting that how one performs or behaves is a simple matter of saying, "I can" or "I can't." Behavior is far more complex than that. Each of us has certain aptitudes and skills that equip us to do a few things a little better than some and some things a little better than most. Any of us who wish to become more competent must keep ourselves as open as possible to experiences and opportunities that could broaden and expand our perceptions of self. By sampling new experiences and by testing ourselves in as wide a variety of ways as possible, we not only increase the possibility of discovering those things that we do a little better than most but also decrease the possibility of being deflated by things we are not particularly good at. Most of us are better than we give ourselves credit for being, and taking on new challenges now and then is one good way to find that out.

HOW WE SEE OTHERS AFFECTED BY HOW WE SEE OURSELVES

Ralph Waldo Emerson insightfully observed, "What we are, that only can we see." This simple aphorism stands as the cornerstone on which are built our most important principles of how we see others. It underscores a widely held view among lay people and psychologists alike that favorableness of attitudes toward the self and others is positively related. It is commonly believed, for example, that unless one is able to love oneself, one cannot love others. Along this line, psychoanalyst Erich Fromm (1956) observed that: "Love of others and love of ourselves are not alternatives. On the contrary, an attitude of love toward themselves will be found in all who are capable of loving others" (p. 174). On the other side of the emotional scale, Fromm (1968) also noted that: "Hatred against oneself is inseparable from hatred against others" (p. 331).

Summarizing from his more than 40 years of experience as a psychotherapist, Carl Rogers (1961) noted a somewhat common phenomenon in many of his clients. Those who feel least capable of reaching their goals tend to be very critical and rejecting of others. On the other hand, Rogers also noted that as people move toward accepting themselves as worthy individuals, they are also inclined to be less critical and more accepting of others.

Recent research suggests that one's self-concept serves as an emotional reference point against which other people are seen and compared (Markus and Smith, 1981; Markus, Moreland, and Smith, 1985). That is, we are likely to judge others as we judge ourselves, which is to say that there is a tendency to evaluate others on the *same dimensions* we use for our own behavior and to assign them the same *values* on those dimensions. Our mental processing, for example, might proceed along the following lines: "If I'm fairly optimistic, I think you're probably fairly optimistic, too." "If I'm somewhat shy, I think you must be, as well." "If I cheat a little bit, you must cheat a little bit, too."

In other words, whatever is most central to us will be what we tend to see as most clearly present (or lacking) in others. For example, Rosenblatt and Greenberg (1988) found that depressed people tend to be drawn to other depressed people, while nondepressed people tend to be drawn to people like themselves—nondepressed. (You can see how this attraction of likes may serve to magnify the problems of depressed people who gravitate toward persons who are also depressed.)

Epstein and Feist (1988) showed that not only is there a relationship between positive self-regard and positive regard for others, but that this is even more likely to be the case when one sees himself or herself as identified with those to whom the positive regard is directed. For example, if you are a self-accepting individual and a member of, say, a flying club or an environmental group, you would likely respond even more positively to other members because of your identification with those groups. All in all, the research findings in this area are quite consistent with the observation of Kuiper and Rogers (1979), who concluded from their investigation of how people encode personal information about others that "how we summarize information about other people is bound up with our own view of self."

Barron (1968) offers some tantalizing evidence to support the idea that what we see in others is a projection of our own self-perceptions. In the process of doing research related to the nature and expression of psychological health, he and his colleagues had to develop some operational conceptions about what a healthy person would probably be like. They then studied subjects chosen for their general effectiveness as persons, and each staff member described each subject on an adjective checklist. The intention was to derive from these checklists a composite staff description of each subject's so-called "soundness as a person." The results were surprising. As it turned out, individual staff members

used quite different adjectives to describe the same person. The most revealing aspect was the great consistency with which staff members described highly effective persons by using exactly the same adjectives that in private moments of good will they could use to characterize themselves. Barron added

Moreover, they tended to describe clearly *ineffective* persons as possessing traits which in themselves they most strongly denied. . . . Thus, one staff member noted for his simple and clear thought processes most frequently described an ineffective person as *confused;* another staff member who is especially well-behaved in matters of duty checked the adjectives *conscientious* and *responsible* most frequently in describing highly rated subjects . . . another staff member who has subsequently been interested professionally in independence of judgment saw effective subjects as *independent* and *fairminded. Each of us, in brief, saw his own image in what he judged to be good.* (p. 12)

It seems to be generally true that our own view of ourselves and our particular life situation serves as an emotional filter through which we view the world around us. There are many examples of how this works. The suspicious person looks for ulterior motives; the trusting person sees honest intentions; the fearful individual sees life's perils and dangers; the brave individual sees life's excitements and adventures; the miserly person looks around to see what to store away; the altruistic person looks around to see what to give away. And so it goes. The way we see ourselves affects how we interpret the world, which may have a great deal to do with making it become more that way for us. It may be that our perception of what is reality becomes, for better or worse, a self-fulfilling prophecy.

Oscar Wilde's observation that "all criticism is a form of autobiography" is perhaps more true than we ever thought. What we seem inclined to see "out there" in the behavior of other people is at times no more than a projection of our own drives and needs and fears. Those who tell us that people are basically untrustworthy and cruel—ignoring the plain fact that they are also dependable and kind—may be saying more about themselves than about others. We tend to see things not as *they* are, but as *we* are.

CAUTION: PERCEPTIONS CAN BE IN ERROR

Before we get into the essence of this section, please read the following sentence:

FINISHED FILES ARE THE RESULT

OF YEARS OF SCIENTIFIC STUDY

COMBINED WITH THE EXPERIENCE OF

MANY YEARS.

Before reading further, count the F's in the sentence. Count them just once.

Now that you've counted, how certain are you of your count? Would you be willing to take some bets on it? If you are like most people, you probably counted three F's. That's what your visual senses told you. But your perception, if that was your perception, is in error—an honest error, but an error nonetheless.

It sometimes happens that our perceptions of people and events are in error, not necessarily because deep emotional needs distort our vision but because we simply have not considered all the facts or data available or we simply overlooked some of the data.

If you originally counted three F's in the above sentence, perhaps you went back and recounted after you read that there were more. Some people recount up to a half-dozen times before finally seeing that there are six F's. The first time through, however, most people—I was one of them—see only three. (There are actually six.)

Why? Perception is the key. Most of us read only those words or phrases that have meaning or give meaning to a sentence. We do this so automatically that it's an almost unconscious process. Thus, we pay particular attention to nouns and verbs because they give a sentence most of its meaning. Since prepositions, such as *of,* are primarily function words that convey little meaning, we tend to read right over them. One reason for erroneous perceptions is that we tend to "see" those aspects of our world that have most meaning for us and to overlook those aspects that have less meaning. You and your friend may witness the same event and come away with different interpretations, not necessarily because of differences in perceptual acuity, but because of differences in the meaning that each of you attached to the event.

Past learning also leads us to errors in perception. For instance, the chances are good that you did not pick up the typographical error in the previous sentence. People regularly see words spelled correctly when in fact they are not. This is the so-called "proofreader's illusion," which is a fine example of the principle that what we know affects what we see. Or, to put it more accurately, what we *think* we see.

Each of the above examples is an illustration of the gaps that can exist in our perceptions of the world around us at any given time. It is as if there is a piece missing from awareness. A hole in attention. We miss seeing what is there to be seen. A blind spot in our perceptual machinery. Actually, because of the architecture of the eye, we really *do* have a blind spot. To see how this works, close your left eye and, with your right hand, hold this book at arm's length in front of you. Focus your right eye on the cross and, very slowly, move the book toward you and back again. Somewhere between about 10 or 15 inches away the circle will disappear from your field of vision.

A blind spot exists because at the back of each eyeball is a point where the optic nerve, connected to the brain, attaches to the retina. This spot lacks the light-receptive cells that line the rest of the retina to register the light streaming through the lens of the eye. As a consequence, there is a gap in the information transmitted to the brain. Our blind spot registers nothing. We aren't ordinarily conscious of our blind spot because what is missed by one eye is picked up by the overlapping vision in the other.

Figure 2-1   *Testing for your blind spot.*

It is, I think, quite revealing and instructive to see one's blind spot; it offers a specific example of a far more subtle, psychological parallel. In a very real way, the blind spot is a fitting physiological metaphor for our failure to sometimes see things as they are in actuality.

Labels Can Misshape Perceptions

Our perceptions may also be in error because of what seems to be a strong inclination to "see" only the labels that get pinned on people rather than to respond to people as individuals. One of the most striking demonstrations of how labels can severely limit and narrow our perceptions of others has been documented in a bold and ingenious field study by Rosenhan (1973), which he wrote up and entitled, appropriately, "On Being Sane in Insane Places." Rosenhan describes how he and seven other people, five men and three women—a psychology graduate student, three psychologists, a pediatrician, a psychiatrist, a painter, and a housewife—feigned certain symptoms of mental illness (they felt "empty," "hollow," and "heard voices") to get themselves admitted to mental hospitals. The ploy worked; they were diagnosed as schizophrenic (the label) and were admitted to 12 different mental hospitals located in five different states on the East and West coasts.

Once in these institutions, Rosenhan and his fellow pseudopatients, according to plan, dropped all pretense of being mentally disturbed and acted in a completely normal manner. Did this change the perceptions of the psychiatric staffs and orderlies? Not at all. Indeed, the staffs frequently interpreted perfectly normal actions on the part of these "patients" as further evidence of their illness. For example, during their hospitalization, Rosenhan and his colleagues took copious notes concerning their experiences. It didn't take long for the *real* patients to notice that Rosenhan and the others were not inmates, but members of the hospital staff reached a quite different conclusion; note taking was simply perceived as further evidence of the patients' unstable mental condition. One nurse, for instance, saw the note taking as a manifestation of an abnormal compulsion.

There was considerable motivation for the pseudopatients because, by prior mutual agreement, they all agreed that the only way out was by their own devices. Essentially, each person had to convince the staff that he or she was sane. The psychological stresses associated with this kind of hospitalization were intense, and all but one of the pseudopatients desired to be released almost immediately after being admitted. Thus, not only were they motivated to behave sanely, but to be paragons of cooperation.

Despite their public "show" of sanity, the pseudopatients were never detected. Rather, the evidence is strong that, once labeled schizophrenic, the pseudopatient was stuck with that label, which may be why the length of hospitalization ranged from 7 to 52 days, with an average of 19 days.

Having once been labeled schizophrenic, there was virtually nothing the pseudopatients could do to overcome the tag. The tag profoundly colored others' perceptions of them and their behavior. A powerful lesson emerging from this study is that once a person is labeled in a certain way, all of his or her behaviors and characteristics are colored by that label.

Consider an example of how this process works: A psychiatrist on rounds with a group of young residents, pointed to a huddle of patients who were sitting outside the cafeteria entrance half an hour before lunchtime. The psychiatrist explained how such behavior was characteristic of the oral-inquisitive nature of the compulsive behavior syndrome. It seemed not to occur to this psychiatrist that there were very few things to anticipate in a psychiatric hospital other than eating. Thus, what was assumed to be strictly abnormal behavior may, indeed, have been normal behavior. It should come as no surprise that when it came time for discharge, each pseudopatient in Rosenhan's study was released with a diagnosis of schizophrenia "in remission," except one, who had a different diagnosis to begin with.

All in all, Rosenhan's story is a striking example of how our perceptions of behavior and events can be shaped entirely (and wrongly) by labels. Labels are a form of stereotyping. They are like little boxes into which we sometimes put people, which leads us to many erroneous perceptions because we unconsciously begin to pay more attention to the box than to the person. Labels cloud individual differences and individual exceptions to the rule. For example, not every young person who commits a delinquent act is delinquent; not every blonde has fun; not every woman is sensitive and nurturing; not every man is insensitive and fearful of feelings; not every democrat is a liberal; not every republican is a conservative.

Then, too, our perceptions are sometimes in error because we may look at things only from our own point of view and fail to see how they may be perceived by another person. For example, I recall an incident involving a youthful art teacher who admonished one of her first-grade pupils for drawing a cow in a certain way because, after all, "Cows just don't look like that." The little boy frowned a bit, examined his cow closely, looked up at the teacher, and said, "Maybe they don't, but I bet if you saw them as I did they would." (Cows, like everything else in a child's world, look quite different from their point of view. Kneel down and look around.)

Schlien (1963) reported a story about a psychologist that perhaps best illustrates some of the things we have been saying about perception: the influence of needs, the impact of self-concept, behavior that is consistent with perceptions, the possibility of misinterpreting behavior if we examine it only from our own point of view, and so on. The story goes like this:

The parents of a small boy were worried. He was quiet, sensitive, lonely, and acted afraid of other children. The parents wanted some professional advice before the child entered school, so they invited a psychologist friend of theirs to the house for an afternoon and dinner so he could observe the boy under natural conditions. Upon arriving, the psychologist asked all the appropriate questions about history and behavior and then took a spot on the balcony where he watched, unseen, the boy play in a garden by himself. The boy sat pensively in the sun, listening to the neighborhood children shout. He frowned, rolled over on his stomach, kicked the toes of his white shoes in the grass, sat up, and looked at the stains. Then he saw an earthworm. He stretched it out on a flat stone, found a sharp-edged chip, and proceeded to saw the worm in half. Many impressions were taking shape in the psychologist's mind, and he made some tentative notes: "Seems isolated and angry, perhaps over-aggressive, or sadistic, should be watched carefully when playing with other children, not have knives or pets." Then he heard the boy talking to himself. He leaned forward and strained to catch the words. The boy finished his separation of the worm; his frown disappeared; and he said, "There. Now you have a friend." (pp. 324–325)

WHY PERCEPTIONS OF "REALITY" DIFFER

Consider the following headline that appeared over an Ann Landers' column.

HE LEFT HER FOR ANOTHER MAN

What is your interpretation of this headline? If it is interpreted one way, the intimation is that a man has left or has deserted some woman to cavort, presumably, with another man, perhaps to go fishing or partying, and, thus, he is a scamp. Read another way, however, he is a good guy, one who has left her for another man who has come on the scene to fill the vacancy and provide superior masculine companionship. The words are the same for any two people who read the headline, but because each person may *perceive* the headline differently, each can have quite different interpretations of its meaning.

For some additional comic relief, consider a few examples of headlines, compiled by Gloria Cooper (1980), that have appeared in various newspapers across the United States, each of which has one of two meanings, depending on one's interpretation. (I think we can be reasonably certain that the headline writers did not have the second meaning in mind.) Clearly, what is "seen" depends on one's perceptions:

DRUNK GETS NINE MONTHS IN VIOLIN CASE

LEGALIZED OUTHOUSES AIRED BY LEGISLATURE

ROBBER HOLDS UP ALBERT'S HOSIERY

NEW MISSOURI U. CHANCELLOR EXPECTS LITTLE SEX

STUD TIRES OUT

STATE DINNER FEATURED CAT, AMERICAN FOOD

In Figures 2-2 and 2-3 are two famous drawings that illustrate why it is possible for two different people to perceive the same object (event, experience, person, even a headline) but yet arrive at different conclusions about it. One is the picture of a woman, and the other is a three-dimensional cube drawn

Figure 2-2   *An ambiguous drawing that can be seen as an attractive young lady or as an ugly witch-like woman.*

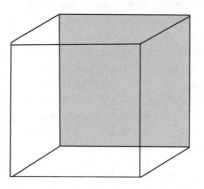

Figure 2-3   *Three-dimensional cube drawn in two dimensions. Notice how the tinted area appears either as an outer or inner surface.*

in two dimensions. A curious phenomenon happens when you look at each of these figures. When you look at the woman, you see either an old, witch-like woman, which is what most people see the first time around, or you see a pretty young woman wearing a boa. When you look at the cube, the tinted area can appear either as an outer surface or an inner surface of a transparent box. When a three-dimensional figure like a cube is drawn in two dimensions, it seems to reverse directions spontaneously, thus making it difficult to know for sure whether the tinted area is in the back or front.

The point is that we cannot see the old woman and the young woman at the same time or the cube's tinted side as being on the outside or inside at the same time. Each is a composite of both, and what we see depends on our shifting idea of what is reality.

What is the "reality" of these drawings? It depends on who's looking at them and for how long and at what moment. There is no "single" reality because the drawings have been so cleverly composed that the same composition seems different to us at different times, and when we see one image, we cannot see the other.

This show of Gestalt trickery may contain an important lesson. It indicates that what we may call our view of life is a shifting image rather than a continuous reality. It can probably be safely said that our lives—like the two pictures—are ambiguous patterns, and although at different times we choose to look at one pattern rather than another, this does not make one any more or less real than the other. Indeed, maintaining our sense of sanity and personal balance very likely depends in part on the acceptance of a certain level of ambiguity in our lives. What we see may not be what others see, and what others see may not be what we want to see. Life, for the most part, is not either/or but both.

Whether in our work, or friendships, or love relationships, we are ready to be perplexed and even angry when the picture turns into the opposite. On Monday, everything seems fine; on Friday, it is barely tolerable. Which is the true picture—the witchlike woman or the pretty woman? We can go a bit crazy trying to decide, until we realize that none of our life situations is so good that we see the pretty woman all the time or so bad that we view the witch all the time.

Perceptions of "reality" may vary widely.

Drawing by C. E. M. Copyright © 1961
by The New Yorker Magazine, Inc.

Reality is not one picture, but two. We cannot see them at the same time, but they are both there. Perhaps if we can accept this idea, we can more easily and graciously bear life's inevitable shades of gray before jumping to hasty conclusions about what is black and what is white, about what is right and what is wrong.

Whether at the level of two people arguing with each other or at the level of two nations fighting each other, it is apparent that there can be both small- and large-scale differences of opinion concerning how we see things. How healthy it would be if we could accept the idea that reality is really a series of subtly changing tones of gray rather than something cast in just one color or another and seen from the same angle and in the same way by all people.

I think that Zukav's (1979) Zen-like description of reality reflects a deep truth about what constitutes its nature and substance:

> Reality is what we take to be true. What we take to be true is what we believe. What we believe is based upon our perceptions. What we perceive depends upon what we look for. What we look for depends upon what we think. What we think depends upon what we perceive. What we perceive determines what we believe. What we believe determines what we take to be true. What we take to be true is our reality. (p. 328)

A THEORETICAL PERSPECTIVE FOR UNDERSTANDING PERCEPTUAL PROCESSES

The theoretical orientation or position we will examine in the remainder of this chapter focuses on humans as social beings who are influenced and guided by the personal meaning they attach to their experiences. In its most simple terms, it is an orientation that seeks to understand humans by studying humans. We can understand astronomy only by being an astronomer; we can understand entomology only by being an entomologist (or perhaps an insect); but we can understand a great deal about psychology merely by being a person, *by being the object of our own study.* This may seem to be self-evident, an obvious direction for psychology to take, but alas, this has not always been the case. Perhaps the following observation by Bugental (1964) may help us understand why:

> Because of our need to compete with the physical sciences, behavioral sciences have skipped over, by and large, the naturalistic stage from which other disciplines developed. We have not been people-watchers as biologists were bird- and bug-watchers. We have moved too quickly into the laboratory and looked only at special populations of people under special circumstances; we have thought we could derive generalizations about human behavior without first gaining the kind of understanding that could come only from years of performing normal tasks. Very few of us make any attempt to use our scientific training to investigate what people are really like when they are being themselves. When one examines the literature in the behavioral sciences, one seldom has the feeling, "that's what it's like to be me." The *person* is usually

missing and the findings have no reality or meaning for us because we cannot find *ourselves.* (pp. 23–24)

As if in answer to the need to put the person back into the behavioral sciences, humanistic psychology has emerged as a major orientation toward the study of human behavior. It represents "the third force" in psychology, insofar as it endeavors to go beyond the points of view of behaviorism and psychoanalysis, the two most dominant perspectives within the broad arena of psychology. The humanistic point of view does not see itself as competitive with the other two systems; rather, it attempts to supplement their observations and introduce further perceptions and insights (Hamachek, 1987).

Since humanistic psychology, phenomenology, and existential psychology are frequently used in the same breath by those who identify with any frame of reference that discusses a psychology of the self, it might be well if we take a look at the meaning of each of these terms and their relationships to each other and to perceptual psychology.

Let's begin with existentialism. This is basically a twentieth-century philosophy that stresses an individual's responsibility for his or her development. It is an introspective theory, which expresses a person's intense awareness of his or her own existence and freedom to choose among behavioral alternatives. A main tenet of existentialism is the idea that people struggle to transcend themselves, to reach beyond themselves. In this sense, the idea of transcendence boils down to our capacity for "dynamic self-consciousness." That is, not only can we think, but we can also think about (criticize and correct) our thinking. Not only can we feel, but we can also have feeling about our feelings. We are not only *conscious,* but also *self-conscious.*

We have already noted that to a phenomenologist, reality lies not in the event but in the phenomenon, that is, the person's *perception* of the event. This is not so different from the existential point of view, which suggests that humans are the determiners of their own natures and definers of their own values. For the phenomenologist, one's perceptions grow out of one's experiences; for the existentialist, one's "essence" or "being" grows out of one's capacity to make choices. Both of these points of view support the idea that what a person becomes is significantly influenced by the choices one makes. This is in opposition to the more deterministic points of view (psychoanalytic or behavioristic), which maintain that a person's "being" is shaped primarily by instinctual drives or outside forces beyond one's control.

Thus, the theoretical perspective that serves as our framework here is one that includes such things as perceptions, choices, and self-concept to be important cogs in the self's machinery of growth. In addition, the self is viewed as the mediating component between the stuff with which one is born (genetic potentials) and the environment in which one grows. To give you an overview for the sort of theoretical thinking that fits this frame of reference, we turn our attention next to a sampling of major theorists who have contributed to this perspective.

CONTRIBUTORS TO A SELF PSYCHOLOGY POINT OF VIEW

Many great names in psychology are either directly or indirectly related to what I'm referring to here as a self psychology perspective. This basically means that they are theorists who have been primarily concerned with human behavior as that behavior is influenced not just by one's past history but also by current psychosocial conditions and inter- and intrapersonal variables. Those who have made significant contributions along this line include theorists such as Alfred Adler, Gordon Allport, Albert Bandura, Eric Berne, Hadley Cantril, Arthur Combs, Charles H. Cooley, Erik Erikson, Eric Fromm, Karen Horney, William James, Kurt Lewin, Abraham Maslow, George H. Mead, Gardner Murphy, Henry Murray, Otto Rank, Carl Rogers, M. Brewster Smith, Harry S. Sullivan, and Donald Snygg.

Because there is neither the necessity nor sufficient space to detail the contributions of each theorist, we will consider a cross-section of their points of view, beginning with the early contributors, to see the variety of ways possible for understanding the development of the self and its various expressions in behavior.

C. H. Cooley (The Looking-Glass Self)

Cooley (1902) was one of the earliest social psychologists to explore the idea of self. He recognized that the social milieu from which a person comes contributes heavily to how a person views himself or herself. With this idea in mind, he developed a theory of the self that was concerned primarily with how the self grows as a consequence of interpersonal interactions. From this, he posited the concept of "the looking-glass self," which is perhaps best expressed in his own words:

> In a very large and interesting class of cases the social reference takes the form of a somewhat definite imagination of how one's self . . . appears in a particular mind, and the kind of self-feeling one has is determined by the attitude toward this attributed to that other mind. A social self might be called the reflected or looking-glass self.
>
> *Each to each a looking glass*
> *Reflects the other that doth pass.*
>
> The self that is most important is a reflection, largely, from the minds of others. . . . We live on, cheerful, self-confident . . . until in some rude hour we learn that we do not stand as well as we thought we did, that the image of us is tarnished. Perhaps we do something, quite naturally, that we find the social order is set against, or perhaps it is the ordinary course of our life that is not so well regarded as we supposed. At any rate, we find with a chill of terror that . . . our self-esteem, self confidence, and hope, being chiefly founded upon the opinions of others, go down in a crash. . . . (pp. 20–21)

We can see here, in the process of self-appraisal by individuals, the importance of their accurate perception and the interpretation of the reactions of other people to them. This idea is nicely reflected in the thoughts of an anonymous writer I ran across, who mused,

> I wonder if the mirror isn't the world's worst invention. The optimist looks into a mirror and becomes too optimistic, the pessimist, too pessimistic. Thus, mirrors increase conceit or destroy confidence. Far better is seeing ourselves as reflected in the expressions on the faces of people we meet during the day. The way you look to others is apt to be nearer the truth than the way you may look to yourself.

George H. Mead (Socially Formed Self)

A somewhat more sophisticated view of the self was developed by Mead (1934), who, as Cooley did, felt it necessary to root the self in the social conditions relevant to the individual and to derive the content of the self from the interaction between individuals and their social world. Mead's self is an *object of awareness* rather than a system of processes. That is, we come to know ourselves as we see others responding to us. Mead's self is a *socially* formed self, which grows in a *social* setting where there is *social* communication. He further suggests that people can have as many selves as there are numbers of social groups in which they participate. For instance, a person may have a family self, which reflects the values and attitudes expressed by his or her family; a school self, which represents the expectations and attitudes expressed by his or her teachers and fellow students; and many other selves.

Harry Stack Sullivan (Reflected Appraisals)

Closely related to the social interaction ideas of Mead and Cooley is the theoretical position of Sullivan (1953), a psychiatrist who developed what has been called an *interpersonal theory* of personality development. As Sullivan sees it, from the first day of life we are immersed in a continual stream of interpersonal situations in which we are the recipient of a never-ending flow of "reflected appraisals." It is through our assimilation of these reflected appraisals that we come to develop expectations and attitudes toward ourselves as individuals. If these appraisals have been mainly derogatory, the self-image is apt to be disparaging and hostile. If, on the other hand, the reflected appraisals have been chiefly positive and constructive, our feelings about ourselves are more inclined to be positive and approving.

Alfred Adler (Life Plan or Life-Style)

The essential pillar of Adlerian psychology, from which the rest of it takes on meaning, is his conception of a "life plan" of the individual, or the purpose, the goal, the "end in view" that determines behavior. Adler's (1927) self is a highly personalized, subjective system through which people interpret and give meaning to their experiences. Unlike Freud, who made the unconscious the center of personality, Adler (who, by the way, was one of Freud's earliest pupils) stressed *consciousness* as the center of personality. He viewed each person as a conscious being ordinarily aware of his or her reasons for behavior. More than that, each person is a self-conscious individual who is capable of planning and guiding his or her actions with full awareness of their meaning for self-realization.

Adler saw every person as having the same goal, namely superiority, but he also saw that there were countless different "life-styles" for achieving that goal. For example, one person may try to become superior by developing her intellect, another may strive to be a Don Juan, and still another puts all his efforts into achieving the body beautiful. The intellectual, the lady-killer, and the muscleman each has an individual life-style. The intellectual seeks knowledge; the Don Juan, women; the muscleman, strength. Each approaches life in such a way as to achieve the end of being more or less superior to those seeking similar goals.

In Adler's view, one's life-style is shaped largely by the specific inferiorities, either fancied or real, that a person has. For example, a man who feels inferior to other men because of his felt lack of physical size (or intellectual ability, or social skills, or perceived handicap of some sort) might choose to devote much of his free time and energy to building a strong, hard body. Or he might choose to develop a specific skill or ability that few others are able to accomplish. The important matter is that a person can choose to set up what Adler called a "life plan" that is directed either to overcome a perceived defect or to compensate for it. It is this setting up of a goal or direction in life that gives meaning to events that might not otherwise make sense. Adler's conception of the nature of personality reinforces the idea that people can choose to be the masters, not the victims, of their fate.

Karen Horney (Moving Toward, Against, or Away from People)

Like Sullivan and Adler, Horney (1945) was another psychiatrist who reacted critically to Freud's instinctivistic and genetic psychology. Horney's ideas sprang from her primary concept of basic anxiety, which she defined as

> . . . the feeling a child has of being isolated and helpless in a potentially hostile world. A wide range of adverse factors in the environment can produce this insecurity in a child: direct or indirect domination, indifference, erratic behavior, lack of respect for the child's individual needs, lack of real guidance, disparaging attitudes, too much admiration or the absence of it, lack of reliable warmth, having to take sides in parental disagreements, too much or too little responsibility, overprotection, isolation from other children, injustice, discrimination, unkept promises, hostile atmosphere, so on and so on. (p. 41)

Any one or a combination of these experiences could predispose an individual to adopt certain strategies of adjustment to satisfy a neurotic need or needs growing from disturbed human relationships. Horney (1942) developed a list of ten needs, any one of which could be acquired as a consequence of disturbed human relationships. She called these needs "neurotic" because they are irrational solutions to the basic problem:

1. *The neurotic need for affection and approval:* This need is highlighted by an indiscriminate need to please others and to do what others want. This sort of person wants the good will of others and is extremely sensitive to signs of rejection and unfriendliness. "If I am rejected I am unworthy."

2. *The neurotic need for a "partner" who will take over one's life:* This individual has a dread of being deserted or left alone and tends to "overvalue" love in the sense of seeing love as the magic potion to solve all problems. "If I am loved I am worthwhile."

3. *The neurotic need to restrict one's life within narrow borders:* Such a person is more inclined to save than to spend, fears making demands on others, and feels a strong necessity for remaining inconspicuous and in the background as much as possible. "If I am cautious I will not be hurt or disappointed."

4. *The neurotic need for power:* This need expresses itself in craving power for its own sake, in an essential disrespect for the feelings and individuality of others, and in a basic fear of uncontrollable situations. There is also a strong belief in the omnipotence of intelligence and reason, along with a denial of the power of emotional forces and even contempt for expressions of emotion. Such persons dread "stupidity" and bad judgment and believe that almost anything is possible through the sheer exertion of willpower. "I rely primarily on my ability to think and reason; emotional people are weak people."

5. *The neurotic need to exploit others:* This person evaluates others primarily in terms of whether or not they can be exploited or used. "Do they have power, position, or authority to do something for me?"

6. *The neurotic need for prestige:* This sort of person's self-evaluation depends on the amount of public recognition received. "If I am recognized by many people, I feel worthwhile."

7. *The neurotic need for personal admiration:* Here we have people with an inflated image of themselves, a need to be admired not for what they possess or present in the public eye but also for the imagined self. Self-evaluation depends on living up to their image and on admiration of it by others. "Even though it is difficult being something I am not, it is worth it for the admiration I receive. Besides, what would happen if people saw me as I really am?"

8. *The neurotic ambition for personal achievement:* In this case there is usually a relentless driving of oneself to higher and higher levels of achievement, usually accompanied by an intense fear of failure. Self-esteem depends on being the very best, particularly in one's own

mind. "If I fail I could never accept myself and neither would others; I had better fight for the number one spot."

9. *The neurotic need for self-sufficiency and independence:* Having felt personal pain in attempts to find warm, satisfying relationships, these individuals turn to distance and separateness as their major sources of security. Usually there is a fear of being hurt, which causes these individuals to act as though other people were not needed. "If I don't get close to people no one can hurt me."

10. *The neurotic need for perfection and unassailability:* These people usually have a deep fear of making mistakes and being criticized and so try to make themselves impregnable and infallible. They are constantly in search of flaws in themselves so that they can be covered up before they become too obvious to others. "If I am perfect, who can criticize me?" (pp. 54–60)

From Horney's point of view, these ten needs are the sources from which inner conflicts develop. The neurotic's need for power, for example, is insatiable: The more that is acquired, the more that is wanted; satisfaction is seldom felt. In a similar vein, the need for independence can never be fully satisfied because another part of the personality cries out to be loved and accepted. The search for perfection is a lost cause from the beginning. In one way or another, all these needs are unrealistic and self-defeating.

Horney (1945, pp. 48–95) later classified the ten neurotic needs under three headings: (1) moving toward people, (2) moving away from people, and (3) moving against people. Each of these interpersonal response traits represents a basic orientation toward others and oneself. For example, a person whose predominant interpersonal trait is one of *moving toward people*

. . . shows a marked need for affection and approval and an especial need for a "partner"—that is, a friend, lover, husband or wife who is to fulfill all expectations of life and take responsibility for good and evil. . . . [He] needs to be liked, wanted, desired, loved; to feel accepted, welcome, approved of, appreciated; to be needed, to be of importance to others, especially to one particular person.

A person whose predominant interpersonal response trait is one of *moving against people* perceives

. . . that the world is an area where, in the Darwinian sense, only the fittest survive and the strong annihilate the weak . . . a callous pursuit of self-interest is the paramount law. . . . He needs to excel, to achieve success, prestige or recognition in any form.

From the person whose interpersonal response trait is *moving away from people,*

The underlying principle . . . is never to become so attached to anybody or anything that he or it becomes indispensable. . . . Another pronounced need is for privacy. He is like a person in a hotel room who rarely removes the "Do Not Disturb" sign from his door. . . . His independence, like the whole phenomenon of detachment of which it is a part, has a negative orientation; it is aimed at *not* being influenced, coerced, tied, obligated.

The three types could be summarized as follows: Compliant types worry about how they can make people like them so they won't be hurt. Aggressive types consider the best defense to be the best offense. Detached types have the philosophy that if they do not get close to people they will not get hurt too badly.

Horney (1945) suggests that the essential difference between a normal and a neurotic conflict is one of degree: ". . . the disparity between the conflicting issues is much less great for the normal person than for the neurotic" (p. 31). In other words, everyone has these conflicts to some degree, but some people, usually because of early experiences with rejection, neglect, overprotection, and other expressions of unfortunate parental treatment, have theirs in exaggerated form.

Carl Rogers (The Fully Functioning Person)

Rogers' self-theory and ideas about the fully functioning individual represent a synthesis of phenomenology as developed by Combs and Snygg (1976), social interaction theory as represented in the writings of Mead and Cooley, and Sullivan's interpersonal theory.

The principle conceptual ingredients of Rogers' theory are the following: (1) the *organism,* which is the total person; (2) the *phenomenal* field, which is the totality of experience; and (3) the *self,* which is a differentiated portion of the phenomenal field and consists of conscious perceptions and values of the "I" or "me."

The self, which is the nuclear concept in Rogers' theory, has numerous features, the most important of which are these: (1) The self strives for consistency; (2) a person behaves in ways that are consistent with the self; (3) experiences that are not consistent with the self are perceived as threats and are either distorted or denied; and (4) the self may change as a result of maturation and learning.

The nature of these concepts and their interrelationships are discussed in a series of 19 propositions formulated by Rogers in his book *Client-Centered Therapy* (1951). Consider seven of the most basic propositions:

1. Individuals exist in a continually changing world of experience of which they are the center. In this sense, each person is the best source of information about him- or herself.

2. Individuals react to their perceptual field as it is perceived and experienced. Consequently, knowledge of a person's experiences is

not sufficient for predicting behavior; one must know how the person perceives the experiences and what they mean to that person.

3. Each individual has a basic tendency to strive, to actualize, maintain, and enhance the experiencing organism.

4. As a result of interaction with the environment, and particularly as a result of interactions with others, one's picture of oneself is formed—an organized fluid, but consistent conceptual pattern of perceptions of characteristics and relationships of the "I" or the "me."

5. Perception is selective, and the primary criterion for selection is whether the experience is consistent with how one views oneself at the moment.

6. Most ways of behaving that are adopted by individuals are those that are consistent with their concept of self.

7. When people perceive and accept into one integrated system all their sensory and visceral experiences, they are in a position to be more accepting and understanding of others as separate and *different* individuals. For example, those who feel threatened by their own hostile or sexual feelings may tend to criticize or move away from others whom they perceive as behaving in sexual or hostile ways. On the other hand, if they can accept their own sexual or hostile feelings, they are more likely to be more tolerant of the expression of such feelings by others. (pp. 483–520)

From this theory of self and from his many years as a practicing psychotherapist, Rogers developed some ideas of what it means to be a "fully functioning person." For the most part, his ideas evolved from his very personal experiences with his clients, whom he saw developing a "self" that was uniquely their own. According to Rogers (1961), people en route to becoming "fully functioning" usually exhibit characteristics such as the following:

1. They tend to move away from facades. That is, they move away from a self that they are *not* and move toward the self they really *are.*

2. They tend to move away from "oughts." In other words, they cease to guide their conduct in terms of what they "ought" to be or "ought" to become.

3. They tend to move away from meeting others' expectations and move toward meeting their *own* expectations.

4. They tend to move away from pleasing others and begin to be more self-directing.

5. They tend to be more accepting of themselves and able to view themselves as persons in the process of "becoming." That is, they are not upset by the fact that they do not always hold the same feelings

toward a given experience or person or that they are not always consistent in other ways. The striving for conclusions or end states seems to decrease.

6. They tend to move toward being more open to their experiences in the sense of not having always to blot out thoughts, feelings, perceptions, and memories that might be unpleasant.

7. They tend to move in the direction of greater acceptance of others. That is, they are more able to accept the experiences of others. (pp. 163–198)

A. H. Maslow (Self-Actualization)

Maslow's (1968, 1970) unique contribution to self psychology lies in his preoccupation with healthy people rather than sick ones and his belief that studies of these two groups generate different types of theory. He felt that psychology had focused too intently on human frailties and not enough on human strengths, that in the process of exploring human shortcomings, it had neglected human virtues. Where is the psychology, Maslow asked, that takes into account such experiences as love, compassion, gaiety, exhilaration, and well-being to the same extent that it deals with hate, pain, misery, guilt, and conflict? Maslow undertook to supply the other half of the picture, the brighter, better half, and to round out a portrait of the whole person.

Maslow's theory of human motivation assumed that needs are ordered along a hierarchy of priority of prepotency. That is, when the more basic needs are satisfied, the next need in the hierarchy emerges and presses for satisfaction. He theorized that each person has five basic needs, which are arranged in hierarchical order of relative prepotency:

1. The physiological needs, that is, hunger and thirst
2. The safety needs
3. The love and belongingness needs
4. The esteem needs
5. The self-actualization needs, that is, the desire for self-fulfillment, for becoming what one has the potential to become

To study what makes healthy people healthy or great people great or extraordinary people extraordinary, Maslow made intensive clinical investigations of people who are, or were, in the truest sense of the word, self-actualizing, that is, moving in the direction of achieving and reaching their highest potentials. People of this sort are rare, indeed, as Maslow discovered when he was selecting his group. Some were historical figures, such as Lincoln, Jefferson, Whitman, Beethoven, William James, and F. D. Roosevelt, whereas others were living at the time they were studied, such as Einstein, Eleanor Roosevelt, Albert

Schweitzer, and some personal acquaintances of the investigator. Maslow was able to sort out 15 basic personality characteristics that distinguished healthy, self-actualizing people from, how shall we say, "ordinary" people. This is not to suggest that each person he studied reflected all 15 self-actualizing characteristics, but each did exhibit a greater number of these characteristics and in more different ways than might be expected in a less self-actualized person. Maslow (1970) describes these individuals as follows (pp. 35–58):

1. They are realistically oriented.

2. They accept themselves, other people, and the natural world for what they are.

3. They are spontaneous in thought, emotions, and behavior.

4. They are problem-centered rather than self-centered people in the sense of being able to devote their attention to a task, duty, or mission that seemed peculiarly cut out for them.

5. They have a need for privacy and even seek it out on occasion, needing it for periods of intense concentration on subjects of interest to them.

6. They are autonomous, independent, and able to remain true to themselves in the face of rejection or unpopularity.

7. They have a continuous freshness of appreciation and capacity to stand in awe again and again of the basic goods of life: a sunset, a flower, a baby, a melody, a person.

8. They have frequent "mystic" or "oceanic" experiences, although not necessarily religious in character.

9. They feel a sense of identification with humankind as a whole in the sense of being concerned not only with the lot of their own immediate families but also with the welfare of the world as a whole.

10. Their intimate relationships with a few specifically loved people tend to be profound and deeply emotional rather than superficial.

11. They have democratic character structures in the sense of judging people and being friendly not on the basis of race or religion but rather on the basis of who other people are as individuals.

12. They have a highly developed sense of ethics and are inclined to choose their behavior with reference to its ethical implications.

13. They have unhostile senses of humor, which are expressed in their capacity to make common human foibles, pretensions, and foolishness the subject of laughter rather than sadism, smut, or hatred of authority.

14. They have a great fund of creativity.

15. They resist total conformity to culture.

This is an impressive list to be sure, and one of the most detailed conceptions of self-actualization yet developed.

IN PERSPECTIVE

This chapter has introduced the nature of perceptual processes and how beliefs, needs, values, stereotypes, and our own self-concept can influence our perceptions of "reality." In addition, we have seen that more frequently than we realize, our perceptions of others are largely projections of our own drives, needs, and fears. Reality is seldom just one thing; it is rich in variation and subtle shades of difference as viewed from different angles by different people. You and your friend may find common agreement in the wider scope of things, but you have wide differences of opinion when it comes to the specifics of whatever the particular "thing" is. Many people, for example, agree that religion, in its broad outline, is probably necessary for people to feel and express their spiritual needs. There is considerable difference of opinion, however, concerning which religion is best suited for this and how those needs should be expressed.

All in all, how we perceive the world determines how we behave in it and feel about ourselves. A large body of research suggests that we humans will go to great lengths in adjusting our perceptions to fit our preconceptions.

Although the following observation by Berelson and Steiner (1964) was made 30 years ago at the conclusion of their monumental review of research related to human behavior, it is still true today:

> In their quest for satisfaction, people are not just seekers of truth, but of deceptions, of themselves as well as others. . . . Thus, they adjust their social perceptions to fit not only the objective reality but also what suits their wishes and needs; they tend to remember what fits their needs and expectations, or what they think others will want to hear . . . in the mass media people tend to hear and see not simply what is there but what they prefer to be told, and they will misinterpret rather than face up to an opposing set of facts or points of view; people avoid the conflicts of issues and ideals whenever they can by changing those around them rather than their own minds, and when they cannot, private fantasies can lighten the load and carry them through; people think . . . that their own group agrees with them more fully than it really does; and if it does not, they find a way to escape to a less uncongenial world. . . . For the truth is, apparently, that no matter how successful people become in dealing with their problems, they still find it hard to live in the real world, undiluted: to see what one really is, to hear what others really think of one, to face the conflicts and threats really present, or, for that matter, the bare human feelings. . . . In short, people live not only with the reality that confronts them but with the reality that they make. (pp. 633–635)

Each of us, it appears, wears glasses of one sort or another. We seem inclined to see the world not as it is, but through the lens of our particular psychology and upbringing and angle of vision. These homemade glasses are infinitely varied. Some are rose colored; others are gray or dark blue; and still others are so narrowly focused that they offer only the tunnel vision of dogmatists and fanatics. It is all a matter of degree, however, for none of us views ourselves or the world without some subjective distortion. Perhaps the best we can do is to remain open to the possibility that the color in which we see the world may not be its real color but one tinted by our own psychological and biological heritage. And to be flexible enough and courageous enough to change when that is necessary.

Each of the contributors who has been discussed here tends to espouse a "dynamic" view of human behavior in the sense of seeing people as active, choosing, conscious organisms whose behaviors are shaped by both internal and external forces. Moreover, they give people credit for not only assigning personal meaning to their perceptions and experiences but also adjusting their behavior so that it is consistent with their personal meanings. This is not to suggest that one's perceptions and, hence, one's personal meanings are always correct. Most of our personal and interpersonal problems arise not from disagreements about reality, but from distortions and misperceptions of reality. To be as accurate as possible in our perceptions, it would be helpful to develop as much insight as we can into ourselves as individuals and the ways in which our needs, values, and beliefs influence how we perceive the world.

Thus, if we are to behave effectively and appropriately, our perceptions of reality must be fairly accurate. When our perceptions of ourselves or others are inaccurate, we are more likely to undertake actions that have little chance of success. Indeed, we seriously reduce our opportunities for engaging in many things we might otherwise do and enjoy if it were not for our misperceptions.

The need for knowing oneself is basic and universal in human experience, not confined to a heroic few or to the giants among us. The need that has been variously labeled "self-acceptance," "self-love," self-understanding," and the like is neither innate nor indistinct in function and origin. It is basically a need for an image of oneself that is accurate enough to be workable and acceptable enough to be enjoyed.

QUESTIONS FOR STUDY, REVIEW, AND REFLECTION

1. What does it mean to say that each person behaves in a manner consistent with his or her "perceptual field?" Give examples of how this works.

2. Can you explain why the adage, "believing is seeing" is more accurate than the even older adage, "seeing is believing?"

3. Beliefs are difficult to change. Reflect for a moment: If someone tried to change your beliefs about religion or your political views, how open do you suppose you'd be?

4. How would you explain the impact of needs and values on perceptions to someone who did not understand the inner workings of that impact?

5. What is a stereotype? What four or five stereotypes do you have that seriously influence your views of particular people? Describe how those stereotypes influence your behavior.

6. What does it mean to say that one's self-concept serves as an emotional reference point against which other people are seen and compared?

7. Can you explain why it is that our perceptions of the world around us are sometimes in error? What are some examples of times when you've been wrong in your perceptions of yourself?

8. When the point was made that there can be more than one reality, what does that mean? How can that occur?

9. What similarities and differences do you see among Cooley's "Looking-Glass Self," Mead's "Socially Formed Self," and Sullivan's "Reflected Appraisals?"

10. In which of Horney's ten neurotic needs do you see bits and pieces of yourself? If to some extent you do identify with any of them, how do you suppose that happened? How would you explain it?

11. Suppose someone asked you to explain the difference between Rogers' and Maslow's contribution to self psychology. What would you say?

REFERENCES

Adler, A. *Practice and Theory of Individual Psychology.* New York: Harcourt, Brace and World, 1927.

Allport, G. W. *The Nature of Prejudice.* Reading, Mass.: Addison-Wesley, 1954.

Barron, F. *Creativity and Personal Freedom.* New York: Van Nostrand Reinhold, 1968.

Berelson, B., and Steiner, G. A. *Human Behavior: An Inventory of Scientific Findings.* New York: Harcourt, Brace and World, 1964.

Bruner, J. S., and Goodman, C. C. "Value and Need as Organizing Factors in Perception." *Journal of Abnormal and Social Psychology,* 1947, *42:* 33–44.

Bugental, J. F. T. "The Third Force in Psychology." *Journal of Humanistic Psychology,* 1964, Spring: 23–24.

Cooley, C. H. *Human Nature of the Social Order.* New York: Charles Scribner's Sons, 1902.

Combs, A. W., Richards, A. C., and Richards, F. R. *Perceptual Psychology: A Humanistic Approach to the Study of Persons.* Lanham, N.Y.: University Press of America, 1988.

Combs, A., and Snygg, D. *Individual Behavior: A New Frame of Reference,* rev. ed. New York: Harper and Row, 1976.

Cooper, G. "Squad Helps Dog Bite Victim." Edited by *The Columbia Journalism Review.* New York: Doubleday, 1980.

Dawson, J. "Socio-Economic Differences in Size Judgments of Discs and Coins by Chinese Primary VI Children in Hong Kong." *Perceptual and Motor Skills,* 1975, *41:* 107–110.

Epstein, S., and Feist, G. J. "Relation Between Self- and Other- Acceptance and its Moderation by Identification." *Journal of Personality and Social Psychology,* 1988, *54:* 309–315.

Fromm, E. *The Art of Loving.* New York: Harper, 1956.

Fromm, E. "Selfishness and Self-Love," in C. Gordon and K. J. Gergen (Eds.), *The Self in Social Interaction,* Vol. I. New York: Wiley, 1968.

Hamachek, D. "Humanistic Psychology: Theory, Postulates, and Implications for Educational Processes," in J. A. Glover and R. R. Ronning (Eds.), *Historical Foundations of Educational Psychology.* New York: Plenum, 1987.

Hastorf, A., and Cantril, H. "They Saw a Game: A Case Study." *Journal of Abnormal and Social Psychology,* 1954, *49:* 129–134.

Horney, K. *Self-Analysis.* New York: W. W. Norton, 1942.

Horney, K. *Our Neurotic Conflicts.* New York: W. W. Norton, 1945.

Howard, J. W., and Rothbart, M. "Social Categorization and Memory for In-Group and Out-Group Behavior." *Journal of Personality and Social Psychology,* 1980, *38:* 301–310.

Keasey, C. B., and Tomlinson-Keasey, C. "Petition Signing in a Naturalistic Setting." *Journal of Social Psychology,* 1973, *89:* 313–314.

Kelley, H. H. "In Warm-Cold Variable in First Impressions of Persons." *Journal of Personality,* 1950, *18:* 431–439.

Kuiper, N. A., and Rogers, T. B. "Encoding of Personal Information." *Journal of Personality and Social Psychology,* 1979, *37:* 499–514.

Levine, R., Chein, I., and Murphy, G. "The Relation of the Intensity of the Need to the Amount of Perceptual Distortion: A Preliminary Report." *Journal of Psychology,* 1948, *25:* 205–222.

Lichtenberg, J. W. "Believing When the Facts Don't Fit." *Journal of Counseling and Development,* 1984, *63:* 10–11.

Linville, P. W., and Jones, E. E. "Polarized Appraisals of Outgroup Members." *Journal of Personality and Social Psychology,* 1980, *38:* 689–703.

Lord, C., Ross, L., and Lepper, M. "Biased Assimilation and Attitude Polarization: The Effect of Prior Theory on Subsequently Considered Evidence." *Journal of Personality and Social Psychology,* 1979, *37:* 2098–2109.

Majasan, J. K. *College Students' Achievement as a Function of the Congruence Between Their Beliefs and Their Instructor's Beliefs.*" Unpublished doctoral dissertation, Stanford University, 1972.

Markus, H., and Smith, J. "The Influence of Self-Schemes on the Perception of Others," in N. Cantor and J. Kihlstrom (Eds.), *Personality, Cognition, and Social Interaction.* Hillsdale, N.J.: Erlbaum, 1981.

Markus, H., Moreland, R. L., and Smith, J. "Role of Self-Concept in the Perception of Others." *Journal of Personality and Social Psychology,* 1985, *49:* 1494–1512.

Marlatt, G. A., and Rohsenhow, D. J. "The Think-Drink Effect." *Psychology Today,* December, 1981, pp. 60–69.

Maslow, A. H. *Toward a Psychology of Being,* 2nd ed. Princeton, N.J.: D. Van Nostrand, 1968.

Maslow, A. H. *Motivation and Personality,* 2nd ed. New York: Harper and Row, 1970.

McClelland, D. C., and Atkinson, J. W. "The Projective Expression of Needs: I. The Effect of Different Intensities of the Hunger Drive on Perception." *Journal of Psychology,* 1948, *25:* 205–222.

Mead, G. H. *Mind, Self, and Society.* Chicago: University of Chicago Press, 1934.

Miller, C. T. "Categorization and Stereotypes About Men and Women." *Personality and Social Psychology Bulletin,* 1986, *12:* 502–512.

Postman, L., Bruner, J., and McGinnus, E. "Personal Values as Selective Factors in Perception." *Psychological Review,* 1948, *55:* 314–324.

Quattrone, G. A., and Jones, E. E. "The Perception of Variability with In-Groups and Out-Groups: Implications for the Law of Small Numbers." *Journal of Personality and Social Psychology,* 1980, *38:* 141–152.

Rogers, C. R. *Client-Centered Therapy.* Boston: Houghton Mifflin, 1951, pp. 483–520.

Rogers, C. R. *On Becoming a Person.* Boston: Houghton Mifflin, 1961.

Rosenblatt, A., and Greenberg, J. "Depression and Interpersonal Attraction: The Role of Perceived Similarity." *Journal of Personality and Social Psychology,* 1988, *55:* 112–119.

Rosenhan, D. L. "On Being Sane in Insane Places." *Science,* 1973, *179:* 250–258.

Rosenthal, R. *Experimenter Effects in Behavioral Research.* New York: Appleton-Century-Crofts, 1966.

Rosenthal, R. "How Often Are Our Numbers Wrong?" *American Psychologist,* November, 1978, pp. 1005–1007.

Ross, L., and Lepper, M. "The Perseverence of Beliefs: Empirical and Normative Considerations," in R. Shweder (Ed.), *Fallible Judgment in Behavioral Research: New Directions for Methodology of Social and Behavioral Science,* No. 4. San Francisco: Jossey-Bass, 1980.

Science Digest, December, 1988, p. 68.

Schlien, J. M. "Phenomenology and Personality," in S. M. Wepman and R. W. Heine (Eds.), *Concepts of Personality.* Chicago: Aldine, 1963.

Skrypnek, B. J., and Snyder, M. "On the Self-Perpetuating Nature of Stereotypes About Women and Men." *Journal of Experimental Social Psychology,* 1982, *18:* 277–291.

Snyder, M. L., and Uranowitz, S. W. "Reconstructing the Past: Some Cognitive Consequences of Person Perceptions." *Journal of Personality and Social Psychology,* 1978, *36:* 941–950.

Suedfeld, P., Bochner, S., and Matas, C. "Petitioner's Allure and Petition Signing by Peace Demonstrators: A Field Experiment." *Journal of Applied Social Psychology,* 1971, *1:* 278–283.

Sullivan, H. S. *The Interpersonal Theory of Psychiatry.* New York: W. W. Norton, 1953.

Zukav, G. *The Dancing Wulimasters.* New York: Morrow, 1979.

Chapter 3

Self-Consistency: Behavioral Expressions and Stability over Time

PROLOGUE

For better or worse, a certain thread of consistency weaves its way through the fabric of our personality that makes us more or less "knowable" to others and to ourselves. It is this thread of consistency that makes us somewhat predictable. Our friends can usually foretell how we might act under certain conditions, and we can make similar predictions about ourselves. Even if we are given to unpredictable mood swings, this fact is noted by others as a predictable aspect of our behavior. Although we may be able to alter our presentation of self, assume different roles and behavior for short periods of time, each of us ultimately expresses that self which he or she really is. A person cannot help but be himself or herself. Which is the whole point of this chapter.

Why is a certain amount of behavioral consistency in ourselves and others important? How and what ways do we express consistency? How consistent is behavior over time? If behavioral consistency really exists, how can we explain the fact that we may behave one way with person A or in situation B but another way with person C or in situation D?

How do people handle those times when their behavior is inconsistent with their beliefs? Is it true that the person we are today is very much like the person we were yesterday and, in addition, a predictor of the person we will likely be tomorrow? In this chapter, we turn our attention to these and related issues. Let's begin with an important question.

BEHAVIORAL CONSISTENCY: WHY IS IT IMPORTANT?

Most of us conduct our day-to-day living on the assumption that there is a reasonably high degree of personal consistency in the behavior of others in our social world. There are at least two good reasons for this. First, there is much less personal strain and anxiety if our social environment is not in a constant state of change. Second, we are in a much better position to monitor the appropriateness of our behavior toward the various people in our lives if their behavior and personality are not constantly changing. If, for example, Jason, who is usually dour and grumpy, suddenly appears happy and cheerful, we may not know quite how to respond. Or if Janet, who has always presented herself as weak and helpless, suddenly becomes forceful and assertive, we may not know how to relate to her because our old responses seem inappropriate. Our ability to arrive at "correct" conceptions of behavior depends on others behaving in a more or less consistent manner. An emotionally inconsistent person is difficult to relate to because we never quite know what to expect next, a condition bound to produce a certain level of tension and unrest. It is not surprising to find that research has demonstrated that, over a variety of conditions, predictable people are better liked than unpredictable people (Gergen and Jones, 1963).

Behavioral consistency is also important because it serves as the foundation for stable human relationships. We may love someone a great deal; we may respect that person highly, but if that individual proves to be too unreliable and too unpredictable, we usually withdraw our emotional investment in the relationship. If the bank in which we keep our money begins to reflect sudden and unpredictable ups and downs in its interest rates, we are not likely to deposit our hard-won dollars to its care. When trust in a bank's stability is missing, so, too, is the willingness to commit what may be important to us, a consideration that no doubt has a large influence on all our investment decisions, whether they involve financial institutions or relationships.

Actually, it is doubtful whether any of us behave in a totally consistent manner across different situations. Consider your own behavior. Are you talkative and outgoing when with friends? Most of us are. But what happens when you are with strangers? Are you inclined to be quieter than usual and perhaps a little shy? No doubt there are times when you are stubbornly resistant, yet you can also be flexibly adaptive. You are on one occasion cheerful and happy, whereas on another occasion you feel sad and gloomy. Do these shifts in feelings and behavior mean that you have no internal consistency? Not at all. It simply means that you are capable of a wide range of feelings and behaviors and that what is felt or expressed depends not only on *you* but also on the situation in which you find yourself—whom you are with, where, and when.

Even though the particular expressions of our behavior may vary depending on the situation, the differences in expression from one situation to another are more a matter of degree than of kind. For example, a person who is basically introverted may be less so with friends, but that person is still basically introverted. The outer behavior may change to some extent, but the basic disposition remains the same.

Psychological research suggests that each of us develops certain primary dispositions and response styles, which we reflect more or less consistently in our behavior (Burns and Seligman, 1989). This sense of inner sameness is important because it allows us to develop a central core of characteristics that becomes the hub of our identity, the basis for our concept of self. A reasonably stable sense of self is crucial to our emotional well-being. We need to feel that we, and others in our lives, are whole and intact, which may be one of the reasons we commonly detect more consistency in our own and other people's behavior than actually exists. Gergen (1968) wryly observed that ". . . we not only see people all in one piece, but we treat them as if they are, and we often punish them if they are not" (p. 300).

Perceptions of Consistency in Others

On the whole, the way we see others tends to be fairly stable, an outcome helped along by our abilities to conceptualize and, thereby, simplify the complex flux of interpersonal relationships in which we find ourselves. For example, as we are exposed to facts and information about another, these perceptions are integrated and reduced into a mind's-eye concept of the sort of individual we believe that person to be. Noting a person's self-effacing manner and submissive behavior, for example, may lead us to conceptualize or picture this person as "shy." This concept is then used as the label for a cluster of observations that serve as the keystone for what we regard as "understanding" the other person. When conceptual judgments are made, they tend to remain intact and unchanging. Once we label a person as shy, aggressive, deceptive, friendly, or whatever, we do not easily give up that perception. Even if later information grossly contradicts our perception of what we believe another person is like, it may be either distorted or misperceived so that it fits what we believe to be true. For example, in an earlier review of research related to this idea, it was found that when persons receive contradictory information about another, they often misconstrue new information so that what they hear or see is internally consistent with what they already believe to be true about the other person (Hamachek, 1982). If, for instance, you hear that your good friend, Lisa, whom you perceive as a gentle, kind, sensitive woman, has said something viciously cutting about Lynn, whom you know only slightly, you may find yourself wondering what Lynn did to deserve it, thus preserving your image of Lisa.

According to social learning theorists, the personality characteristics that are attributed to others are more often in "the eye of the beholder" than in the person observed, which is another reason why we tend to see others behaving in generally consistent ways. There are at least four explanations for how we maintain the illusion of consistency, if not actual consistency in the behavior of others:

1. Our preconceptions of how people behave may lead us to generalize beyond our actual observations. That is, we may unconsciously support our observations with information from what Schneider (1973) called our "implicit personality theories" of what traits and behaviors go together. Our stereotypes of how a "feminist" or a "used car salesperson" or a "conservative" behaves may influence us to see what we expected to see, thus causing us to attribute greater consistency to a person's actions than our observations warrant. Research related to interpersonal perceptions points clearly to the idea that the stronger our preconceived notion about a particular person or group, the more likely it is that we will "see" what our preconceptions have prepared us to see rather than what is actually there (Anderson, 1974; Howard and Rothbart, 1980). Naturally, this makes it *seem* as if there is a high degree of consistency in the perceived person's behavior. For example, if you perceive a particular person as basically untrustworthy, there is little he or she can do that will not be seen in that light. Which is why, by the way, it is so difficult to regain another person's trust once it is lost.

2. Many personal qualities remain fairly constant—manner of speaking, style of dress, physical appearance, expressive gestures, political affiliation, religious beliefs, and so on. Constancies of this sort help to create an impression of consistency in personality.

3. Inasmuch as the behavior of another person is such a central feature of any interpersonal situation, there is a tendency to overestimate the extent to which behavior is caused by a personality characteristic and to underestimate the importance of situational forces (Bem and Allen, 1974). If we observe someone behaving aggressively on one occasion, we tend to assume that the person has an aggressive disposition and will behave similarly on other occasions—even though the situational factors may be quite different.

4. Our own presence may influence people to behave in certain predictable ways. Thus, our acquaintances may appear to behave consistently because our presence influences the behavior we're observing. How often have you heard, in response to your descriptions of a person, "But no one else sees me that way"? Or how often have you heard stories about the child who is a holy terror at home but a perfect angel at his grandparents'? To the mother, the child is consistently bad; to the grandmother, consistently good. The child is perceived as consistently bad or good, as the case may be, but his behavior may be more a function of whom he is with than a basic personality characteristic. For example, the mother may constantly nag and criticize, which causes the child to behave negatively. The grandmother, on the other hand, may be more accepting and loving,

which tends to bring out the best in the boy. Both mother and grandmother see him behaving consistently one way or the other, but they may not consider how their own behavior influences the boy's. It is in ways like this and others we've examined that people tend to be seen as stable and consistent.

Perceptions of Consistency in Ourselves

Just as there is less personal strain when others we relate to are not in a constant state of change, so, too, is it less taxing when our own personality is reasonably stable. Being able to predict our behavior with a degree of accuracy is comforting because it frees us from worrying unnecessarily about how we might behave under certain conditions. It is when we cannot anticipate how we might behave or what we might say that makes us most nervous. A struggling tenth grade student expressed the problem in the following way during an interview I had with him:

> The thing that bothers me most is me. Isn't that stupid? I don't even know who me is. Every now and then I think I know, but I keep changing. My girlfriend— I should say, my ex-girlfriend—broke up with me because she says I was always breaking my promises. Couldn't trust me, she said. I think she's right, actually. I did break promises. The thing I don't know is how I can keep a promise if I can't even tell when I'm making it whether or not I can keep it. Isn't that stupid?—I can't even tell that.

The young man was right, of course; it *is* difficult to carry out a promise (which is, after all, an explicit declaration that we will do or refrain from doing something that we ourselves have specified) when he doesn't know himself well enough to make that sort of declaration (prediction) in the first place.

For most of us, our everyday experiences have taught us that it is possible to make predictions about our own and others' behavior. Many times our soothsayings ring true, which suggests a certain unity of personality. This unity grows out of our need to be consistent with our concept of who we are as persons.

However, our predictions about our own and others' behavior are not always correct because, of all things, we are not always perfectly consistent. How many times, for example, have you heard yourself say things like "I couldn't have been myself when I said that" or "I don't know what possessed me to do such a thing." It is as if at certain moments we are introduced to an aspect of our being that has been hidden from view, repressed into the deeper regions of our unconscious. Thus, the quiet and somewhat self-effacing, shy woman who lashes out in rage may have great difficulty understanding how she could have expressed herself in such a manner. Recently, I read a newspaper account of a man described as a somewhat religious, upper income, conservative person, who was charged with shoplifting a sweater from a local department store. When asked why he did it, he replied, "God, I don't know, I don't know. I've never done this before. I don't know the man who did this."

Perhaps inside each of us there are components of our being that lie dormant, held in check because their expression runs counter to how we see ourselves. Occasionally, those dormant components break through, and we surprise ourselves—and sometimes others—with what comes out. However, the very rarity of such occurrences reflects the need for unity and consistency of behavior.

Without being aware of it, each of us projects a certain personality "style" that makes us more or less knowable and predictable to ourselves and others, an idea we turn to next.

PERSONALITY STYLE AND EXPRESSIONS OF CONSISTENCY

When we talk about personality style, we are referring to the sum total of all that one is and does, to a person's *characteristic patterns of perceiving and responding*. Each painter and composer has a style all his or her own; so, too, each lawyer, secretary, ballplayer, teacher, novelist, chairperson, and mechanic. From style alone, it is possible to recognize the stories by Hemingway, the mysteries of Agatha Christie, the musicals of Rogers and Hammerstein, the paintings of Picasso, the comedy of Arsenio Hall, the quarterbacking of Joe Montana, or the cooking of one's wife (or husband, as the case may be). Each of these activities carries its own unique mark. Although another person's art may resemble that of Picasso's, no one but Picasso can paint exactly like Picasso. An artist, it is said, is not a special type of person, but every person is a special type of artist. You might say that each person's artistry is projected more or less consistently in his or her characteristic ways of behaving. With this as a working concept, let's turn our attention now to some of the evidence that indicates how various perceptual styles and response styles are ultimately linked to the organized unity of the individual personality. First, we need to make an important distinction between two kinds of behavior.

Expressive Versus Coping Behavior

Not everything we see in another person's behavior is indicative of the deeper person within. Sometimes it is more on the order of a *coping* behavior, which is apt to be more consciously chosen and situationally determined. For example, on a first date or in a very formal situation or during a job interview, much of what we say or do is carefully selected and consciously monitored. At a formal dinner party, we are usually more aware than usual of manners, keeping food on our plates and off the table (and ourselves), using the right fork, and so forth. In other words, we cope, and our cautious, self-conscious behavior reflects our efforts. We would, for example, be ill advised to generalize about a person's table manners based on what we observed at the dinner party.

Coping behavior, then, is a conscious effort to adjust to a current situation. Expressive behavior, on the other hand, is most likely to occur in those things we do spontaneously and unconsciously. That is, each of us has developed a highly characteristic and consistent style of talking, writing, sitting, walking, gesturing, laughing, and relating to others. At a distance, we spot a friend by her gait. We recognize the presence of a friend in a crowded theater by his laugh. We identify persons over the phone not so much by what they say but from their voices and manner of speaking. Our expressive behavior is perhaps the most irrepressible part of our nature. Our coping behavior is variable, and it depends on *what* we have to do. But *how* we do it—our expressive behavior—grows more out of our primary dispositions and attitudes. This expressive aspect of our personality is reflected in the way we perceive the world around us, an idea we will examine next.

Consistencies Between Perceptual Style and Personality

As William James long ago pointed out, if four men go to Europe—a politician, an artist, a businessman, and a playboy—they will see, hear, note, and remember entirely different scenes and events. And each of them will do so in a manner entirely consistent with how his unique emotional makeup predisposes him to perceive the world. Each of us develops characteristic ways, which Klein (1951) identified as "perceptual attitudes," of dealing with how we see things, regardless of content and sensory modality. Basically, this means that each of us develops certain ways of perceiving the world that are consistent with our particular personality. Let's turn to some specific illustrations of how this might work.

LEVELERS AND SHARPENERS

Some of us, for example, are *levelers,* whereas others are *sharpeners.* Holzman and Gardner (1959) proposed this "leveling-sharpening" continuum as a way of explaining how personality and perceptual style interact and how this differs among individuals. *Leveling* refers to the inclination to overlook or "level" perceptual differences among objects; that is, this sort of person tends to see things in terms of their sameness or similarity rather than in terms of distinctions between them. In contrast, *sharpening* is a way of looking at things in terms of their differences. A sharpener, for example, would have less trouble than a leveler in picking out the embedded figures in Figure 3-1. Levelers also have more trouble finding hidden faces in puzzle pictures, and they report less contrast in pictures of differing brightness. Thus, there seems to be some evidence to suggest that different people have different perceptual styles that characterize them in many different situations. Personality studies have found that levelers tend to avoid competition (perhaps as a way of avoiding sharp distinctions in performance?), to be the dependent one in relationships, and to be self-oriented. Sharpeners are inclined to be more competitive and exhibitionistic and to have high achievement needs (Israel, 1969). You might say that

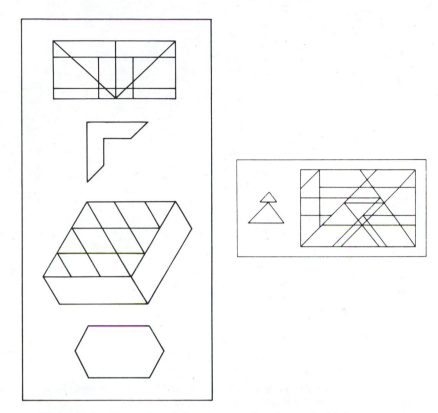

Figure 3-1   *Examples of drawings used in the Embedded Figures Test. The objective is to identify the simple figures in the more complex ones.* Sharpeners *do this more quickly than do* levelers. *Are you able to locate the simple figures?*

sharpeners look for ways to emphasize the differences in themselves and others, whereas levelers seek to smooth out the differences.

FIELD DEPENDENT AND FIELD INDEPENDENT

Are you the kind of person who is emotionally open and who enjoys being with others, or do you prefer nonsocial situations in which you can keep your feelings pretty much to yourself? Odd as it may sound, your response to questions of this sort could probably be predicted from how you performed on certain spatial orientation tasks. Before reading further, look at Figure 3-2, and do the simple tasks requested there.

The small task in Figure 3-2 is one of the perceptual tests used by Witkin and Goodenough (1977) to measure a person's orientation perception. Personality dimensions called *field dependent* and *field independent* have been proposed that are thought to reflect a person's preference for depending on

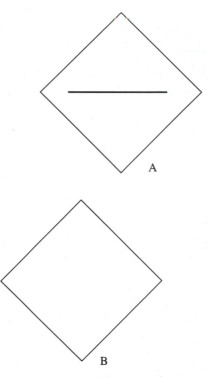

Figure 3-2   *Look at Frame A, and then consider Frame B. Now draw a rod in Frame B so that it is upright with respect to gravity.*

internal or external sources of information in *both* perceptual and social situations (Eliot, 1961; Witkin, Moore, and Goodenough, 1977). In other words, there is a certain consistency between the way we perceive and orient ourselves to the spatial/physical world around us and to the social/interpersonal world in which we find ourselves.

One of the tests for assessing field dependence and field independence in perception is judging when lines are vertical (aligned with gravity) in situations in which there is conflicting visual information. You can see one version of those tests in Figure 3-3 in which people are asked to adjust the tilt of the rod (as in A of Figure 3-3) so that it is upright with respect to gravity. Figure 3-3 depicts the two major ways that people have responded to this task. You can see that some people are able to do this quite accurately despite the tilt of the frame (B). They are called "field independent" because they seem to *depend* more on their own *internal* sensing to define "vertical" and are able to ignore the visually contradictory information from the tilted frame. Other people, however, adjust the rod so that it is tilted more toward the orientation of the frame (C). They are referred to as "field dependent" because they seem to *depend* more on the *external* field of information provided by the frame and less on their internal sensing. (What was your response in Figure 3-2?)

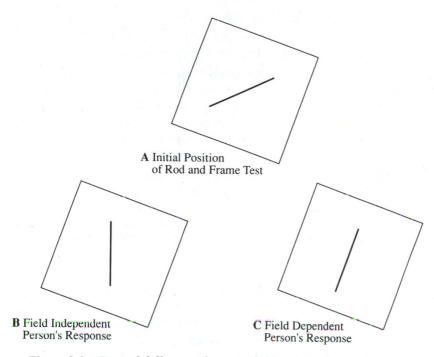

A Initial Position
of Rod and Frame Test

B Field Independent
Person's Response

C Field Dependent
Person's Response

Figure 3-3 *Typical differences between field-independent and field-dependent persons' responses.*

Although tested individuals varied in their tendency to be field dependent or field independent, it was noted that a given individual's perceptual style tends to remain fairly constant in a variety of test situations. For example, field-independent people can usually find the embedded figures in Figure 3-1 more rapidly than can field-dependent people.

To summarize, our perceptual style, like the way we sign our names, is a highly expressive aspect of our behavior. We do it automatically and unconsciously. In the process, we end up presenting a reasonably coherent, consistent picture of ourselves to others. Consider, for example, the following broad description of the behavioral continuums discussed in this section. Note how the behaviors associated with each tend to cluster together in natural groupings. (Keep in mind that the descriptions you are about to read are polarized distinctions, which in real life are apt to be less exclusive and more apt to fall along a continuum from "just like me" to "somewhat like me" to "not at all like me.") Which one(s) fit you as you know yourself?

1. A *field-dependent* person tends to (a) look to others, for what is right and wrong; (b) be somewhat fearful of, and passive toward, authority figures; (c) be friendly and outgoing but quite conscious about whether he or she is liked by others; (d) be somewhat conventional,

conservative, and hesitant about expressing angry or aggressive feelings; (e) have self-esteem problems; (f) have more interpersonal prejudices; and (g) choose careers that are people oriented.

2. A *field-independent* person tends to (a) be less reliant on others for feelings of self-worth; (b) be reasonably self-confident and self-accepting; (c) be able to express angry feelings as well as caring feelings in relationships; (d) rely more on his or her judgments of right and wrong; (e) have fewer interpersonal prejudices; and (f) choose careers in mathematical, scientific, or analytic professions.

3. A *sharpener* is a person who tends to (a) look for ways to "sharpen" the distinctions between people and situations; (b) look for the contrasts that underscore how people, events, and situations differ from each other; and (c) be somewhat competitive and achievement oriented, as if to "sharpen" the performance differences between himself or herself and others.

4. A *leveler* is a person who tends to (a) look for ways to "level" out the differences between people and situations; (b) be somewhat self-oriented as opposed to achievement oriented, as if to minimize performance distinctions between himself or herself and others; and (c) be somewhat passive and dependent in relationships, as if to keep things "level" and uncontested.

It's not often that any particular individual will fit perfectly into any one of these behavioral categories; we humans are too complex to be pigeonholed in any simple way. However, most people do find themselves somewhat more identified with, or recognizable in, one or two categories than the others. In your own case, for example, do you see how your identification with a certain category could be the motivational undercurrent for a certain amount of consistency in your behavior?

Locus of Control and Behavioral Consistencies

Before reading further, you may find it revealing to respond to the ten-item inventory in Table 3-1. There are no right or wrong responses as such. A response is "right" if it feels right to you. Check off your responses in either column A or B and then we will discuss what they may mean.

Probably no other dimension of personality has been studied more thoroughly or with more rigor in the past 25 years than the locus of control variable (Rotter, 1990; Strickland, 1989). Depending on whether our locus of control is internal or external, we perceive our lives as being directed by either ourselves or outside forces.

Consider, for example, your responses to the locus of control inventory. If most of your responses were in the A column, your locus of control may be more *internal* than *external*. If, on the other hand, most of your responses were

Table 3–1   Locus of Control Inventory

Julian Rotter is the developer of a 29-item scale for measuring an individual's degree of internal or external control. The sample items below are taken from an earlier version of the test but were not used in the final version. There are ten statements here. In each instance, choose the one you agree with the most. Is your locus of control internal or external? Check your choice on the right.

A I More Strongly Believe That:	B OR	A	B
1. Promotions are earned through hard work and persistence.	Making a lot of money is largely a matter of getting the right breaks.	___	___
2. In my experience I have noticed that there is usually a direct connection between how hard I study and the grades I get.	Many times the reactions of teachers seem haphazard to me.	___	___
3. The number of divorces indicates that more and more people are not trying to make their marriages work.	Marriage is largely a gamble.	___	___
4. When I am right I can convince others.	It is silly to think that one can really change another person's basic attitudes.	___	___
5. In our society a man's future earning power is dependent upon his ability.	Getting promoted is really a matter of being a little luckier than the next guy.	___	___
6. If one knows how to deal with people they are really quite easily led.	I have little influence over the way other people behave.	___	___
7. In my case the grades I make are the result of my own efforts; luck has little or nothing to do with it.	Sometimes I feel that I have little to do with the grades I get.	___	___
8. People like me can change the course of world affairs if we make ourselves heard.	It is only wishful thinking to believe that one can really influence what happens in society at large.	___	___
9. I am the master of my fate.	A great deal that happens to me is probably a matter of chance.	___	___
10. Getting along with people is a skill that must be practiced.	It is almost impossible to figure out how to please some people.	___	___

The original and longer version of this test is presented and discussed in the following source: J. B. Rotter, "Generalized Expectancies for Internal Versus External Control of Reinforcement," *Psychological Monographs,* 1966, *80:* Whole No. 609.

in column B, perhaps you have more of an *external* than an *internal* locus of control. "Locus of control" refers to a person's beliefs about control over life's events. Some people feel that life's outcomes are predominantly the consequences of their own actions. These people are labeled *internals.* Others feel that their outcomes in life are determined by forces beyond their control, such as fate, luck, chance, and other people. These people are labeled *externals.* As shown by Rotter's (1966) Internal-External Scale, locus of control represents a continuum along which different people reflect varying degrees of internality and externality. People are seldom completely one way or the other, but most people do tend to lean toward one end of the continuum. The direction of the lean determines the direction of the behavioral consistency we might expect.

Since locus of control refers to people's implicit, generalized conclusions about what it is that controls their lives, we might reasonably predict that internals will be more consistently assertive than externals in their attempts to control, master, manipulate, and otherwise cope with their environment in effective ways. Studies show that this is, in fact, the case.

Do you prefer games of chance or skill? Would you rather engage in an activity in which your final ranking depended on your luck or your knowledge? Lefcourt's (1982) review indicates that internals prefer activities involving skill and strategy, whereas externals are more inclined to choose activities involving luck and chance. The preference is quite consistent with the locus of control orientation. Internals want the control that comes from within (the use of skill), whereas externals give control to outside factors (luck, chance). When you have done well on an academic task—written assignment or exam—are you able to assume responsibility for your success, or are you inclined to pass it off as luck or unexplained good fortune? If you can take credit for it, as pointed out by Findley and Cooper (1983) and Stipek and Weisz (1981), you are likely to be an internal. It works the other way, too. That is, internals are less likely to blame outside factors for their own failures than are externals (Hochreich, 1975; Phares, Wilson, and Klyver, 1971). As pointed out by Phares (1979), people with an internal belief are more able to take credit for their work because according to this kind of belief one is, after all, responsible for one's success (or lack of it). Externals are less able to pat themselves on the back because of their haunting suspicion that the success really wasn't of their doing.

If you're a smoker, have you ever tried to quit? As it turns out, smoking is another behavior that can be related to the external-internal continuum. And again, we find evidence of consistency between the personality type and the behavior. Lefcourt's (1982) research review showed that nonsmokers are more apt to be internals than smokers. Smokers often say they wish they weren't *controlled* by their smoking. Control is a central issue. Externals are more apt to give in to it ("I just can't help myself"), and internals are less likely ("I can control this if I choose").

Even eating is related to the internal-external continuum, and the weight of the evidence (pun intended) strongly suggests that the person who overeats is apt to have an external locus of control. Research shows that there are marked differences between the obese (from 14% to 75% overweight) and those of normal weight not only in the amount they eat, but also in the cues that trigger eating (Rodin and Slochower, 1976; Tom and Rucker, 1975). In general, overweight persons seem more responsive to external food cues such as the sight, smell, and taste of food than they are to internal physiological hunger signals. In other words, for people with severe weight problems, the condition of their stomachs has little to do with their eating behavior. The practical implications of these findings seems clear: If you're overweight and have a difficult time resisting food while it's around, the best thing to do is not have it around in the first place. A friend of mine, who wages an ongoing but friendly battle of the bulge, is fond of saying, "If I don't see it, I won't eat it. If I don't smell it, I don't want it."

Are you the kind of person who, when in the hospital or in the doctor's office for a checkup, asks many questions about your condition, what it means, how it happened, what to do about it, and so forth? As discovered by Seeman and Evans (1962), this is quite characteristic of patients who score high as internals. Speaking of hospitals and doctors, there is an impressive array of evidence suggesting that one's perceptions of control have significant implications for health, especially in conditions that might ordinarily further a feeling of less control. It is a well-documented medical fact that loss of control can produce heightened reactions to stress, thus making a person more susceptible to disease and illness (Cousins, 1989). In order to reduce the possibility of the adverse effects of stress on postoperative surgical patients, Langer, Janis, and Wolfer (1975) "taught" preoperative surgical patients that they could control their pain and distress by focusing on the positive, optimistic outcomes of their experience. They were, in other words, taught to process their situation from more of an internal locus of control perspective. It worked. These patients were judged by their nurses, both pre- and postoperatively, to be significantly less anxious and better able to cope with distress than patients without such cognitive control preparation. Not surprisingly, they were also less likely than other patients to want sedatives or pain killers following surgery. Similarly, it has also been found that nursing home patients who are given more control over basic decisions affecting their lives are both psychologically and physically better off than patients who do not have this sense of control (Langer and Rodin, 1976; Rodin and Langer, 1977).

All in all, the volumes of research related to locus of control suggest that our intrapsychic and interpersonal orientation to the world around us, whether it be internal or external, is a fairly good predictor of the ways we are likely to react emotionally and cognitively to life's circumstances. Understanding the idea of locus of control, then, is another way to understand behavioral consistency. Like currents in a river, different behaviors in the same individual have a tendency to flow in similar directions. Externals are more easily manipulated, rely more on luck and chance, and seem generally more responsive to what happens outside the self than to what is going on inside. For internals, the behavioral flow is toward mastering their environment by trying to find out as much as they can about it, by relying on their personal skills, and by paying attention to their own inner feelings. Although the relationship between locus of control and behavior is by no means a perfect one, being sensitive to the direction of one's internal-external orientation can give us a starting point for understanding and predicting the way that we and others are likely to respond to the contingencies of everyday living.

Outer Expressions of the Inner Person: Hidden Consistencies

The private, hidden person we are on the inside is expressed in more ways and more frequently than we may realize. The inner person we think we camouflage so well telegraphs his or her presence in our written expression, speech patterns, art preferences, assorted expressions of high dominance or low dominance behavior, and even the way we cross the street.

In an effort to be more precise in the measurement of relationships between graphic responses and personality, Mira (1958) developed a standardized series of graphic tests for what was termed a "myokinetic psychodiagnosis." For example, a subject starts to copy a simple design, for instance, a staircase. As soon as he is underway, a shield is placed in front of his eyes so that he can no longer see what he is doing, but he continues copying. In this way, the coping behavior is reduced, and the expressive component becomes more prominent. Mira believed he could identify certain deep tendencies in the personality by observing the expressive graphic behavior. For instance, a marked drift *away* from the body, in the case of lines drawn to and from the body, was related to aggressive attitudes toward others, whereas an *upward* drift was related to self-directed aggression. In addition, Mira found that elated people exaggerate upward movements, whereas depressed people tend to overdo movements toward the body. Thus, one can see the consistency between a person's inner feelings and his or her outer expression.

Although it is only a matter of degree, there does seem to be a relationship between personality and a person's written expression. Consider, for example, the musical scores in Figure 3-4. One is by Beethoven, another by Mozart, and a third by Bach. If you know anything about the music of these three men, which score do you think was written by whom? Perhaps you can see the unities: the tempestuousness of Beethoven (I), the spritely fastidiousness of Mozart (II), and the ordered and steady flow of Bach (III). These qualities were reflected not only in their music and graphic style but in their personal lives as well.

The three samples in Figure 3-5 of Richard Nixon's handwriting over a five-year period are visual examples of the congruency that may exist between a person's inner feelings and something as simple as a personal signature. There is even evidence to suggest that there are relationships between our choice of words and the person deep within. For example, Doob (1958) found that people who are active, analytic, and discriminating in handling their day-to-day living tend to use more adjective and adverb modifiers and more active verbs than people less active and analytic. Active people, it seems, are not passive in relating either to their environment or in their use of speech. There

I

II

III

Figure 3-4 *Musical manuscripts of Beethoven, Mozart, and Bach.*
From W. Wolff, *The Expression of Personality,* New York: Harper, 1943.

Nixon Handwriting Reflects Pressure

New York [Aug. 14, 1974]—(AP)—Former President Nixon's signature tells it all, according to a handwriting analyst.

Felix Lehmann studied three examples of Nixon's signature—the first from shortly after Nixon took office in 1969, the second several months ago and the third shortly before he resigned from office.

"Tremendous capitals show pride, but the long thread at the end of his name shows he wants to leave room to maneuver," Lehmann said of the first signature. "The striving for recognition and ambition are overpowering in his handwriting."

The second example:

"He goes from an appearance of clarity to being wishy-washy . . . But in this signature there is still hope."

And Lehmann's analysis of the third signature:

"There's nothing left. Only a shadow. His ambitions are over. A shapeless stroke, ambiguity. A disintegration of personality, a person sinking within himself."

Figure 3-5 *Samples of Nixon's handwriting over a five-year period during his presidency.*

From *Denver Post*, August 14, 1974. Reprinted by permission of AP.

tends to be a consistency of expression between their active lives and their active use of the language.

All things being equal, your preference for certain kinds of art is probably related to where you might place yourself on the conservative-liberal continuum. The prototypical conservative has been variously described as conventional, conforming, antihedonistic, religious, authoritarian, punitive, ethnocentric, militaristic, dogmatic, superstitious, and antiscientific, whereas the prototypical liberal is characterized as the antithesis of these behaviors and attitudes (Wilson, 1973). Inasmuch as people who are typically conservative in the usual sense tend to be more conventional and concrete, we might expect them to prefer simple and representational paintings, whereas people who are more typically liberal would prefer paintings that were complex and abstract. This is exactly what Wilson, Ausman, and Mathews (1973) found in their study of conservatism and art preferences. Additionally, they found that the simple-complex dimension discriminated between the liberals and conservatives more strongly than the abstract-representational dimension. That is, the conservatives' ratings of the complex paintings indicated that these paintings were not just preferred less but were actively *disliked*. Apparently, the value that conservatives place on order, simplicity, and security is as observable in their choice of paintings as it is in their choices elsewhere on the political-religious-social spectrum. Remember, people are seldom entirely liberal or totally conservative; rather, they tend to lean in one direction or the other.

If you're a woman, would you describe yourself as a high-dominance person (strong, self-assertive, self-confident), or do you see yourself as more of a low-dominance person (passive, shy, somewhat uncertain)? In his early research in which he investigated the personalities of these two types of women, Maslow (1939) found interesting consistencies between the personalities of each of these two groups of women and their other behaviors. High-dominance women reflect their dominant, assertive characters in a variety of ways. They choose foods that are saltier, stronger tasting, sharper, and more bitter—for example, strong cheese rather than mild; foods that taste good even though ugly and unattractive, such as clams; foods that are novel and different, such as snails or fried squirrel. They are less picky, less easily nauseated, less fussy about unattractive or sloppily prepared food, and yet more sensuous and lusty about good food than are low-dominance women. These same qualities are apparent in other areas, too. For example, the language of high-dominance women is tougher, stronger, harder; the men they choose are tougher, stronger, harder, and their reaction to people who try to take advantage of them is tougher, stronger, and harder. In still other research, Maslow (1942) found that the high-dominance woman is more apt to be pagan, permissive, and accepting in all sexual realms. She is less apt to be a virgin, more apt to have masturbated, and more apt to have done more sexual experimentation. In other words, her sexual behavior is consistent with what seems to be a general personality characteristic, for here, too, she is apt to be dominant in terms of being more forward and less inhibited.

There is even the intriguing likelihood of hidden consistencies between the personalities of personality theorists and the theories they derive. Harvey Mindess (1988) explored this possibility in his analysis of a number of prominent psychologists, which included Sigmund Freud, Carl Jung, B. F. Skinner, Carl Rogers, and Milton Erickson. He began with a basic question: "How is the theory a function of the theorist's own personality?" The outcomes of his analysis are revealing. For example, Mindess points out that Freud's own relationship with his parents provided a prototype for the Oedipal complex; his love for his mother was intense, bordering on lust, and his feeling for his father was, at the very most, ambivalent. "That he came to 'discover' these qualities in others was merely an extension of himself" (p. 53). The point is further made that the development of a personality theory is not simply a matter of attributive projection, but defensive projection as well. Thus, one of the unconscious motives for projecting one's personality on to humankind as a whole is a validation of one's own personality, especially those aspects one has cause to doubt oneself. One cannot, after all, be blamed for character flaws that are immutable aspects of human nature. This argument is developed most revealingly in the case of Skinner, who claimed in his autobiographical writings that he discovered the truth of behaviorism while struggling to cope with his early failure as a fiction writer. This failure, as Skinner saw it, was not due to deficits in personal talent, but rather the inevitable result of the circumstances in which he found himself. He analyzed his personal circumstances in a manner consistent with his behavioristic theory, that is, causes of behavior are located *outside* the self, not *inside*. (One might suspect that this self-serving analysis was a particularly liberating experience for Skinner.)

Inasmuch as Mindess uses only the logic of deductive reasoning, it would be difficult to prove or disprove his conclusions. To the extent, however, that the signature of who we are is written on all that we do, it does not seem at all improbable that we will find a high degree of consistency between the theorist and the theory. In fact, this is exactly what Johnson and his colleagues (1988) found to be the case in their investigation of relationships between the philosophical world views of 119 behavioral scientists who were divided into four groups based on their theoretical persuasions. In the words of the researchers, "The upshot of both the present study and previous research is that scientists exhibit individual differences in beliefs, attitudes, assumptions, cognitive style, and methodological preferences, all of which constitute aspects of their overall personality style" (p. 853). It would appear that even at the level of scientific inquiry, an activity often regarded as a purely rational and empirical enterprise, the theoretical position of a scientist is not just a statement about his or her objectively derived beliefs, but, at a deeper level, a subjective reflection of who he or she is as a person.

Next time you cross the street, take note of how you do it. Even in this natural, spontaneous act there are reflections of the inner person. Consider the findings of Kastenbaum and Briscoe (1975), who staked out a busy street in a major city and ranked 125 men and women according to the amount of risk they took in getting across. They were rated on the basis of such factors as whether or not they watched traffic lights, kept an eye out for oncoming cars, stayed within the crosswalk or scurried from behind parked cars, and other indications of recklessness or caution. After the subjects were observed and rated, they were interviewed to find out something about their personalities and attitudes. Although there were all types of people in all categories, generally the young and single took greater risks than those who were older and married. The safest street crossers were more aware of their actions and considered themselves generally safer, more self-protecting people. The less cautious reported they had been barely aware of even crossing the street. One thing to be said for the risky crossers is that they were not deluding themselves. They neither wanted nor expected to live as long as did the cautious pedestrians. The researchers concluded, "Seeing how a person crosses the street, we can make a number of 'good guesses' about his marital status, mental contents, driving habits, suicidal history, etc." By no coincidence, it seems we each cross the street much as we make our way through life, a finding unlikely to curb interest in such matters.

This, then, is some of the evidence that supports the idea that the personality has a unitary organization. In its simplest terms, it suggests that an individual's "personality style" reflects a degree of unity and congruency across many different expressive behaviors. Consider a simple example of behavioral congruency: John F. Kennedy entitled his book *Profiles in Courage*, and Richard Nixon entitled his book *Six Crises*. What do these titles suggest about the world view of each of these men and his approach to life?

However forceful the evidence may be, we must be cautious in our judgments of others for two reasons: (1) behavioral consistency is never perfect; and (2) we can too easily misinterpret a person's inner state if we are insensitive to that person's primary motives or if that person hides his or her real feelings with masquerading behavior. For example, we sometimes misinterpret shyness for snobbishness and self-confidence for conceit. A ready smile and a firm handshake are not necessarily valid indicators of honesty and integrity; indeed, the confidence man and the shyster are adept at such cues. However, there is little we do or say that is not, in some way, a reflection of the deeper values and primary motivations that lie within. A common thread, known as self-concept, weaves its way throughout the fabric of each person's personality, which ties it together and helps it to function as a unified whole. By remaining alert and sensitive to the myriad of perceptual, bodily, and graphic response styles available to us, we are better able to see how seemingly unrelated behaviors are, although different, really interconnected strands of the same emotional cloth.

COGNITIVE DISSONANCE: WHEN BEHAVIORS AND ATTITUDES CLASH

Have you ever said something you didn't really believe or acted in a way that was quite contrary to your actual views? Probably you have. We all go through moments like this. These are the times when how we behave is at odds with our basic attitudes or beliefs, which, as elaborated by Festinger (1957), Wicklund and Brehm (1976), and Cooper and Fazio (1984), is the basis for a very influential view in social psychology known as the *theory of cognitive dissonance*.

Dissonance theory begins with a simple truism: We humans do not like inconsistency. Specifically, we tend to feel uncomfortable with inconsistency among our various attitudes, on the one hand, or between our attitudes and our behavior on the other. When this happens, we usually experience an unpleasant emotional state known as *dissonance,* which we can reduce in basically one of two ways: (1) change our attitudes so they are consistent with the behavior or (2) change our behavior so it is consistent with our attitudes.

For example, let's say that John reads a persuasive book on the importance of conserving natural resources and reducing pollution and decides to give time and money to causes designed to promote greater public consciousness about environmental issues. Six months before the pro-environmental commitment, John bought an older but nicely preserved pre-antipollution vintage sports car, which he drives back and forth to work and which he enjoys enormously. Suddenly, John is caught between what he values (clean air) and what he drives (an air polluter). According to cognitive dissonance theory, John is in the middle of a huge inconsistency between his attitudes and behavior. What can be done about it?

Since cognitive dissonance is an unpleasant psychological condition, John would probably look for ways to reduce it. There are at least four kinds of rationalizations involved: (1) He could attempt to *add consonant elements,* that is, ideas or thoughts that support his pro-environmental attitudes. For instance, he remembers that his sports car gets better gas mileage than his previous car, which, therefore, allows him to save gas and reduce pollution compared to his former car. (2) He could attempt to minimize the importance of his particular behavior by thinking about the fact that several million commuters travel back and forth to work each day, thus making his own driving seem trivial in the larger scheme of things. (3) He could alter his driving habits; for example, he could drive less by taking public transportation or by joining a car pool, if that was possible. (4) Or he could alter his pro-environmental attitudes by concluding that he doesn't really care about the issue as strongly as he thought.

What to Do If the World Doesn't End

John's case is hypothetical and is used to illustrate some of the basic principles of cognitive dissonance theory. An example of what can actually happen when there is an inconsistency between beliefs and behavior is documented by Festinger, Riecken, and Schacter's (1956) investigation of a religious group who predicted the earth's destruction. The head of that group, Mrs. Marion Keech, claimed to have received messages in the form of "automatic writing" from beings on the planet Clarion who informed her that the world would end in a giant cataclysm before dawn on December 21. The group members believed that only they would be saved when flying saucers from Clarion would come to whisk them off to safety. Some left their jobs, some left college, some left their spouses—all to prepare for the final hours and their ride into the cosmos.

On the day of the predicted cataclysm, the chosen few were waiting at their designated places for the saucers to rescue them. When the saucers did not arrive at the time predicted, dissonance was produced. What the group believed would happen and what actually happened were inconsistent events, and to reduce the dissonance, the development was interpreted as a test set up by the gods to see if true believers could withstand uncertainty. Subsequent word was received that flying saucers would come at a later time. Then, when they did not come as predicted, when several other predictions about their arrival were also proved wrong, and when grave doubt began to surface concerning the coming of the catastrophic flood, the really true believers had a problem. Indeed, they were in a state of dejected puzzlement until they came by the happy construction, conveyed to them in another message in automatic writing to Mrs. Keech, that, because of the faith and steadfastness of the followers, the gods had decided to spare the world and to rearrange the divine plan. Thus, the dissonance was relieved, and the events, as they were happening, were consistent with a new belief or idea. However, to keep it effective in relieving the dissonance, it had to be built up to more credible proportions. Consequently, the true believers exerted strong efforts, through news releases and missionary work, to publicize the great turn of events that had occurred and to win more converts to the cause. Through investing additional efforts in support of the interpretation of what had happened, they made the new interpretation seem even more believable. By changing both their beliefs (the gods were testing them) and their behavior (they renewed their evangelical efforts), the dissonance was resolved by aligning a new set of beliefs with a new set of behaviors. And, once again, their behaviors and beliefs matched up.

In a somewhat similar incident, studied by Hardyck and Braden (1962), an evangelical Christian group believed that the world would be destroyed in a nuclear holocaust by a certain date. Anticipating the worst, 103 members of this group spent 42 days and nights in a bomb shelter before they recognized that the world had not come to an end. There was a clear difference between what they believed would happen and what actually happened. Was their belief shaken? Not at all. They reentered the nonholocausted world believing more strongly than ever that God was in touch with them. They simply reinterpreted the event to mean that God had postponed the holocaust because of their strong show of faith. Rather than emerging from the shelter with shaken beliefs, they walked away with firmer convictions.

Dissonance Reduction Through Drinking or Selective Recall

The bottom line is this: People do not like to feel dissonance or inconsistency with themselves. Not only is it psychologically uncomfortable, but also, as Fazio and Cooper (1983) showed, it increases people's level of physiological activation, that is, causes feelings of restlessness and uneasiness. It's a well-known fact of life that when people feel unpleasant, uneasy, or unhappy they sometimes turn to drugs—alcohol is a favorite—to ease the pain. Steele, Southwick, and Critchlow (1981) wondered if drinking would lessen the unpleasant feelings people have when faced with inconsistency between their attitudes and behavior. To test this possibility, they took a group of students who, on the basis of an attitude assessment questionnaire, were opposed to a large tuition hike at their university. The students were then divided into two groups, one of which was to write down arguments supporting the increase and the other to list arguments opposing it. Those students who had to write the favoring arguments found themselves engaged in counterattitudinal behavior and, thus, felt considerable dissonance. After the arguments were written, participants were asked to taste and rate several substances. For some, it was either beer or vodka-laced cocktails; for others, it was either distilled water or coffee. Then, the participants' attitudes about the tuition hike were measured again. The results showed clearly that participants who wrote the counterarguments and who drank water or coffee felt a high degree of dissonance; that is, they felt uncomfortable, uneasy, and inconsistent with their own values. What they drank had little effect on how they felt. However, participants who wrote the counterarguments and who drank the alcohol felt a *low* degree of dissonance; that is, they felt less tense and less inconsistent. (By the way, the amount of alcohol consumed was quite small; no one was anywhere near being intoxicated.)

These findings suggest why drinking may be particularly attractive to people whose behavior conflicts with their beliefs. When there is conflict between these two aspects of one's being, there is dissonance. Alcohol relieves the discomfort of the dissonance, at least temporarily, which may be one of the reasons that some people grow dependent on alcohol as a source of relief.

Another way to reduce cognitive dissonance is to "remember" selectively only those aspects of an experience that are in one's best interests. This is not necessarily done consciously, and it is very much like the defense mechanism described as repression in Chapter 1. We can see how it works in an experiment by Buss and Brock (1963), who asked a number of men and women who had previously said they were opposed to the use of electric shock in scientific research to participate in an experiment in which they believed they were administering electric shock to induce learning. Just before the experiment began, they were asked to read a statement purporting to emanate from medical authorities. One version stated that electric shocks were extremely harmful, and the other stated that they were, in fact, beneficial. After the experiment, participants were asked to recall the content of the communication. Consistent with cognitive dissonance theory, there was significantly *less* recall of the medical statement that said that shocks were harmful. In other words, forgetting the negative material made it easier for the participants to accept the fact that they had administered an electric shock to other persons and, thus, enabled them to reduce the dissonance between what they believed and what they had done. It is also an excellent example of how we selectively recall experiences and events to protect our self-concepts.

The point should be clear. Dissonant ideas and behavior produce conflict and tension. In the quest for an overall unity of personality, changing our behavior or attitude to make it consistent with what we have already done is a course through which most of us seek to reduce the dissonance and ensure some degree of "sameness" on a day-to-day basis. We each have a need to feel like a whole person, a person whose various aspects of psychophysical existence are integrated into a coherent sense of self. Because of this need, we develop a self-concept that functions both as an emotional barometer that helps us define ourselves to ourselves and as a navigational aid that helps us chart the route we wish to take with our lives. We can understand better the psychodynamics of behavioral consistency by looking at its relationship to self-concept theory, an idea we turn to next.

BEHAVIORAL CONSISTENCY WITHIN THE FRAMEWORK OF SELF-CONCEPT THEORY

In broad terms, self-concept theory provides a conceptual framework for understanding and predicting people's behavior by taking into account the way they perceive themselves. Basically, the theory suggests that people tend to behave in a way consistent with their self-perceptions. Lecky (1945), one of our early self-concept theorists, developed the idea that normally functioning people strive for consistency in all aspects of their lives, something that can only be accomplished by behaving in a manner consistent with their concept of self:

> Behavior expresses the effort to maintain integrity and unity of the organization. . . . In order to be immediately assimilated, the idea formed as the result of a new experience must be felt to be consistent with the ideas already present in the system. On the other hand, ideas whose inconsistency is recognized as the personality develops must be expelled from the system. There is thus a constant assimilation of new ideas and the expulsion of old ideas throughout life. (p. 135)

Rogers (1947) observed that the integration of various aspects of an individual into a unified concept of self "is accompanied by feelings of comfort and freedom from tension." Rogers (1951) further said that one major way of preserving unity of the self is by filtering one's experiences so that they are either

> ". . . (a) symbolized, perceived and organized into some relationship to the self, (b) ignored because there is no perceived relationship to the self-structure, (c) denied symbolization or given a distorted symbolization because the experience is inconsistent with the structure of the self." (p. 503)

This proposition states, in effect, that perceptions are selective, and the primary criterion for selection is whether the experience is consistent with one's self-picture. Once the self is formed, it works hard to preserve and protect its image.

A somewhat related idea is found in Erikson's (1980) concept of *identity,* which he theorized to be an especially important occurrence during adolescence as one attempts to bring the sense of one's own identity into closer unity with one's social relationships:

> The sense of ego identity is the accrued confidence that one's ability to maintain inner sameness and continuity . . . is matched by the sameness and continuity of one's meaning for others. (p. 94)

Extending Erikson's idea a step further, Allport (1961) suggested that one's ability to maintain inner sameness and continuity is more likely to occur when one is ego- or "self"-involved in whatever the experience at hand happens to be:

> . . . thoughts and behavior have greater consistency when they relate to what we consider to be warm, central, and important in our lives than they have when they are not so related. (p. 384)

There is research to support Allport's view. For example, public opinion polls show that people who feel strongly about an issue will be quite consistent in endorsing all the propositions related to it. If they feel less strongly involved (less "self"-involved), they are more likely to be variable and inconsistent (Cantril, 1943). They are in a word, less predictable. Epstein (1980) theorized that our self-concept is actually a self-theory, something that we unwittingly develop because we need it to live our lives. Like any good theory, its basic function is to help us formulate and test hypotheses, although unlike most theory testing, this is something we do at a subconscious level. Epstein suggested that our self-theory, together with what he calls our "theory of reality," has three basic functions: (1) to assimilate the data of experience, (2) to maintain a favorable pleasure-pain balance, and (3) to optimize self-esteem.

How Our Self-Schemas Affect Behavior

Our self-concept is basically a kind of schema or set of schemas that forms the basis of our particular theory of self. To understand the underlying mechanism of how self-schemas work, consider the following questions: Are you honest? Kind? Ambitious? Lazy? Sexy? Witty? Intellectual? The list could go on, but you get the idea. Most of us have little difficulty answering questions of this sort because our experiences and input from others over time have enabled us to form a reasonably stable conception of our own personality along many different dimensions, such as those in the preceding questions. The word *many* should not be read as *all,* however. Although our self-schema may be clear and well developed with respect to certain traits, such as intellectualism, laziness, and honesty, it may remain ambiguous or unclear in terms of others, such as, for example, being conservative or liberal. In any case, self-schemas are formed and consolidated into our concept of self-perceptions.

Markus and Sentis (1982) suggested that self-schemas help us (1) select certain aspects of situations that seem particularly noteworthy, (2) organize and integrate our thoughts on these matters, (3) make inferential guesses about other things that may happen, and (4) remember experiences and events that are relevant to our self-concepts. Interestingly, research by Markus (1977) illustrates the extent to which our self-schemas influence us to behave in ways that are consistent with how we see ourselves. On the basis of a variety of personality measures, she was able to divide a sample of women into three different groups: (1) those who saw themselves as strongly independent persons, (2) those who saw themselves as quite dependent persons, and (3) those who did not see themselves as particularly independent or dependent. Among other things, Markus asked each of the women to select those adjectives in a list of adjectives that were or were not characteristic of her. The findings were revealing. Women who saw themselves as highly independent were the quickest to apply the adjectives suggesting "independent" to themselves, whereas those whose self-schemas were organized more around being dependent were fastest in deciding that "dependent" adjectives fit their personalities. In another study, women were given fake scores on a supposed test of suggestibility. The results showed that women with strong, clear conceptions of themselves were most inclined to reject test feedback that was inconsistent with how they saw themselves. Women with weaker, less definitive self-conceptions, on the other hand, were more apt to be "suggested into" believing bogus feedback about themselves. Markus concluded that the schemas these people had about themselves enabled them to process rapidly external information relevant to their self-concepts. By responding to subconsciously embedded schemas (e.g., "I am independent" or "I am dependent"), they could quickly decide whether particular adjectives applied to them, could readily remember instances in which they had acted in ways that fit this schema and could predict behavior along the same lines, and could also easily reject descriptions of themselves that didn't fit their self-schemas.

These findings are replicated in other areas of behavior. Some people, for example, see themselves as failures because they haven't done as well as they had hoped to. With this self-schema, they are much more disposed to see threats to and negative evaluations of themselves in their surroundings (Kleinke, 1978). Even their attributions—i.e., what they "attribute" the failure to—can be affected by their self-conceptions. Strickland's (1989) review shows clearly that, whereas persons with a history of success are inclined to take personal credit for any future success, those who have a negative view of themselves typically attribute whatever successes they have to external factors—either they were just lucky or the task was easy. Our interpretations of the things that happen to us are often consistent with our particular self-schemas.

To summarize, self-concept theory suggests that we will "act like" the person we perceive ourselves to be. Our self-concept reflects a consolidation of innumerable clusters of "schemas," or representational ideas we have developed about ourselves. Seeing ourselves as shy, we tend to behave in quiet and reserved ways; seeing ourselves as levelheaded, we tend to behave rationally and hold our feelings in check; seeing ourselves as "just an average, ordinary person," we tend to behave in average ways, seldom doing anything extraordinary. Our self-perceptions are a form of self-labeling, which we turn into self-fulfilling prophecies by behaving in ways that confirm both their existence and validity.

From our own point of view, our behavior always has a certain sameness and consistency. Whether we are at a party with dozens of people or on a walk in the woods by ourselves, we tend to retain a continuous sense of personal identity. Is our behavioral consistency best accounted for by the possibility that we are a certain "type" of person or by the possibility that we have acquired certain traits that predispose us to behave in one way or the other? Let's turn our attention to each of these possibilities.

TYPE THEORIES AND THE ISSUE OF BEHAVIORAL CONSISTENCY

Basically, type theorists are seeking to understand and predict behavior by classifying people according to a limited number of central characteristics that are thought to influence a broad range of behaviors. To the extent that we have certain preconceived notions about blondes, redheads, republicans, democrats, sensitive men, or assertive women, we, in our own way, are "type" theorists. That is, on the basis of what we see as a very central characteristic of a person, we may consciously or unconsciously *stereotype* that person, which is, essentially, a standardized and oversimplified opinion or attitude that we feel describes all people who fit the stereotype.

Efforts to classify behavior according to certain alleged "types" go back deep in time, one of the earliest being that of the Greek physician Hippocrates, who in about 400 B.C. proposed that there were four basic temperaments: choleric (irritable), melancholic (depressed), sanguine (optimistic), and phlegmatic (listless). Inasmuch as he was a physician during the golden age of Greek medicine, it is not surprising that he related each of his types or "temperaments" to corresponding bodily fluids, which he called "humors." The choleric type, for example, was thought to have too much yellow bile, the melancholic type too much black bile, the sanguine type too much blood, and the phlegmatic type too much phlegm.

Although Hippocrates' topology seems simplistic and unsophisticated to us, certain stereotypes about possible relationships between people's personality and their physical makeup persist even today. How often do we guess that fat people are jolly and outgoing, that thin ones are somewhat timid and shy, or that muscular persons are bold and confident?

Sheldon (1954) attempted to type people according to specific body builds, which he called "somatotizing." Three basic types—and variations of each—emerged from this system: (1) the thin, long-boned, poorly muscled *ectomorphic* type (described as sensitive, solitary, and cerebral); (2) the well-muscled and athletically built *mesomorphic* type (described as assertive, daring, and independent); and (3) the heavy and fat *endomorphic* type (described as relaxed, self-indulgent, and approval seeking). After years of interviewing and observing a group of young male subjects, Sheldon reported that there was a positive relationship between somatotype and personality, a conclusion that most contemporary psychologists do not fully accept. A major question remains: Do certain body builds "cause" certain personality "types" or do people's expectations for how certain physical types should behave lead to a kind of self-fulfilling prophecy? At best, the answer to the question is ambiguous, which leaves the door open to typing people, many times erroneously, along the lines just suggested.

Jung's (1921) analytic theory represents a different kind of topology altogether. Whereas Hippocrates and Sheldon focused on different physical types, Jung focused on two basic attitudinal types, specifically, introversion and extraversion. As Jung saw it, persons who are more introverted tend to be oriented toward their inner life, are inclined to be quiet and retiring, and tend to minimize interactions with others. Extraverts, on the other hand, tend to be more externally oriented, that is, more social, outgoing, and the like. In Jung's theory, every individual possesses the innate workings necessary for both introversion and extraversion, but over time, people develop a preference for one or the other. Jung argued that when that happens people become types, either introverts or extraverts, which predisposes them to behave in typically introverted or extraverted ways in most situations. Jung's theory is much more complex than this, particularly that part concerned with how these types may be related to rational functions like thinking and feeling or to less rational functions like sensation and intuition. For our purposes, however, it is enough to know that introversion and extraversion are two major psychological types used by both lay persons and psychologists to classify people according to a certain type.

Which leads us to ask an important question.

How Accurate Are Type Theories in Predicting Behavior?

A psychological theory is useful for predictive purposes only to the extent that it is both broad enough to account for a wide range of behaviors and specific enough to allow for individual differences in their expression. Type theories are broad enough, in fact so broad, that individual variations of a particular type are washed out. Hippocrates thought that *everybody* could be classified as choleric, melancholic, sanguine, or phlegmatic. But people are far too complex to be typed in such simple ways. We are not always *just* irritable, depressed, optimistic, or listless. We have a myriad of other choices for behavior, and we can behave in more than one way at once. Moreover, we can behave differently in different situations. Type theories help us recognize extreme behaviors, such as, for example, introversion and extraversion, but they are not very useful in helping us understand, say, the ambivert, who is neither introverted nor extraverted but somewhere in between.

When we pay too much attention to types, either personally derived stereotypes or theoretically conceived psychological types, we may miss the consistency in behavior that is there because (1) we are looking for our preconceptions of behavior rather than actual behavior (e.g., not all blondes have fun, not all redheads are hot tempered, not all sensitive men are weak, and not all assertive women are unfeminine), and (2) the behavior we see may not be covered by the "type" we have in mind (e.g., how do we perceive the republican who is more liberal than conservative or the democrat who is more conservative than liberal?).

Thus, the extent that behavioral consistency can be accounted for by the fact that an individual is a certain "type" or an aggressive "type" or a friendly "type" does not give enough information. First, there are many different expressions for any one of those behaviors; and second, any one of those behaviors may interact with other aspects of your "type," called *traits,* an idea we turn to next.

BEHAVIORAL CONSISTENCY
AS EXPLAINED BY TRAIT THEORIES

Whereas type theories assign people to one category or another, trait theories of personality view people as having many characteristics, or "traits," that exist simultaneously. By definition, a trait is a persisting component or dimension of personality that influences behavior. Each trait is seen as a quality or characteristic that some people have more or less of than other people. Traits usually fall along a continuum ranging from high to low, with many degrees in between. There are no doubt as many traits attributed to people as there are adjectives to describe their behavior. Some of the more common examples of traits associated with everyday behavior are aggressive-passive, warm-cool, trusting-suspicious, practical-imaginative, relaxed-tense, honest-dishonest, and loyal-disloyal. There are many, many other possibilities, but this gives you an idea of what the trait concept is all about and how traits tend to line up along a continuum.

According to consistency theory, once various traits are established, people will behave in ways consistent with those traits across different situations. Identify people's basic traits and then it will be possible to predict people's behavior, or so went the argument of early trait theorists.

This idea was seriously challenged by the findings uncovered by Hartshorne and May (1928) in their early studies of deceit among children. In their research, children were provided with opportunities to commit a range of "immoral" acts, such as lying, cheating, and stealing. In addition, they gave children the opportunity to commit these acts in a variety of settings, including at athletic contests, at a party, and in the home.

When this study was conducted, most psychologists would have predicted that the children would be consistently honest or dishonest in their behavior.

For example, according to the psychoanalytic theories that were popular in the first 50 years of the twentieth century, children with a well-developed conscience (superego) would probably refrain from stealing, cheating, or lying in nearly all situations, whereas children with a poorly developed conscience would be sorely tempted and succumb with regularity. In fact, this didn't happen. Only minimal consistency was noted. Children who lied or cheated in one situation were not especially likely to lie or cheat in another, which was an apparent contradiction of the idea of self-consistency. Hence, the researchers concluded that there is no general personality factor or trait such as honesty, but that honesty is specific and situational, a position contrary to the behavioral consistency idea postulated by self-concept theory.

Do we conclude, then, that behavioral consistency does not exist? Not when looked at from another perspective.

Primary Motives and Dominant Values as Factors in Behavioral Consistency

As behavioral consistency theory developed over time and as its assumptions were refined, it became increasingly apparent that traits do not exist as separate, unrelated psychic entities. Trait theory and research has helped us see that each individual is a unique constellation of traits and that *no one* trait accounts for behavior (Allport, 1966; Buss and Finn, 1987). Rather, our behavior is determined by the *interrelationships* among traits. Our understanding of how various traits influence our behavior is deepened further when we realize that some of our traits and values are more central and dominant, whereas others are more secondary in their overall influence.

As mentioned earlier, Hartshorne and May concluded that because children who cheated in one situation did not always cheat in another, behavioral consistency did not exist. From the perspective of interacting traits, some of which are dominant and others less so, the apparent inconsistency may lie in the fact that it is *only to the observer* that the child's behavior is unpredictable. From the point of view of the person doing the behaving, behavior stems from and is determined by a set of values distributed along a definite hierarchy of dominance. For example, a person might keep money that a stranger dropped on the sidewalk but would never think of doing so if it were lost by a cherished friend. The explanation for the perceived inconsistency could be that loyalty is more a dominant value for the person in question than honesty. Hence, he behaves in an honest fashion because he is loyal, not because he is honest.

Since most situations to which we react are complex events, they bring into play a multiplicity of motives and values. Usually, however, the dominant value system prevails, and the resulting behavior is logical, if not always justifiable, from the standpoint of the person doing the behaving. For example, the student who cheats in one instance but not in another may still be self-consistent. If her dominant values center around high achievement, she may be willing to risk cheating if she suspects she is in serious grade trouble. If, on the other hand, she places honesty above high achievement in her hierarchy of values, she might sooner fail than cheat and even feel a bit self-righteous about passing up what she considers to be a golden opportunity to copy from someone else's paper during an exam.

Of course, to pursue the example a step further, if a student's dominant value is honesty and if she *does* cheat, she would have to deny her dishonesty ("I didn't look on purpose") or rationalize it ("everyone else was, so I had no choice") to avoid the inevitable guilt, a somewhat predictable outcome when one's behavior and personal beliefs fail to match up.

We are sometimes wrong in our observations and predictions about others, not necessarily because they behaved inconsistently but because our perceptions of them were in error. For example, consider G. B. Shaw's *Pygmalion* (most of us know it better as *My Fair Lady*), in which Eliza Doolittle, an ignorant flower girl, is taken on by Professor Higgins for speech training. He not only teaches her to speak in an educated manner, but also finds that she unquestioningly obeys his every order. If he tells her to act like a servant, she does so; like a lady, and she does so. On the surface, it seems that Eliza has no consistency at all in her personality. Underneath, however, there is one unifying explanation for her conduct: She is in love with the good professor. Her love is her primary motivation. Viewed in this light, her behavior lacked unity because of a misperception on our part and not because of her inconsistency. Although she was absurdly inconsistent in her manners of speech and behavior, she was highly consistent in her love for Professor Higgins. Once we know this, we are tapping a deep primary motivation, which, from Eliza's point of view, unifies much of her behavior.

Another example of how behavioral consistency can be misconstrued by mistaken perceptions is cited by Allport (1961):

> There is the case of a thirteen-year-old girl who was referred for counseling because she used excessive makeup on her face. This habit seemed sadly at variance with her scholarly nature. Her teacher felt something must be "wrong." The apparent split in the girl's personality was readily explained. She had a heavy crush on her teacher, who was herself scholarly and enjoyed a high natural complexion. The little girl was entirely [consistent] in her striving to be like her beloved teacher. (p. 384)

In every personality, there are primary motives of major significance and others of minor significance. Occasionally, a primary motive is so outstanding in a person that it deserves to be called a *cardinal* motive. Allport (1961) suggested that such a prominent quality could also be called ". . . the eminent trait, the ruling passion, the master sentiment, the unity-theme, or the nadir of life" (p. 365). Tolstoy's passion for the "simplification of life" or Einstein's search for a "unified field theory" or Gloria Steinem's fight for equal rights for women or the struggle of Martin Luther King, Jr., to make his "dream" a reality or Mother Teresa's dedication to the plight of the poor or Gandhi's vision of a unified commonwealth might be examples of cardinal motives that brought a high degree of unity to behavior. Sometimes, however, we have to look hard for that one cardinal motive that might unify what otherwise seems like inconsistent behavior.

Take the case of Rebecca, a 32-year-old elementary schoolteacher, who has trouble sustaining long-term relationships with men. When she is with a man, she can be warm, giving, empathic, and quite loving. On other occasions, however, and even with the same man, she can be cold, withholding, and quite self-centered. Do these contradictions in behavior mean that she lacks primary motives and dominant values? Not at all. She has two opposing behavioral patterns, one of which is warm and giving, the other cold and withholding. Once we know Rebecca better, we begin to see that these two different behavior patterns spring from one overreaching primary motive. The outstanding fact about her personality is that she is a self-centered egotist who is warm and giving when this behavior will serve her own best interests. This cardinal self-centeredness expresses itself in warm, congenial, loving behavior when she wants something—usually attention or admiration—or in cold withholding behavior when she is less needy. Sooner or later most of the men in her life sensed the expediency of her motives and simply refused to be manipulated and used by her in this selfish manner.

Or take the case of nine-year-old Jeremy. His mother approached me after a meeting to talk about the trouble she was having with him. She explained that at school he was "a quiet, well-mannered little boy who behaved pretty well" but that at home he was "unruly, hard to handle, and frequently sasses both his father and me." He was, the mother concluded, "two different boys." Jeremy's behavior did seem to be inconsistent. At school, his primary motivation seemed to be to behave well; at home, it was to behave poorly. Was there a deeper, more central motive? After several counseling sessions with both mother and father, it turned out that there was indeed. Jeremy was starved for attention and found that one way to get it was to be good at school and bad at home. Although his surface behavior seemed inconsistent (good at school, bad at home), both behaviors were quite consistent with the underlying central motive, which was to get attention. The parents discovered that they were not giving Jeremy very much attention when things were going well but that they were giving him lots of attention when he misbehaved, little realizing that they were reinforcing the very behavior they wished to extinguish. Once they were aware of this pattern, they started giving him more attention when his behavior was positive, which not surprisingly brought out more of his positive qualities at home.

To summarize, traits are the particular components that together make up one's personality and that fall along a continuum from high to low. According to consistency theory, we tend to behave in a manner that is more or less consistent with the traits we have come to identify as part of our concept of self. Some of our traits are secondary, in terms of their influence on our behavior, while others are more central or primary to the way we see ourselves; and still others are so important as to deserve the label *cardinal* traits because of their pervasive and overriding influence in our lives. Although people seldom behave in perfectly consistent ways, there is probably more consistency in behavior than meets the eye. The expression of contradictory behaviors does not necessarily mean that a person is behaving inconsistently; it may mean only that we have failed to correctly spot the deepest (most primary or most cardinal) motive that is operating. Which leads us to an important question.

How Can We Recognize a Person's Primary Motives and Dominant Values?

Although there are other means for doing this, two routes in particular are helpful for recognizing a person's deeper motives and values.

First, take note of the events that a person reacts to emotionally. For example, if Allen is easily upset when someone questions his intelligence, this may be a sign that it is important for him to be regarded as intelligent and that intelligence ranks high on his scale of central values. If Alice becomes quickly defensive when someone challenges her religious views, this could be a sign that religious values play a primary part in her life and that she does not care to have something so important to her questioned. Although there may be other reasons for Allen's and Alice's responses, the point to be considered here is that a person's spontaneous emotional responses to unplanned occurrences can be good clues about the nature of the deeper person residing below surface behaviors.

Second, pay attention to how a person responds to crises and accidents, the upsetting catastrophes, small and large, that any of us may have at one time or other—death of a relative, divorce, loss of a job, health problems, financial loss, and so forth. Some people handle crises or tragic occurrences with courage, resolve, and purpose; others handle those circumstances with a sense of helplessness, hopelessness, and despair. These two opposites remind me of a verse that used to hang in my grandparents' living room:

> *It's easy enough to be pleasant*
> *When life flows along like a song,*
> *But the person worthwhile*
> *Is the one who can smile*
> *When everything goes dead wrong.*

If you want to know what characteristics are dominant in an individual, observe that person when everything does, indeed, go dead wrong; it can be a rich source of clues about that person's underlying nature.

THE CONTRIBUTION OF SOCIAL LEARNING THEORY

If you are a person known to your friends as the life of the party, the incurable wit, the one with a thousand jokes, chances are good that when you attend some somber occasion, such as a funeral, you are capable of being quite serious, reserved, and unfunny. If, on the other hand, you are generally viewed as a quiet, introverted person chances are good that when you are in the company of good friends and at a good party, you are capable of being far more outgoing and spontaneous. Does this mean that if you are the jokester in the crowd who is suddenly unfunny at a funeral or that if you are the introvert who cuts loose at a party, there is no consistency to your behavior?

From the point of view of type or trait theories, it would be difficult to explain these behavioral differences because each assumes that if we behave one way in one situation, we will behave in somewhat similar ways in other situations. Perhaps each of the preceding examples can be explained by the existence of a more primary motive and dominant value, and if we looked long enough we might be able to find it. For example, the primary motive may be a deep need for acceptance, which we endeavor to win by responding in whatever way the situation warrants.

This is precisely where social learning theory begins to fit into the picture. Up to this point, the idea of behavioral consistency has been explained primarily in terms of *person variables,* those intrapsychic components to which a person responds that are essentially internal. Mischel (1983a, 1984) seriously challenged the emphasis placed on person variables when, after reviewing many studies designed to measure consistency of behavior, he found that the behaviors noted in one situation were only weakly related to behaviors noted in another. He saw, for example, that measures of such traits as honesty, self-control, dependency, and aggression in one situation correlated only about + .30 with similar measures in another, which is not very high when we consider that a perfect correlation is + 1.00. Mischel's major criticism of type and trait theories was that, by overemphasizing person variables, they overlooked those possible aspects of the *situation* that contributed to the way one chose to behave. What was needed, said Mischel, was a point of view that considered the contribution of both the person *and* the situation. Enter social learning theory, a position described by Bandura (1977) as one that

> . . . approaches the explanation of human behavior in terms of a continuous reciprocal interaction between cognitive, behavioral, and environmental determinants. . . . This conception of human functioning neither casts people into the role of powerless objects controlled by environmental forces, not free agents who can become whatever they choose. Both people and their environment are reciprocal determinants of each other. (p. vii)

Mischel (1986) observed that social learning approaches to personality "pay less attention to motivational and dispositional constructs and instead look at behavior, and the functional relations between what the person does and the psychological conditions of his or her life" (p. 303).

Consistency from a Social Learning Point of View

The position advocated by social learning theory is called *reciprocal determinism,* a label accurately reflecting the idea that variables in the person, situation, and behavior all continuously interact with each other, as seen in Figure 3-6. It is within the context of this ongoing interaction between the person and the situation that learning occurs—learning that teaches one to remain the same as one is at the moment or that teaches one to make an appropriate change.

Consider a few examples. From a social learning perspective, people are most likely to behave in ways that have been reinforced in the past. For example, if Bobby punches the smaller boy next door and thus gets the boy's candy bar—and if he manages to avoid being punished for this behavior—he is likely to behave aggressively with the same boy and other small boys. In addition, he may learn from his experience that it is profitable to hit smaller children in a variety of circumstances, such as when he wants to play with someone else's toys or ride someone else's skateboard. This is an example of *behavioral generalization;* Bobby learns to be aggressive in a variety of situations when he wants something. In a similar way, Betty may learn that the way to get what she wants from her mother is to cry a lot.

Social learning theory would not, however, predict that Bobby will be aggressive all the time or that Betty will consistently cry when she wants her way. If, for instance, Bobby's successes with smaller boys go to his head and if he tries to bully a somewhat bigger boy, he may get a punch in the nose. Or if he tries pushing around the little boy next door and gets caught by his parents, he may be grounded for a few days. In other words, if his aggressive tendencies are punished rather than rewarded, he may not be so likely to try them again. Similarly, Betty may discover that her crying is rewarded when her mother is very busy and tired but not when she is more relaxed and less harried. With time, Betty will learn to respond to an important aspect of the situation—her mother's mood—before crying. Through a process known as *discrimination,* Billy and Betty learn to discriminate between situations in which, in this case,

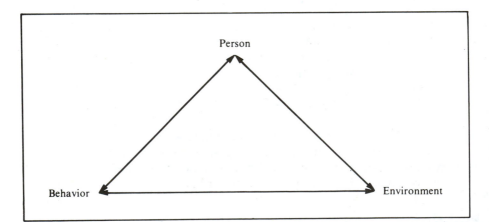

Figure 3-6   *Reciprocal interaction between the person, environment, and behavior.*

behaving aggressively or acting like a spoiled child is likely to be rewarded and those in which such behavior will not.

Thus, the processes of generalization and discrimination help to explain why the particular traits of behaviors we show in one situation may not be the same as in another. We tend to behave in similar ways in different situations to the extent that similar behavior has positive consequences. Inasmuch as most social behaviors (such as assertiveness or passivity) are not reinforced in the same way in all circumstances, we may not find a high degree of consistency in their expression from one situation to another. For example, in classroom A, the teacher may expect the students to be quiet and mostly listen. Even assertive students may appear passive under those conditions. In classroom B, the teacher may encourage students to speak up and voice their ideas. We might find even the usually passive students behaving more assertively in this situation.

The research findings of Endler and Hunt (1966) underscore strongly the interactive aspects of the person and the situation. A large group of people responded to a series of questionnaires designed to determine the kinds of situations that evoke anxious feelings, the way the individual responds to the situation, and the intensity of the response. The anxiety-provoking situations ranged from something as innocuous as "You are starting on a long automobile trip" to "You are about to take an important exam" or "You are on a ledge high on a mountainside." Subjects were asked to imagine each situation and describe how he or she would respond by marking a number of possible reactions (e.g., "hands tremble," "feel tense," "can't concentrate") and noting the intensity of the reaction on a five-point scale ranging from "not at all" (0) to "very much" (5). The analyses revealed that individual differences and situations by themselves accounted for only a small percentage of the variability among scores. By far, the greatest source of variability was the *interactions* of the two with each other and the response mode.

A similar questionnaire was devised to measure the components of hostility, this time by asking about the kinds of situations that evoked anger and the individual's response to each situation (Endler and Hunt, 1968). Again, it was the interactive aspects of the person with the situation that were most revealing. For example, two people may receive equally high scores on a test of anxiety, but one person is anxious in the face of physical danger, whereas the other, quite calm in that situation, is very anxious in interpersonal situations, such as giving a speech or taking an exam.

Whether one behaves in an anxious way or maintains a calm demeanor across different situations depends to some extent on the situation, how it is perceived, one's concept of self, one's expectations, and one's past history with similar situations. If, for example, speaking in front of a group of peers is something about which I feel anxious, chances are that my anxiety will be transmitted to my audience, who may reflect my anxiety by sitting more tensely in their seats and showing more concern in their faces, which I will interpret as all the more reason to feel anxious. If, on the other hand, speaking to a group of strangers does not cause me to feel anxious, the chances are equally good that my relaxed bearing will be reflected by a relaxed audience, which will tend to reinforce my own calm attitude.

The environment influences the person, and the person influences the environment, which is the central theme of social learning theory in regard to behavioral consistency—which brings us to an important question.

Trait Theories or Social Learning Theory—Which is Right?

There are data to support both sides. Consider, for example, the illustration of a person who seems hostile and independent at times and passive and dependent at other times. Is this person really an aggressive individual who just plays at being passive, or is this basically a warm, somewhat passive person who uses aggression as a defense mechanism? Both trait theories and social learning theory would say that this person can have all these characteristics— passivity, warmth, dependence, aggressiveness, and hostility. Social learning theory helps us understand that what an individual displays at any *particular* time depends on *where* the person is, *whom* the person is with, and *what* the person is doing. From a social learning perspective, each of these aspects of a person may be a quite genuine and real aspect of one's total being (Mischel, 1986).

Thus, a case for behavioral consistency can be made from either side of the fence, but a stronger case can be made when both sides are considered. Trait theories alert us to the idea that each of us is characterized by certain behavioral tendencies or traits that make us more or less recognizable to others. Social learning theory reminds us that the particular *expression* of these behavioral tendencies will depend on the situation in which we find ourselves. Thus, we may behave differently in one place than we do in another not because we are suddenly different persons, but because different situations draw out different aspects of our personalities.

Even though our behavior is not exactly the same from one situation to another, we are seen by others, and by ourselves, as pretty much the same person today as we were yesterday. There is a strong core of consistency, even though specific behaviors may change. And this leads us to an important question.

HOW CONSISTENT IS BEHAVIOR OVER TIME?

Imagine, for a moment, that, from the time of your birth to now, a special motion picture crew has randomly filmed your day-to-day living for at least one hour per week. The film is edited into a four-hour encapsulation of your life, and you are invited to a sneak preview. You are the uncontested "star" of this production, surrounded by a supporting cast of parents or parent figures, siblings, assorted relatives and family members, friends, foes, and loved ones.

What do you suppose you would see in such a film? You would see yourself grow up, of course. And you would see obvious changes in height, weight, girth, and body proportions. But would the essence of the person you saw in the first hour be the same person you saw in the third and fourth? Would you recognize the child and adolescent of the first half hour in the man or woman of the last half hour? Would the personality traits you began to show at age five be similar to those most dominant in you now? Or would you expect to see so many changes between the child you once were and the person you are now that you would have trouble understanding how the two are connected?

Actually, if you really could see such a film, you would probably have two kinds of surprises. First, you would no doubt be surprised to see the many similarities between the person you once were and the person you have become. And second, you would be surprised to see the many changes in all aspects of your being that have occurred without your ever being aware of them.

If we could view such a film of our lives, would we, on the whole, see more in the way of behavioral consistency over time or would we see more in the change? Is our sense of personality identity, our feeling of being essentially the same person over time, a delusion, a fiction of our imagination designed to trick us into a false sense of continuity, or is it a reality held together by a stable core of self-conceptions? Although the research evidence is by no means unequivocal, some very persuasive data on the side of consistency has been gathered over

We may be more like Snoopy than we realize.

Reprinted by permission of UFS, INC.

the past 50 years or so. Let's consider first some of the evidence for behavioral consistency that begins in childhood.

Behavioral Consistency in Childhood and Adolescence

Signs of behavioral consistency begin at an early age. The core of who we are as individuals forms early and has roots that go back deep in time. There are indications that, even in the first two years of life, we begin showing consistently connected outer signs of the person emerging within. In early research related to this issue, Shirley (1933), for example, found that the 25 children who were closely observed during their first two years of life showed a rather high degree of consistency in the general pattern of their month-to-month behavior. It was noted, for instance, that although their behavior changed as they matured, there were always "identifying earmarks." A given expression of behavior "would lapse only to be supplemented by another that apparently was its consistent outgrowth." For example, one baby was distinctive at an early age for his "apprehensive watching" and, at a later age, showed similar fearful behavior by hiding behind his mother and by his reluctance to play and talk in the presence of a stranger. As you can see, even though the specific responses are different (timorous crying, apprehensive watching, hiding behind his mother), each seems to reflect a fearful expression. If we try to compare specific responses, we fail to see that the underlying consistency can express itself in different ways and at different times.

Shirley also suggested that certain aspects of personality are inborn and persist from age level to age level. In his words:

> Both constancy and change characterize the personality of the baby. Traits are constant enough to make it plausible that a nucleus of personality exists at birth and that this nucleus persists and grows and determines to a certain degree the relative importance of the various traits. Some change is doubtless wrought by environmental factors, but this change is limited by the limitations of the original personality nucleus. (p. 56)

Moving up the developmental ladder, Martin's (1964) investigation of 53 middle-class nursery school youths revealed a high degree of constancy in the social behavior of these children. These children's behavior was rated over a two-year period in seven response categories: dependency, nurturance, aggression, control-dominance, autonomous achievement, avoidance-withdrawal, and friendship affiliation. Only nine of the 53 children reflected profile instability during the two-year period. Martin concluded that

> . . . during a period in the life span when instrumental behavior is demonstrably changing, in response to modifications in individual capabilities and social expectations, and—more specifically in the nursery school setting—a pattern of individual social behavior that is strikingly unchanging emerged. It

is as if each child has his own *behavioral economy* which persists through time. (p. 465)

A high degree of persistence in "ascendence-submission" was found by Stott (1957), who studied more than 100 children over a period of about 12 years. They were initially assessed while in nursery school on a scale of ascendence-submission ranging from extreme bossiness to extreme submissiveness, and 12 years later, they were observed in the various recreational clubs they attended. Stott found that ". . . persistence of pattern was more frequent than change during the period covered" and that 87% of the children ". . . showed no consistent pattern of change." When changes did occur, they were temporary in most instances, with a subsequent return to an earlier pattern. It would appear that, all things being equal, bossy nursery school children and their more submissive age-mates also tend to remain that way during their early growth years, a finding consistent with Martin's in his shorter, two-year study.

Cited frequently among studies of consistency and change from childhood into adolescence is an investigation by Neilon (1948), who, after a 15-year interval, followed up the individuals who were studied by Shirley from birth to two years of age. Neilon collected extensive autobiographical sketches of 15 of the original 19 children at the age of 17 years—ten boys and five girls. Descriptive sketches of the infant and adolescent personality were prepared independently and presented to psychologists who knew none of the children. The psychologists were asked to match the infant sketch with what they believed to be the corresponding adolescent personality. (It should be noted here that although Neilon and her associates knew the names of the children who had participated in the original study, they did not know which child was represented in each of Shirley's published biographies because of the use of pseudonyms in publication.) After the psychologists finished matching, Shirley's original data were then consulted for the real names of the children. The psychologists succeeded in matching the girls so successfully that their results could be obtained by chance less than once in a million times. With the boys, they were correct to an extent that could occur by chance only once in 4,000 tries. Although great individual differences existed for individual children, one girl being matched correctly by all ten judges and another by none, it was evident that there was considerable consistency in personality over a 15-year period. In other words, *many characteristics that were evident in early childhood persisted into late adolescence.* This is impressive evidence on the side of consistency, but Neilon's small sample size should make us appropriately wary of generalizing too far.

Consistency of behavior in childhood is by no means certain. For example, Escalona and Heider (1959) made predictions based on observations of 31 infants and then tested these predictions against behavioral data gathered five years later. Predictions were made for many different aspects of behavior, and the outcomes were similarly focused. A successful prediction is illustrated in the following protocol for Terry:

> Prediction, item 41:
>
> Have thought that he will be very vocal in the sense of talking with a great deal of eagerness. Outcome: He talked freely, usually with enjoyment and often with a sort of urgency. (pp. 205–206)

There were, however, also predictive failures, as illustrated in the protocol for Janice:

> Prediction, item 35:
>
> I expect Janice to understand and use language with perfectly good competence. I would be surprised if her verbal abilities as measured by tests exceeded average standards for her age. Outcome: Achieved superior scores on vocabulary and verbal comprehension items. (p. 175)

Predictions were, in general, more successful with certain children than with others. With one child, the predictions were 92 percent successful; at the other extreme, there was a child for whom only 33 percent of the outcomes agreed with the predictions. Some aspects of behavior were more accurately predicted than others, particularly those having to do with life-style and adaptation to sex roles. Predictions that dealt with more specific characteristics, such as competitiveness or shyness, were less accurate.

It is a well-known fact that one's willingness to postpone immediate gratification is related to the ability to set long-term goals and to a higher level of personal maturity (Funder, Block, and Block, 1983; Mischel, 1983b). In a ten-year longitudinal study involving 95 children who were nursery school age at the beginning of the investigation, Mischel, Shoda, and Peake (1988) found that children who were able to delay gratification longer at four and five years of age became adolescents who were better able to cope with frustration and stress and who were rated as more academically and socially competent, verbally fluent, attentive, and planful. In other words, those children who behaved more maturely in nursery school were likely to be the same ones who were showing more signs of maturity as adolescents.

To sum up, it looks as though certain behaviors, such as assertiveness and dominance, on the one hand, and passiveness and withdrawal, on the other hand, along with the capacity to delay gratification, are fairly consistent behavioral expressions in the same children over time. Remember, however, that this is a statistical generalization, and there can be many individual exceptions. In addition, we need to be mindful of the fact that, although there are many signs of behavioral "sameness" in children as they grow up, there will be many changes in both the substance and expression of their behavior. This is not so surprising when we consider that children, immersed as they are in a constant stream of interactions and feedback, and caught in rapid currents of physical change, are highly susceptible to developmental strains caused by the unexpected swirls of emotional eddys that occur in the flow of everyday living, sometimes causing significant behavioral changes.

Let's turn our attention now to the question of stability of certain childhood behaviors into the adult years. What degree of consistency might we expect to find between the child we once were and the adult we have become?

Childhood Behaviors that Persist into Adulthood

One of the most extensive studies of consistency over time was undertaken by Kagan and Moss (1962), who studied the stability from infancy to adulthood of such aspects of behavior as passivity, aggression, striving for achievement, and sexuality. Assessments were made during four childhood periods and again when some of the subjects were between 19 and 29 years old. Infant ratings for the 89 subjects were compared with self-ratings and scores on various personality tests and the results of interviews in adulthood. One characteristic that proved to be relatively stable was passivity. This trait generally became evident during the second year, and it was expressed in various ways during the school years by, for example, timid behavior in social situations, avoidance of dangerous activities, and conformity to parents. The investigators believe that they have reasonable grounds for the hypothesis that the foundations for ". . . extreme degrees of passivity, or its derivatives, in late childhood, adolescence and adulthood are established during the first six years of life" (p. 83). Males were more stable when it came to aggressive behavior, and females were more stable in terms of dependency. Both males and females reflected stability from the standpoint of achievement behavior; the evidence suggests that the period from six to ten years of age is important in establishing this form of motivation, a finding that has significant implications for the importance of helping students develop positive learning attitudes in the early elementary years. Regarding the overall study, Kagan and Moss concluded that

> Many of the behaviors exhibited by the child aged six to 10, and a few during the age period three to six, were moderately good predictors of theoretically related behaviors during early adulthood. Passive withdrawal from stressful situations, dependency on family, ease-of-anger arousal, involvement in intellectual mastery, social interaction anxiety, sex-role identification, and pattern of sexual behavior in adulthood were each related to reasonably analogous behavioral dispositions during the early school years. . . . These results offer strong support for the generalization that aspects of adult personality begin to take form during early childhood. (pp. 266–288)

Consistencies have also been found between some of the early signs of unhealthy behaviors in childhood and their expression of adulthood. Birren (1944), for example, found that the symptoms of 38 psychotic adults corresponded closely to the pattern of traits they exhibited as children in a child guidance clinic. These findings closely resemble those from a study by Robins (1966), who analyzed the emotional status of over 500 persons seen 30 years earlier in a child guidance clinic; he also found a high degree of consistency of antisocial behavior between childhood and adulthood. For example, 61% of those who were seriously antisocial as children were exhibiting equally serious antisocial behavior as adults. Robins also found that the level of childhood antisocial behavior not only predicted sociopathy but also predicted which schizophrenics and alcoholics would be combative and acting out and which would be relatively quiet and retiring.

In a 20-year longitudinal study, Block (1981) collected extensive personality data on 70 men and 76 women when the subjects were in junior high school. These same persons were studied again in their late teens, in their mid-30s, and during the late 1960s when they were all in their mid-40s. The data bank Block had to draw from was immense, including everything from attitude checklists filled out by the subjects to transcripts on interviews with the subjects and their teachers, parents, and spouses; different sets of material were gathered during each of the four time periods. Clinical psychologists, working independently of each other, made summary ratings of each subject's personality, which Block then compared with at least three other psychologists' ratings and found that there was a high degree of agreement among them. To avoid potential bias, the materials for each subject were carefully segregated by age level, all comments referring to the person at an earlier age were removed from the file, and no psychologist rated the materials for the same subject at more than one time period.

From this painstaking methodology emerged a striking pattern of stability. On virtually every one of the 90 rating scales used, there was a statistically significant relationship between subjects' ratings when they were in junior high school and when they were in their 40s. On the whole, the most self-defeating adolescents were the most self-defeating adults; cheerful teenagers tended to be cheerful 40 year olds; those with mood fluctuations in junior high school were still having mood swings in midlife.

Thus, what we see in high school students' behavior is an indication of what we will see in their adult behavior. An interesting individual example of this can be seen in the life of former TV evangelist, Jim Bakker, who so successfully solicited millions of dollars for his PTL television ministry. As pointed out by Shepard's (1989) biographical analysis, Bakker's flair for the stage and skills in raising big dollars were evident as early as his sophomore year in high school when he produced three financially successful annual talent shows in his school's 1,100-seat auditorium. What is hinted at in the child is evident in the man. (Of course, not *everything* evident in the man is hinted at in the child. In Bakker's case, for example, there is no evidence that he had played fast and loose with the talent show monies as he had with PTL's.)

Overall, it looks like we can expect to find a reasonable degree of behavioral consistency from childhood and adolescence into adulthood. For example, if we note that a child enjoys reading books for entertainment, likes school, is fairly sociable, and is quite self-confident, chances are fairly good that this same child will grow into an adult who reads books and newspapers regularly, has some kind of post-high-school education, is still fairly self-confident, and has a circle of friends (Haan, 1981). If the child is a boy, we may be able to make some reasonable predictions about his adult aggressiveness, and if the child is a girl, we may be able to make predictions about her dependency as an adult from knowing how dependent she was as a child (Kagan and Moss, 1962).

The behaviors we see in childhood and adolescence point to the possibilities of what we may see in adulthood, but not in any absolute sense. It would probably be safe to say, however, that the more extreme and persistent the behaviors we see in childhood and adolescence, the more likely it is that those behaviors will persist into the adult years. It is clear that children and adults respond to changing roles, changing environments, and changing demands with changes in behavior, or even with alterations of basic personality characteristics, which is why there can be significant differences between one's adult and childhood behaviors.

Let's turn our attention now to a final question.

How Consistent is Behavior During Adulthood?

In some very basic ways, the person we are in our 20s foreshadows the person we are likely to become in our 70s. An impressive array of evidence has accumulated over the past 20 years or so suggesting that there is a reasonably strong consistency of personality from young adulthood into the later years. Important work in this area has been done by Costa and McCrae (1980, 1986), who in two separate studies, collected personality test data on such overall dimensions as extraversion and neuroticism as well as on more specific traits, such as gregariousness, assertiveness, anxiety, and depression. In one study, over 400 men, ranging in age from 25 to 82, filled out a test battery in the mid-1960s and then completed another battery ten years later, in the mid-1970s. In a second study, more than 200 men between the ages of 20 and 76 completed test batteries three times, separated by six-year intervals. Three major personality dimensions emerged in which people show the greatest consistency between young adult and later adult years:

1. *Extraversion and introversion:* The highest degrees of stability, ranging from .70 to .84, were found for these two dimensions, which assess gregariousness, warmth, and assertiveness. Men who were more extraverted in their younger days—outgoing, active, excitement seeking, and people centered—were very likely to be so in their later years. On the other hand, those who were more introverted in their younger days—solitary, quiet, less people centered—were likely to be so in their later years as well. Although it is not without exception, the outgoing or quiet 20-year-old is the outgoing or quiet 40-year-old who is the outgoing or quiet 80-year-old.

2. *Neuroticism:* Almost as much constancy was found in the domain of "neuroticism," which includes such specific traits as depression, anxiety, hostility, and impulsiveness. Those scoring high in neuroticism (compared to those scoring low) typically start out their lives feeling more anxious, more often depressed, more self-conscious, more impulsive, and more hostile, and they are inclined, it appears, to end up that way, too. Neurotics are likely to be complainers throughout life. They may complain about different things as they get older—for example, worries about love in early adulthood, a "midlife crisis" or sexual problems in their 40s, health problems in late adulthood—but they are still complaining. The less-neurotic person reacts to the same problems with greater equanimity.

3. *Openness to experience versus rigidity:* Evidence for consistency on this dimension is the weakest of the three, but there is enough to support the possibility that some people are consistently more "open to experience," in the sense of being willing to try new things, to take risks, and to make big changes. This dimension represents a rather broad continuum, which may be why it shows the weakest consistency. It is not likely that any of us are either completely open to every experience that comes along or completely closed. Still, it does suggest that people tend to lean in one direction or the other and that this "lean" is stable over time.

Impressive evidence for behavioral consistency deep into life and over a 40-year span emerged from a unique longitudinal study by Maas and Kuypers (1974). For this study, in-depth interviews were conducted with 95 women and 47 men (average age 70) to gather information about the kind of persons they had become, their health, and how they were living. This information was then compared with survey data from the Institute of Human Development at the University of California (Berkeley) that had been gathered from the same persons for a project started in 1929. Some of the major findings emerging from this study are the following:

1. "Pathology" in old age has more visible roots in early adulthood than does "strength." However, early adulthood pathology does *not* lead inevitably to pathology in old age.

2. There was strong evidence that many of the persons interviewed, found to lead a similar life-style or having a similar personality in their later years, were also alike in their young adulthood.

3. Old age does not usher in problems that are necessarily new but tends, if anything, to highlight or underscore problems that have long-term antecedents.

4. Health problems among elderly persons are likely to be clearly foreshadowed in the early adult years. For example, where the

investigators found life-styles marked by social withdrawal, they also found strong indications of various expressions of illness and disability. Between 30 and 70 years of age, there was a strong relationship between physical well-being and psychological health. Anxious, fearful persons, for example, are apt to have more health problems than assertive, autonomous persons, and this tends to be true no matter how old or young they are.

5. A general conclusion from this study is that if one is healthy emotionally and psychologically at age 30 years, one is likely to stay that way at age 70. The reverse is also true. Young adults who are depressed, fearful, rigid, and sickly are still troubled in life's last years. Whether one is healthy and glad or sickly and sad, it appears that old age merely continues what the earlier years have launched.

Results of recently completed longitudinal research is helping us understand some of the possible reasons underlying the connection between psychological health in the early years and physical and emotional well-being later on. For example, Burns and Seligman's (1989) analysis of data collected on 30 subjects over a 52-year period pointed to some suggestive clues. They found that those people who constantly blamed themselves for unhappy life events and who, in addition, believed that their unhappiness and ill-fortune would probably never change were more likely to be the ones at risk for depression, lower achievement, and physical illness. Burns and Seligman described these people as those who were inclined to reflect an "explanatory style" for interpreting life experiences that was consistently more negative and pessimistic. In a related study, Peterson, Seligman, and Vaillant's (1988) analysis of data collected on 99 subjects over a 35-year period revealed that the more pessimistic a person is at age 25 years, the poorer his or her psychological and physical health was apt to be at age 45 and 65.

Both of these studies suggest that one's attitude toward life is apparent in early adulthood (its roots no doubt go deeper) and remains fairly stable over time, particularly if it is negative. We can only speculate, but perhaps one reason for this has to do with the idea that negative attitudes (outlooks, points of view, beliefs) are essentially defensive in nature, designed to protect one from anxiety, opposing points of view, and the unexpected. To give them up is to feel unprotected and exposed, something that for some people may be a scary possibility. Hence, the readiness to both expect and see the worst in case evasive action is necessary.

Overall, both of these studies point to evidence suggesting that those afflicted with more physical or psychological health problems in their later years are likely to be those who are pessimistic, self-blaming, and hostage to the idea that there is little they can do to change their lives or their circumstances. (Let us be clear that there is a vast difference between blaming oneself, which is little more than self-castigation and a form of self-pity, and acknowledging one's errors or shortcomings and taking responsibility for fixing whatever needs repair.)

All in all, the studies we've just reviewed, along with findings from other research (Conley, 1984; Costa, McCrae, and Arenberg, 1980; McClelland, 1981), indicate that behavior tends to be reasonably consistent over time. All things being equal, the person we are in our younger years resembles the person we become in our later years. In fact, Finn's (1986) analysis of 459 men over a 30-year period suggests that, as we age, behavioral patterns stabilize and personality traits grow increasingly more resistant to change.

Although a strong case can be made for behavioral consistency, it is important to keep in mind . . .

A NOTE OF CAUTION ABOUT CONSISTENCY OF BEHAVIOR OVER TIME

Personality can and does change. The findings do *not* indicate that personality characteristics are *completely* formed during childhood and adolescence. Also, even though a general dispositional trend may be established early, the manner in which it is expressed, indeed whether it is expressed directly at all, may continue to be quite susceptible to change. Clinical and psychotherapeutic literature, for example, abounds with evidence suggesting that adults can change not only their general life-styles but specific behavior as well (Garfield, 1981). Whereas basic aspects of personality such as anxiety or emotionality, friendliness, and eagerness for novel experiences tend to remain relatively stable throughout life, other traits, such as alienation, morale, and feelings of satisfaction can change greatly. In his analysis of data collected on 388 men and women over a 45-year period, Conley (1985) found that these traits change so much that there is virtually no relationship between their levels when adults are in their 20s and when they are in their 60s. Perhaps a reason for this is that these are traits that are more likely to be influenced by external conditions. Thus, they are more subject to change as life conditions change.

Levinson's (1981) research is another case in point. His findings suggest that each adult moves through alternating periods of stability *and* change. During the stable periods, we create what Levinson calls a *life structure,* a network of roles and relationships, including work and family ties, inner feelings about ourselves, and aspirations that fit together in an overall picture. It is during the transitions that change is most likely to occur as we reexamine our life structure and decide whether to modify it or maintain it. The ladder of adult stages when change is most apt to take place is shown in Figure 3-7.

Each of these transition periods is thought to have a particular focus. For example, Levinson suggested that each of us faces (or has faced) an inevitable midlife transition, which includes three major tasks:

1. Reappraise the adult years and evaluate what has been worthwhile and what has been left out.

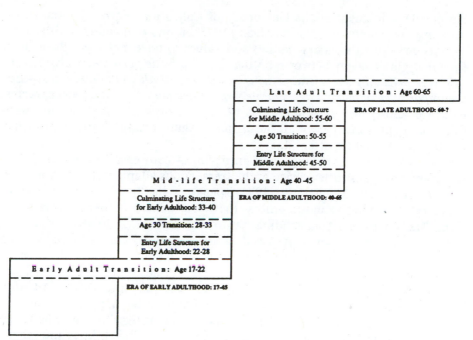

Figure 3-7 *Developmental periods in the eras of early and middle adulthood.*

From *The Seasons of a Man's Life* by Daniel Levinson et al. Copyright © 1978 by Daniel L. Levinson. Reprinted and adapted by permission of Alfred A. Knopf, Inc.

2. "Integrate" the great polarities, such as young-old, destruction-creation, masculine-feminine, and attachment-separateness. This is the time in life when we begin to deal with our own aging and death and to be dependent as well as independent.

3. Create a new "life structure" to give one's life a sense of personal meaning and direction that will serve over the next transitional period.

Although not all researchers in human development agree with either Levinson's methodology (he bases his findings on extensive interviews with small samples of men and is doing similar research with women) or his findings, his pioneering efforts have caused professionals and lay persons alike to question the idea that there is little change in our basic personality once the pattern has been established.

Although stability of personality was a major finding emerging from a 40-year longitudinal study involving 521 people conducted at the Institute of

Human Development at the University of California (Berkeley), one of the institute's psychologists, Norma Haan (1972), found that many healthy individuals do adjust their personalities and values to reflect changes throughout the life cycle. It might be worth noting that *two basic personality characteristics were prized by successful persons at all ages. Both young and old stressed the importance of being a dependable, productive person.* These two characteristics, reliability and capability, may be the very essence of stable and well-functioning personality. For all the criticism against it, the Puritan ethic may not be such a bad idea after all.

One of the most striking—and gratifying—features of studies of consistency and change is the evidence of the tremendous adaptability of human beings. For example, MacFarlane (1974) speaks of the ". . . almost incredible capacity" of the individual to process the ". . . welter of inner-outer stimulation." Many of the most outstanding mature adults in the group MacFarlane and her associates studied had bypassed or overcome difficult situations, even though ". . . their characteristic responses during childhood or adolescence seemed to us to compound their problems." MacFarlane went on to note that she and her associates had failed to appreciate the maturing utility of many painful, strain-producing, and confusing experiences. On the other hand, many subjects who ". . . early had had easy and confidence-inducing lives" and who had been free from severe strains and had exhibited very promising abilities and talents were ". . . brittle, discontented, and puzzled adults" (pp. 115–126).

For the most part, we humans tend to be reasonably consistent and predictable; what chaos there would be if this were not the case. It seems to be generally true that in matters closely related to our primary motives and dominant values, we tend to be more consistent over time and from situation to situation. For example, people who place a high value on learning and knowledge do not suddenly cease reading and searching just because they are no longer in school. People who are highly spiritual do not stop living in a spiritual mode when their sabbath day is over. People with a strong need for domination and power do not abruptly give up that need when they go home at night.

Most of us, it appears, have a certain direction in which we are headed. The farther along we go, the more momentum we gather and the harder it is to alter our course. To a very large extent, each of us behaves in a manner that is consistent with the person we see ourselves as being, which becomes a self-fulfilling prophecy. Our self-image creates a kind of emotional environment, which like the clothes on our back, we take with us wherever we go. If our environment is drab and negative, created by haunting self-doubts and sustained by low self-worth, people coming in contact with that environment may instinctively pull back and edge away, thus underscoring what we suspected in the first place—people don't seem to like us very much. If, on the other hand, our emotional environment is open and receptive, generated by a friendly outlook and maintained by positive self-attitudes, people coming into that environment may instinctively draw closer and remain longer, reinforcing what we felt in the first place—people like us and we like them. More than we may realize, we are who we are—and stay that way, for better or worse—because we create, through our behavior, the very conditions that give life to a continual cycle of self-fulfilling prophecies, thereby confirming our worst fears or our highest hopes for ourselves and others.

IN PERSPECTIVE

Each of us behaves in a manner that is more or less consistent with the sort of person we conceive ourselves to be. If we see ourselves as uncoordinated, we are not likely to do many things of an athletic sort; if we have confidence in our intelligence, we may seek out opportunities for new learning; if we doubt our ability, we might avoid a particular course or curriculum. Our self-perceptions are a form of self-labeling, which we convert into self-fulfilling prophecies by behaving in ways that confirm both their existence and validity.

Almost everything we do is related to that central core of behavioral characteristics that mark each of us as a unique individual. Our perceptual style, in terms of how we "see" things, is related to how we view ourselves and our own particular personality makeup. No matter how we respond, whether it be with something as simple as our handwriting or as complex as our choice of an occupation, we reflect something of the nature of our feelings about ourselves in a more or less unified and predictable way. Whether we are aware of it or not, we tend to function as whole persons, with the various facets of our behavior linked together in a continuous loop of interacting connections.

Efforts to predict people's behavior in light of their "type" of personality have not been fruitful because the type categories were too broad to be of much value. Trait theories have not been much more helpful because the traits a person might reflect in one situation do not always appear in other situations. Social learning theories have helped us to see that situational and trait variables interact with each other, which has enabled us to see that behavior can *appear* to be inconsistent with past behavior because the situation is different, and thus, the person is, too. The way we behave is not just a consequence of *who* we are, but *where* we are.

The closer we come to truly understanding another person's primary motives and dominant values (not to mention our own), the better able we are to see the consistency in behavior and the unity of personality. Expressions of consistency can change with time, even though the primary motives may remain the same. For example, the fearful child at one year of age cries a great deal; at age five, he is less vocal but runs away from threatening situations; at age 15, he is quiet and somewhat of a loner; at age 25, he is shy, introverted, and perhaps busy at some job where contact with people is minimal. The consistency of behavior is not always in the overt action, but in the perception. Once we understand, for example, that the boy's primary motive is to avoid the threat he feels when he is too close to people, we can see that there is considerable unity in his behavior over time, even though its expression has been modified.

Probably none of us can be counted on to behave in a completely consistent manner day in and day out. Behavioral consistency does not come in absolutes, but in degrees. When our behavior is inconsistent with our attitudes, we usually feel an uncomfortable cognitive dissonance, which is an internal red flag that waves when we run against the grain of our basic beliefs. When that happens, we restore order by changing either the behavior or the belief, usually whichever is the easiest to do.

The evidence we have looked at suggests that most people strive for and exhibit some measure of personal consistency and unity in their everyday lives. This is not surprising because behaviorally inconsistent people have considerable disharmony in both their intrapsychic lives and interpersonal dealings. By being sensitive, patient observers of what is going on below the surface of behavior, we can learn to see many outer signs of inner consistencies both within ourselves and others.

The purpose of understanding something about the nature and expressions of self-consistency and stability of behavior over time is not merely an academic one. The evidence suggests that basic personality styles begin early in life, which means that, whether we are teachers or other professional people or parents, we can be alert to early signs indicating the possible direction of a child's growth. Too often we wait for children to "grow out of" their shyness or aggressiveness or lack of motivation or speech problem or whatever, without realizing that we are confusing the symptom of a possible personality defect with what is frequently called "just a stage they're going through." Behavior that is established early and reinforced while the child is young is likely to remain stable over time and serve as the seedbed in which one's primary motives and dominant values are nurtured. This fact would suggest that if we are to be forces of positive change, we must begin our efforts to encourage healthy growth outcomes while children are going through their formative years. Psychologically tuned elementary teachers working in conjunction with parents and extended guidance and counseling programs in the elementary grades would be a sound step in the right direction.

Consistency gives us a sense of stability and security, while the possibility of change offers hope for being more than we are, an important component in the overall mixture that constitutes psychological growth.

QUESTIONS FOR STUDY, REVIEW, AND REFLECTION

1. If you were asked to explain why behavioral consistency was important in ourselves and others, how would you respond?

2. Think about your own concept of self—the way you see yourself. What three or four core qualities or dominant values are most central to your concept of self? What would you say if you were to explain to

someone how those dominant values aid you in being consistent on a day-to-day basis?

3. How would you explain the differences between levelers and sharpeners and between field-dependent and field-independent people? How would you classify yourself in relation to these categories? What examples can you give to support your classifications?

4. What four or five adjectives would likely be chosen to describe you by people who know you well? (It would be interesting to get feedback of this sort from friends.) What four or five adjectives would you choose for yourself? Are they similar? Different? Whose expectations do you try hardest to live up to? What does this suggest about the location of your locus of control?

5. How is the theory of cognitive dissonance related to behavioral consistency? That is, what is it about the idea of behavioral consistency that is central to dissonance theory?

6. How would you explain the basic differences between trait theories and type theories? Why does each theory fail to explain behavioral consistency?

7. How has social learning theory helped us to explain why people might behave in a predictable manner in one instance—i.e., are consistent with the personality characteristics we think they have—but seem to behave unpredictably in another instance?

8. If you were to write a two-page description of the sort of person you are today, in terms of social behavior, emotional expressions, and intellectual best, and if you compared it with the description provided by people who knew you during the first ten or so years of your life, what do you suppose you would discover? (This could make for an interesting conversation between you and the people who knew you in your younger years.)

9. If you were asked to write a two-page summary of the major conclusions of research related to studying the consistency of behavior over time, what would you write?

(Note: If you ever have a chance to see the film 28 Up, *you might want to do so. It is a 1985 British Academy-Award-winning documentary produced by Michael Apted that traces the lives of 14 children—10 boys and four girls—by combining footage of films made at seven, 14, 21, and 28 years of age. The effect is like time-lapse photography. The children seem to sprout, bud, and blossom into maturity in seconds. Families spring up beside them. Here they are at ages 21 or 28 talking about their hopes and dreams and feelings about themselves, and*

suddenly we are whisked back in time to when they were age seven or 14 and responding to the same questions. The film is more than watching the participants respond to questions: It is watching them live, play, work, and think about themselves in different time zones of their lives. A fascinating film.)

REFERENCES

Allport, G. W. *Pattern and Growth in Personality.* New York: Holt, Rinehart and Winston, 1961.

Allport, G. W. "Traits Revisited." *American Psychologist,* 1966, *21:* 1–10.

Anderson, N. H. "Cognitive Algebra: Integration Theory Applied to Social Attribution," in L. Berkowitz (Ed.), *Advances in Experimental Social Psychology,* Vol. 7. New York: Academic Press, 1974.

Bandura, A. *Social Learning Theory.* Englewood Cliffs, N. J.: Prentice-Hall, 1977.

Bem, D. J., and Allen, A. "On Predicting Some of the People Some of the Time: The Search for Cross-situational Consistencies in Behavior." *Psychological Review,* 1974, *81:* 506–520.

Birren, J. E. "Psychological Examinations of Children Who Later Became Psychotic." *Journal of Abnormal and Normal Psychology,* 1944, *39:* 84–95.

Block, J. "Some Enduring and Consequential Structures of Personality," in A. I. Rabin, J. Aronoff, A. M. Barclay, and R. A. Zucker (Eds.), *Further Explorations in Personality.* New York: Wiley, 1981.

Burns, M. O., and Seligman, E. P. "Explanatory Style Across the Life Span: Evidence for Stability Over 52 Years." *Journal of Personality and Social Psychology,* 1989, *56:* 471–477.

Buss, A. H., and Brock, T. C. "Repression and Guilt in Relation to Aggression." *Journal of Abnormal and Social Psychology,* 1963, *66:* 345–350.

Buss, A. H., and Finn, S. E. "Classification of Personality Traits." *Journal of Personality and Social Psychology,* 1987, *52:* 432–444.

Cantril, H. *Gauging Public Opinion.* Princeton, N. J.: Princeton University Press, 1943.

Conley, J. J. "Longitudinal Consistency of Adult Personality: Self-Reported Psychological Characteristics Across 45 Years." *Journal of Personality and Social Psychology,* 1984, *74:* 1325–1333.

Conley, J. "Longitudinal Stability of Personality Traits: A Multitrait-Multimethod-Multioccasion Analysis." *Journal of Personality and Social Psychology,* 1985, *49:* 1266–1282.

Cooper, J., and Fazio, R. H. "A New Look at Dissonance Theory," in L. Berowitz (Ed.), *Advances in Experimental Social Psychology,* Vol. 17. New York: Academic Press, 1984.

Costa, P. T., Jr., and McCrae, R. R. "Still Stable After All These Years: Personality as a Key to Some Issues in Adulthood and Old Age," in P. B. Baltes and O. G. Brim, Jr. (Eds.), *Life-Span Development and Behavior.* New York: Academic Press, 1980.

Costa, P. T., Jr., and McCrae, R. R. "Personality Stability and its Implications for Clinical Psychology." *Clinical Psychology Review,* 1986, *6:* 407–423.

Costa, P. T., Jr., McCrae, R. R., and Arenberg, D. "Enduring Dispositions in Adult Males." *Journal of Personality and Social Psychology,* 1980, *38:* 793–800.

Cousins, N. *Head First: The Biology of Hope.* New York: E. P. Dutton, 1989.

Doob, L. W. "Behavior and Grammatical Style." *Journal of Abnormal and Social Psychology,* 1958, *56:* 398–401.

Eliot, R. "Interrelationships Among Measures of Field Dependence, Ability, and Personality Traits." *Journal of Abnormal and Social Psychology,* 1961, *63:* 27–36.

Endler, N. S., and Mc V. Hunt, J. "Sources of Behavioral Variance as Measured by the S-R Inventory of Anxiousness." *Psychological Bulletin,* 1966, *65:* 336–345.

Endler, N. S., and Mc V. Hunt, J. "S-R Inventories of Hostility and Comparisons of the Proportions of Variance from Persons, Responses, and Situations for Hostility and Anxiousness." *Journal of Personality and Social Psychology,* 1968, *9:* 309–315.

Epstein, S. "The Self-Concept: A Review and the Proposal of an Integrated Theory of Personality," in E. Staub (Ed.), *Personality: Basic Aspects and Current Research.* Englewood Cliffs, N. J.: Prentice-Hall, 1980.

Erikson, E. H. *Identity and the Life Cycle: A Reissue.* New York: Norton, 1980.

Escalona, S., and Heider, G. M. *Prediction and Outcome: A Study in Child Development.* New York: Basic Books, 1959.

Fazio, R. H., and Cooper, J. "Arousal in the Dissonance Process," in J. T. Cacioppo and R. E. Petty (Eds.), *Social Psychophysiology.* New York: Guilford Press, 1983.

Festinger, L. A. *A Theory of Cognitive Dissonance.* Evansville, Ill.: Row, Peterson, 1957.

Festinger, L., Riecken, H. W., and Schacter, S. *When Prophecy Fails: A Social and Psychological Study of a Modern Group That Predicted the Destruction of the World.* New York: Harper and Row, 1956.

Findley, M. J., and Cooper, H. M. "Locus of Control and Academic Achievement: A Literature Review." *Journal of Personality and Social Psychology,* 1983, *44:* 419–427.

Finn, S. E. "Stability of Personality Self-Ratings Over 30 Years: Evidence of an Age/Cohort Interaction." *Journal of Personality and Social Psychology,* 1986, *50:* 813–818.

Funder, D. C., Block, J. H., and Block, J. "Delay of Gratification: Some Longitudinal Personality Correlates." *Journal of Personality and Social Psychology,* 1983, *44:* 1198–1213.

Garfield, S. L. "Psychotherapy: A 40-Year Appraisal." *American Psychologist,* 1981, *36:* 174–183.

Gergen, K. J., and Jones, E. E. "Mental Illness, Predictability, and Affective Consequences as Stimulus Factors in Person Perception." *Journal of Abnormal and Social Psychology,* 1963, *63:* 95–104.

Gergen, K. J. "Personal Consistency and the Presentation of Self," in G. Gordon and K. J. Gergen (Eds.), *The Self in Social Interaction.* New York: Wiley, 1968.

Haan, N. "Personality Development From Adolescence to Adulthood in the Oakland Growth and Guidance Studies." *Seminars in Psychiatry,* 1972, *4:* 399–414.

Haan, N. "Common Dimensions of Personality Development: Early Adolescence to Middle Life," in D. H. Eichorn, J. A. Clausen, N. Hann, M. Honzik, and P. H. Mussen (Eds.), *Present and Past in Middle Life.* New York: Academic Press, 1981.

Hamachek, D. *Encounters With Others: Interpersonal Relationships and You.* New York: Holt, Rinehart and Winston, 1982.

Hardyck, J. A., and Braden, J. "Prophecy Fails Again: A Report of a Failure to Replicate." *Journal of Abnormal and Social Psychology,* 1962, *65:* 136–141.

Hartshorne, H., and May, M. A. *I: Studies in Deceit.* New York: Crowell-Collier and Macmillan, 1928.

Hochreich, D. J. "Defensive Externality and Blame Projection Following Failure." *Journal of Personality and Social Psychology,* 1975, *32:* 540–546.

Holzman, P. S., and Gardner, R. W. "Leveling and Repression." *Journal of Abnormal and Social Psychology,* 1959, *59:* 151–155.

Howard, J. W., and Rothbart, M. "Social Categorization and Memory for In-Group and Out-Group Behavior." *Journal of Personality and Social Psychology,* 1980, *38:* 301–310.

Israel, N. R. "Leveling-Sharpening and Anticipating Cardiac Response." *Psychosomatic Medicine,* 1969, *31:* 499–509.

Johnson, J. A., Germer, G. K., Efran, J. S., and Overton, W. F. "Personality as a Basis for Theoretical Predictions." *Journal of Personality and Social Psychology,* 1988, *55:* 824–835.

Jung, C. G. "Psychological Types," in *Collected Works,* Vol. 6. Princeton, N.J.: Princeton University Press, 1971. (First German Edition, 1921)

Kagan, J., and Moss, H. A. *From Birth to Maturity: A Study of Psychological Development.* New York: Wiley, 1962.

Kastenbaum, R., and Briscoe, L. "The Street Corner: A Laboratory for the Study of Life-Threatening Behavior." *Omega,* 1975, *6:* 33–44.

Klein, G. "The Personal World Through Perception," in R. R. Blake and G. V. Ramsen (Eds.), *Perception: An Approach to Personality.* New York: Ronald, 1951.

Kleinke, C. L. *Self-Perception: The Psychology of Personal Awareness.* San Francisco: W. H. Freeman, 1978.

Langer, E. J., Janis, I. L., and Wolfer, J. A. "Reduction of Psychological Stress in Surgical Patients." *Journal of Experimental Social Psychology,* 1975, *11:* 155–165.

Langer, E. J., and Rodin, J. "The Effects of Choice and Enhanced Personal Responsibility for the Aged: A Field Experiment in an Institutional Setting." *Journal of Personality and Social Psychology,* 1976, *34:* 191–198.

Lecky, P. *Self-Consistency: A Theory of Personality.* New York: Island Press, 1945.

Lefcourt, H. M. *Locus of Control: Current Trends in Theory and Research,* 2nd ed. Hillsdale, N. J.: Erlbaum, 1982.

Levinson, D. J. "Exploration in Biography: Evolution of the Individual Life Structure in Adulthood," in A. I. Rabin, J. Aronoff, A. M. Barclay, and R. A. Zucker (Eds.), *Further Explorations in Personality.* New York: Wiley, 1981.

Maas, H. S., and Kuypers, J. A. *From Thirty to Seventy.* San Francisco: Jossey-Bass, 1974.

MacFarlane, J. L. "Perspectives on Personality ·Consistency and Change From the Guidance Study." *Vita Humana,* 1974, *7:* 115–126.

Markus, H. "Self-Schemata and Processing Information About the Self." *Journal of Personality and Social Psychology,* 1977, *35:* 63–78.

Markus, H., and Sentis, K. "The Self in Social Information Processing," in J. Suls (Ed.), *Social Psychological Perspectives on the Self.* Hillsdale, N. J.: Erlbaum, 1982.

Martin, W. E. "Singularity and Stability of Profiles of Social Behavior," in C. B. Standler (Ed.), *Readings in Child Behavior and Development.* New York: Harcourt, Brace and World, 1964.

Maslow, A. H. "Dominance-Feeling, Personality, and Social Behavior in Women." *Journal of Social Psychology,* 1939, *10:* 33–44.

Maslow, A. H. "Self-Esteem (dominance-feeling) and Sexuality in Women." *Journal of Social Psychology,* 1942, *16:* 259–294.

McClelland, D. C. "Is Personality Consistent?" in A. I. Rabin, J. Aronoff, A. M. Barclay, and R. A. Zucker (Eds.), *Further Explorations in Personality.* New York: Wiley, 1981.

Mindess, H. *Makers of Psychology: The Personal Factor.* New York: Human Sciences Press, 1988.

Mira, E. *M. K. P.—Myokinetic Diagnosis.* New York: Logos, 1958.

Mischel, W. "Alternatives in the Pursuit of the Predictability and Consistency of Persons: Stable Data That Yield Unstable Interpretations." *Journal of Personality,* 1983a, *51:* 578–604.

Mischel, W. "Delay of Gratification as Process and Person Variable in Development," in D. Magnusson and U. P. Allen (Eds.), *Interactions in Human Development.* New York: Academic Press, 1983b.

Mischel, W. "Convergences and Challenges in the Search for Consistency." *American Psychologist,* 1984, *39:* 351–364.

Mischel, W. *Introduction to Personality,* 4th ed. New York: CBS College Publishing, 1986.

Mischel, W., Shoda, Y., and Peake, P. K. "The Nature of Adolescent Competencies Predicted by Preschool Delay of Gratification." *Journal of Personality and Social Psychology,* 1988, *54:* 687–696.

Neilon, P. "Shirley's Babies After Fifteen Years: A Personality Study." *Journal of Genetic Psychology,* 1948, *73:* 175–186.

Peterson, C., Seligman, E. P., and Vaillant, G. "Pessimistic Explanatory Style is a Risk Factor for Physical Illness: A Thirty-five-year Longitudinal Study." *Journal of Personality and Social Psychology,* 1988, *55:* 23–27.

Phares, E. J. "Defensiveness and Perceived Control," in L. C. Permuter and R. A. Monty (Eds.), *Choice and Perceived Control.* Hillsdale, N. J.: Erlbaum, 1979.

Phares, E. J., Wilson, K. G., and Klyver, N. W. "Internal-External Control and Attribution of Blame Under Neutral and Distractive Conditions." *Journal of Personality and Social Psychology,* 1971, *18:* 283–288.

Robins, L. N. *Deviant Children Grown Up: Summation and Interpretation of Results.* Baltimore: Williams and Wilkens, 1966.

Rodin, J., and Langer, E. J. "Long-Term Effects of Control-Relevant Intervention with the Institutional Aged." *Journal of Personality and Social Psychology,* 1977, *35:* 897–902.

Rodin, J., and Slochower, J. "Externality in the Obese: Effects of Environmental Responsiveness on Weight." *Journal of Personality and Social Psychology,* 1976, *33:* 338–344.

Rogers, C. R. "Some Observations on the Organization of Personality." *American Psychologist,* 1947, *2:* 358–368.

Rogers, C. R. *Client-Centered Therapy: Its Current Practice, Implication, and Theory.* Boston: Houghton Mifflin, 1951.

Rotter, J. B. "Generalized Expectancies for Internal Versus External Control of Reinforcement." *Psychological Monographs,* 1966, *80:* Whole No. 609.

Rotter, J. B. "Internal Versus External Control of Reinforcement: A Case History of a Variable." *American Psychologist,* 1990, *45:* 489–493.

Schneider, D. J. "Implicit Personality Theory: A Review." *Psychological Bulletin,* 1973, *73:* 294–309.

Seeman, M., and Evans, J. W. "Alienation and Learning in a Hospital Setting." *American Sociological Reviews,* 1962, *27:* 772–783.

Sheldon, W. H. *Atlas of Man: A Guide for Somatotizing the Adult Male of All Ages.* New York: Harper and Row, 1954.

Shepard, C. E. *Forgiven: The Rise and Fall of Jim Bakker and the PTL Ministry.* New York: Atlantic Monthly Press, 1989.

Shirley, M. M. *The First Two Years: A Study of Twenty-Five Babies (Vol. III). Personality Manifestations.* Institute of Child Welfare Monograph Series, No. 8, Minneapolis: University of Minnesota Press, 1933.

Steele, C. M., Southwick, L. L., and Critchlow, B. "Dissonance and Alcohol: Drinking Your Troubles Away." *Journal of Personality and Social Psychology,* 1981, *41:* 831–846.

Stipek, D. J., and Weisz, J. R. "Perceived Personal Control and Academic Achievement." *Review of Educational Research,* 1981, *51:* 101–137.

Stott, L. H. "Persistency Effects of Early Family Experiences Upon Personality Development." *Merrill-Palmer Quarterly,* 1957, Spring, *3* (Special Issue, Seminar on Child Development).

Strickland, B. R. "Internal-External Control Expectancies: From Contingency to Creativity." *American Psychologist,* 1989, *44:* 1–12.

Tom, G., and Rucker, M. "Fat, Full and Happy: Effects of Food Deprivation, External Cues, and Obesity on Preference Ratings, Consumption, and Buying Intentions." *Journal of Personality and Social Psychology,* 1975, *32:* 761–766.

Wicklund, R. A., and Brehm, J. W. *Perspectives on Cognitive Dissonance.* Hillsdale, N. J.: Erlbaum, 1976.

Wilson, G. D. *The Psychology of Conservatism.* London: Academic Press, 1973.

Wilson, G. D., Ausman, J., and Mathews, T. R. "Conservatism and Art Preferences." *Journal of Personality and Social Psychology,* 1973, *25:* 286–288.

Witkin, H. A., and Goodenough, D. R. "Field Dependence and Interpersonal Behavior." *Psychological Bulletin,* 1977, *84:* 661–689.

Witkin, H. A., Moore, C. A., Goodenough, D. R., and Cox, P. W. "Field-Dependent and Field-Independent Cognitive Styles and Their Educational Implications." *Review of Educational Research,* 1977, *47:* 1–64.

Chapter 4

Self-Concept as Influenced by Growth, Appearance, and Developmental Outcomes

PROLOGUE

The foundation of our self-image is our body image. This is not so surprising when you consider that children's initial contacts with life and the world around them are essentially visceral and tactile in nature. Among children's first discoveries are their hands and feet, and among their first sensations are the varied pains and pleasures of their own bodies. An endless stream of physical experiences provide the nucleus for a growing sense of self. It is highly likely, for example, that a child's first distinction between "me" and "you," between "I am running" and "she is running," is formed on the basis of early and ongoing sensitivity to his or her own body responses and assorted muscular reactions while growing up. To a very large extent, children define themselves in terms of what they can accomplish physically. How often do we witness young children seeking the validations of those in their immediate vicinity with requests to "Watch me," "Look at what I can do," "Watch how fast (far, long) I can run (jump, swim underwater, throw a ball, hold my breath")? When children besiege us with requests of this sort, they are showing us not only what they can do but, in a deeper and less-conscious way, who they are. Adults and other children respond to these requests affirmatively or negatively and sometimes not at all, which for better or worse, contributes to a child's developing sense of self.

What begins as a purely physical self expands slowly with time and becomes integrated into a more complex psychological self. Our body image does not constitute the whole of the psychological self, but it is a highly significant aspect of it. A central idea to be developed in this chapter is that our experiences with our body, as a psychological object, are infused widely into our lives. The various components of our physical self—height, weight, girth, hair and skin color, complexion, and general body proportions—contribute significantly to the effect associated with our self-perceptions. The physical shell that houses the person within is a perceptual reality from which we cannot escape. Whether we think we are too tall or too short, too fat or too thin, attractive or not attractive enough affects the feelings we have about ourselves, which, in turn, affects others' feelings toward us. Our attention in this chapter, then, focuses on an examination of the relationship between self-concept and physical growth, appearance, and developmental outcomes.

BODY TYPE AND PERSONALITY: HISTORICAL ROOTS

More than 2,500 years ago Hippocrates suggested that there are basically two kinds of human beings, the long thins and the short thicks. Although not scientifically precise descriptions, almost all classifications of body type since that time have had nearly the same basis. During the 1920s, for example, Kretschmer (1925) used a somewhat similar classification in his controversial but influential hypotheses about the relationship between body build, temperament, and mental illness. He theorized that people could be typed as *asthenic* (thin and frail), *pyknik* (short, soft, rounded), *athletic* (muscular), or *dysplastic* (one type in one segment and another somewhere else), this latter category being for people who could not be classified in one of the first three. It was an elaborate theory but fell by the wayside for lack of consistent research findings to support it.

Sheldon's (1954) work during the 1950s represents the last major effort to develop a method of classifying personality on the basis of physical characteristics. Rejecting the idea that individuals can be divided into distinct physical types, he classified people along a continuum ranging from *ectomorphic* (tall, thin) to *mesomorphic* (athletic, muscular) to *endomorphic* (heavy, rotund). Figure 4-1 shows these three physical types and their variations.

In rating a person's physical characteristics, Sheldon's system uses a seven-point scale for each of the classifications in the order of endomorph, mesomorph, and ectomorph, with high numbers indicating more of a particular component. For example, a rating of 6-5-2 would describe a rounded but relatively muscular and sturdy individual. A typical professional wrestler might fit this description.

Sheldon's rating system was accepted easily enough, but he got into trouble by assigning certain psychological characteristics to particular physical types. According to Sheldon, the predominately rounded, heavy endomorphic person is one who loves to eat, seeks bodily comforts, and is happy and outgoing. The predominately athletic mesomorphic person is described as energetic and direct in manner; and the somewhat lanky, thin ectomorphic person is classified as sensitive and fearful.

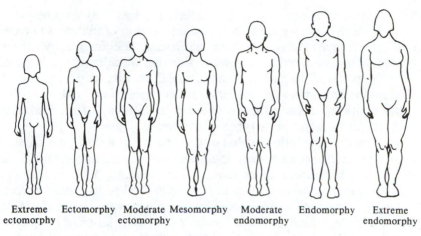

| Extreme ectomorphy | Ectomorphy | Moderate ectomorphy | Mesomorphy | Moderate endomorphy | Endomorphy | Extreme endomorphy |

Figure 4-1 *Examples of differences in body build.*

This system of "somatotizing" individuals has been strongly criticized (Hammond, 1957; Humphreys, 1957). The fact is, not all endomorphs are happy and outgoing; not all mesomorphs are athletic and direct; and not all ectomorphs are sensitive and introverted. Both Kretschmer's and Sheldon's theories break down because there are simply too many exceptions to any given generalization. As we shall see, there *are* relationships between certain body types and personality, but they are neither as direct not as simple as physical type theories would have us believe.

When considering possible links between body type and personality, we are, of course, touching on possible cause-and-effect relationships. Would it be accurate to conclude that certain body types, or structures or proportions or whatever you care to call them, *cause* certain personality effects? Probably not. At the moment, the best we can do is speculate that the components of one's body structure help determine not only what people can do but also what they and those close to them expect that they should be able to do. This should not be so surprising. After all, the most obvious and observable part of our entire being is the body shell in which we house our private world and personal existence. Whether we like it or not, the fact is we have a strong tendency to stereotype and categorize each other according to the cues available to us. And one of the most prominent cues is body structure.

Let's turn our attention now to what we know about how different body structures are perceived and some of the common stereotypes that are associated with certain body types.

PERSONALITY STEREOTYPES ASSOCIATED WITH DIFFERENT BODY BUILDS

The first thing we observe about another person (and that person about us) is his or her general appearance and overall body structure, particularly when meeting someone for the first time. In fact, the less well we know another person, the more likely we are to form an impression of that person based on physical appearance (Miller, 1970). In the absence of knowing anything about the person within, perhaps it is not surprising that we call up certain personality stereotypes based on outer appearances. There are, as it turns out, some rather common and somewhat universal stereotypes related to body build and personality lurking in the subconscious minds of many of us. Consider, for instance, the three major body types illustrated in Figure 4-2.

Now, look over the following list of adjectives and assign each adjective to the body type that it seems to describe best: aggressive, happy-go-lucky, tough, passive, weak, adventurous, quiet, tense, competitive, good natured, ambitious. Perhaps you can see how particular adjectives are linked to certain preconceptions about how people who resemble these body types are expected to behave.

You might find it interesting to compare your association of body type and personality characteristics with Brodsky's (1954) early research findings in this area. What he did was to sample how 150 male college students—half were white, half were black—responded to five 15-inch silhouettes of males, representing (1) endomorph (short, chubby), (2) endomorphic (muscular, but short and heavy), (3) mesomorph (muscular, athletic), (4) ectomesomorphic (muscular, but tall and thin), and (5) ectomorph (tall and thin). A questionnaire was administered containing such questions as the following: Which one of this group of five men is most aggressive? What one is least aggressive?

Personality characteristics were usually assigned by the respondents to the "pure" silhouettes: endomorph, mesomorph, and ectomorph, such as in Figure 4-2. One of the interesting findings was that there were no important differences in the way the two groups responded, lending weight to the idea that cultural stereotypes exist in aligning certain personality characteristics with particular body types. The major findings can be summarized as follows:

> More than one-third of the respondents labeled the *endomorph* (short, chubby) silhouette as representing the man who probably eats the most, makes the worst soldier, the poorest athlete, can endure pain the least well, would be least likely to be chosen leader, would be the least aggressive, would drink the most, be least preferred as a personal friend (but, ironically, would have many friends), and would probably put his own interests before those of others.

> The *mesomorph* (muscular, athletic) fared more favorably. The respondents said that he would make the best athlete and the most successful military leader. They chose him as the man who would likely be elected as leader. He was also judged to be a nonsmoker and to be the most self-sufficient. He was most preferred as a friend and was judged to have many friends. Respondents also said that he would be the most aggressive, would endure pain the best, would be least likely to have a nervous breakdown, and would probably drink the least.

> The stereotype of the *ectomorph* (tall, thin) was judged to be the one most likely to have emotional problems, to eat the least and the least often, to be a heavy smoker, to be the least self-sufficient in the sense of needing friends the

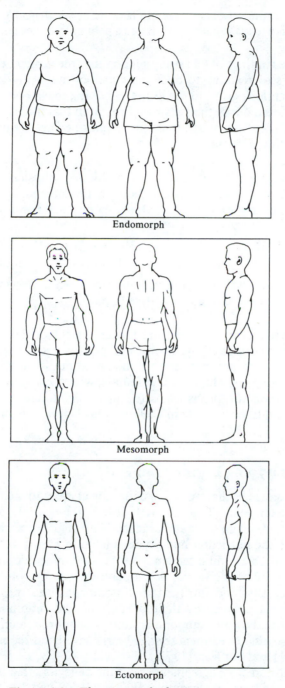

Figure 4-2 *Three major body types.*

most (but, unfortunately, was judged to have the fewest friends), to hold his liquor the worst, to make a poor father, and a poor military leader.

All in all, the findings of this study suggest that there may be characteristic stereotyped ways of reacting to different types of male physiques, with the most positive reactions given to the athletic-looking mesomorph. DeJong and Kleck (1986) pointed out in their review of research that males who are associated with one of the three body builds just mentioned are typically perceived as having the following traits:

1. *Endomorphic (soft, fat, round):* old-fashioned, physically weak, talkative, warmhearted, sympathetic, good natured, agreeable, trusting, needy, people oriented, loving physical comfort, and loves to eat.

2. *Mesomorphic (muscular, athletic, strong):* masculine, adventurous, self-reliant, energetic, competitive, liking exercise, and bold.

3. *Ectomorphic (tall, thin, fragile):* ambitious, tense, nervous, stubborn, quiet, liking privacy, and sensitive to pain.

The stereotypes of the good-natured, plump person; the fragile-looking, bespectacled bookworm; and the strong, competitive mesomorph may not be very scientific descriptions, but they are the broad outline of expectations for the behavior of young and old, male and female, with these general body types. For example, parents are probably more apt to encourage a more muscular mesomorphic child to participate in athletics than one who is more fragile and ectomorphic.

Physical Stereotyping Begins at an Early Age

The physical stereotypes that we've been looking at are evident among children as young as six to ten years of age. Staffieri (1967), for example, discovered that boys this age are already in close agreement when assigning certain personality characteristics to the particular body types shown in Figure 4-2. For example, there was a remarkable similar tendency for the endomorphic silhouettes to be described as socially offensive and delinquent, the ectomorphic silhouettes as retiring, nervous, shy, and introverted. Ectomorphs and mesomorphs were chosen as the most popular by their peers, whereas endomorphs were less popular, knew that they were unpopular, and were more rejecting of the body image. Similar results for elementary-aged girls have been reported by Caskey and Felker (1971) and Staffieri (1972).

Adults are also in close agreement about the behaviors that fit certain body types among young boys. For example, Walker (1962) had 125 preschool children rated by their teachers on 64 behavioral items. What he found was that there were more significant relationships between body build and behavior for boys than for girls. That is, on the basis of body build data, the teachers could better predict how boys might behave than how girls might behave—which suggests that physical factors may be more important in affecting the behavior of boys and others' expectations for their behavior. At least for children between the ages of four and about 12 years or so, our cultural stereotypes and expectations concerning physique and behavior seem more firmly established for males. The mesomorphic (athletic) body build, particularly among preschool boys, showed the strongest relationship to the behavioral ratings. The teachers seemed more certain about how those boys might behave and, thus, were in higher agreement among themselves when assigning ratings to the mesomorphic boys. Generally, those boys were seen as popular, likeable, strong, and independent. You may be interested in knowing that subsequent research involving parents' ratings of the same children tended to confirm the observations made by the teachers (Walker, 1963). That is, both teachers and parents are inclined to perceive the same general behavior in children of certain body types, particularly among boys.

Body Build and Personality: Behavioral Implications

Body build and personality do seem to be related. It is difficult to know for sure why these relationships are somewhat more pronounced for boys than for girls, but these possible explanations come to mind: (1) Adult expectations for boys' behavior are more specific; that is, boys are supposed to "behave like boys," which means participation in a certain amount of rough and tumble and large muscle activities—running, biking, soccer, football, and the like—and showing a certain amount of boldness, daring, and competitiveness. Of course, boys who are neither too soft and round nor too thin and fragile, but who are more lithe and muscular, are apt not only to be more successful in those things, but also to be *expected* to be more successful. When expectations are added to natural potential, it is a powerful mix. (2) Expectations for how boys are to behave are something about which there is relatively high agreement. That is, most adults are in reasonably close accord with the idea that boys should "behave like boys," even though this ideal has lost some of its traditional "macho" quality in recent years. General adult agreement about how boys are to behave adds up to a cultural expectation that is reasonably specific, uniform, and supported by the sheer number who reinforce it. (3) When judged on the basis of physical appearance, young girls are usually allowed considerably more latitude. That is, it is more acceptable for little girls to engage in rough and tumble activities, play softball, soccer, and the like than it is for little boys to play house and push a doll buggy. On the other hand, it is also acceptable for little girls *not* to get involved in rough and tumble activities or play left field in a softball game. Generally, young girls have a broader range of behavioral options from which to choose and freedom to do so without penalty, whereas boys are generally expected to stay within a narrower range of prescribed expectations. Thus, the right kind of body proportions are more important for a boy because they enable him to do better the things he is expected to do; body proportions are less important for a girl because expectations for how she is to behave are not so narrowly defined.

However, the evidence does suggest that the broad-shouldered, muscular, narrow-hipped boy and the well-proportioned girl are more likely to win social approval and acceptance on the basis of pure physique than are boys or men and girls or women who are either too heavy or too thin and too tall or too short. High self-confidence and self-esteem are frequently associated with mesomorphic physiques in males and females, particularly as they move away from their childhood years. Although things like, say, leadership qualities, social approval, or high self-esteem are not *caused* by having a nice build or a well-proportioned figure, they may, in fact, be among the positive gains that *result from* a more mesomorphic appearance. Considering the feedback a person both gives and receives on the basis of purely physical appearances, it is not difficult to see how our physical proportions can influence our feelings about ourselves simply by affecting how other people react toward us. The overweight person who grows up in the face of assorted descriptive monikers like "Tubby," "Chubby," "Fatso," or "Lard" or the thin individual who is variously addressed as "Bony," "Skinny," or "Beanpole" is hardly encouraged to develop self-confidence and self-esteem in the same way as a person who is not markedly overweight, underweight, too tall, or too short. If used for a long enough period of time, the names that were originally meant to describe a person's physique can also describe and define, to some extent, his or her personality. Thus, the little boy or girl who frequently hears adjectives like "delicate" or "fragile" may, in fact, grow up to be that kind of person—somewhat fragile and vulnerable with a low threshold for pain, stress, or frustration. Some children are reminded of how weak they are; others are encouraged to be strong. What adjectives did you hear as you were growing up?

All in all, one's body build has a powerful potential for eliciting specific social responses, either positive or negative. How we feel about ourselves depends, to some extent, on how we feel about the basic body structure and physical boundaries of the body shell in which we reside. Adolescents are particularly vulnerable when it comes to physical stereotyping and variations in body build, a topic we turn to next.

VARIATIONS IN THE PACE OF GROWTH: PSYCHOLOGICAL AND SOCIAL EFFECTS

It is a well-documented fact that the timing of puberty and the marked physical changes that herald its onset are subject to wide individual differences (Brooks-Gunn and Warren, 1989; Lerner, Lerner, and Tubman, 1989). Figure 4-3 shows the percentage of boys and girls who can be expected to reach puberty and physical maturity between nine and one-half and 17½ years of age. You can see that there are wide individual differences as to when puberty begins and physical maturity is reached.

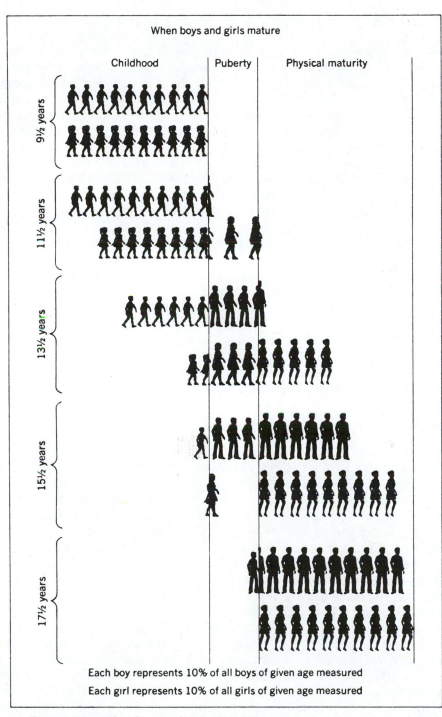

Figure 4-3 *When boys and girls mature.*

Most boys begin their growth acceleration at about 12 years, reach a growth peak between 13½ and 14 years, and then decline sharply to pre-growth-spurt rates by about 15½. Growth goes on at a slower pace for several years thereafter. On the average, boys grow about 8 inches between the ages of 11 and 15 years and increase their weight by about 12 pounds. The average girl begins her stint of rapid acceleration at about age ten years, reaches a peak between 11½ and 12, and then decreases to pre-growth-spurt rates by about age 13. On the average, girls grow about 4 inches between the ages of 11 and 14 years and add about 10 pounds in weight.

Other dramatic changes are occurring in both sexes. For example, the low forehead becomes higher and wider, the mouth widens and the lips fill out, and the slightly receding chin begins to assert itself. The nose grows larger and loses much of its pudginess. The large head, characteristic of the childhood years, seems to become smaller in proportion to the total body length. (It does not actually get smaller, but appears to because the trunk extremities are growing so rapidly.) Because of these critical changes, most youngsters between the ages of 11 and 13 years look increasingly like the adults they are growing into, as least as far as facial features are concerned.

The physical changes that occur during adolescence are vast and varied. The individual differences in physical growth have been found to affect personal and social adjustment not only during the developmental years, but beyond that time as well. Because the effects of early and late growth are different for boys and girls, perhaps we can more clearly see these differences if we separate the sexes and examine them one at a time.

Effects of Early Versus Late Maturation in Boys

It would no doubt simplify matters if all boys the same age grew at about the same rate, but, as with all other aspects of growth, there is a wide range of individual differences. At 13 years of age, John may have the body of a 17-year-old boy, while Charles, who really is 17, looks more like most 13 year olds. What are the effects of these differing growth rates in John and Charles? (You can get an idea of what a fast-maturing and a slow-maturing boy of the same age look like in Figure 4-4.) Inasmuch as both boys and girls tend to be enormously preoccupied with their appearance and body changes, rate of growth has both short- and long-term effects. On the whole, research has consistently found that, for boys in particular, maturing slightly ahead of one's peers is accompanied by distinct social advantages (Gross and Duke, 1980; Lerner and Foch, 1987; Mussen and Jones, 1958; Petersen, 1987). Faster-growing boys such as John, for example, tend to have more positive self-concepts. On the whole, they are inclined to be more independent, self-confident, and self-reliant than their slower-growing peers. In addition, they report higher levels of personal satisfaction and more positive feelings about themselves. Perhaps a reason for this is that they tend to be more widely accepted and liked by both peers and adults. All of these findings may help explain why early-maturing boys tend to be more matter-of-fact about

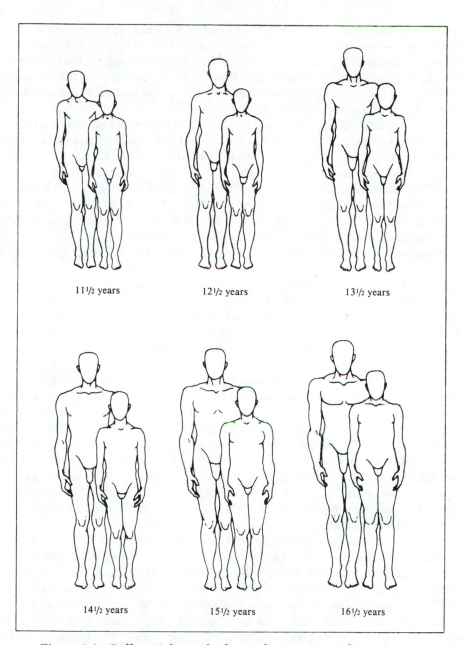

11½ years   12½ years   13½ years

14½ years   15½ years   16½ years

Figure 4-4 *Differential growth of an early-maturing and a late-maturing boy.*

From F. K. Shuttleworth, "The Adolescent Period: A Pictorial Atlas." *Monographs of the Society for Research in Child Development* (Ser. no. 59). 14 (1949).

themselves and why they have less need to strive for status and recognition. This general air of confidence may be one of the reasons why they are frequently chosen for leadership positions in high school. Research suggests that boys who mature early are poised, relaxed, good natured, and relatively stable. Clausen (1975) noted that boys who mature at an average age have about as many relative advantages as those who mature early.

Slower-maturing boys such as Charles, on the other hand, tend to have a somewhat more difficult time of it (Lerner and Foch, 1987; Mussen and Jones, 1958; Petersen, 1987; Weatherly, 1964). Boys who mature late tend to be anxious, tense, and dependent. In addition, they are more likely to behave in childish, affected, attention-seeking ways, which might explain why they are apt to be less accepted by their peers, more dominated by their parents, and chosen for so few leadership positions. During adolescence, at least, late-maturing boys suffer as many disadvantages as early-maturing boys enjoy advantages.

Although life for slower-maturing boys is somewhat dismal to begin with, the picture brightens as they catch up and move into young adulthood. Findings from ongoing longitudinal and in-depth studies indicate that early maturers perhaps pay a price for their moment of glory in adolescence and that late maturers are compensated for their early agonies (Peskin, 1973; Siegel, 1982). As adults, early maturers tend to be anxious about not doing well or not being liked, concerned about appearances, and somewhat rigid about how they live their lives.

On the other hand, those same insecure, anxious late-maturing boys tend to be more expressive, curious, and flexible as adults. Surprisingly, they are apt to have better senses of humor and to handle ambiguous situations more easily than their faster-growing cohorts, a behavior that reflects their flexibility. Perhaps one reason why former slow-growing adolescent males enjoy a few adult advantages over their peers is that they have had to work a bit harder to survive in a tough world. In the process, they probably have had greater reason to learn about the importance of curiosity, flexibility, and a sense of humor in order to do that. In addition, late-maturing boys simply have more time to prepare for their status as an adult.

To summarize: Early-maturing boys do seem to enjoy certain personal and interpersonal advantages in adolescence primarily because both others' perceptions of them and expectations for them are positive. This obviously helps them feel good about themselves. On the positive side, this frequently lends itself to competitive advantages (check out the sizes of those on the football and basketball teams, for example). On the negative side, it sometimes means that the adolescent boy responds to expectations sometimes determined more by size and appearance than by other aspects of maturing. Later-maturing boys appear, and sometimes behave, younger than they are, which only makes it more difficult for them to survive in the fickle social world of their peers.

Overall, late maturation during adolescence is more of a handicap than an advantage. Early maturity, on the other hand, is a two-sided coin. On the positive side, it can lend itself to certain competitive and social advantages. On the negative side, it sometimes puts the adolescent boy in the unfair position of having to respond to unrealistic expectations that may be determined too much by size and appearance and too little by ability and motivation. All in all, however, the early-maturing boy is likely to have a better time of it in terms of both certain physical advantages and a more positive self-concept as he moves through his adolescent years.

Let us not forget to note that, in any particular case, the effects of early or late maturation may be significantly modified by the individual's psychological history and present circumstances. For example, some very late-maturing boys are so talented in some specific areas (music, math, athletics, and so on) that their stature is hardly noticed. On the other hand, being a fast grower is no guarantee of instant social status and popularity. Some boys' physical growth spurts ahead of their coordination, and they end up stumbling all over themselves. Other fast-growing boys may be unmotivated, unimaginative, or simply lack the social finesse to be popular or accepted at any height or weight. Being an average or fast grower may give a boy the initial edge, but unless he has other personal qualities to accompany his size, he is as likely as anyone to flounder around in his interpersonal relationships and to struggle to maintain a positive self-concept.

Effects of Early Versus Late Maturation in Girls

The outcome of early or late maturation for girls is somewhat more complex than is the case for boys. (Figure 4-5 will give you an idea of the growth differences between the typical early-maturing and late-maturing girls.) Whereas a faster-maturing boy tends to be heavier and taller than his peers, a faster-growing girl may only be stockier and heavier, but not necessarily taller than her peers. This may cause self-image problems, inasmuch as a heavier, stockier body runs counter to the tall and trim ideal, at least in North America (Dion, 1986). Early-maturing girls encounter another problem. Because girls begin to mature sooner than boys, something that faster growers do on an even earlier schedule, rapidly developing girls look especially conspicuous in the sixth and seventh grades. (A quick look at the faster-growing girls between ages 11½ and 12½ in Figure 4-5 will help you see why.) This can trigger two problems: (1) Since faster-growing girls in those grades look very much unlike their female counterparts, they feel self-conscious and different. As expressed by an early-maturing young lady while discussing personal feelings about her own growth experience, "I didn't like what was happening to me at all. I felt like I was a woman before I was through being a girl, and I was only in the sixth grade." (2) Another problem, particularly for those girls who developed rapidly in the sixth, seventh, and eighth grades, is the difficulty they have interacting with boys in their own age group. Although they have reached puberty and are ready to socialize with boys, most boys have not yet made that transition. It

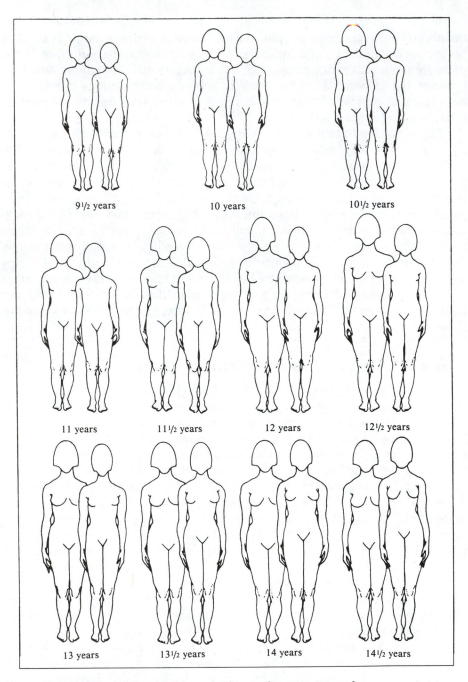

Figure 4-5 *Differential growth of an early-maturing and a late-maturing girl.*

From F. K. Shuttleworth, "The Adolescent Period: A Pictorial Atlas." *Monographs of the Society for Research in Child Development* (Ser. no 59). 14 (1949).

should not surprise us when we find an early-developing seventh-grade girl look favorably and hopefully at a tenth-grade boy.

The early-maturing boy is welcomed into the ready-made roles of school leader and athlete. Both parent and peers (and coaches) admire him. The welcome mat to maturity is much smaller for early-maturing girls. Rather than see her blossoming physique as simply a sign of early maturity, it is more likely to be viewed as a source of potential sexual trouble. Parents might brag about a son's manly muscles; they are not as likely to crow about a young daughter's curvaceous proportions.

Overall, research shows that, for girls, as opposed to boys, the rate of physical maturation is a much less influential variable that mediates self-concept and personality development (Brooks-Gun and Petersen, 1983; Hamachek, 1980). Why should this be? One possible reason might be related to the fact that the cultural sex-role prescription for males in our society is relatively clear and is one that places a high value on attributes associated with physical strength, coordination, and athletic deftness, especially in the adolescent and young adulthood years. For girls, however, the feminine sex-role prescription is less definite and stereotyped and is, therefore, not as likely to be connected to any specific pattern of physical attributes. In addition, whereas people seem to respond more to a boy's or a man's total physical makeup, the response to a girl's or a woman's physical makeup is apt to be more specific. That is, the physical qualities of a young woman capable of eliciting a favorable response include her face, bosom, hips, legs, and total proportion (although not necessarily in that order). For example, one adolescent girl might have a pretty face and very little else, but this could be sufficient to win her many signs of approval. Another girl may have an extremely attractive figure and only very plain facial features, but her nice legs or shapely form may be quite enough to win her some social approval. In other words, it may be more possible for a female than for a male to elicit positive responses to different parts of her body so that even though she may fall short in one area, she can make it up in another. When it comes to the physical side of the self, girls may be judged more in terms of how they *look* and boys more in terms of how they *perform*. Thus, a tentative speculation about why the rate of physical maturation has a less-dramatic effect on girls than boys is that girls have greater flexibility for altering or changing their looks than boys do for altering or changing their performances.

Slow but steady progress is being made in destereotyping what young girls and women are "supposed" to be. Indeed, one of the healthy outgrowths of the women's liberation movement seems to be a gradual shift in social expectations away from traditional, stereotyped views about what constitutes "masculine" and "feminine" behavior to a more realistic stance that recognizes that a girl can be strong and assertive without being masculine and that a boy can be warm and sensitive without being effeminate. As social expectations change, adolescent boys and girls and men and women may feel free to develop more aspects of the total self that each can become rather than just certain culturally accepted aspects of it.

THE EFFECTS OF BODY IMAGE ON SELF-CONCEPT

The concern about appearance, shape, and body proportions that begins in adolescence has been found to continue deep into one's adult life (Cash, Winstead, and Janda, 1986; Cash and Pruzinsky, 1990; Wright, 1989). This is not surprising. After all, the most visible part of the self is our physical body. Our physical appearance is the one personal characteristic that is accessible to others in almost all social interactions. Occupying, as it does, a substantial portion of our visual and auditory fields, we see and hear a lot of ourselves. And so do others. To a very large extent, our self-concept develops out of the reflected appraisals others have of us. People respond not only to what we say and do, but also to our appearance—clothes, grooming, and physical attributes. In a very important way, our bodies occupy a central role in our own and others' perceptions.

The particular way a person perceives his or her physical body—whether distorted or not—may have important psychological consequences. An adolescent boy, for example, may be so concerned about his lack of coordination that he refuses to try out for athletics or even attend dances; a woman may be so sensitive about her breast development that she is hesitant to date or appear in a bathing suit; a man or woman could be so narcissistically attached to his or her own body development that each neglects other aspects of growth, such as social and intellectual development. Perception of the body relates intimately to larger conceptions of the self. Fisher's (1986) research in this area points to a clear parallel between the way people appraise themselves as persons and the way they evaluate their bodies. It is not easy to separate one's body from one's sense of self. Along this line, I'm reminded of the remarks made by one of my students during a class discussion on body image—a part-time salesman who lost 25 pounds through exercise and healthier eating over a four-month period:

> It's hard to explain how I feel, but one thing I do know is that I don't mind looking in the mirror anymore. I used to hate mirrors. I didn't even look at myself in store window reflections. But I like what I see now—well, except for this stomach that's still pretty flabby. What I mean is, I seem to like me—as a person—better. I've also noticed an interesting thing happening in my work. My sales record has gotten increasingly better the past three months. I'm not conscious of doing anything particularly different, but *I do know I feel less, what should I say, ashamed around people and more confident in myself.*

This man is saying what many people say after an improvement in their body image. Not just a change in an external body shell occurs, but also change in the more internal and deeper sense of self. The feeling of shame that he mentioned is something that can easily develop if one hears enough times that one is too fat or too skinny or too plain looking or whatever. Feeling ashamed grows out of the failure to meet another person's expectations, whereas confidence grows out of successfully meeting our own standards. This gentleman spent most of his life consuming too much food but neglected to take into account the inevitable consequences of that behavior. Not coincidentally, when he stopped blaming others for the fact that he ate too much—"others" referring primarily to his mother and wife: "They feed me too much!"—he was in a position to do something about a problem that was basically his own. And that gave him control over it. By moving the responsibility from "out there" to "in here," he was able to start changing his body image, which, in time, enabled him to develop a healthier self-image.

A client of mine, a woman in her late 20s, experienced a dramatic change for the better in her self-concept after a visit to a cosmetologist, who taught her how to use makeup to best effect, and to a hairstylist, who showed her several ways she might do her hair to take advantage of her particular facial structure. Like many women—and men, too, for that matter—she had never been taught how to present herself in more appealing ways. Her mother was a rather plain woman who believed in neither makeup nor hairstyling, and she was embarked on a similar course, but unhappily so. However, through modifying her outer appearance, she changed her inner feelings, and her therapy progressed at a rapid rate. You may be interested to know that within three weeks of learning how to use makeup and having her hair styled, she had a portrait of herself taken—the first ever in her life. In her words:

> You know, I didn't even have my picture in my high school yearbook. I used to hate to have my picture taken. I felt that a camera would make me see myself too clearly or something. I think I always wanted the camera to take a picture of the person I wanted to be, but all it did was take a picture of the person I was. But, you know, I kind of like the person I see now.

I do not mean to suggest that all it takes to change the psychological self is a modification of the physical self. I do mean to suggest, however, that sometimes a person's personal and interpersonal difficulties spring from body-image problems and not self-image problems per se. When this is the case, we need to do as much as we can to encourage changes in the body image so that the owner of that image can be more at peace with it. When this happens, change in self-image sometimes occurs quite naturally. Along these lines, Maltz (1970), a plastic surgeon, observed:

> Upon starting the practice of plastic surgery many years ago, I was amazed by the dramatic, sudden changes in personality which often took place when a facial defect was corrected . . . changing the physical person seemed to create an entirely new person . . . fearful people became bold, the angry became friendly, the self-effacing were now outgoing. (p. 7)

Body image is more or less important to some people than it is to others, but there are few instances, indeed, where it is not important at all. A thriving multibillion dollar cosmetics industry and perennial best-selling diet and exercise books are testimonials to the intense interest we have in looking good and, for increasing numbers, in feeling good, as well. When considering body image and the question of what looks good and what does not, we are confronted with the issue of attractiveness, which brings us to an interesting topic to explore.

FACTORS THAT INFLUENCE PERCEPTIONS OF PHYSICAL ATTRACTIVENESS

Standards for what constitutes physical attractiveness vary not only from culture to culture, but from one time period to another within the same culture. (The next time you have a chance, you might find it interesting to look back through the family photo albums of the past 30 years or so to get an idea of how dramatic those changes in standards can be.) A recent Gallup survey reported by Britton (1988) shows clearly that the thinness mania that's gripped American women since the 1960s is finally losing its hold. For both men and women, skinny is passé, muscular and fit is the new silhouette of choice.

Each culture transmits effectively, and fairly uniformly, criteria for what constitutes physical attractiveness, a fact documented by Berscheid and Walster (1974). Actually, it is not surprising that most of us would agree on what is and what is not attractive in other people. From the time we were impressionable children, Disney movies and illustrators of children's books have taught us that the gentle and charming heroines such as Cinderella, Sleeping Beauty, and Snow White—as well as the dashing princes who win their hearts and everlasting love—all look alike. With their oval faces, big eyes, regular features, clear complexions, and supple, athletic bodies, they reflect a perfect alignment of innocence, form, and movement. Think about how these charmers compare to depictions of wicked witches, mean stepmothers, and sinister villains, characters whose features are variously punctuated with irregular features, squinty eyes, pointed chins, and warty noses, and who, on top of their shaky demeanors, are constantly associated with evil intentions and selfish motives.

Cunningham (1986) made an interesting discovery after having a group of male undergraduates rate the facial attractiveness of 50 females from college yearbooks and from the yearbook section of a Miss Universe beauty pageant program. Women rated the highest tended to be those with childlike features such as large and widely spaced eyes, prominent cheekbones, high eyebrows, small nose, small chin, and a large smile (Cinderella?).

As far back as 1883, Sir Francis Galton set out to find what made an attractive face attractive in the first place. Using a technique called composite portraiture, he superimposed a large number of faces on a single photographic plate, using very brief exposure times. He ended up with faces for both men and women in which the features of all the faces were averaged, thus eliminating individual differences and peculiarities. As reported in an interesting book by Wilson and Nias (1976), the result was an artistically striking face. With his photographic trickery, Galton was able to show that what we regard as a nice-looking face is somewhat oval-shaped with regular, typical features (Snow White?). A less attractive face is more apt to be one with a surprise or two (the Wicked Witch?).

What is or is not attractive or nice-looking can be significantly affected by the clothes we wear, an idea we turn to next.

What We Wear: Reflections of the Inner Person

How we adorn the body shell in which we live can significantly affect both our self-perceptions and the perceptions others have of us. I had some quite practical lessons about this simple truism during my college days when hitchhiking was my main ticket between the University of Michigan and home. Remembering from my courses in social psychology that people tend to form impressions, particularly first impressions, on the basis of what is immediately observable to them, I made it a point to dress neatly and conservatively on my many thumbing sojourns. I think it is interesting to note that I usually made the trip within about a half hour or so of the time it would have taken me if I had driven the 300 miles myself. I don't know whether to attribute my good fortune to a neat, conservative dress style or to the hopeful look on my face. No doubt both played a part. I frequently asked people why they had stopped. Many replies fell into the, "Well, you looked presentable" category. One man replied, "I don't know—you just looked safe to me." I concluded from my considerable hitchhiking experiences that even if clothes and appearance make a difference nowhere else, they do seem to matter if one plans to thumb his or her way along the road of life.

The clothes we wear are statements about who we are. In order to test this possibility, Rosenfeld and Plax (1977) asked 240 men and women to fill out questionnaires about their preferences and attitudes toward clothing, gave them an extensive battery of personality tests, and then checked for patterns that seemed to go together. Consider some of the major findings: Women who scored high on "exhibitionism" tended to be more radical and liked the idea of showing a little cheesecake, whereas women who wanted to keep themselves well covered were timid, sincere, and had more feelings of inferiority. Exhibitionistic men were characterized as aggressive, outgoing, and confident but relatively unsympathetic and unaffectionate. On the other hand, men who liked to dress with all bases covered had high self-concepts and not surprisingly, were more guarded about revealing things about themselves. As you might guess, men who dressed with an eye to practicality, believing that this was more important than beauty, tended to be inhibited and cautious. For women, these characterizations were reversed. Those women who looked to practicality in dress were clever, enthusiastic, confident, and outgoing. Women who thought that beautiful clothes were more important tended to be more self-centered, independent, and detached. More than we realize, clothes are outer signs of the deeper and sometimes less-conscious feelings we have about ourselves.

Clothes can influence others in subtle but powerful ways. Consider a few interesting examples of how this works. An enterprising research team, for instance, arranged to have a 31-year-old male model approach an intersection crowded with other pedestrians and either obey or violate the traffic signal. An interesting thing happened. When he walked against the red light while dressed neatly in a coat and tie, significantly more people would follow his example in disobeying the stop signal than was the case when he was dressed in plain, everyday work clothes (Lefkowitz, Blake, and Mouton, 1955).

Somewhat similar results were obtained by Bickman (1971) in a novel experiment that involved placing a dime in pay phone return slots and then having men and women in two kinds of dress approach persons using these phones with the following request: "Excuse me, I think I might have left a dime in this phone booth a few minutes ago. Did you find it?" Half of the time, the men wore suits and ties, and the women wore neat dresses and dress coats. The other half of the time, the men wore work clothes, and the women appeared in generally unkempt-looking skirts and blouses. Significantly, more people returned the dime when they were approached by the well-dressed men and women.

Not surprisingly, the clothes that salespeople wear may also affect how much they sell. Young (1979), for example, found that when the salesmen in a men's store wore suits, the average value of their sales was 43% higher than when they wore short sleeves and a tie and was 60% higher than when they wore an open-collar shirt. The seven salesmen in this study were observed over a three-month period in a store that let them dress pretty much as they chose, and every salesman wore each combination on several occasions during that period. Since every salesman increased his sales when wearing a suit, age and experience could not be seen as influencing the sales. Nor were the salesmen with high sales records working in parts of the store with high-priced items because all the salesmen covered the entire store. We cannot conclusively say that the appearance-enhancing effect of suits *caused* the sales increase because other factors may have been at work. For example, the salesmen may have dressed casually when they were not feeling well and may have sold poorly for that reason; or wearing suits may have bolstered their confidence and, hence, their performance. But no matter how we tailor the real explanation, clothes remain an important factor.

Clothes, it seems, are an important component of the self that we project to both ourselves and others. When we dress casually, we usually feel and behave more casually; when we dress formally, we tend to feel and behave more formally. What is on our backs can influence inner feelings and outer behavior. What we wear does matter. We may want others to accept us for who we really are, but who we are is perceived by the beholder as a total package, and clothes, it appears, are the wrappings.

Height Is No Tall Story

Height—or our lack of it—is an aspect of the overall self we present to the world that seems to affect others' perceptions of us more so than it does our perceptions of ourselves. For example, Cash, Winstead, and Janda (1986) found in their survey of the body image perceptions of 2,000 people that 80% of the men and 77% of the women were satisfied with their height. On the other hand, when people evaluate others, height becomes more important. For example, in a study that required 140 corporate recruiters to choose between two hypothetical job applicants having the same qualifications and differing only in height (one man was 6 feet, 1 inch; the other was 5 feet, 5 inches), the shorter man was favored by only 1% of the recruiters; 27% had no preference, and 72% *would hire the tall man* (Kurtz, 1969).

We may even have an unconscious inclination to think that persons in positions of high social status are taller than they really are. An illustration of this is reflected in the findings of Wilson (1968), who conducted a simple research project by introducing a "Mr. England" to five similar groups of college students. To one group, this person was introduced as "a student from Cambridge"; to a second, he was "a demonstrator in psychology from Cambridge"; to the third, "lecturer in psychology from Cambridge"; to another, "a senior lecturer from Cambridge"; and to the last group, "Professor England from Cambridge."

After Mr. England had gone, students were asked to estimate his height to the nearest 1/2 inch, presumably for use in a statistics exercise. As Mr. England climbed the ladder of success, he gained a full 5 inches in the eyes of the students! On the other hand, the course instructor, whose height was also estimated, was perceived to remain the same in height. Perhaps it is not surprising that from 1990 to 1968, the man elected U. S. president was always the taller of the two candidates. It is worth noting that Nixon, Carter, and Reagan (also Ford) are all taller than average for American males, and George Bush, of course, towered over his 1988 presidential rival (and eventual loser), Michael Dukakis, by about 6 inches. Hassel (1974) pointed out the interesting fact that, of the eight presidential assassins since 1835, only John Wilkes Booth could claim average stature. (The average American male, by the way, is 69 inches tall, and the average American female is 63.6 inches [Roberts and Herman, 1986].)

Height, it seems, does make a difference in how we are inclined to perceive others, particularly men. Not only is there an inclination to ascribe more positive attributes to tall men, but there is even a tendency to see men of high social status as taller, bigger, if you will, than they really are. Although there are probably many reasons for why this occurs, one may have to do with the natural tendency to equate greater size with greater power and strength. When you consider that we spend the first ten to 14 years of our lives surrounded by bigger, stronger adults, who can exercise their power and authority in benign and hostile ways, it is not so surprising that we automatically and unconsciously equate greater status with height or height with status. Perhaps the reason this occurred more with men than women is because the men in our lives, by comparison, were usually bigger than the women and *looked* more powerful. It will be interesting to see what happens to perceptions of women's size as they assume more and more positions of power and authority.

Perhaps one of the reasons we tend to equate tallness with superior power and status is because in each of us there resides remnants of the child we once were, a child who spent the first ten years or so of life looking up at, and being dependent on, people who literally were bigger and stronger than us.

If you are a bit shorter than you would like to be, whether you are male or female, it may be well to remember that you don't have to be tall to be *perceived* as tall. As demonstrated by "Professor England," it is the height of our accomplishments and not the height of our bodies that can make the greater difference in how we are perceived.

Weight Weighs Heavily

A steady diet of diet books and a plethora of quick weight loss clinics expanding at a faster rate than most waistlines are symbolic of the massive concern that millions of people have about the pounds they carry. Whereas height is not an issue for the majority of men and women, weight definitely is. Forty-one percent of the men and 55% of the women in Cash, Winstead, and Janda's (1986) survey expressed dissatisfaction with their weight, the majority wishing they had less of it. No other physical characteristic except skin color is so problematic in our society. Just as there is the tendency to perceive leaner, athletically built persons as emotionally tougher and in more control, there is also the inclination to perceive heavier people as weaker and in less control. DeJong and Kleck's (1986) review of literature reveals that, whereas other kinds of physical problems that people suffer are generally attributed to misfortune and elicit a certain amount of sympathy and understanding, excessive body weight is often associated with laziness or lack of will power. Of course, as any thoughtful person is aware, no particular person or group has exclusive rights to laziness or low will power. Unfortunately, however, once a particular stereotype is formed, it is difficult to shake because physique and certain physical characteristics are so intrinsically connected with the identity of persons. Because we tend to see ourselves as we see other people perceiving us, it is not hard to see why and how weight may be associated with self-image difficulties.

There is no simple answer to the problem of being overweight. (You might be interested in estimating the implications of your own weight by determining your "body-mass" index, something easily done by following directions in Figure 4-6). One theory suggests that overweight people are "biologically determined" to be pudgy because their bodies contain an excessive number of fat cells (Nisbett, 1968); another theory suggests that overweight persons are "externals," whose eating is determined by outside cues such as sight, smell, and the taste of food (Schachter and Rodin, 1974). Actually, no *single* theory is able to account for why certain people have weight problems. Rodin's (1981) review points clearly to the idea that onset and degree of excessive weight are determined by a combination of genetic, metabolic, psychological, and environmental factors.

One fact seems clear: It is easy to put on extra pounds but more difficult to take them off. As most weight-conscious people know, 3,500 calories results in about 1 pound of body weight. (The word "calorie," by the way, comes from *calor,* the Latin word for heat. Defined scientifically, a calorie is the amount of heat that will raise the temperature of 1 kilogram of water 1°, from 15° to

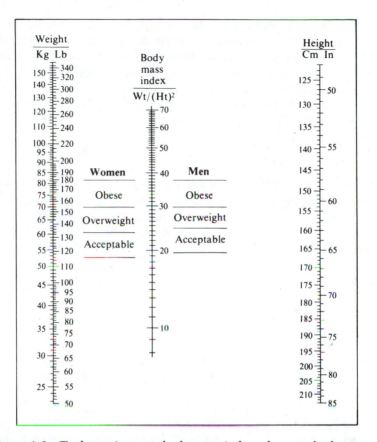

Figure 4-6 *To determine your body-mass index, place a ruler between the body weight (left-hand column) and the height (right-hand column), using either the metric or avoirdupois scales. The body-mass index is the point at which the line connecting the weight and height crosses the body-mass-index column in the middle.*

Copyright © 1978, George A. Bray, M. D.

16° C. Thus, when we use the word "calories," we're referring to invisible units of heat that measure the energy stored in food.) Everything we do involves a certain expenditure of heat and, therefore, of caloric energy. Even sleeping burns calories. For example, one hour's sleep will burn about 50 calories if you weigh about 125 pounds or about 60 calories if you weigh about 150 pounds. Don't, however, rush off to take a nap thinking that you will wake up slimmer and trimmer. We sleep to refurbish the body, not to reduce it.

Whereas one hour's worth of sleep would burn about 60 calories if you weigh 150 pounds, a one-half hour job or brisk walk would burn about 300 calories, which is why exercise is a very fine way to shed extra pounds, particularly if it is aerobic and done at least three to four times per week for 30-minute sessions. You can, by the way, get a pretty good idea about the number of calories burned while walking or jogging 1 mile by multiplying your weight times .73. Not only are more calories burned *while* exercising, but also more calories than usual are burned *after* exercising because one's basal metabolism remains elevated for four to six hours following a workout (Silver, 1985). In addition, there is substantial evidence to show that by enhancing the self's physiology, something that can be helped along by regular exercise and sensible eating, the self's *psychology* can be changed for the better (Hamachek, 1986).

No Close Shaves Here

If you're a man and sport a certain amount of facial hair, you may be happy to know that evidence has been reported in several studies suggesting that greater virility, confidence, sophistication, and maturity are attributed to bearded than to clean-shaven men (Freeman, 1969; Vernis and Roll, 1970). In an effort to study this area in a more controlled way, Pellegrini (1973) enlisted the help of eight men between the ages of 22 and 25 years who were photographed at four different stages: full beard, goatee, moustache, clean shaven. College students, giving their impressions of the men in the photographs, consistently gave higher ratings to the men with the most facial hair. Full-bearded men were generally judged as more masculine, mature, self-confident, and liberal than clean-shaven men. Men with mustaches and goatees fell in between. Perhaps only college students are that favorably inclined toward men with beards, but it was suggested by Pellegrini (a man, by the way) that inside many men "there is a beard screaming to be let out." (It would be interesting to see whether these 1973 results would be any different today. What do you think?)

There is, however, a wide range of opinion among woman about the alleged attractiveness of a facial foliage, so if you're a man, it might be advisable to first check with the lady in your life before tossing out your razor.

Proportions Shape Perceptions

A Gallup poll of 1,037 adult men and women reported by Britton (1988) pointed to an overriding finding: Skinny is on the way out, muscular is on the way in. Women were asked four questions:

> Which of the following physical characteristics describe you best?
>
> Which of the following best describe the kind of body you would like to have?
>
> What do you think men find most attractive in a woman?
>
> What traits best describe the kind of man who is most attractive to you?

Similar questions were asked of men. In answering, each person was free to choose from 50 attributes related to height, weight, breast size, chest and shoulder size, dress size, body tone, body size, hair color and type, eye color, and skin condition.

The first thing noted from the data was that the average man and woman have bodies that are, well, average. He's 5'10" and 172 pounds with a 33-inch waist; she's 5'3" and 134 pounds and wears a size 10 or 12 dress. A startling finding emerging from this survey was that there were so many men and women who *liked* being average. Although women *think* men like them lean, a full 65% of men say that their ideal woman has an average body type; only 18% of men think thin is heavenly.

Men and women are in agreement when it comes to body type—both think that average body proportions are preferable to those with leaner lines. Men and women do disagree, however, about how strong a woman should be. An overwhelming 59% of men like a soft à la Monroe, compared to 20% who are fond of the Fonda look. Regardless of what men want, however, today's woman clearly wants to be stronger. In fact, the more education she has, the more likely it is that she will prefer having a hard body ideal over being a marshmallow. A full 65% of college-educated women want a muscular tone, compared to only 27% of women without a college degree. Britton (1988) quotes the observations of Brett Silverman, who has studied the relationship between body ideals and culture:

> Women today are achieving in ways commonly thought of as masculine, so it's not so strange that they want to be muscular—so they can compete on a masculine level. The new hard-body ideal could be similar to the older drive for thinness, which may have been a way for women to try to look less feminine while becoming more competitive. It's as if achieving women have felt they had to aspire to angular male models in place of womanly curves. Thinness has been the rage in America during times when the women's movement was at its peak—the 1960s and the 1920s. There was even an exercise movement and an outbreak of eating disorders in the '20s—very similar to what's happened lately . . . . But there's a good thing about the new trend: Unlike the fashion for thinness, the trend toward masculinity still allows women to keep their natural curves. It's undeniable that many successful, visible women—Cybill Shepard, Madonna, Kathleen Turner, Anjelica Houston, to name a few—have both a muscular cut and cleavage. (p. 70)

The body alignment that both men and women prefer and are attracted to is neither too small nor too large but more moderately proportioned. When women are asked about the proportions they are attracted to in a man, the majority tend to favor a small waist, small buttocks, moderately sized legs, and broad shoulders (Horvath, 1981; Lavrakas, 1975). If you can picture a Tom Cruise or Smoky Robinson shape here, you understand the idea. Studies of male judgments about female attractiveness fall along similar lines; that is, most men are attracted to females with medium-sized breasts, medium-sized legs and buttocks, and narrow hips (Horvath, 1979; Kleinke and Staneski,

The average man:	Men want to be:	Men think that women want a man:	Women actually want a man:
5' 10" 172 lb. 33-in. waist Medium-width shoulders and chest Hairy or smooth chest (half say each) Lean build Brown eyes Short, straight, dark hair Tanned or untanned (half say each), clean-shaven	5' 11" 171 lb. 33-in. waist Medium-to-broad shoulders and chest Hairy or smooth chest (half say each) Muscular build Brown or blue eyes (half say each) Short, straight, dark hair Tanned, clean-shaven	6' 173 lb. 32-in. waist Broad shoulders Broad chest Hairy chest Muscular build Blue eyes Short, curly, dark hair Tanned, clean-shaven	5' 11" 171 lb. 33-in. waist Medium-to-broad shoulders Hairy chest Muscular build Brown or blue eyes (half say brown, half blue) Short, curly, dark hair Tanned, clean-shaven

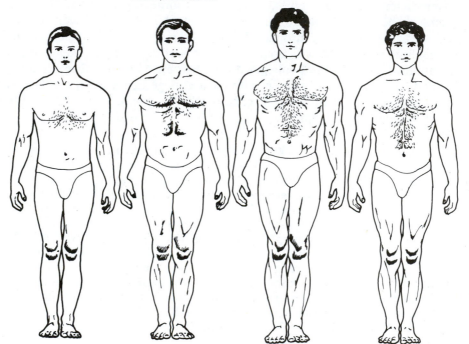

Figure 4-7 *Perceptions of men's proportions.*
From A. G. Britton, "Thin Is Out, Fit Is In." *American Health,*
July/August, 1988, pp. 66–71. Illustration by Nazan Akyavas.

1980). The shape of a Candice Bergen or a Velicia Rechard might fit this image. You may find Figures 4-7 and 4-8 revealing when it comes to assessing what the average man and woman looks like compared to what they want to be and also what men and women think the other looks for compared to what the other really *wants.*

The average woman:	Women want to be:	Women think men want a woman:	Men actually want a woman:
Dress size 10 to 12	Dress size 8	Dress size 8	Full rear, medium-width hips, small-to-medium waist
5' 3 1/2"	5' 4 1/2"	5' 4"	
134 lb.	123 lb.	118 lb.	
Average-sized breasts	Average-sized breasts	Large breasts	5' 4"
Average body type	Average body type	Thin body type	121 lb.
Soft body tone	Muscular body tone	Soft body tone	Medium-sized breasts
Brown eyes	Brown or blue eyes (half say each)	Blue eyes	Average body type
Short, straight, brown hair	Brown hair, wavy and curly: no clear preference for length	Long, wavy blond hair	Soft body tone
Some wrinkles, blemishes or freckles (half have a problem	Smooth, tanned skin	Smooth skin	Blue eyes
Not tanned		Tanned	Long, wavy hair (half say blond, half brown)
			Smooth, tanned skin

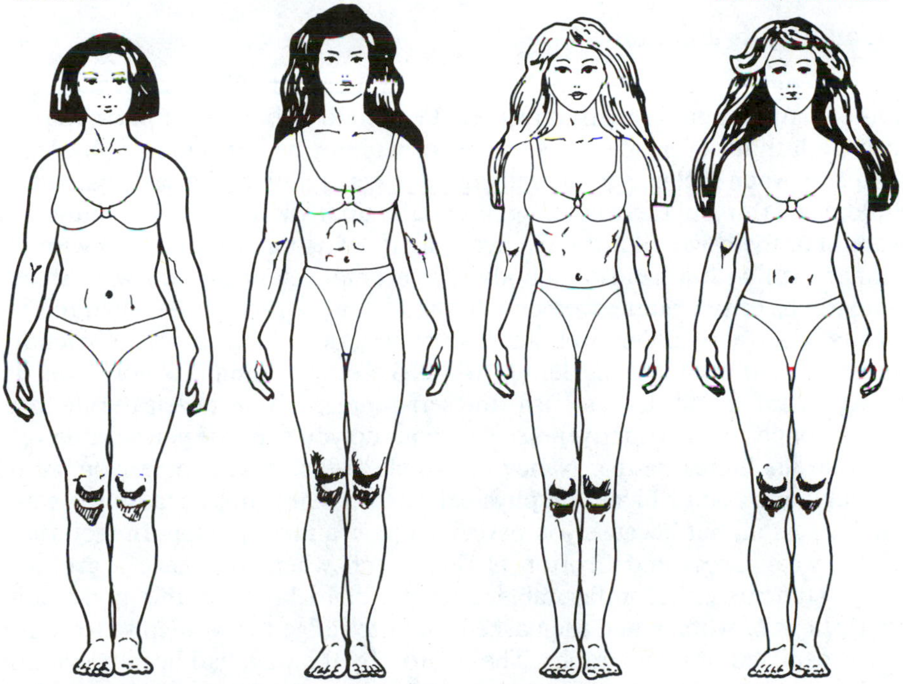

Figure 4-8 *Perceptions of women's proportions.*
From A. G. Britton, "Thin Is Out, Fit Is In." *American Health,* July/August, 1988, pp. 66–71. Illustration by Nazan Akyavas.

What we perceive as attractive in the opposite sex is sometimes linked to our personal values or personality. For example, Beck, McLean, and Ward-Hull (1976) found that women who enjoyed physical activity and participated in sports tended to prefer the large-sized man, whereas women who had more "traditionally feminine" interests in home and family tended to prefer the moderate-sized man. Overall, male smallness was favored more by socially reserved women. Wiggens, Wiggens, and Conger (1968) found evidence to support the old idea that in judging the attractiveness of women, some men are "breast" men, "buttocks" men, or "leg" men. Perhaps it is no surprise that men who tend to be extraverted and exhibitionistic—who have a greater need to be the center of attention—are the ones who are most likely to prefer large-busted women.

Overall, however, both men and women prefer moderate body proportions in each other. Body assemblies like those of Arnold Schwarzenegger or Dolly Parton, although pleasant enough to look at, are not what most people would rate as attractive in the usual sense of the word. Whether you are a man or a woman, it would appear that a large chest has less appeal than a small derriere, which is, you might say, the bottom line in this matter.

Personality Is a Factor

Physical considerations are not the only attributes that affect our own perceptions of another person's attractiveness. Personality also plays a part. You and I can both think of people we know who may not be particularly physically attractive, when it comes to measuring up to certain objective criteria, but we would never think of them as being physically unattractive. Without our being aware of it, their overall attractiveness might have more to do with a winning manner than with a handsome body. For example, suppose you were shown photographs of two young women who had been judged, unbeknown to you, as equally attractive. One woman, Nancy, was described to you as friendly, energetic, helpful, and considerate, while the other woman, Nicole, was described as unfriendly, lazy, selfish, and self-centered. Your task is to rate them in terms of physical attractiveness. To whom do you suppose you would probably give the higher rating, Nancy or Nicole? Like most people, you would probably rank Nancy higher on physical attractiveness not because she was a prettier person, but because you perceive her as a nicer person. In fact, that's exactly what Gross and Crofton (1977) found when they gave a group of college students either unfavorable, average, or highly favorable personality descriptions of women and then asked them to judge the women's attractiveness as depicted in photographs. The photos, by the way, had been previously rated by others as being attractive, average, or unattractive. You can see in Table 4-1 that the more favorable the personality description, the higher the ratings of physical attractiveness. For example, the most physically unattractive women received higher ratings when their personality descriptions were positive than they did when their descriptions were merely average or unfavorable. On the other hand, the women who had been judged as most attractive, but whose personality descriptions were unfavorable received lower ratings than other attractive women whose descriptions were average or more favorable. The essential message from this research: Perceptions of physical attractiveness are not just a function of physical features, but of personality characteristics, as well.

Table 4–1

Previous Ranking of Photographs	Mean Physical Attractiveness Rating with Personality Description		
	Unfavorable	*Average*	*Favorable*
Unattractive	2.78	3.47	4.80
Average	4.50	4.91	6.04
Attractive	5.13	5.73	5.90

Adapted from A. E. Gross and C. Crofton, "What Is Good Is Beautiful." *Sociometry,* 1977, *40:* 85–90.

Elephant Man, the extraordinary film that dramatically portrayed the life of John Merrick, who was grossly disfigured by a congenital disease (fibromatosis), illustrates, I think, the central point of this section. I remember that moment in the film when the audience was exposed to their first sight of this utterly misshapen man, twisted and distorted beyond recognition, it seemed. There was a group gasp, so shocking was the initial sight. By the end of the film, however, Merrick's appearance was a secondary matter and barely important as the deeper qualities of his character emerged in the audience's consciousness—his gentle way, his sensitivity, and his keen intelligence. First impressions were revised and fears dispelled as the noble content of Merrick's inner being surfaced from behind a grotesque mask. How he looked became less important than who he was.

A Final Thought

Each of the factors we've just examined—dress preferences, height, weight, beards, body proportions, and personality—has the potential for affecting self-concept development directly or indirectly, If, for example, we view certain aspects of our body or appearance with pleasure or displeasure, the affects of that perception will have a direct effect on us. No middle person is involved. On the other hand, when others respond to us, their response will be influenced, at least to some extent, by what they see on the surface, especially when meeting us for the first time or during the early phases of a relationship. The people who come in and out of our lives give us all sorts of verbal and nonverbal signals about who they think we are and what kind of person they believe us to be, influenced, initially at least, by their perceptions of the physical self we present. Life is a mirror; it reflects back whatever we present to it. Each reflection is a small building block used in the construction of one's concept of self.

So far, we've focused on how certain body types, pace of growth, and physical attributes are associated with perceptions of physical attractiveness. Let's turn our attention now to how attractiveness (or lack of it) can influence our own or others' behavior.

Physical characteristics can sometimes play a big part in affecting how others respond to us.

Reprinted by permission of UFS, INC.

ATTRACTIVENESS AND ITS EFFECTS ON BEHAVIOR

When we make judgments of other people, most of us would like to feel that we are not unduly swayed by such considerations as whether a person has a pretty face or a plain one, a handsome profile or an ugly one, or such factors as weight, height, body proportions, or manner of dressing. It is as though we would like to be free of these surface features so that we can see the "real" person who resides at a deeper level. If, for example, a random sample of men and women were asked what it is about the opposite sex that attracts them, most would cite such qualities as "personality," "intelligence," "character," "sincerity," and the like ahead of "looks" or physical attractiveness. In fact, appearance and physical attractiveness are usually ranked somewhere in the middle (Chaiken, 1986).

Most of us probably agree that it is probably not such a good idea to judge a book by its cover. That's what we say. But that's not necessarily what we do.

We Are Attracted to the Attractive

Covers are more important than we may like to believe. Although on one level we say that physical attractiveness shouldn't play a big part in our feelings toward others, it may be more crucial than we realize. For example, in an interesting test of this idea, Walster and her colleagues (1966) randomly matched 376 men and 376 women—all college students—for a blind date and then asked them whether they would date the same person again. Both sexes gave significantly more preference to dates who had previously been rated (unknown to the participants) as physically attractive. In fact, the more physically attractive the date, the more he or she was liked. Although the researchers looked hard for other factors, based on the results of personality tests, that might possibly predict the attraction, they could find none. It was not intelligence, masculinity, femininity, dominance, submissiveness, sensitivity, sincerity, or the like but only physical attractiveness that determined whether or not a couple liked each other and actually repeated their date.

Two subsequent studies, each with different college-aged populations, found that the partner's *perception* of the physical attractiveness of the date corresponded higher with the "desire to date again" response than did any of the other perceived characteristics of the partner, including similar "interests," "character," "personality," and so on (Brislin and Lewis, 1968; Tesser and Brodie, 1971). In light of these findings, it is not surprising that attractive males and females were the most likely to be chosen as dates from a commercial video-dating service (Green, Buchanan, and Heuer, 1984).

Attractiveness not only influences who likes whom well enough to date again, but also is a fairly good predictor of which couples will stay together the longest. White (1980), for example, found that physical attractiveness was a very important factor in long-term relationships; but in this case, it was the *similarity* of the attractiveness of the two people that was crucial. Pairs who were well matched in physical attractiveness were more deeply involved with each other some nine months after beginning the relationship than were couples who differed from each other in physical attractiveness.

It is clear from the research on dating couples that attractiveness plays a powerful role in attracting people to each other and in keeping them together for longer periods. Attraction dynamics might also help explain why . . .

A Man May Work Harder for a Beautiful Woman's Approval

Found in our social folklore is the idea that a beautiful woman can pretty much wrap a man around her little finger. Some imaginative research done by Sigall and Aronson (1969) showed that there may be a kernel of truth to this belief.

A group of college men were interviewed by a woman who was made to appear physically attractive in one phase of the study and physically unattractive in the second phase. In the unattractive phase, a naturally beautiful woman was given a somewhat oily complexion; was dressed in sloppy clothes; and wore a frizzy, blonde wig. Posing as a graduate student in clinical psychology, she conducted the interviews so that half the men received highly favorable evaluations and the other half highly unfavorable evaluations. How did the men respond? When the woman was homely, the men were somewhat indifferent to whether they received good or poor evaluations, and in both cases, they liked her a fair amount. However, when she was beautiful, they liked her a great deal when they got favorable evaluations, but when they got unfavorable evaluations, they disliked her more than under the other condition. There was also another interesting finding. Although the men who were evaluated negatively by the beautiful woman said they didn't like her, they nonetheless expressed considerable interest in talking to her again in a future experiment! Apparently, the negative feedback from the attractive woman was so important to their sense of self-worth and self-esteem that they wanted the opportunity to change her mind.

Thus, it may be that a man's self-worth is more vulnerable to an attractive woman's negative evaluation because, even though he doesn't like her, he may believe that her perceptions of him could be accurate. Remember, one of the perceptions of attractive people is that they are smart and capable (Dion, 1986). Hence, he may be motivated to try to change her evaluation because there is the lingering suspicion that she may have a point, and he wants a shot at changing her mind so that he can feel better about himself.

It would be interesting to see what the results would be if Sigall and Aronson's design was turned around so that women were getting the positive and negative evaluations from attractive and unattractive men. What are your hunches about this? Do you think women would reflect similar behaviors, or not?

All in all, the voluminous research done in the area of physical attractiveness points to a clear conclusion . . .

Attractive People Are Better Liked

Physical attractiveness plays an important role in determining who likes whom in both the short and long run. And this is not a dynamics that is apparent only between men and women. Consider the findings from a study by Dion, Berscheid, and Walster (1972), who showed a group of college students photographs of three college-aged people—one was physically attractive, the second was average, and the third was unattractive. The students then rated each of the three people in the photographs on 27 different personality traits and also assessed the subjects' probability for future happiness. The results showed that physically attractive people were assigned by far the most desirable traits and given the greatest chance for happiness, and this was true whether men were rating men, men were rating women, women were rating men, or women were rating women. Apparently, our penchant for liking physically attractive people cuts across sex boundaries. We are inclined, it seems, to like attractive people regardless of our sex *or* theirs.

Attractiveness dynamics are apparent even among nursery school children. For example, after having children rated on a physical attractiveness scale by independent judges, Dion and Berscheid (1974) administered a sociometric test to find out who liked whom among the children themselves. The physically unattractive boys were viewed as more aggressive and were not as well liked as the physically attractive boys; in fact, unattractive boys were more frequently mentioned when the children were asked to name classmates that "scared them."

It seems that whether we are young or old, male or female, when we perceive another person as attractive we tend to like that person more, at least initially. One of the reasons for this may be our inclination to associate almost automatically certain positive personality traits with an attractive appearance. For example, in the Dion, Berscheid, and Walster (1972) study mentioned previously, the respondents consistently reported that they thought that good-looking people were generally more sensitive, kind, interesting, strong, poised, sociable, and exciting than were less attractive people.

These are glowing adjectives, indeed. You might think that if we see attractive people as having these lofty qualities we would be inclined to view ourselves as somewhat plain by comparison. Not so, as discovered by Marks, Miller, and Maruyama (1981) when they asked people to compare themselves to several other people on a variety of traits. Participants consistently rated attractive people as being more similar to themselves. Could it be that there is a general tendency to view ourselves as being more like attractive people than unattractive people? If so, our positive regard for those who are good-looking may not be due so much to their physical attractiveness as to their perceived similarity to us. When glowingly describing that attractive other person, we may be secretly revealing traits that we feel belong to us.

We may also like attractive people because we recognize that being associated with them helps us look good. For example, when Sigall and Landy (1973) asked people to evaluate a man seated with either an attractive or unattractive woman, he received far more positive ratings when seen with the attractive woman. Kernis and Wheeler (1981) found that the effect of being associated with an attractive person is even more powerful when one is seen as a friend of that person, as opposed to being merely seen with him or her.

Thus, it may be that we like attractive people more because we see them as having many positive qualities, these qualities being more or less similar to what we see in ourselves. Also, because we look good (or maybe better, at least) when connected in some way with attractive people, we may like them more because of what we get by association. (We see this, for example, among political candidates, who are particularly fond of having their pictures taken with popular movie stars and athletes.) On the other hand, if we see a particular attractive person as having positive characteristics but are not able to see some of those same traits in ourselves, and are not able to be associated with that person to get some of the run-off benefits, we might feel twinges of jealousy or envy. These may be inner signals of low self-worth, signs that we might be underestimating ourselves or overestimating the other person.

It Helps to Be an Attractive Student

Attractiveness can even affect who makes the honor roll. Consider the outcomes of a study by Clifford and Walster (1973), who arranged to have 400 fifth-grade teachers evaluate the same report card. Each card itemized the students' grades in eight subjects over six grading periods, along with a report of their performance in personal development and work and study habits. Posted in the corner was a picture of a child, one of an attractive boy or girl or one of an unattractive boy or girl. The results clearly indicated that when the children were good-looking, the teachers were more apt to guess that they had higher IQs, had parents who were interested in their education, and got along better with their peers than did the less attractive children.

Even more alarming results were obtained when Dion (1972) gave 200 female teacher-candidates written descriptions of alleged misbehaviors committed by either a seven-year-old boy or girl, along with the child's photograph clipped to the corner. When the report included a photograph of an attractive child, the students were inclined to excuse the misdeed or see it as an isolated incident. For example, a misbehaving, but attractive, child might elicit a comment such as "She appears to be a charming little girl . . . she plays well with everyone, but like anyone else, a bad day can occur. Her cruelty . . . need not be taken too seriously." But when the same report was attached to the photograph of an unattractive child, the raters were more inclined to assume that the naughtiness was a typical incident and a reflection of generally bad behavior. Although the attractive little girl was still seen as "charming," in spite of misbehaving, an unattractive girl, guilty of the same misbehavior, received comments such as "I think the child would be quite bratty and would be a problem to teachers . . . would probably try to pick fights . . . all in all, a real problem." The women in Dion's study also believed that unattractive children were characteristically more dishonest than their attractive classmates.

There is even evidence suggesting that attractive female students may get higher grades *because* they are attractive. To test this idea, Landy and Sigall (1974) prepared two essays, one well written, the other disorganized and simplistic in its ideas. They made 30 copies of each essay and attached pictures, supposedly of the author, to 20 of them: an attractive woman in ten cases, an unattractive one in the other ten. Ten essays in each group had no picture. The essays were then graded by 60 male college students. Attractive writers swept the ratings across the board, and they most surpassed the unattractive writers when the poor essays had been *deliberately prepared* by the researchers as examples of poor responses! Of course, we have to keep in mind that these were males evaluating females, which may have had a natural biasing effect, and also, they were not professional teachers, who we hope would be more swayed by the form of the response than of the writer.

The results of the three studies we've just examined serve to remind us, particularly if we are teachers, that our perceptions of beauty may unfairly shape our expectations for performance, especially if we harbor the implicit assumption that the attractive students are usually more able.

Good looks help out not only in the classroom but in the courtroom as well, another way that attractiveness can influence behavior.

Good-Looking Defendants Are Given More Breaks

Although justice is supposed to be blind, there is evidence to suggest that beauty in the courtroom may affect the final verdict. As a test of this, Sigall and Ostrove (1975) asked 120 male and female college students to read the account of a crime committed by a woman, whose picture was attached, and then suggest an appropriate punishment. One group of students read a report with a photograph of a beautiful woman attached; another group read the same account but with a picture of a homely woman attached; still another group of students read the same report without knowing what the defendant looked like.

An analysis of the suggested punishment revealed that at least the lack of beauty didn't *increase* the length of sentence; that is, the homely offender fared no worse than her anonymous counterpart. The attractive woman, however, did get special treatment. When the crime was a $2,200 burglary, she got off easy, but when the crime involved inducing a middle-aged bachelor to invest $2,200 in a nonexistent organization, beauty hurt her case. In this instance, the attractive woman received a slightly stiffer sentence than either the homely woman or the anonymous defendant. In other words, if attractive women use their looks to help them commit a crime, their beauty will hurt them in court. In other cases, their attractiveness may help shorten their prison stay. Physical attractiveness *can* work in an offender's favor—which is of course, why lawyers want the defendants they represent to look their scrubbed-up, dressed-up best in court. This can, however, work to the detriment of the accused if that person is viewed as having used his or her beauty in devious ways for illicit gains.

Even rapists may get a break if they are good looking. Using 60 male and 60 female college students as mock jurors, Jacobson (1981) found that when the alleged rapist was unattractive, 82% of the "jurors" found him guilty, as compared to only 57% when he was attractive. When the attractive suspect was convicted, he received an average jail term of ten years, versus nearly 14 years for the homely suspect.

A good many controlled studies have tested the effect of attractiveness or unattractiveness on jurors' decision making, and time and again, the findings indicate that when attractive defendants are found guilty, they are more likely to receive lighter sentences than unattractive defendants involved in similar crimes (Michelini and Snodgras, 1980). This also tends to be true in actual courtrooms, a trend uncovered by Stewart's (1980) analysis of relationships between sentencing and attractiveness of 67 defendants: Although 75% of the unattractive defendants received prison sentences, only 45% of the attractive defendants were recipients of a similar fate. Crime may not pay, but it apparently doesn't cost quite so much if the crook is good-looking.

Possible Social Hazards of Attractiveness

Although attractiveness has it benefits, it can also have its downside, for example, there is a good bit of data suggesting that attractive people are often perceived as vain, snobbish, materialistic, and unsympathetic (Cash and Duncan, 1984; Dermer and Thiel, 1975).

Attractiveness also can interfere with one's popularity. In a study involving college students, for example, it was found that the most-attractive students were often the *least* liked students. The most-popular students, on the other hand, were attractive but were not the *most* attractive (Krebs and Adinolfi, 1975). In addition, there is evidence suggesting that handsome men are more apt to be avoided by other men. Along these same lines, moderately attractive women are more likely to be satisfied with their social lives than are their more- or less-attractive peers (Reis, Nezlek, and Wheeler, 1980). It has also been found that among elementary school boys—sixth graders in this case—those who are very attractive have less influence over their peers than those who are less attractive (Langlois and Stephan, 1981). In other words, moderate amounts of physical attractiveness may enhance one's social position, but too much may get in the way because of the possible feelings of resentment, jealousy, or envy it sometimes triggers in others.

Although we might expect that attractive people would have higher self-esteem than their less-attractive counterparts, the relationship between these two characteristics is weak and inconsistent (Maruyama and Miller, 1981). A possible reason for this is that attractive people, as children and adults, receive so much attention and praise that they tend to wonder whether it's really true: "People only seem to pay attention to the way I look and fail to see what I can do." (The late Marilyn Monroe frequently commented that people were more interested in her looks than in her ability as an actress.) Less attractive individuals, on the other hand, may be more likely to assume that any praise that comes their way is sincere and deserved.

As a way of testing these possibilities, Major, Carrington, and Carnevale (1984) arranged to have a group of attractive and unattractive undergraduates write a short essay that was evaluated by another student. One segment of students was led to believe that the evaluator would be watching them as they wrote, while another segment was led to believe that the evaluator would not see them. The experiment was rigged so that all subjects received a positive evaluation from an opposite-sex observer. An interesting find emerged.

Attractive subjects were more likely to accept and believe the positive evaluation if they were not seen by the evaluator, while unattractive subjects felt the positive evaluation was deserved if they had been observed. How can these findings be explained? In real life, most social interactions take place with others who *are* aware of how we look. Less attractive people may receive less praise, but they give considerable weight to the praise they do receive. More attractive individuals are recipients of more praise but tend to discount it because they doubt its sincerity. For that reason, attractiveness and self-esteem are not strongly related. Remember, however, that this is a generalization based on group results. As in all psychological research involving people, there are many individual exceptions.

Attractiveness as a Trigger for Self-Fulfilling Prophecies

How we treat people affects how they come to think about themselves. Our inclination to associate positive qualities with a physically attractive person may work something like a self-fulfilling prophecy; that is, we see in that individual what we expect to see and then behave toward that person in a manner consistent with the expectation, which helps to make it come true.

Evidence for this phenomenon emerged from a cleverly designed study by Snyder, Tanke, and Berscheid (1977). In one-half of the study, a group of college-aged men were each given a biographical information form with a picture of an attractive woman attached. In the second half, another group of men were each also given a biographical information form but with a picture of an unattractive woman attached. After examining the information, each man filled out a questionnaire designed to assess the extent to which his impression of the woman reflected general stereotypes linking physical attractiveness and personality characteristics. Then, each man engaged in an unstructured conversation over an intercom system (microphone and earphones) with the woman he thought corresponded to the biographical form and picture given to him. The researchers were interested in finding out whether or not the men's conception of who they were talking to influenced their conversations.

Remember, the woman a man talked to and the woman in the picture were different, he only thought they were the same. Consider the results. To begin with, men who thought they would be talking to an attractive woman were more apt to have preconceptions about her being more sociable, poised, sexually warm, and outgoing than men who thought they were going to talk to the unattractive woman. An interesting and telling find emerges. Men who interacted with women whom they considered to be physically attractive were more sociable, sexually warm, interesting, bold, outgoing, and socially adept than men interacting with supposedly unattractive women. And even more important, the women who were perceived (unbeknown to them) to be physically attractive *actually behaved in a more friendly, likable, and social manner than the women perceived as unattractive.* In other words, the stereotypes that the men had that derived from the pictures truly functioned as self-fulfilling prophecies. The men behaved toward each woman in a manner that was consistent with how they expected attractive or unattractive women to behave, thus encouraging each woman to behave as expected and, in turn, helping the expectations to come true.

The revealing aspect of this evidence is that such preferential treatment could be the beginning of a cycle of a self-fulfilling prophecy. That is, if people are treated well or poorly, as the case may be, it affects how they perceive themselves and how they perceive their personal qualities. Thus, attractive children and adults may come to think of themselves as "good" or likable because they are continually treated that way. Conversely, unattractive people—young and old—may begin to think of themselves as "bad" or unlikable because they are continually treated that way. Ultimately, people may begin to behave in a manner consistent with this self-concept, a way that is consistent with how they were treated to begin with.

Whatever our role may be in working with others, it would probably be a good idea to keep a watchful eye on our preferences for this person or that one so that we aren't caught in the trap of believing, as seems easy to do, that only that which is beautiful is good.

IN PERSPECTIVE

Beginning with Hippocrates' observation 2,500 years ago that humankind fell into two general categories—the long thins and the short thicks—there have been ongoing efforts to classify humans according to various body types and to associate those types with certain personality characteristics. For the most part, those efforts have failed. We humans are simply too complex to fit neatly into stereotypic associations between specific body structures and certain personality characteristics. This is not to say that there are no relationships between certain body types and personality. Research has shown that relationships do exist but only in very general ways and with many exceptions to any specific findings.

Body build and physical appearance do not cause us to behave in one way or another. Rather, these components of our being affect, to some extent, how others respond to us, which may very well influence our behavior. There is hardly a thing about our physical appearance whether it be height, weight, hair color, eyes, or the clothes we wear, that does not in some way influence how others see us. This is not so surprising. In the absence of knowing more about a person's inner feelings, or family history, or values, or intellectual capacity, we make judgments based on what we see. Generally speaking, the less well a person knows us, the more likely that person is to judge us on the basis of external appearances, a phenomenon that is apparent even among nursery school children. However, as relationships between people develop—if they develop at all—physical appearance becomes less crucial and personality variables play an increasingly larger part.

Not only is appearance important in eliciting either positive or negative feedback, but so, too, is the rate at which a person grows. Physical maturity at an early age is a distinct advantage for a boy, and research suggests that these advantages are likely to persist into his adult years as well. True enough, his slower-growing peers eventually catch up with him physically but not necessarily in certain psychological gains. The outcome of early or late maturation for girls is more difficult to predict, although the general weight of the evidence suggests that fast-growing girls, like fast-growing boys, have more advantages and are somewhat better off then their slower-growing counterparts.

Research clearly and consistently points to the idea that attractive people, whether in school, in the courtroom, or in the dating scene are viewed as more likeable, more generally laudable in more ways than less attractive people. Part of the reason for this lies in our inclination to see ourselves as more like attractive people than unlike them, which suggests that our positive regard for good-looking people may be due as much to their perceived similarity to us as it is to their physical attractiveness. Thus, when we applaud the virtues of attractive people, we may be privately applauding our own. Nobody ever said that our self-perceptions were unbiased.

How we feel about ourselves is related to how we feel about our bodies. Although having a nice figure or a well-proportioned body does not guarantee a healthy, positive self-concept, research does suggest that the feedback we receive from the world around us is determined, at least in part, by our physical shell. More than we may be aware, we seem inclined to put each other in certain personality categories based on physical appearance.

Actually, the body image we have depends less on what we're born with and more on what we do with what we have in the first place. If we don't like it, body image is something we can modify. Sensible eating habits, a regular exercise program, and good grooming can work wonders in assisting any person toward a more positive body image and self-concept.

Appearance does not necessarily make a person, but it does, for better or for worse, tend to reflect the person who lives within. The first thing we notice about another person is how he or she looks, in terms of overall appearance. If we like what we see, it can help to set in motion a positive cycle of expectations and responses that enhances growth-promoting interactions. On the other hand, if our initial impressions are more negative, we may unwittingly start a negative cycle of expectations and responses that leads to growth-inhibiting interactions. By remaining alert to our inclination to judge people—"type" them, actually—on the basis of physical appearance, we stand a better chance of short circuiting some of the wrong ideas we sometimes arrive at about people before we really get to know them. This seems particularly necessary for those of us who work in people professions such as psychology, counseling, social work, nursing, and teaching, areas where our success and effectiveness depends heavily on the having accurate perceptions of those we deal with.

In sum, body image is an important aspect of one's self-image. A person's physical self is the outer shell that houses all his or her inner feelings, and as such, it deserves to be recognized and understood for its potential for eliciting social responses that contribute to an individual's overall concept of self.

QUESTIONS FOR STUDY, REVIEW, AND REFLECTION

1. For the next day or so, pay close attention to how other people's general appearance affects your response to them, including those you know well and those you know barely at all. When it comes to physical appearance, what is it about others that affects you the most?

2. If asked why certain personality characteristics have come to be associated with endomorphic, mesomorphic, and ectomorphic body types, how would you respond?

3. What does research say about the psychological advantages and disadvantages associated with being a fast- or slow-maturing boy and girl? What affect did your own adolescent pace of growth have on your overall development?

4. Why are height and weight so influential in shaping people's perceptions of each other? What parts do your own height and weight play in your feelings about yourself?

5. What does research suggest about what men and women prefer in each other when it comes to body proportions and size?

6. How can a person's personality influence our perceptions of that person's physical attractiveness? If asked to explain the dynamics of this relationship, how would you respond?

7. Can you explain why physical appearance plays a more important part in the earlier phases of knowing someone than in later phases?

8. If you were to make a presentation about why it is that so many positive qualities are associated with attractive people, what five or six major points would you include?

9. Attractiveness also has its hazards. Can you explain what some of these might be?

10. Can you explain how the phenomenon of self-fulfilling prophecies could be related to perceptions of attractiveness or unattractiveness?

REFERENCES

Beck, S. B., McLean, P. M., and Ward-Hull, C. I. "Variables Related to Women's Somatic Preferences of the Male and Female Body." *Journal of Personality and Social Psychology,* 1976, *34:* 1200–1210.

Berscheid, E., and Walster, E., "Physical Attractiveness," in L. Berkowitz (Ed.), *Advances in Experimental Social Psychology,* Vol. VII, New York: Academic Press, 1974.

Bickman, L. "The Effect of Social Status on the Honesty of Others." *Journal of Social Psychology,* 1971, *85:* 87–92.

Brislin, R. W., and Lewis, S. A. "Dating and Physical Attractiveness: A Replication." *Psychological Reports,* 1968, *22:* 976.

Britton, A. G. "Thin is Out, Fit is In." *American Health,* July/August, 1988, pp. 66–71.

Brodsky, C. M. *A Study of Norms for Body Form-Behavior Relationships.* Washington, D. C.: The Catholic University of America Press, 1954.

Brooks-Gunn, J., and Petersen, A. C. (Eds.). *Girls at Puberty: Biological and Psychological Perspectives.* New York: Plenum, 1983.

Brooks-Gunn, J., and Warren M. P. "How Important Are Pubertal and Social Events for Different Problem Behaviors and Contexts?" Paper presented at the biennial meeting of the Society for Research in Child Development, Kansas City, April, 1989.

Cash, T. F., and Duncan, N. C. "Physical Attractiveness Stereotyping Among Black College Students." *Journal of Social Psychology,* 1984, *122:* 71–77.

Cash, T., and Pruzinsky, T. (Eds.). *Body Image.* New York: Guilford Press, 1990.

Cash, T. F., Winstead, B. A., and Janda, L. H. "The Great American Shape-Up." *Psychology Today,* April, 1986, pp. 30–37.

Caskey, S. R., and Felker, D. W. "Social Stereotyping of Female Body Image by Elementary Age Girls." *Research Quarterly,* 1971, *42:* 251–255.

Chaiken, S. "Physical Appearance and Social Influence," in C. P. Herman, M. P. Zanna, and E. T. Higgins (Eds.), *Physical Appearance, Stigma, and Social Behavior: The Ontario Symposium,* Vol. 1. Hillsdale, N. J. Lawrence Erlbaum, 1986.

Clausen, J. "The Social Meaning of Differential Physical and Sexual Maturation," in S. Dragastin and G. H. Elder, Jr., (Eds.), *Adolescence in the Life Cycle.* New York: Wiley, 1975.

Clifford, M. M., and Walster, E. "Effect of Physical Attractiveness on Teacher Expectations." *Sociology of Education,* 1973, *46:* 248–258.

Cunningham, M. R. "Measuring the Physical in Physical Attractiveness: Quasi-Experiments on the Sociobiology of Female Facial Beauty." *Journal of Personality and Social Psychology,* 1986, *50:* 925–935.

DeJong, W., and Kleck, R. E. "The Social Psychological Effects of Overweight," in C. P. Herman, M. P. Zanna, and E. T. Higgins (Eds.), *Physical Appearance, Stigma, and Social Behavior: The Ontario Symposium,* Vol. 3. Hillsdale, N. J.: Lawrence Erlbaum, 1986.

Dermer, M., and Thiel, D. J. "When Beauty May Fail." *Journal of Personality and Social Psychology,* 1975, *31:* 1168–1176.

Dion, K. "Physical Attractiveness and Evaluation of Children's Transgressions." *Journal of Personality and Social Psychology,* 1972, *24:* 207–213.

Dion, K. "Stereotyping Based on Physical Attractiveness: Issues and Conceptual Perspectives," in C. P. Herman, M. P. Zanna, and E. T. Higgins (Eds.), *Physical Appearance, Stigma, and Social Behavior.* Hillsdale, N. J.: Lawrence Erlbaum, 1986.

Dion, K., and Berscheid, E. "Physical Attractiveness and Peer Perception Among Children." *Sociometry,* 1974, *37:* 1–12.

Dion, K., Berscheid, E., and Walster, E. "What Is Beautiful Is Good." *Journal of Personality and Social Psychology,* 1972, *24:* 285–290.

Fisher, S. *Development and Structure of the Body Image,* Vols. 1 and 2. Hillsdale, N. J.: Lawrence Erlbaum, 1986.

Freeman, D. G. "The Survival Value of the Beard." *Psychology Today,* 1969, *3:* 36–39.

Green, S. K., Buchanan, D. R., and Heuer, S. K. "Winners, Losers, and Choosers: A Field Investigation of Dating Initiation." *Personality and Social Psychology Bulletin,* 1984, *10:* 502–511.

Gross, A. E., and Crofton, C. "What Is Good Is Beautiful." *Sociometry,* 1977, *40:* 85–90.

Gross, R. T., and Duke, P. M. "The Effect of Early vs. Late Maturation on Adolescent Behavior." *Pediatric Clinic of North America,* 1980, *27:* 71–77.

Hamachek, D. "Psychology and Development of the Adolescent Self," in J. F. Adams (Ed.), *Understanding Adolescence: Current Developments in Adolescent Psychology,* 4th ed. Boston: Allyn and Bacon, 1980.

Hamachek, D. "Enhancing the Self's Psychology by Improving Fitness Physiology." *Journal of Human Behavior and Learning,* 1986, *3:* 2–12.

Hammond, W. H. "The Status of Physical Types." *Human Biology,* 1957, *29:* 223–241.

Hassel, C. V. "The Political Assassin." *Journal of Political Science and Administration,* 1974, *7:* No. 4.

Horvath, T. "Correlates of Physical Beauty in Men and Women." *Social Behavior and Personality,* 1979, *7:* 147-151.

Horvath, T. "Physical Attractiveness: The Influence of Selected Torso Parameters." *Archives of Sexual Behavior,* 1981, *10:* 21–24.

Humphreys, L. G. "Characteristics of Type Concepts with Special Reference to Sheldon's Topology." *Psychological Bulletin,* 1957, *54:* 218–228.

Jacobson, M. Reported in "Newsline," *Psychology Today,* October, 1981, p. 17.

Jones, M. C., and Mussen, P. H. "Self-Conception, Motivations, and Interpersonal Attitudes of Early- and Late-Maturing Girls." *Child Development,* 1958, *29:* 491–501.

Kernis, M. H., and Wheeler, L. "Beautiful Friends and Ugly Strangers: Radiation and Contrast Effects in Perception of Same-Sex Pairs." *Personality and Social Psychology Bulletins,* 1981, *7:* 617–620.

Kleinke, C. L., and Staneski, R. A. "First Impressions of Female Bust Size," *Journal of Social Psychology,* 1980, *110:* 123–134.

Krebs, D., and Adinolfi, A. "Physical Attractiveness, Social Relations, and Personality Style." *Journal of Personality and Social Psychology,* 1975, *31:* 245–253.

Kretschmer, E. *Physique and Character,* 2nd ed. W. J. H. Spratt trans. New York: Harcourt, Brace and World, 1925.

Kurtz, D. L. "Physical Appearance and Stature: Important Variables in Sales Recruiting." *Personnel Journal,* December, 1969, pp. 981–983.

Landy, D., and Sigall, H. "Beauty is Talent: Task Evaluation as a Function of the Performer's Physical Attractiveness." *Journal of Personality and Social Psychology,* 1974, *29:* 299–304.

Langlois, J., and Stephan, C. W. "Beauty and the Beast: The Role of Physical Attractiveness in the Development of Peer Relations and Social Behavior," in S. Brehm, S. Kassin, and F. Gibbons (Eds.), *Developmental Social Psychology,* Oxford: Oxford University Press, 1981.

Lavrakas, P. J. "Female Preferences for Male Physiques." *Journal of Research in Personality,* 1975, *9:* 324–334.

Lefkowitz, M., Blake, R., and Mouton, J. "Status Factors in Pedestrian Violation of Traffic Signals." *Journal of Abnormal and Social Psychology,* 1955, *51:* 704–706.

Lerner, R. M., and Foch, T. T. (Eds.). *Biological-Psychological Interactions in Early Adolescence: A Life-Span Perspective.* Hillsdale, N. J.: Lawrence Erlbaum, 1987.

Lerner, R. M., Lerner, J. V., and Tubman, J. "Organismic and Contextual Biases of Development in Adolescence: A Developmental View," in G. R. Adams, R. Montemayor, and T. P. Gullota (Eds.), *Biology of Adolescent Behavior and Development.* Newbury Park, Calif.: Sage, 1989.

Major, B., Carrington, P. I., and Carnevale, P. D. J. "Physical Attractiveness and Self-Esteem: Attributions for Praise from an Other-Sex Evaluator." *Personality and Social Psychology Bulletin,* 1984, *10:* 43–50.

Maltz, M. *The Magic Power of Self-Image Psychology.* New York: Pocket Books, 1970.

Maness, B. "What Do You Really Know About Exercise?" *Today's Health,* November, 1975, p. 17.

Marks, G., Miller, N., and Maruyama, G. "Effect of Targets' Physical Attractiveness on Assumptions of Similarity." *Journal of Personality and Social Psychology,* 1984, *41:* 198–206.

Maruyama, G., and Miller, N. "Physical Attractiveness and Personality," in B. Maher (Ed.), *Advances in Experimental Research on Personality,* Vol. 10. New York: Academic Press, 1981.

Michelini, R. L., and Snodgras, S. R. "Defendant Characteristics and Juridic Decisions." *Journal of Research on Personality,* 1980, *14:* 340-350.

Miller, A. G. "Role of Physical Attractiveness in Impression Formation." *Psychonomic Science,* 1970, *19:* 241–243.

Mussen, P. H., and Jones, M. C. "The Behavior-Inferred Motivation of Late- and Early-Maturing Boys." *Child Development,* 1958, *29:* 61–67.

Nisbett, R. E. "Determinants of Good Intake in Human Obesity." *Science,* 1968, *159:* 1254–1255.

Pellegrini, R. J. "Impressions of the Male Personality as a Function of Beardedness." *Psychology,* 1973, *10:* 29–33.

Peskin, H. "Influence of the Development Schedule of Puberty on Learning and Ego Functioning." *Journal of Youth and Adolescence,* 1973, *2:* 273–290.

Petersen, A. C. "Those Gangly Years." *Psychology Today,* September, 1987, pp. 28–34.

Reis, H. T., Nezlek, J., and Wheeler, L. "Physical Attractiveness in Social Interaction." *Journal of Personality and Social Psychology,* 1980: *38:* 604–617.

Roberts, J. V., and Herman, C. P. "The Psychology of Height: An Empirical Review," in C. P. Herman, M. P. Zanna, and E. T. Higgins (Ed.), *Physical Appearance, Stigma, and Social Behavior.* Ontario Symposium, Vol. 3. Hillsdale, N. J.: Lawrence Erlbaum, 1986.

Rodin, J. "Current Status of The Internal-External Hypothesis for Obesity." *American Psychologist,* 1981, *36:* 362–372.

Rosenfeld, L. B., and Plax, T. G. "Clothing as Communication." *Journal of Communication,* 1977, *27:* 24–31.

Schachter, S., and Rodin, J. *Obese Humans and Rats.* New York: Halsted, 1974.

Sheldon, W. H. *Atlas of Men: A Guide for Somatotyping the Adult Male at All Ages.* New York: Harper and Row, 1954.

Siegel, O. "Personality Development in Adolescence," in B. B. Wolman (Ed.). *Handbook of Developmental Psychology.* Englewood Cliffs, N. J.: Prentice-Hall, 1982.

Sigall, H., and Aronson, E. "Liking an Evaluator as a Function of Her Physical Attractiveness and Nature of the Evaluations." *Journal of Experimental Social Psychology,* 1969, *5:* 93–100.

Sigall, H., and Landy, D. "Radiating Beauty: Effects of an Attractive Partner on Person Perception." *Journal of Social Psychology,* 1973, *28:* 218–224.

Sigall, H., and Ostrove, N. "Beautiful but Dangerous: Effects of Offender Attractiveness and the Nature of the Crime on Juridic Judgment." *Journal of Personality and Social Psychology,* 1975, *31:* 410–414.

Silver, N. "How to Eat More and Weigh Less." *American Health,* March, 1985, pp. 110–113.

Snyder, M., Tanke, E. D., and Berscheid, E. "Social Perception and Interpersonal Behavior: On the Self-Fulfilling Nature of Social Stereotypes," *Journal of Personality and Social Psychology,* 1977, *35:* 656-666.

Staffieri, J. "A Study of Social Stereotype of Body Image in Children." *Journal of Personality and Social Psychology,* 1967, *7:* 101–104.

Staffieri, J. "Body Build and Behavioral Experiences in Young Females." *Developmental Psychology,* 1972, *6:* 125–127.

Stewart, J. E., II. "Defendant's Attractiveness as a Factor in the Outcome of Criminal Trials: An Observational Study." *Journal of Applied Social Psychology,* 1980, *10:* 348–361.

Tesser, A., and Brodie, M. "A Note on the Evaluation of a 'Computer Date.'" *Psychonomic Science,* 1971, *23:* 300.

Vernis, J., and Roll, S. "Primary and Secondary Sex Characteristics." *Psychological Reports,* 1970, *26:* 123–126.

Walker, R. N. "Body Build and Behavior in Young Children: I. Body Build and Nursery School Teachers' Ratings." *Monographs of the Society for Research in Child Development,* 1962, *27:* No. 3.

Walker, R. N. "Body Build and Behavior in Young Children: II. Body Build and Parents' Ratings." *Child Development,* 1963, *34:* 1–23.

Walster, E., Aronson, E., Abrahams, D., and Rottman, L. "Importance of Physical Attractiveness Dating Behavior." *Journal of Personality and Social Psychology,* 1966, *4:* 508–516.

Weatherly, D. "Self-Perceived Rate of Physical Maturation and Personality in Late Adolescence." *Child Development,* 1964, *35:* 1197-1210.

White, G. "Physical Attractiveness and Courtship Progress." *Journal of Personality and Social Psychology,* 1980, *39:* 660-668.

Wiggens, J. S., Wiggens, N., and Conger, J. C. "Correlates of Heterosexual Somatic Preference." *Journal of Personality and Social Psychology,* 1968, *10:* 82–90.

Wilson, G., and Nias, D. *The Mystery of Love: The Hows and Whys of Sexual Attractiveness.* New York: Quadrangle/The New York Times Book Co., 1976.

Wilson, P. R. "Perceptual Distortion of Height as a Function of Ascribed Academic Status." *Journal of Social Psychology,* 1968, *63:* 361–365.

Wright, M. R. "Body Image Satisfaction in Adolescent Girls and Boys: A Longitudinal Study." *Journal of Youth and Adolescence,* 1989, *18:* 71–84.

Young, E. Reported in "Newsline," *Psychology Today,* August, 1979, p. 29.

Chapter 5

Self-Concept as Related to Parent-Child Relationships, Family Experiences, and Genetic Considerations

PROLOGUE

Meet four youngsters.

Katie is a friendly, happy 14 year old who experiences her world as a warm and exciting place. She is a slightly above-average student, participates in girls' athletics, comes from a loving home, and has many friends. She seems in all ways a normal, happy human being.

Thomas is a 16 year old high school dropout who never did very well in school, who has never seemed to like himself or others very well, and who always seems to be picking himself up from one fight after another. His mother works odd jobs; his father, a high school dropout himself, is frequently unemployed and drinks heavily.

Stephanie is an intelligent, creative ten year old who consistently achieves below her potential. Both of her parents are college graduates and are deeply concerned about her lethargic attitude about school. They try to be encouraging and supporting without being pushy, but so far nothing has seemed to work.

Eric is an extremely active eight year old who cannot seem to sit still. Although he appears to be a happy enough child, he causes both himself, his teacher, and others trouble because of his disruptive behaviors. He has an older brother and sister, both of whom are self-disciplined youngsters doing well in school. His mother and father are concerned, loving parents who seem at their wits end in knowing what to do.

There are the inevitable questions: How did these youngsters get this way? What determines the course of a child's emotional, social, and mental development? Is the outcome of a child's developmental years the by-product of the child-rearing styles of parents? Or is it due primarily to accidents of heredity, the roulette wheel of genes and chromosomes? Is it the quality of family life, the impact of friends, the stresses of our culture, or is it that a child is simply "born that way?" What is it that causes one child to be outgoing and another passive, friendly or aggressive, hyperactive or self-disciplined, focused on achievement and future goals or mired in self-depreciation and an attitude that says "I can't?" Why do some children, although faced with deep emotional hardships, bend but never break, while others seem to bend and crumble in the face of what seems to be far lesser stress?

There are no easy answers to complex questions like these. However, once we know something about a child's parentage and environmental circumstances, we are at least in a position to make some informed predictions about what may happen to individual lives. Perhaps it would help to think about it this way: Children are like sponges; they soak up everything in their environments. They do so innocently and uncritically. The words they hear, the sights they see, the experiences they are part of, all of these events contribute to the emotional foundation on which they build a concept of self that guides their lives. Remember, however, that like a sponge, what a child soaks up will depend on what is in the surroundings. A sponge living in polluted, contaminated water will absorb a quite different experience than one living in clear, pristine conditions. Similarly, a child who lives with rejection, put downs, too little love, and too much punishment will absorb a quite different emotional environment than a child who lives with acceptance, affirmations, adequate love, and fair discipline.

Thus, what a child becomes depends both on what he or she is born with in terms of genetic potential and on the environmental conditions within which he or she is raised. A child's nature—the stuff of its genes and chromosomes—cannot be separated from its nurture, and in this chapter, we will examine inputs of each of these factors to a child's self-concept formation.

The way children are raised, whether by natural parents or other caretakers, constitutes an important aspect of nurture's contribution to how they feel about themselves and others. When we look at ourselves closely and honestly, we are able to see traces, and sometimes strong reflections, of our parents' behaviors and attitudes that we have unconsciously assimilated into our own psyches. The methods used by parents to affect their children's lives have changed in some interesting ways over the years, something we want to look at first.

EARLY IDEAS ABOUT HOW
CHILDREN SHOULD BE RAISED

There has never been a scarcity of viewpoints about the best way to raise children. Although 2,300 years ago there were no psychologists around to dispense advice to desperate parents, a couple of Greek philosophers, Plato and Aristotle, had, among their many other views, ideas about how to raise children, too (Jensen and Kingston, 1986). Plato, for example, fearing that most adults in his time were too corrupt and unfit for child rearing, advocated that all children be separated from their parents at an early age. He further advocated that these children be raised by the State and evaluated at different times to see whether they would be best suited as workers, managers, military leaders, or legislators. (Sounds a bit more like a colony of bees than a society of humans.)

Plato's student, Aristotle, was somewhat more advanced in his thinking, believing, as he did, that only those individuals who were the most capable should be raised by the State and prepared as future leaders. He felt that family life was too important a source of personal and social stability to be overlooked. In addition, Aristotle further recognized that the individual differences among parents' child-rearing techniques was necessary to accommodate the needs of children, who were quite different from each other.

Actually, there are some interesting similarities between the views of Plato and Aristotle and our contemporary ideas about child rearing. Plato, for example, felt that parenting styles that were overly restrictive or excessively permissive were detrimental, a fact borne out by contemporary research. Aristotle recognized that children's uniqueness should be considered when implementing child-rearing plans and that the family unit was an important source of social stability.

On the whole, there is general agreement that treatment of children in past centuries was much less humane than we know it to be in present times. Aries (1962), for example, found that the concept of childhood hardly existed during the Middle Ages. Children were dressed as adults, were viewed as miniature adults, and were involved in adult activities such as music and education. Childhood games and play were virtually nonexistent. Being a kid wasn't much fun.

With the help of another philosopher, Englishman John Locke, the seventeenth century saw an increased emphasis on the importance of childhood and the child's place in the family (Maccoby, 1980). In Locke's view, not only were children *not* miniature adults, but they were born void of thoughts, ideas, and sin. They were, in effect, blank slates, and parents were encouraged to be patient, thoughtful, and truthful in dealing with a child's curiosity. Physical punishment was deemed unnecessary if parents behaved as they should.

During the eighteenth century, the emotional importance of childhood was helped along even further by the writings of still another philosopher,

Frenchman Jean-Jacques Rousseau (1974), who promoted the ideas that children should be allowed to grow as nature dictates and that they should not be taught before they are ready to learn, ideas that are now commonplace. In Rousseau's view, young children are not ready or able to reason or to form judgments; thus, to be strict and demanding would only arouse hostility. Like Locke, Rousseau stressed parental understanding and thoughtful care, thereby deemphasizing the need for stringent disciplinary practices. In the big picture, there were more signs of, and cultural permissions for, explicit expressions of parental gentleness and love during the eighteenth century.

Developmentalism and Calvinism in Early America

Sunley (1955) has suggested that views like Locke's and Rousseau's fall under the heading of what is called "Early Developmentalism." Basically, this represents an orientation to child rearing that promoted the idea that children went through necessary developmental stages and that punishment was a cruel consequence for failing to fit certain adult preconceptions about their behavior. In this framework, parents were seen as facilitators of a child's growth and not as creators.

Developmentalism ideas carried into early nineteenth-century America and competed directly with viewpoints about raising children that grew out of Calvinism. During the early 1800s, for example, some of the major ideas about raising children grew out of particular assumptions that certain groups had about human nature and its depravity. Parents influenced by Calvinistic thinking believed that newborns were already damned as a result of "original sin" and, as a consequence, both evil and rebellious. (You can see how diametrically opposed this belief is to Locke's point of view.) Thus, locked into a perception of a child's innate evilness, parents of good intention saw little choice but to *defeat* the child, to bend the child's satanic will with hard work and frequent and often severe punishment. The idea was, in a very real sense, to break the child's will so that he or she would submit to parents and to God. Consider a few examples of how this was done:

> One mother, writing in the *Mother's Magazine* in 1834, described how her sixteen-month-old girl refused to say "dear mamma" upon the father's order. She was led into a room alone, where she screamed wildly for ten minutes; then she was commanded again, and again refused. She was then whipped, and asked again. This kept up for four hours until the child finally obeyed. Parents commonly reported that after one such trial the child became permanently submissive. But not all parents resorted to beatings to gain this end. One mother spoke of "constant thorough gentle drilling," which consisted partly of refusing to give the child an object just out of its reach, however much it cried. Another mother taught submission and self-denial at one and the same time by taking objects away from the child. Strictness in diet and daily routine was apparently frequently an accompaniment to obedience training. (Sunley, 1955, p. 161)

In Chapter 2, we discussed how and why people behave in terms of what they "believe" to be true. The preceding excerpt is a striking example of how a belief—in this instance, in a child's innate sinfulness—served as the rationale for treating a child harshly. Maccoby (1980) notes that this idea was so prevalent among certain factions at the time that two states—Connecticut and Massachusetts—passed laws legalizing the death penalty for chronically disobedient children. There is no record I am aware of indicating whether any child was ever inflicted with this punishment, but it does reflect the extent to which deeply held beliefs about what is, or is not, good or right can promote unreasonable and cruel behaviors.

The attitude about the "evilness of the child" was around for a long time and in fact was still apparent during the early 1900s. As the Calvinist view was gradually diluted by developmentalist ideas about children and new approaches to child rearing and as damnation was no longer a foregone conclusion, the focus of parenting slowly changed. It became the parent's responsibility to keep the child from *learning* sin, a refocusing that had dramatic effects on child-rearing practices and attitudes. These attitudes about how children learn to be sinful and what parents could do to combat these evil tendencies are no better illustrated than in Wolfstein's (1951) analysis of the advice given to parents in a 1914 edition of the U. S. Children's Bureau pamphlet *Infant Care*. Wolfstein made the following observations about what mothers were told at that time:

> The infant appeared to be endowed with strong and dangerous impulses. These were notably auto-erotic, masturbatory, and thumb-sucking. The impulses "easily grow beyond control" and . . . "children are sometimes wrecked for life." The mother was warned that the baby may achieve the dangerous pleasures to which his nature disposes him by his own movements or he may be seduced into them by being given pacifiers to suck or having his genitals stroked by the nurse. The mother . . . is further told that masturbation "must be eradicated . . . and that the child should have his feet tied to opposite sides of the crib so that he cannot rub his thighs together." Similarly for thumb-sucking "the sleeve may be pinned or sewed down over the fingers of the offending hand for several days and nights. . . ." (pp. 15–25)

Although we may now wonder how thumb sucking and masturbation could be viewed with such alarm, if we believed, as some parents in the early 1900s did, that these were behaviors that could "easily grow out of control," we can begin to understand why parents were concerned about these things.

Of course, not all parents behaved as the 1914 pamphlet suggested, but there was, nonetheless, a general emotional attitude about how to bring up children that made the interactions between parents and children a bit more impersonal than is the case today. This factor is reflected about as thoroughly as it can be in a 1928 book written by the famous behavioristic psychologist John B. Watson, *Psychological Care of Infant and Child.* Consider a few typical passages from that book, which parents, eagerly looking for guidance, read in the late 1920s:

There is a sensible way of treating children. Treat them as though they were young adults. Dress them, bathe them with care to circumspection. Let your behavior always be objective and kindly firm. Never hug and kiss them. Never let them sit in your lap. If you must, kiss them once on the forehead when you say good-nite. Shake hands with them in the morning. Give them a pat on the head if they have made an extraordinarily good job of a difficult task. Try it out. In a week's time you will find how easy it is to be perfectly objective with your child and at the same time kindly. You will be utterly ashamed of the mawkish, sentimental way you have been handling it.

In conclusion, won't you then remember when you are tempted to pet your child that mother love is a dangerous instrument? An instrument which may inflict a never healing wound, a wound which may make infancy unhappy, adolescence a nightmare, an instrument which may wreck your adult son or daughter's vocational future and their chance for marital happiness. (pp. 81– 82, 87)

The Watsonian parent, as you can see, was relatively free of the usual emotional expressions and overt affectional contacts that have come to be accepted as a normal part of our contemporary child-rearing culture. Although parents of the early twentieth century were encouraged to care for and love their children, they were reminded to retain a certain air of detachment and objectivity. It was not easy to shake the idea, built up for centuries, that children were undeserving of too much attention or love (they were evil and had to be broken), which would spoil them (they could learn to be evil).

As time went on, the basic tenants of Developmentalism were extended by new ideas about raising children. The first complete turnabout of the Watsonian trend was Ribble's *The Rights of Infants* (1943), in which she asserted that depriving children of such basic human interactions as fondling, hugging, kissing, and other forms of body contact was as serious as denying them nourishment or sunshine. She further maintained that these interactions, often lumped together as "tender loving care," were necessary for the physical, intellectual, and emotional growth and well-being of any child. Support for Ribble's position came fast. A new "softer," warmer approach became more popular. The ideal home or school in the 1940s and early 1950s was organized around greater acceptance of children's needs for gratification and more opportunities for freedom and self-expression. Allowing children to express more of their own feelings and needs became the thing to do. Indeed, Spock's very influential edition of *Baby and Child Care* (1947) not only advocated these practices in infancy, but encouraged their extension into the child's developmental years as well.

However, by the mid-1950s the pendulum was beginning to swing back again. For example, comparing the changes in child-rearing practices from 1940 to 1955 in his later edition of *Baby and Child Care* (1957), Spock stated, "Since then a great change in attitude has occurred, and nowadays there seems to be more chance of a conscientious parent's getting into trouble with permissiveness than with strictness." Those opposed to softer and more permissive modes of child rearing are fond of pointing to the 1960s and early 1970s as examples of what can happen to youth when toughness is missing and firm discipline lacking. Halleck (1972), for example, hypothesized that because of the more relaxed, permissive approach to child rearing in the 1940s and 1950s, we turned out a generation of spoiled, greedy youth who were unable to tolerate much frustration without showing an infantile response. Hence, there arose such phenomena as the irreverent and so-called "hippie" movement; assorted temporary, explosive takeovers of college and university administrative offices; loud, sometimes volatile, protests against the Vietnam War; and, of course, an enormous civil rights uprising, which in various ways continues today. Of course, the other side of this coin is that these events are examples of what can happen when children are raised in a manner that encourages them to question authority rather than to fear it, to express their feelings rather than suppress them. There is no simple explanation for why the youths of any particular generation behave as they do, nor should we act as though there is.

Whatever the case, the 1960s and early 1970s were marked by a continual tension between the adult world and that of the child and adolescent. It was as if the child-rearing culture was caught in the middle of the toughness and firmness it had practiced for hundreds of years and the softness and permissiveness with which it had been experimenting.

Contemporary Trends

Although contemporary approaches to child-rearing are not returning to heavy-handed discipline, there are indications suggesting that parents' attitudes toward child-rearing are less easy going than in the 1940s and early 1950s and less ambivalent about an approach, which seemed to be the case in the 1960s and early 1970s. If anything, the current emphasis is on being understanding but firm rather than being too permissive or excessively harsh. If, for example, three-year-old Jeffrey is frightened by loud thunder, instead of a parent responding with, "Now stop that crying. There's nothing to be afraid of, it's just a loud noise," a parent now is encouraged to try to understand the child's *perceptions* of what is happening and respond with something like, "I know that loud thunder can be scary—come over and sit by me for a minute" or "Ooh, that is loud isn't it? What does it sound like to you?"

The emphasis on understanding the child is not a sign that we are returning to a permissive child-rearing ethic. With delinquency and adult crimes on the rise and a return to a more-conservative political-social climate, there seems to be little patience these days for philosophies that talk only about children's freedoms and rights without also emphasizing their obligations and responsibilities. Indeed, as we will see later in this chapter, children who tend to do well in school and to have high self-esteem are more apt to have parents who are firm rather than permissive.

Today's parents are advised to be more sensitive not only to their children's feelings but to their own feelings as well. Whereas earlier approaches to child rearing encouraged parents to focus on their children's behavior, contemporary

Being a firm parent has its hazards.
Reprinted by permission of Universal Press Syndicate.

modes encourage and teach a greater awareness of the underlying feelings that may be motivating the behavior in the first place. Earlier in this chapter, for example, we saw how parents in the early 1900s were advised to eradicate masturbation by whatever means possible before it "grows out of control and wrecks children for life." Contrast that advice with the contemporary offering to parents by Seymour and Rhoda Fisher, psychiatrist and psychologist, in *What We Really Know About Child Rearing* (1976):

> If your own values and religious beliefs make you feel you cannot tolerate [masturbation], face up to that fact squarely. It will probably be less confusing and ultimately less disturbing to the child if you openly and directly prevent him

from masturbating than if you resort to sneaky strategies to stop him. . . . If intellectually you see no reason why you should disapprove of masturbation, but find that when your children play with their genitals it upsets you and results in your "indirectly" stopping them (for example, trying to distract them) face up to the fact that part of you is opposed to masturbation. It then makes sense for you to keep an eye on yourself and to screen out all the sneaky disapproving acts that you can. When you are tempted to communicate that masturbation is potentially dangerous, restrain yourself. When you are about to launch into an elaborate stratagem for distracting your child from his genitals, stop yourself. Your resolve will probably not prevent him from sensing some of your disapproval, but it may help by decreasing the number of irrational messages about sex with which he has to cope. It is almost impossible to conceal from your kids how you feel emotionally about any particular issue. (p. 103)

Notice that parents are not told that they should or should not stop their children's masturbation but rather they are advised to pay attention to their own convictions and feelings and to deal with the issue directly and openly. This acknowledges what child development research has made increasingly clear over the years: Children learn not only from adult verbal messages, but also from the emotional signals that adults transmit unconsciously through their behaviors, moods, and hidden meanings. For example, most of us can tell within a minute or so of being with someone to whom we are emotionally close whether or not something is wrong with that person. The words may be missing, but body language is loud and clear. It is a language we learn at a very young age in order to understand our environment and to protect ourselves from it if necessary. When it comes to how children learn, an old adage comes to mind, "More things are caught than taught."

Contemporary parents are advised to be firm but fair, to be less fearful of using their parental power, but to couple this power with healthy dosages of parental love and understanding. Fifty or more years ago, parents seemed to feel that the way to cure the fault was to attack the child. Times have changed. I think today's parents are generally more receptive to the idea that if anything is to be attacked it is the underlying problem. A disease is cured by finding its cause, not flailing at its symptoms.

There seems to be little doubt about the idea that what children become is very much influenced by how they are raised, which brings us to an important question.

WHAT INFLUENCES PARENTS TO "PARENT" THE WAY THEY DO?

Unlike lower animal life, there is nothing to suggest that human parents instinctively know "how to parent." Some new parents are not even sure how to *hold* a baby, much less how to raise it. Indeed, once pregnancy is confirmed, many new parents-to-be go to special classes just to learn how to *have* a baby. (I was once one of those parents, so I know what I'm talking about.) Because raising children is much too complex to run by a simple instinctual system, there are at least three basic influences that affect parent-child relationships: (1) experiences with one's own parents, (2) one's socioeconomic status, and (3) the child's personality. Let's briefly examine each of these factors.

Experiences with One's Own Parents

It is no surprise that those who were our primary caretakers have a major impact on our own parenting behavior. We are not only witnesses to their child-rearing methods but also recipients, both good reasons for being more or less like them in raising our own children. Depending on how things went in our growing years, this may be good news for some but bad news for others.

You might get some feeling for the extent of your parents influence in your life by looking at how closely your ideas about children resemble theirs—or not, as the case may be—in such key areas as how children should behave, the kind of religious exposure they should have, the value they should place on education, the way they should be disciplined, and so on. Speaking of discipline, Blackwelder and Passman (1986) found remarkable similarities in how that was handled in families spanning three generations. Although, to be sure, there were some individual exceptions, the overall conclusion was that more often than not a family's disciplinary style had roots that went back as deep as three generations.

In a similar vein, Harris (1959), in his early study of the backgrounds of normal children, observed that what happened to the mothers as children (fathers were not included in this study) was also happening to their own children, and what was happening to their parents was also happening to them as parents. He found, for example, that mothers who felt close to their own mothers and who were reasonably satisfied with their mother's child-rearing methods and attitudes were likely to use those methods as a guide to raising their own children. Another group of mothers, however, had strong, negative feelings toward their mothers—usually because those mothers were seen as excessively controlling, strict, and interfering—and they made conscious decisions to do their parenting differently. Unfortunately, this was frequently expressed by going too far the other way and having too few rules and being too lenient.

Along this line, Spock (1971) made the interesting observation that his own mother, who bore five children between 1903 and 1913, rebelled very much against the stern Victorian propriety of her parents and offered her own children a more balanced diet of firmness and permissiveness. Just as there are certain parents who, as a result of being raised too dictatorially as children, decide to allow their own children more freedom, there no doubt are still other parents who, because they were given so little guidance as they grew up, choose to exercise more control over their children's lives. It is as if they look back and see that they could have profited from more direction in their *own* lives as they were growing up and do not wish to make the same mistake of being too permissive.

The continuity of parenting practices from one generation to the next is seldom a conscious process and is always a matter of degree. Through the very powerful and daily process of unintentional teaching, parents pass on to their children those fundamental child-rearing attitudes transmitted to them by their own parents. What happens between children and their parents during their developmental years will greatly influence, for better or worse, their own behavior as parents later on.

Influence of Parents' Socioeconomic Position

One of the things that make people different from each other in all societies is their *socioeconomic status* (SES). Actually, this is a label for a combined index that lumps together people's education, income, and occupation, which gives us an idea of an individual's overall SES position. Thus, a high SES person is well educated, has a relatively high income, and has a high-status occupation, usually in the professional, managerial, or business-owner ranks; a low SES person has less education, has a relatively low income, and is in the unskilled or semiskilled labor market.

Sociological research has shown that there are fairly clear differences in parenting practices among families at different points on the SES continuum (Hess, 1970; Kohn, 1977; Willerman, 1979; Zussman, 1977). (Remember, we are talking here about families as a group at any particular point on the SES scale. There are many individual variations of healthy and unhealthy child-rearing approaches among families *within* a particular grouping.)

Child rearing occurs within a social context, and particular parenting behaviors and attitudes are associated with different SES groupings. Consider four rather consistent differences that have been noted between high and low SES parents, differences, by the way, that have been found for both black and white families:

1. Higher SES parents talk to their children more, use complex language, and reason with them more. Lower SES families do less of these things.

2. Higher SES parents tend to show more explicit warmth and affection to their children. Lower SES parents are less demonstrative in these ways.

3. Higher SES parents tend to stress happiness, creativity, ambition, independence, curiosity, and self-control. Lower SES parents are more likely to stress obedience, respect, neatness, cleanliness, and staying out of trouble.

4. Higher SES parents tend to be more democratic and to be either permissive or authoritative, to use induction (that is, point out the effects of a child's actions on others or ask the child how she or he would feel in the other's shoes), and to be aware and responsive to their children's point of view. Lower SES parents tend to be more controlling, power-assertive, authoritarian, and arbitrary in their discipline, and they are more likely to use physical punishment.

It would not be accurate to conclude that parents' SES position is the *cause* of either positive or negative self-concept development in children. Rather, it would be more accurate to say that parents within certain SES groupings have developed particular behavior patterns that are somewhat consistent with their educational backgrounds and occupation. Kohn (1963), for example, theorized that adults develop certain patterns of behavior that facilitate job performance, behaviors that are then reflected in the way they treat their children and in the way they expect their children to behave. Consider it this way: People in high-status jobs tend to be self-directed. They know that their success depends on their own skill, initiative, and perseverance, and they are more likely to deal with ideas and interpersonal relationships than with physical objects. Thus, in dealing with their children, they are more likely to use the very skills they use in their jobs—reasoning, negotiation, and positive reinforcement—and to emphasize self-reliance.

On the other hand, the psychosocial conditions of lower SES people are more subject to the shifting moods of the economic climate, perhaps the strength of their unions, and the current demands for their skills, conditions that create stress and a low sense of personal control over one's life. Thus, in raising their children, they are more likely to reflect feelings of helplessness, low self-esteem, and frustration, which, over time, their children adopt, through identification as their own feelings.

Although these are generalizations that would be difficult to apply to individual cases, the point we want to remember is that all children are raised within a certain socioeconomic milieu shared by their parents and many others like them. Children raised in comfortable, roomy middle-class neighborhoods with lawns to play on experience a quite different climate of values, attitudes, and parenting behaviors than those raised in tense, crowded tenement buildings with the street as their playground. Once one becomes part of a certain SES position, it is difficult to escape either its physical reality or the mentality that governs it. It would not be accurate to say that children who *have* more (more money, opportunity, status, healthy parenting, and so on) are always the ones who *become* more. However, we can say with greater accuracy that children who *have* more, in the way of a higher SES position, have a *greater likelihood* of becoming more, in terms of opportunities for doing something positive with their lives and feeling better about themselves.

So far, we have discussed how both one's child-rearing history and socioeconomic status can influence one's parenting style. As parents, we are not only *actors,* but we are *reactors,* which is why . . .

A Child's Temperament Has a Strong Impact

Raising a child is a two-way street. New research strongly suggests that although we play an important part in shaping children, they shape *us* as well. For example, Betty is viewed by those who know her as a "natural mother." She enjoys being a parent and seems composed and in command of that role. Even when her 18-month-old son, Brian, is cranky and irritable, she is able to deal with him calmly and with affection.

On the other hand, Betty's neighbor, Kate, seems always to be in a state of frustration and tension. She seems impatient with her 20-month-old daughter, Kim, and is easily angered by her; and late in the evening, she appears distracted and depressed.

Betty and Kate are similar in many ways. Both are regarded as stable, competent adults, untroubled by financial pressure, and participants in good marriages. The difference between Betty and Kate as mothers lies not in *their* personalities but in those of their *children.* Mary's son, Brian, is a contented child—easy to care for, sleeping and eliminating on schedule; generally responsive and pleasant, he offers his parents plenty of positive feedback for their efforts in his behalf. In contrast, Kim seems always cranky and irritable, cries easily, and appears unreceptive to even the most heroic efforts to calm and amuse her. In sharply different ways, each mother is being influenced and shaped by her child's temperament and behavior. From the very beginning, parents' child-rearing approaches depend greatly on the nature of the child born to them, not just on some innate strength—or weakness—buried deep in the parental breast.

Children begin shaping their parents from the time they are born. For example, one particularly striking behavioral difference among newborns that usually has an immediate effect on parents is their response to cuddling. Schaffer and Emerson's (1964) study of 37 newborns revealed that there they could be divided into two groups: *cuddlers* and *noncuddlers.* Mothers of cuddlers said things like "He just cuddles right into you"; "She cuddles right back"; and "He'll let me cuddle him for hours." Mothers of noncuddlers, on the other hand, said things like "Try to cuddle him and he'll just kick and thrash, and if you persist he'll begin to cry"; "She won't allow it—she just fights to get away." As you might gather, mothers of cuddlers felt satisfied and warmly attached to their babies, while mothers of noncuddlers were more inclined to feel frustrated and to wonder what was wrong. Is it difficult to imagine which of those two groups of mothers might feel less satisfied and perhaps be less patient with their infants?

In their studies of more than 200 children from the time they were infants until they were seven years old, Thomas and Chess (1977) found that babies show distinct individual differences in temperament during the first week of life that was independent of their parents' handling or personality styles. They found, for example, both remarkable differences and constancies among these children in characteristics such as mood, responsiveness to people, attention span, persistence, and adaptability to new situations.

Two-thirds of the hundreds of babies studied fell into one or another of three categories: *easy, difficult,* and *slow to warm up.* The easy children, about 75 percent of the sample, were happy, regular in sleeping and eating habits, and not easily upset. The difficult children (about 10 percent) were often fussy, fearful of new people and situations, intense in their reactions, and irregular in sleeping and feeding habits. The slow to warm up children (about 15 percent) were relatively fussy and inactive and tended to withdraw or react negatively to novel situations, although their reactions became more positive with experience. By age seven years, more children in the "difficult" group had developed serious emotional problems than those in the other two groups.

It is altogether likely that the parents of these hard-to-manage children sometimes responded to their behavior with frustration and anger, thus increasing the irritability that the children had in the first place. An excellent example of how children influence their parents is found in a study by Buss (1981), who measured the activity levels of 117 children at age three and again at age four years. When the children were five years old, they were placed in an experimental setting in which either their mothers or their fathers watched as they performed a battery of cognitive tasks. Parents were encouraged to assist in whatever way they chose. Parents of active children got into frequent power struggles with their children, tended to intrude physically, and generally had a difficult time establishing good working relationships. In contrast, relationships between parents and less active children were more peaceful and harmonious. Although it is not possible to say exactly which comes first, an active parent or an active child, a peaceful parent or a peaceful child, it is clear that each acts on the other to draw out the characteristics that were there in the first place.

Another example, although tragic, of how children can influence the behavior of their parents can be found in the case histories of abused children. Of all the infant's characteristics, the one that researchers find most predictably to invite abuse is low birth weight. Klein and Stern (1971), for example, examined the hospital records of 51 abused children and found that nearly one-fourth of them had weighed less than 6 pounds at birth—over three times as many as one would expect to find in a random sampling of newborns. The underdeveloped newborn often violates the common parental expectations that the baby will be attractive and lovable. Sometimes it is neither. Feeding disturbances are common, and these babies are more irritable and fussy, and in addition, slower in muscular development, speech, and socialization during the first two years. They are likely candidates to be among those babies who are difficult and unsoothable, the very kind of babies who, as Korner (1979) has noted, are over represented among abused children.

I think it is reasonable to assume (although there is as yet no research) that a parent who is *already* inclined to be punitive and rigid might be even more likely to be that way with a temperamentally difficult child. Other parents, whose inclination is to be tolerant and understanding, might behave quite differently. Thus, it is possible that a child's temperament and the parent's personal inclinations combine to create an emotional climate that, when positive, can be emotionally beneficial for both parent and child. If negative, however, it could have devastating effects.

What does it mean when we refer to a child's "temperament?" Does this refer to a child's inborn nature, or is a child's temperament basically a reflection of the kind of environment—or nurture—to which it is exposed? These are important questions, ones that lead us to ask . . .

WHAT IS NATURE'S CONTRIBUTION TO A CHILD'S TEMPERAMENT?

It is a well established genetic fact that heredity contributes significantly to such characteristics as the color of one's eyes, hair, and skin and to other obvious physical attributes such as height, weight, and stature.

But what about differences—and similarities—in personality characteristics or in what is sometimes referred to as one's temperament? There is intriguing and persuasive new research data suggesting that the core of many of our personality traits—the determinants of whether we're shy or extraverted, traditional or conservative, or even if we're cheerful or gloomy—is influenced by the genes embedded in the coils of the 46 chromosomes that our parents pass on to us at conception. The question today is no longer whether one's heredity influences personality, but rather how much and in what ways?

It is within the family that the alchemy of nurture and nature brews its strongest magic, and by studying families of twins and adopted children, psychologists have been busy trying to understand the ingredients of that brew. In an effort to do this, researchers at the University of Minnesota have been gathering data on more than 350 pairs of twins who have been subjected to extensive testing since 1979, including analyses of their blood, brain waves, intelligence, allergies, and personality traits.

Thomas Bouchard, Jr., who runs the Minnesota Center for Twin and Adoption Research, has found some remarkable similarities between twins reared in completely different families and communities. Some examples:

1. Separated four weeks after birth in 1940, identical twins Jim Lewis and Jim Springer grew up 45 miles apart in Ohio. When reunited in 1979, they discovered both drive the same model blue Chevrolet, chainsmoked Salems, chewed their fingernails, and owned dogs named Toy. Each vacationed frequently at the same three-block strip of beach in Florida. When tested for such personality traits as flexibility, self-control, and sociability, they responded almost exactly alike (Leo, 1987).

2. Although many of the separated pairs of identical twins had differing types of jobs and educational levels, repeated similarities have been found in hobbies and interests—one pair were deputy sheriffs, one pair were volunteer firefighters, a male pair had similar basement workshops, and a female pair had strikingly similar kitchen arrangements. Two identical twin women reared apart found that each has a son who won a statewide mathematics contest, one in Wyoming, the other in Texas (Holden, 1987).

3. Bouchard and McGue's (1981) review of studies that involved nearly 100,000 twins and biological and adoptive relatives make it clear that heredity also has a strong influence on individual IQ scores. They

found, for example, that identical twins reared apart were more similar in IQ than fraternal twins raised together, underscoring the idea that genes play an important part—but by no means all of it—in determining IQ.

When research with twins is carried out, it is done in one or more of the following four categories: identical twins raised in the same family, identical twins raised apart, fraternal twins reared together, and fraternal twins reared apart.

Remember that identical twins are the result of the fertilization of a single egg that splits in half shortly after conception, while fraternal twins are the product of *two* fertilized eggs. Identical twins have in common all their genes; fraternal twins, on average, half. The important reason for studying twins is that it allows a comparison between twins raised separately and those raised together in the same home, which allows researchers to determine the relative importance of heredity and of environment in their development. Studies of this kind allow researchers to control for heredity, particularly in the case of identical twins who share all their genes and who are raised apart. Thus, by knowing the amount of genetic input, it is possible to make more valid inferences about environment's part in shaping one's development.

Researchers at the University of Minnesota have focused their investigations on 11 basic personality traits and have found differences between twins, particularly identical twins reared apart, to be smaller than had been assumed (Bouchard, 1984; Tellegen, et al., 1988). In Table 5-1, you will find a breakdown of those 11 personality traits and Coleman's (1986) analysis of the approximate percentage that heredity has been estimated to contribute in each instance.

Among the traits found most strongly influenced by heredity are traits referred to as "social potency" and "traditionalism." Other traits that have been found to be more than 50 percent influenced by heredity include "qualities such as one's vulnerability to stress, creativity, feelings of alienation and well-being, and even one's tendency to avoid harm."

The inclination to be aggressive, to achieve or be ambitious, and the need for order in one's life are among those traits that appear to be somewhat less influenced by heredity, although the genetic impact is still in the 40-percent range. This suggests that environment can play better than a 50-percent part in determining how these traits are expressed. The need for personal intimacy or social closeness appears to be the least determined by heredity among the traits tested; about two-thirds of this characteristic has been found to be determined by life experience. The capacity for intimacy or social closeness apparently is strongly affected by the quality of interactions in the family. The more children experience physical and emotional closeness in their families, the more likely this trait will be developed, and those children who have the strongest inherited tendency may have the greatest need for social and emotional closeness as adults.

Table 5–1   THE DEGREE TO WHICH 11 KEY PERSONALITY TRAITS ARE ESTIMATED TO BE INFLUENCED BY HEREDITY

Personality Trait	Heredity's Approximate Contribution
SOCIAL POTENCY (Extraversion)	61%
Tends to be the outgoing, take-charge type who likes being the center of attention.	
TRADITIONALISM (Obedience)	60%
Tends to obey rules and authority; favors strict discipline and high moral standards.	
STRESS REACTION (Worrier)	55%
Feels vulnerable and sensitive; tends to get easily upset and to worry.	
ABSORPTION (Creative)	55%
Has vivid imagination; enjoys esthetic and artistic experiences; sees things in new ways.	
ALIENATION (Suspicious)	55%
Tends to feel unliked, mistreated, and used; thinks "world is out to get me."	
WELL-BEING (Optimistic)	54%
Inclined to have a cheerful disposition; feels confident and upbeat.	
HARM AVOIDANCE (Fearful)	51%
Tends to avoid experiences that include risk and danger; prefers safe route even if tedious.	
AGRESSION (Hurtful)	48%
Tends to be physically aggressive and vindictive; may give appearance of one "out to get the world."	
ACHIEVEMENT (Striver)	46%
Works hard; strives for mastery; tends to put work and accomplishments ahead of other things.	
CONTROL (Planful)	43%
Likes to plan carefully ahead; tends to be cautious and plodding, rational and sensible.	
SOCIAL CLOSENESS (Intimacy)	33%
Prefers emotional intimacy and close ties; turns to others for assistance and comfort.	

Adapted from D. Coleman, "Major Personality Study Finds That Traits Are Mostly Inherited," *New York Times,* December 2, 1986, pp. C1, C2.

Notes of Caution About Nature's Contributions

To begin with, it is important to realize that no single gene is believed to be responsible for any particular behavioral trait. No one believes, for instance, that there is a single gene for "social potency" or "vulnerability to stress" but rather that there is a whole host of genetic combinations that, when mixed with one's personal experiences, lead to endless possibilities for how certain traits are expressed. Although a few diseases such as sickle-cell anemia and Huntington's disease are caused by single genes that have their effects regardless of the environment or other genetic considerations of the individual, the complexity of human behavior makes it unlikely that any single gene will determine a human trait in a similar way. Robert Plomin (1989), a leading researcher in behavioral genetics, has observed that ". . . genetic effects on behavior are polygenic and probabilistic, not single gene and deterministic" (p. 110).

It is important to keep in mind that what is called *heritability* is simply the amount (ratio) of observed (or "phenotypic") variance of a particular trait that is due to genetic inheritance. Heritability of physical attributes or behavioral traits is estimated by analyzing patterns of correlations among people who are related in different ways (Falconer, 1990).

A popular misinterpretation of the concept of heritability occurs when we attempt to make judgments about how much a certain trait in a single individual is due to genetic or environmental factors. For example, although there is a correlation of about .80 between parents' height and their children's eventual height, it would be incorrect to conclude that a 5-foot-tall person received 48 inches from his or her parents (60 inches × .80 = 48), and another 12 inches from the environment (60 inches × .20 = 12). It is vitally important to understand that heritability describes the relative importance of genetic similarities or differences among a *group* of individuals rather than any one person.

Thus, we are no more able to predict the precise degree of temperament heritability in a particular individual than we are able to foretell that person's exact height. There are two reasons behind why our forecasting is limited. One, parents' genetic contributions to any particular physical attribute or behavioral characteristic are simply too complex to calculate exactly. And two, environmental factors have the power to modify genetic predispositions. There is a final note of caution: Biology is *not* necessarily destiny. Although new evidence points to the power of genes in shaping one's behavior, there is no evidence to suggest that environment is less important. If anything, new knowledge is moving us toward thinking about nature *and* nurture rather than nature *versus* nurture. The cumulative evidence suggests that it's not full-blown personality traits that are inherited, but rather predilections. In other words, although we might start out nudged in a certain direction by our genes, how *far* we go is greatly affected by all those other factors that fit under the general heading of environment. When asked how environment allowed for the expression of genetic differences, Sandra Scarr (1984) replied:

It has to do with "reaction range." Each person has a range for potential development. For example, a person with "medium-tall" genes for height who grows up in a poor environment may be shorter than average. In a good nutritional environment, the person would grow up taller than average. But no matter how well-fed, someone with "short" genes will never be taller than average. It works the same way with shyness, intelligence, and almost any other aspect of personality and behavior. (pp. 59–61)

The major picture emerging from twin studies going on in the United States and other parts of the world suggests that nature and nurture each contribute, on average, about 50 percent to children's development (Segal, 1990; Tellegen et al., 1988). Heredity's contribution can vary greatly in individual cases. For example, a child who, at an early age, shows strong innate tendencies to be overly aggressive might be helped to be less so through exposure to parents and other adults who are basically loving people capable of being firm, fair, and patient. Or a young child who shows early signs of being excessively introverted (passive, shy) might be helped to be somewhat more assertive by adults who are supportive and encouraging. On the other hand, an environment that is essentially punitive and rejecting might make an innately aggressive child even more so. Experiences with teasing, punishing adults might make an innately shy child even more so.

It is not easy to determine whether a given trait such as shyness, aggressiveness, or, say, vulnerability to stress is being influenced primarily by the environment or partially by heredity. Kagan (in Ellis and Robbins, 1990) suggested that the earlier a particular trait is observable in an infant's or young child's behavior, the more likely it is that that characteristic may be genetically influenced (primarily because the environment has had less chance to shape it). The advantage of being aware of possibilities of this sort is that it gives parents and other adults in a child's life an opportunity to make better decisions about how to deal with certain behaviors in terms of encouraging or discouraging their expression. What one inherits can have a powerful effect on one's overall development. I do want to stress, however, that the environment has an overwhelming influence on how and in what ways one's genetic potential gets expressed. Thus, what makes a difference is not just what a child is born *with,* but what it is that a child is born *into,* a consideration to which we now turn our attention.

SOURCES OF NURTURE: CHILD-REARING PRACTICES AND OUTCOMES

A child born into this world is a marvelous piece of genetic engineering, nine months in the making (usually), and comprises about one trillion cells. (If you would like an idea of how much growth occurs during nine months of fetal development, think of it this way. At the rate of one count per second night and day, it would take 32,000 years to count to one trillion, longer than there has been civilization on earth.) Each infant arrives with a certain genetic potential or "readiness" to be a certain kind of person in terms of basic physical and psychological characteristics. This is a child's nature, the way he or she is by virtue of chance combinations of thousands of genes.

Nurture is the sum total of all that a child experiences after birth. In a sense, it is the experiential broth that nourishes a child's nature. Parents, or whoever a child's major caretakers happen to be, are vitally important contributors to that broth, adding as they do the emotional seasonings that help to determine the palatability of growth experiences to a child.

Parents' contributions to the nurture side of a child's development are expressed primarily through the way they choose to raise their children. I think it's safe to say that all parents, unless they are psychologically impaired, want to give their children the best they can. In spite of these good intentions, however, children don't always turn out for the best. Some grow up angry and suspicious; others, anxious and fearful; and some, unhappy, shame-ridden adults who are caught in a web of low self-esteem and unremitting self-criticism. On the other hand, many children turn out to be reasonably happy, productive adults, able to acknowledge their strengths, willing to face their flaws, and capable of contributing their small share to making this world a little better place in which to live.

Inevitable questions arise: Which kinds of families produce which kinds of children? What do families do in their child-rearing behaviors that make the difference one way or the other? Are particular "styles" for raising children more likely to produce positive outcomes than others? Or does the way children are raised really make that much difference? Let's turn our attention to these questions.

Major Styles of Child Rearing

Although there are no simple answers to complex questions like the ones just raised, child-rearing research in recent years has provided some fairly clear ideas about the outcomes we might expect from the different ways children are raised. Through her longitudinal research on relationships between child-rearing practices and children's behavioral outcomes, began in 1959, Diana Baumrind (1967, 1968, 1980, 1989) has identified three major approaches to child rearing used by most parents. Each is associated with its own particular emotional tone, which may help us understand why children in different families may be so unlike each other. Keep in mind that these descriptions represent "pure" strains of each type. It's not likely that any given parent will adhere purely to any one style, but will tend to favor one kind of parenting style more often than other possibilities. Let's briefly consider each of them.

Authoritarian Parenting.   This style characterizes parents who feel it is important to shape, control, and evaluate the behavior of children against a set standard of conduct, usually an absolute standard, sometimes theologically motivated and formulated by a higher authority. This style is favored by parents who operate according to rather rigid standards of conduct; who favor punitive, forceful measures of discipline; and who value strict obedience as a high virtue. Parents of this sort work hard to teach their children respect for authority, respect for work, and respect for the preservation of order and tradition. Authoritarian parents do not encourage a great deal of give and take, believing, rather, that they know best about what is right.

Authoritative Parenting.   Parents who use this style make an effort to relate to their children in a rational, issue-oriented manner; to encourage verbal give and take; and to rely more on parental reason than parental muscle to accomplish their goals. Still, these parents are able to be quite firm when there is a need for firmness, and they use their parental power when necessary. They expect the child to conform to adult requirements, but they attempt to balance their special rights as adults against their children's individual interests. Parents of this sort do not regard themselves as infallible but also do not base decisions primarily on their children's desires.

Permissive Parenting.   This is a style used by parents who are inclined to behave in a rather easygoing, nonpunitive, and accepting manner toward most things their children do. Children are usually given a voice in family decisions and rules, but there are few demands on them for household responsibility and orderly behavior. Permissive parents tend to allow children to regulate their own activities as much as possible but do not particularly encourage them to behave according to externally defined standards. The child is pretty much the center of things.

Of note, at least in passing, although the data supporting its existence are not strong enough to classify it as a major approach to child-rearing, in a few lucky families (only eight of the 95 studied) parenting was so smooth that it was referred to as *harmonious*. These families had neither permissive, authoritative, nor authoritarian parenting styles. They were manned by parents who seemed to *have* control—in the sense that the children did as their parents expected them to do—but they very seldom *exercised* control. It was as if parents and children tacitly agreed that rooms needed to be clean, the table set, clothes hung up, the garbage taken out, consideration shown to each other, and so forth. Children in these families seemed to pull their own weight in the business of day-to-day living as if doing it on their own accord rather than because their parents demanded it. This pattern was distinguished by an atmosphere of harmony, equanimity, and rationality in parent-child relations. Accordingly, values like power, achievement, control, and order were deemphasized in favor of congeniality and fairness. It is worth noting that this harmonious pattern frequently broke down when children failed to "intuit" or anticipate the parents' wishes. In the absence of this intuitive spirit of cooperation on the part of the child, the harmonious

Good parents are able to weather many storms.
Reprinted by permission of Universal Press Syndicate.

parent would be forced to exert authoritative or authoritarian control or simply lapse into a permissive mode.

In a sense, we could say that every family is "harmonious" when things are running smoothly. It is only when things do not go smoothly that a family's dominant pattern is forced to the surface. As near as I can tell from reading the literature, those parents who were labeled "harmonious" did not necessarily have exceptional parenting skills but rather may have had exceptional children, the kind who make parenting easy. It is worth noting, however, that even in harmonious families there may be lapses into authoritarian, authoritative, or permissive modes when crises emerge, which suggests that, when the chips are down, one of the three primary child-rearing modes tends to surface.

Behavioral Outcomes Associated with Different Parenting Styles

Again, remember that no parent fits a given category all the time; no one is always permissive or always authoritarian or authoritative or harmonious. These are relatively broad categories reflecting dominant patterns that reliably distinguish certain parenting styles from one another.

Both authoritative and authoritarian parents demand socially responsible behavior (following certain rules, listening when talked to, controlling impulses, behaving, and so forth) from their children but encourage it in different ways. Authoritarian parents, for instance, tend to assume a stance of infallibility and to set many rules, requirements, and restrictions, usually by fiat. The message is "You will do it this way because I say so." We can find an example of this style in an interesting report by Mantell (1974), who studied the parent-child relationships of 25 war resisters and 25 Green Berets, a group of volunteer Special Forces soldiers honed for active combat in Vietnam. Whereas the war resisters were more apt to come from homes characterized by helpfulness, mutual respect, freedom, and democratic give and take, Green Berets were much more likely to come from homes where they were expected to be neat and clean, well-mannered, and, certainly, obedient to superiors. When asked to describe his father, one Green Beret responded,

> My father was . . . a stern disciplinarian, I would say. When he told me to do something, it wasn't my normal course of action to ask him why. 'Cause often as not he would say, "Because I told you so."

This response is quite different from that given by a war resister, who in response to a request to describe his home, said,

> The basic idea was that any order given I should be able to ask a reason for it and get a rational response.

It is not difficult to see why the Green Berets were the Green Berets or why the war resisters were the war resisters. One group was accustomed to following orders, and the other group was accustomed to questioning why orders were given in the first place, a typical difference between those who grow up in authoritarian and authoritative homes.

Permissive parents are different still. They neither demand socially responsible behavior nor are they particularly aggressive in rewarding it when it does occur. They issue few directives, and those that are issued are seldom enforced by either physical means or verbal influence. Indeed, permissive parents seem to make it a point to avoid confrontations when the child disobeys. Children of permissive parents, particularly boys, are found to be clearly lacking in socially responsible and achievement-oriented behavior. One reason is that in the absence of negative sanctions ("This is something you must not do") or positive expectations ("I expect you to listen when the teacher talks"), the child is left with the impression that either there are no rules to follow or, if there are, it is okay to go ahead and disobey them anyway. Indeed, Siegel and Kohn (1959) found that when adults do not react at all to a child who disobeys or breaks an existing rule, the child is even more likely on subsequent occasions to repeat that same behavior. If, for example, a seven-year-old boy punches his four-year-old sister every time he's mad at her, his behavior is not likely to change unless someone older, and presumedly wiser, steps in and points out that hitting one's sister simply is not allowed under any circumstances. Some children might misbehave not because they're necessarily "bad," but because no one has ever taught them correct or more appropriate behavior, something that can happen easily enough with permissive parents at the helm.

Baumrind, along with Baldwin (1949), Coopersmith (1967), and Sears, Maccoby, and Levin (1957) have noted a reasonably consistent pattern of behavioral outcomes associated with authoritarian, authoritative, and permissive child-rearing styles.

Children from Authoritarian Homes Tend to Be

1. Less developed—especially boys—concerning being independent and socially responsible. (They have learned to be dependent on authority and, as a consequence, typically have fewer opportunities for making the necessary personal choices that lead to social responsibility.)

2. Low in self-esteem (perhaps the result of too few opportunities to test their own wings in their own ways).

3. Weak in establishing positive relationships with peers; frequently sad in mood (perhaps the consequences of being disparaged, given too little freedom, and receiving not enough interpersonal warmth).

4. Obedient or restrictive and cruel; lacking in spontaneity and curiosity. (It is not uncommon to find that exposure to expressions of arbitrary power assertions leads to overly obedient behavior, out of fear, or to resistance and cruelty, out of anger, and to a lack of spontaneity, perhaps because of a lack of enough opportunity to feel happy and free.)

Children from Authoritative Homes Tend to Be

1. Independent and socially responsible. (They have had many opportunities for making their own decisions, for standing up and being heard, and for contributing to the family enterprise.)

2. Making plans, as opposed to aimless wandering; fairly dominant; and fearless. (This is probably an outgrowth of learning to do things for themselves rather than simply following someone else's directions; it is an attitude that says "I can" rather than "I can't.")

3. High in self-esteem (a feeling that comes from being loved and knowing it, being valued as a person, and living up to expectations that were reasonable and reachable).

On the Other Hand, Children Raised in More Permissive Homes Tend to Be

1. Undercontrolled, in the sense of being able to hold their impulses in check or to delay gratification. (They are used to having their own way because permissive parents tend to make few demands on them or to enforce the ones they do make.)

2. Overly aggressive. (This is related to their undercontrolled impulses. They want what they want when they want it, an attitude encouraged by parents who feel that children should be free to express themselves.)

3. Immature (an outgrowth, no doubt, of being raised in an environment in which expectations for impulse control and behaving appropriately are low and children are very much the center of attention).

4. Low in social skills and leadership potential (very likely the consequence of not having to grow beyond their own egocentric world of self-focused desires and needs, which tends to alienate others).

5. Low in the ability, or at least the willingness, to set goals and go after them. (This is something we might expect to see in those raised in an environment of low expectations, low demands, and low enforcement. Setting goals and developing a certain self-discipline may not seem either important or necessary to children who have pretty much what they want and from whom little is expected.)

No conclusive pattern of behaviors can be easily attached to the harmonious style. The general feeling of equanimity, rationality, and fairness pervading it makes it sound like the best of what might be found in an authoritative home with a dash of permissiveness added for good measure. And there is the important observation that the children in harmonious homes are exceptional to begin with—cooperative, sharing, loving—which suggests that these children may be as much, if not more, the *cause* of harmonious parenting as they are the result of it.

To sum up, research strongly indicates that both authoritarian control and permissive noncontrol tend to inhibit children's opportunities to engage in vigorous interaction with other people. Both overcontrolling authoritarian parents and undercontrolling permissive parents suppress the development of a healthy self-concept, one by making too many demands, thereby blocking independent judgment, and the other by making too few, thereby failing to challenge children to higher levels of growth.

In our discussion about how children are raised, the idea of how they are controlled—managed, interacted with, disciplined, taught, and so forth—is an important one. Basically, there are two general categories of control that we want to examine.

Consequences of Strict Versus Firm Parental Control

Restrictive control is associated with the extensive use of proscriptions and prescriptions covering virtually all areas of children's lives, which severely limits their opportunities for testing themselves in new ways and becoming independent. How vastly parents differ can be seen in the following observations of two mothers with five-year-olds (Sears, Maccoby, and Levin, 1957):

MOTHER A:	I don't want him to leave our own little area. I spent a whole summer chasing him and licking him, and putting him in bed, and we have accomplished it. He must come right home from school and play around here; that is the one thing I do enforce.
MOTHER B:	We live very closely together (neighboring houses), and the children are apt to be all here or all there, and it bothers my mother (child's grandmother) dreadfully. Sometimes she will say to me, "You don't know where she is," and I'll say, "Oh, she's around someplace," and Mother says, "But you're not sure." (pp. 276–277)

Children raised along the lines of A's philosophy hear many, many injunctions admonishing them not to touch, not to be noisy, not to go far, not to interrupt, not to get dirty, and on and on. They are overprotected and over-bossed. Children raised in this manner remind me of a story I heard about a shy, quiet first-grade boy, who when asked his name by the teacher, responded, "Johnny Don't." The teacher, looking puzzled, said to him, "Well, that's an interesting name, but it is different from the one I have listed for you in my records. Are you sure that's your name?" "Oh yes," the shy little boy answered, "my mom and dad have been calling me that since I was a baby."

Damon's (1983) review of related research indicates that children raised by highly restrictive parents tend to be obedient, polite, and nonaggressive, particularly if the parents are warm and accepting. These are behaviors in children that we may applaud and hope to see more of; however, they tend also to be associated with children who are timid and not particularly tenacious in pursuing their goals, something that is even more likely to be true if parents are restricting and authoritarian.

Children raised by highly restricting parents receive a variety of messages, which when reduced to their common elements, say to the child, "You need watching; you're not to be trusted; you need my guidance; you can't do it on your own." You can see how attitudes like this may inhibit not only children's behavior but their spirit and drive as well. High restrictiveness, particularly when accompanied by authoritarian or hostile behavior, may foster self-doubt and dependency, both of which can be significant roadblocks to developing a healthy self-concept.

Firm control is different in both emphasis and tone. Whereas restrictive control relies primarily on mandates and threats, firm control stresses reason and expectations. For example, *restricting* parents might say things like "You can't go out until your homework is done" or "If you leave the yard, you will not be allowed out for the next three nights" or "I don't want to see you playing with Brian or you're going to get it." On the other hand, *firm parents* might say things like "Your homework is important—be sure you do it" or "Stay around the yard; we're going to eat shortly" or "Your friend Brian has a tendency not to answer his mother—I expect you to come when I call."

You can see that it is a difference in shading rather than a dramatic change in color. Restricting parents seem not to trust their children—hence, the imposition of restrictions and threats to keep them in line. With firm parents, it seems not so much a lack of trust as simply a deeper understanding that children will be children and that they are not necessarily bad or forgetful or mischievous because they are untrustworthy but because they are immature and still learning the rules of the game. Thus, the emphasis is on what they are *expected* to do because it is the *right* thing rather than on what they had better *not* do because it is the *wrong* thing.

It is not surprising, then, to find that children raised by a firm hand, as opposed to a restricting one, are more able to control aggressive impulses (they have less to be angry about), more likely to have higher self-esteem (feeling trusted helps them feel worthwhile), and more apt to have greater self-confidence (they have learned to meet expectations, which builds confidence, rather than to fear consequences, which erodes it).

Children are more likely to respond in positive ways to their parents' efforts to exercise control when the attachment bonds between them are securely grounded in trust and love. Let's briefly turn our attention to how the dynamics of attachment work and, in addition, look at how attachment outcomes may affect long-term emotional development.

ATTACHMENT TO PARENTS: DYNAMICS AND IMPLICATIONS

The capacity and willingness to behave and think independently is a typical characteristic of children with healthy self-concepts. Independence behavior is a trait that develops slowly over time, nourished by experiences that teach children that their world is usually safe and predictable, and that when it isn't, they can count on certain people for protection and refuge. For children to develop a healthy sense of independence, they first have to go through a period of *attachment,* which is an important emotional link, an "affectional bond" as

Bowlby (1980) called it, between the infant and the parents. During the early months of an infant's life, parents and infant develop a mutual, interlocking pattern of attachment behaviors. For example, the baby signals her needs by crying or fussing; she responds to being held by cooing or smiling; she looks at the parents when they look at her. In other words, parents and infant enter into a kind of two-person "dance," each reciprocating the other's look, gaze, smile, cooing sounds, and touch with responsive eagerness.

Findings from attachment research make it clear that certain parental behaviors such as sensitivity, acceptance, cooperation, and accessibility are crucial to secure attachment in infancy and continue to be important if children are to develop the courage and confidence to be increasingly independent (Ainsworth, 1982). Other research by Londerville and Main (1981) and Pastor (1981) showed that parental qualities such as warmth, supportiveness, and gentleness are important additives to the blend of parental behaviors necessary for positive attachment. On the other hand, parental qualities such as withholding support, coldness or aloofness, and harshness interfere with secure attachments between parent and child.

A secure attachment is the precursor to the development of healthy independence because *the nature of a child's attachment to his or her parents serves as a kind of emotional base from which the world can be explored or not, as the case may be.* For example, Hazan and Durrett (1982) found that securely attached children explored a new space more independently and thoroughly than did children who were rated as insecurely attached.

Before reading further, you may find it both interesting and revealing to do the small ranking exercise in Table 5-2. Considering what you know about

---

Table 5–2   WHAT IS YOUR ATTACHMENT ORIENTATION?

Read each of the statements below and rank them from 1 to 3 in terms of how you feel each applies to you, especially with regard to love relationships. (A ranking of 1 suggests it closely applies to you and a rank of 3 suggests it applies to you least of all.)

Rank

a. _____   I find it relatively easy to get close to others and am comfortable depending on them and having them depend on me. I don't often worry about being abandoned or about someone getting too close to me.

b. _____   I am somewhat uncomfortable being close to others; I find it difficult to trust them completely, difficult to allow myself to depend on them. I am nervous when anyone gets too close, and often love partners want me to be more intimate than I feel comfortable being.

c. _____   I find that others are reluctant to get as close as I would like. I often worry that my partner doesn't really love me or won't want to stay with me. I want to merge completely with another person, and this desire sometimes scares people away.

From C. Hazan and P. Shaver, "Romantic Love Conceptualized as an Attachment Process," *Journal of Personality and Social Development*, 1987, *52:* 511–524.

yourself in love relationships, how would you rank the three statements in Table 5-2?

Basically, attachment behavior refers to a psychological bonding between infants and their primary caretakers that reflects both the nature and the quality of their relationships to each other. There are, however, differences among children in the attachments they form that may have long-term consequences for their later adult love relationships, a possibility we explore next.

Children's Attachment Patterns and Subsequent Adult Love Relationships

There are three major patterns of attachment that researchers have identified in infants' and young children's behaviors (Ainsworth et al., 1978), which have been described as follows:

1. *Secure attachment:* This is most likely to occur when the primary caregivers were consistently available and responsive to the individual's needs in early childhood. (About 60 to 65 percent of all children studied fall into this category.)

2. *Avoidant attachment:* This category describes children whose parents were essentially unresponsive or overly rejecting. (About 20 percent are in this category.)

3. *Anxious/ambivalent attachment:* This characterizes children whose parents were sometimes available and responsive to needs and sometimes unavailable or who actually erected obstructions to need satisfaction. (About 10 to 15 percent fit this category.)

The point to remember here is that we are talking about those very early and primary attachments that children have with the emotionally important person/persons in their lives. A child's relationship with his or her parents is, in a very real sense, that child's first love relationship. Is it possible that the course of that relationship provides the emotional map that unconsciously influences the direction of subsequent love relationships in adult life?

In an effort to see whether there might be any truth to this idea, Hazan and Shaver (1987) studied three romantic attachment orientations:

1. A *secure attachment* founded on trust that needs would be met.

2. An *avoidant style* produced by an unresponsiveness to needs.

3. An *anxious/ambivalent* style generated by inconsistent responsiveness to needs.

Using a "Love Quiz" given to university students and to readers of a Denver newspaper, the investigators asked questions that probed respondents' most significant romantic relationships as well as background information such as age, level of education, and so forth. Other questions related to their perceptions of love ("Intense romantic feeling is common at the beginning of a relationship, but it rarely lasts forever") and to their perceptions of themselves ("People often misunderstand me or fail to appreciate me"). Still other questions asked respondents to assess how they related to their parents and how their parents related to each other. The quiz also included the three statements in Table 5-2, and each respondent answered in terms of which one best described him or her.

University students and newspaper readers responded in a similar fashion. About 55 percent of all respondents checked the first statement in Table 5-2, indicating a secure attachment, 25 percent checked the avoidant statement listed second, and 2 percent endorsed the third statement, identifying themselves as leaning toward anxious/ambivalent attachment behavior. It is interesting to note that the proportion of adult responses in each attachment category correspond closely to the proportions of children that Ainsworth (1978) and her co-workers found associated with those same attachment categories. This is important because it suggests—but does not prove—that subjects' choices among the alternatives were nonrandom and may have been determined by the same kinds of forces that affect the attachment styles of children.

Keeping in mind the attachment style you ranked as number 1 in Table 5-2, what follows is a brief summary of what Hazan and Shaver found from their research involving 728 men and women:

1. When characterizing their most important love relationship:
   a. *secure* types described it as especially happy, friendly, and trusting and emphasized their willingness to accept and support their partner despite the partner's faults. (It was also noted that their relationships lasted longer: 10 years on the average, compared with 4.9 years for those classified as anxious/ambivalent and 6.0 years for those who fell in the avoidant category.)
   b. *avoidant* types expressed a fear of intimacy, along with experiencing jealousy and many emotional highs and lows.
   c. *anxious/ambivalent* types viewed love as involving obsession, a strong desire for reciprocal closeness, many emotional highs and lows, and extreme sexual attraction and jealousy.

2. When describing how love works in relationships:
   a. *secure* types said that romantic feelings wax and wane but at times reach the intensity felt at the start of the relationship and that in some instances romantic love never fades.
   b. *avoidant* types said that the kind of head-over-heels romantic love seen in movies and books does not exist in real life and that it is rare to find a person one can really fall in love with.

    c. *anxious/ambivalent* types claimed that it is easy to fall in love and that they frequently feel themselves beginning to fall, although (like the avoidant) they rarely find what can be called "real love."

3. When it came to identifying the origins of attachment orientations:

    a. for *secure* respondents, the source of adult attachment patterns was easily traceable to early parent-child interactions. By in large, mothers and fathers were seen as loving and responsive to each other and to their children, just the kind of behaviors that encourage secure attachment in childhood.

    b. *avoidant* types said that their mothers were rejecting, unhumorous and unlikable.

    c. *anxious/ambivalent* persons saw their mothers as too intrusive and their fathers as unfair, although they did have some nice things to say about their parents. Consistent with the label "ambivalent" their feelings toward their parents ran hot and cold.

I have spent this time discussing childhood attachment and its implications for subsequent adult behavior in love relationships because it is such a striking example of how certain aspects of early parent-child relationships can have long-term repercussions. Perhaps it is not surprising that children's eventual love relationships as adults should reflect so many of the remnants of the nature and quality of the emotional attachments that they experienced with their parents.

Secure-attachment people, for example, usually have parents who formed a positive bond with them. Coming, as they usually do, from homes where the primary caretakers were responsive, warm, and loving, they may be more likely as adults to be that way themselves in their love relationships, thus increasing the possibility that they will get the same in return.

On the other hand, *avoidant-attachment* individuals seem less concerned about love. They are more likely to be among those who did not form close emotional attachments during childhood because their parents were less responsive and more emotionally distant. As a consequence, they learned to live without love and the emotional closeness that goes with it. Because they have had fewer opportunities for forming attachments and little faith in lasting love relationships, their chances of finding a satisfying love may be greatly reduced.

Anxious/ambivalent people tend to be clingy and demanding, always, it seems, searching for reassurance because they have problems accepting that they really are loved. Presumably, they end up this way because their parents were inconsistent and emotionally unpredictable when it came to loving them and taking care of their basic needs. Thus, for them, love relationships tend to rollercoaster through an endless series of up and downs, seldom remaining level and consistent, a pattern that reflects the emotional uncertainties they experienced in childhood.

Caution: Early Attachment Patterns Are Not Destiny

Because one has had an avoidant or an anxious/ambivalent attachment history does not automatically mean that one is doomed to have difficulties in subsequent adult love relationships. It only suggests that the likelihood may be greater. Nor are people with roots in secure attachment histories guaranteed that their love relationships will be lasting and smooth. What can be said is that their relationships have a better chance of being healthy, which may enhance their lastingness, if not their smoothness. Life is too complex and people too complicated for us to be able to say that any particular life event or cluster of life experiences has the power to inalterably and forever fix one's destiny. What is learned at one point in time can be unlearned and reprogrammed with new learning at a later point in time. Thus, change for the better or, alas, the worse is always possible.

The point that I hope stands out in all of this is that children's earliest love relationships with their parents or other primary caretakers may unconsciously affect their attitudes about, and receptivity to, later adult love relationships. The things that children learn early in life have a greater chance of being absorbed into the self's belief system because there is little in the way of either prior knowledge or experience to challenge the emotional credibility of what they are assimilating during their youthful formative years.

The extent to which children are affected by their parents depends on the degree to which children are able to *identify* with their parents, an idea to which we now turn.

DYNAMICS OF SEX TYPING AND IDENTIFICATION: PROCESSES AND OUTCOMES

Identification is a concept derived from psychoanalytic psychology about how a personality evolves and forms over time. Essentially, identification is a largely unconscious process through which growing children come to think, feel, and behave in ways similar to the primary people in their lives. In its simplest terms, identification is a process whereby a child unconsciously absorbs the personality and behavioral expressions of his or her parents and, in many ways, behaves as if he were his parents. Children's self-concepts are built on the foundation of their earliest and most primary identification with people (or a particular person) who were the most emotionally significant to them.

The identification process is facilitated by *modeling* or *imitative* behaviors, which are efforts on the child's part to copy certain specific parental behaviors. A three-year-old boy perches on a stool by the bathroom sink, lathers up, and with an empty razor shaves like Dad; a five-year-old girl watches her mother making cookies and copies her every movement in preparing the cookie batter for baking; a seven-year-old boy or girl accidentally and painfully stubs a toe and expresses his feelings with several well-chosen expletives (as Mom or Dad have been known to do). Each of these is an example of imitative behavior. It is through this process of consciously imitating specific behaviors, attitudes, mannerisms, and interests of the emotionally important people around them, parents typically but not always, that children gradually and unconsciously construct the basic framework around which an entire personality will be built. Like soft sponges, children indiscriminately absorb all aspects of the emotional-social environment around them, and over time, through the process of identification, they become *like* that environment and its people in very basic ways. If most children, with no formal instruction, are able to learn how to use a very complex language by the time they are three, is it difficult to see that they very likely have also soaked up many of the basic attitudes, values of their primary caretakers?

Sex typing involves both imitation and identification but refers specifically to the process through which children acquire the psychological and social behavior considered appropriate to their own biological sex in a given society. Not surprisingly, of all aspects of a child's self-concept, one of the most important is the discovery of and attitude toward his or her own sex. Part of a growing child's self-image is the knowledge that "I am a boy" or "I am a girl"—an awareness that occurs somewhere between 18 months and three years of age—and that knowledge carries rather specific implications for how children feel about themselves and how others treat them.

Sex typing and identification probably begin at the moment of birth. Parents typically want to know, first of all, "Is it a boy or a girl?" The answer to this question does more than satisfy nine months of curiosity. It sets in motion a chain reaction of stabilized and stereotyped ideas about how little boys or girls, as the case may be, should be treated. American boys get blue things and girls get pink ones. Friends and relatives give the boy tiny trousers to grow into and adorn the girl in frilly frocks. A girl baby is admired for her delicate features and a boy baby for his husky appearance.

We can get an idea of how this chain reaction of preconceptions begins from the results of an interesting study by Rubin, Provenzano, and Luria (1974), who asked 30 pairs of parents, within 24 hours after their first child was born, to "describe your baby as you would to a close friend or relative." They also had the parents fill out a questionnaire, rating the baby on 18 objective scales such as firm-soft, big-little, and relaxed-nervous. Next, they obtained data from the hospital records listing each baby's weight, height, and Apgar score (a doctor's rating of a newborn's color, muscle tonicity, reflex irritability, and heart and respiratory rates).

Although Rubin and his colleagues found that none of these objective ratings showed any real differences between the 15 male and 15 female infants, the parents knew better. For example, parents of daughters thought their babies were significantly softer, finer textured, smaller and more attentive than did parents of boys. This was true of both fathers and mothers, but the fathers went further, reeling off great differences in other aspects of the infants' looks and behavior, suggesting that fathers' preconceptions of sex differences may be stronger and deeper.

The point is, children are not born into a neutral world. Parents, other adults, and older children in their lives have rather specific ideas about how little boys and girls are to behave (although in this age of more liberated thinking, these ideas are not so narrow as they once were), which has the effect of reinforcing appropriate sex-role adoption. These ideas also nudge children toward appropriate *gender identity,* which is a boy's and girl's awareness and acceptance of his or her basic biological nature as a male or female.

By age three, most children are able to label themselves correctly as *boy* or *girl.* By age four, most children can use the labels *boy* and *girl* correctly in more general ways. For example, they use the right pronouns to refer to people (*he, she, him, her*) and can classify and group dolls or pictures according to sex differences; four year olds also begin to show more marked preferences for toys and activities associated with their own sex. Most four year olds, however, do not ordinarily realize that their sex is a permanent part of themselves, nor have they clearly associated sex with role distinctions. The truth in this is nicely illustrated in a story told by comedian Robert King:

> My niece was about four years old, and she was playing in the kitchen with the boy next door who was the same age. The boy said to my niece, "You want to wrestle?" My niece said, "I can't wrestle; I'm a girl." The boy said, "Oh, well, you wanna play football?" "I can't play football," she said; "I'm a girl." "Well, do you want to throw the baseball around?" And my niece said, "How many times do I have to tell you—I'm a girl?" The boy said, "Oh, all right. Wanna play house?" And my niece said, "OK, I'll be the father."

By about age five or six years, most children have figured out that gender is constant. They also have a reasonably clear idea of their own sex and of the stereotypical "female" and "male" role and characteristics. At about the same time or a little later, children begin to understand the relationship between genital differences and sexual identity. It is also at about age five that the child begins to show consistent imitation of and identification with adults of the same sex.

Which brings us to our next consideration.

PARENTS' ROLE IN CHILDREN'S IDENTIFICATION

Parents are enormously important in shaping a child's sex-role preference and identification. The most fortunate children are those who have so adequate a father (male model) and mother (female model) that they come early to prefer the sex role dictated by their physiology, move naturally and easily into its rehearsal, and eventually identify thoroughly with it.

The girl who has made a female identification is the girl who has happily and willingly adopted femaleness as her way of life. She thinks of herself as a female; she accepts and likes her biological status, its advantages and disadvantages; and she assumes the responsibility and challenge that being female demands. For this to happen, she must be *identified with* (love, respect, and in many ways imitate) her mother or mother figure to be consistently and genuinely *female identified.*

The identification process for a boy is very much the same, except, of course, that he aligns himself emotionally with the father or father figure as the person with whom he is primarily identified.

Parental Behaviors That Encourage Positive Identification

In various research efforts designed to explore possible relationships between parental behaviors and children's identification outcomes, three characteristics of parents tend to stand out: warmth, availability, and power (Moulton et al., 1966; Mussen and Rutherford, 1963: Sears, 1953). The major findings from that research suggests that

1. boys of fathers who are warm, affectionate, nurturing, and available tend to be more closely identified with their fathers and to engage in more sex-role appropriate behavior than boys whose fathers were distant and cold.

2. boys who behave more effeminately are more likely to come from homes in which the *mother,* but not the father, is high in warmth.

3. highly feminine girls are more likely than girls low in femininity to perceive their mothers as significantly warmer, more nurturing, and more affectionate.

Parental warmth is a factor in a child's identification with a parent because it is an emotional quality that encourages and allows a child to feel *close* to the parent, a quite necessary prerequisite to becoming *like* that parent. Warm parents, by virtue of their commitment to the child's welfare, their responsiveness to the child's needs, their willingness to spend time with the child, and their capacity to be sensitive to the child's emotional states, make it easier for the child to develop a strong parental attachment, which has been found to make children more "teachable" at a later time in terms of paying more attention to their parents and learning more readily from them (Matas, Arend, and Stroufe, 1978).

A common theme in these findings is that parental warmth binds children to their parents in a positive way: it helps make the children emotionally responsive to their parents and more willing to accept their guidance. When the parent-child relationship is warm and affectionate, parents are in a better position to exercise what control is needed without having to risk alienating their children with heavy-handed discipline.

Parental power—power in the sense of being firm, authoritative, not giving in easily—is an important part of the package because, as noted by Baumrind (1989), sometimes a show of force is necessary in order for the voice of reason

Relationships like this one can help build positive identifications between parents and children.

Reprinted by permission of UFS, INC.

to be heard. Children can more easily identify with parents who combine power with warmth and availability because they comfortably project the idea that they can be trusted to both love *and* protect, qualities to which children eagerly respond.

What Boys and Girls Need for Healthy Identification

The overall picture that emerges suggests that for the boy to have a fair shot at developing into an autonomous, reasonably assertive male who accepts his masculinity and sexuality as part of his self-concept, he must be able to identify to a considerable degree with his father or another emotionally important male (or males). Sometimes, in the absence of the actual father, an uncle or grandfather or older brother or even a "big brother" from the community Big Brother–Big Sister Program is able to take the role of an emotionally significant male in a boy's life.

The existing evidence supports the notion that boys identify more completely with fathers who are warm, available, and powerful, particularly when this "power" (size, strength, total presence, ability to make decisions, and so on) is primarily benevolent. They have much more difficulty developing an emotional closeness with punishing fathers. I think the idea about the kind of father with whom a boy is able to identify is nicely captured in a quote I came across some years ago by former baseball player Pete Rose, who was describing his feelings about his father in an interview:

> My dad was tough, man. He had more guts than any two guys I've ever known. But he was *mild-mannered* [Italics mine]. There are three things in my life I never saw: never saw my dad smoke, take a drink of hard liquor or argue with my mom. . . . My dad was really something else. There I'd be, a hundred-thousand-dollar ball player, and he'd be waiting for me outside the clubhouse to let me have it for not hustling enough (*Sports Illustrated,* 1975).

Rose's father was obviously available to him, he was powerful but mild mannered—another way of expressing warmth, perhaps—and he was some-one Rose admired, good reasons all for holding him in esteem and closely identifying with him. (In spite of having what seems to be a positive relation-ship with his father, Rose still had big problems later in his life as a compulsive gambler and has served time for illegalities stemming from that problem. I mention this only to underscore the fact that many things can go wrong in one's life even though one may have had exceptional parents.)

But what happens when mothers are the primary source of warmth and power in the lives of boys? One thing that sometimes happens—remember, *sometimes* happens; it is not an automatic given—is that boys from these homes reflect more feminine sex-role preferences than boys from father-dominant homes, a finding that emerged from Hetherington's (1965a) research with boys and girls between the ages of four and 11. The idea is sometimes expressed that mother-dominated boys will grow out of whatever feminine sex-role preferences they have as they get older and feel a certain amount of social pressure from their male peers to change their ways. Hetherington's research did not find this belief to be true. If anything, boys from homes where mothers had the most power showed *more* feminine sex-role preferences as they got older, which suggests that their identification with, in this instance, the mother had a more persuasive impact on their overall behavior patterns than peer pressure.

The matter of which parent has the most power does not seem to play such an important part in the sex-role development of girls. Other research by Hetherington (1965b), for example, showed that father-dominance made it easy for the girl to identify to some extent with the father but did not disturb the primary process of same-sex identification with the mother. Thus, the mother-daughter and father-daughter similarity in mother-dominant homes did not differ signifi-cantly. It is worth noting that *neither* the sons nor the daughters in mother-dominant homes identified with the passive father, who exhibited little power.

For girls, healthy sex-role identification is best encouraged by a warm and nurturing mother and a strong and caring father. Research indicates rather clearly that when the father plays an active and competent masculine role in the family, his daughter is more likely to feel closer to him and to incorporate certain of his "masculine" behaviors into her own personality makeup (Lynn,

1979; Parke, 1981). As discovered by psychiatrist Seymour Fisher (1972), there is another advantage girls may have who grow up feeling emotionally close to their fathers. He found that highly orgasmic women were more likely to have been raised by men who were "real fathers" to their daughters, that is, men who were dependable, caring, but yet demanding that their daughters meet certain moral standards and expectations. Implicit in this seems to be the idea that a strong, dependable, masculine father is able to provide the sort of trust that a daughter can take into subsequent relationships with men. This is important because when there is a problem of not being able to trust men, its roots sometimes go back deep in time when, as a growing girl, a woman may have been hurt, betrayed, disappointed, and, in other ways, psychologically or physically abused by her father or father figure.

All in all, the evidence from both clinical and empirical research suggests that a girl does not have to be as closely identified with her mother as the boy does with his father to experience appropriate sex-role identification, probably for two reasons. One, boys are usually more strongly pressured and, hence, motivated to behave in traditionally sex-role appropriate ways. And, two, girls have more leeway for behaving in different ways as they grow up. For example, young boys can wear spacesuit outfits or play ball, but they would be laughed off the block if they wore dresses or played with dolls. Little girls, on the other hand, can wear either outfit or play either game without being criticized. Girls may play with boys without censure, but boys are still made fun of if they play with girls too much. It's apparently all right for preschool boys and girls to play with each other—sex lines haven't been drawn yet—but by the time they begin elementary school this changes. (One six-year-old boy was overheard saying to his buddy, "I plan on enjoying these years before girls turn into the opposite sex.")

In sum, let us say that to encourage maximum self-concept integration, boys need every opportunity possible to identify with a father figure during their developmental years and girls with a mother figure. A boy learns how to be a man and to accept his "maleness" *by being around a man he values and feels close to.* A girl learns how to be a woman and to accept her "femaleness" *by being around a woman she values and feels close to.* Both boys and girls seem to profit from a certain amount of "cross-identification" with the parent of the opposite sex, a process that can help each of them understand the feelings and point of view of that half of the population whose biology and psychology are different from their own.

The processes we've been examining are reflections of what goes on between parents and children in the context of intact families. What happens to children when parents divorce?

WHEN FAMILIES BREAK UP: EFFECTS ON BEHAVIOR AND SELF-CONCEPT

Divorce is never a pleasant experience, at least in the short run. Lives are disrupted, people hurt, and major adjustments must be made in all spheres of one's life. According to the U. S. Census Bureau (1988), the divorce rate has doubled in the last decade, and more divorces than ever before involve families with children. Between 1910 and 1960, only 25 percent of children lost a parent through divorce or death. Now, however, it is estimated that 40 to 50 percent of children born in the 1990s will spend part of their childhood in a single parent household. Inasmuch as nearly 50 percent of marriages between young adults concludes in divorce, it is not difficult to see why so many youngsters end up in single parent households. Yesterday's conventional wisdom was that even though people were unhappily married they should remain together "for the sake of the children." Contemporary conventional wisdom is of a different mind: Couples in miserable marriages might well *divorce* for the sake of the children because a home life that is unhappy for the adults is unhappy also for the children, and if divorce promotes happiness for the parents, the children will benefit as well. Is there any truth to this belief?

The answer is, it depends. It depends on how much conflict there was in the family to begin with, how long it was going on, how old the children are when parents divorce, and how much contact the children have the the absent parent —usually the father—after the divorce. What seems to make the largest difference to the child is not so much that a separation or divorce has occurred but rather *how it is handled by the adults involved.* For example, one of the major conclusions reached by Judith Wallerstein (in Wallerstein and Blakeslee, 1989 —Sandra Blakeslee is, by the way, a professional writer, not a co-investigator) from her 15-year tracking of 60 families, most of them white, middle to upper-middle class and their 131 children—who were between two and 18 years old at the time of the divorce in 1971—was that children who fared the best were those whose parents continued to make parenting a priority. In those cases in which divorced parents put their differences aside and allowed children to have a continuing relationship with both of them, the youngsters progressed fairly well in their own personal growth. In fact, Wallerstein noted that children exposed to open conflict, where parents in intact families continue to fight and argue openly, turn out less well adjusted than children from divorced families.

However, no matter how well a divorce is handled, research indicates that almost *all* children show signs of at least short-term distress and disruption when parents separate (Hess and Camera, 1979; Hetherington, Cox, and Cox, 1982). During the first two years or so following a divorce, it is not uncommon for children to become more defiant; more negative; and somewhat more depressed, angry, or aggressive. Their school performance sometimes suffers, at least for awhile, and because of the stress involved, they may have more illness than usual. The effects of divorce seem to be greater on boys, particularly in the short term, something we might expect as they adjust to less-frequent contact with their fathers.

The age of children at the time of divorce also affects their adjustment to it, although the evidence is by no means unequivocal. Wallerstein and Blakeslee (1989) reported that whereas nursery-school-aged children showed more fearfulness and general regressiveness to infantile behavior, older children showed more sadness and anger. Over the long term, however, there was no indication that younger children had a more difficult time adjusting to the change. In fact, Wallerstein noted that most of the younger children—those who were between two and one-half and six years old when the investigation began, had few memories of life before the divorce and were emotionally more stable than their older siblings. This may be because younger children have to make less of an adjustment from the way things were—they haven't been around long enough—to the way things are in postdivorce days.

I think it is important to keep in mind that the troublesome behaviors we sometimes see in children following divorce—sadness, anger, negativism, regression, or whatever—are not necessarily symptoms of maladjustment, but rather expressions of coping, of putting inside feelings on the outside. Adults involved with these children can help the process with liberal doses of patience, reassurance, and understanding.

How Are Children Affected in the Long Run?

Although divorce is usually a painful experience for everyone involved, it by no means automatically dooms children to a life of maladjusted despair. For example, Weiss's (1979) study, involving over 200 single parents, showed that children of divorced parents sometimes become more self-reliant and responsible as a result of their increased participation in household decisions. As Weiss said, "They grow up a little faster."

In her 10-year follow-up in 1981, Wallerstein found that 45 percent of the children—many by then young adults—were doing well; they had emerged as competent, able people making their own mark in the world. But 41 percent were doing poorly; they were entering adulthood as self-doubting and sometimes angry men and women. The remaining 26 percent were strikingly uneven in their adjustment to the world. The jury is still out on how they will fare in the long run.

Because of a boy's need for a father or father figure with whom to identify during his childhood, we can understand why boys in father-absent homes may face special problems as they grow up. Although girls in father-absent homes do not usually have the same kind of behavioral problems that boys do, they have been found to experience difficulties in their male relationships. For example, in her study of the effects of early paternal deprivation on the behavior of adolescent girls, Hetherington (1972) was able to observe the behaviors of three groups of girls: (1) those whose mothers had divorced when the girls were very young, (2) those whose fathers had died when the girls were very young, and (3) those who had grown up in regular family conditions. None of the girls had brothers, and all were doing reasonably well in school. Here's a brief overview of what Hetherington found:

1. Girls who came from homes with divorced parents:
   a. sought more attention from males than did girls in the other two groups.

   b. were more likely to take a harsher view on how others should be punished; for example, they expressed harsher views about how prisoners should be treated.

   c. were more likely to hang around places where young males could be found—gymnasiums, machine shops, stag lines at school dances.

   d. dated earlier and more frequently than did girls from the other two groups and were more likely to have had sexual intercourse.

   e. when interviewed by an adult male, they tended to sit close to them in a somewhat open, sprawling posture; leaned more toward him, smiled more often, and looked more often into his eyes than did other girls.

   f. had mothers who were more likely to have negative attitudes toward their ex-husbands, themselves, and life in general.

2. Girls who came from homes where the father had died:

   a. tended to avoid males and stayed away from the typical male gathering places.

   b. had a more lenient view on how others (prisoners) should be punished.

   c. were inclined to sit farther away from male interviewers, smiled less often, and had less eye contact.

   d. tended to start dating much later than normal and seemed more sexually inhibited than the other two groups.

   e. had mothers who reported little or no conflict with their husbands before death. (It may be that the memories they have are so softened by the pain of the loss that what they end up with is a somewhat idealized version of the past.)

As I interpret these findings, the general picture that emerges is one suggesting that girls from divorced families look for ways to *replace* the loss of male input into their lives, while girls from father-deceased families seem generally more hesitant about, and perhaps fearful of, *repeating* a loss that was very painful. This, of course, does not happen in all cases, but it does alert us to some of the possible deeper motivations that may be driving the behaviors of girls who come from homes where the father may be absent because of divorce or death. If, for example, we know that 14-year-old Joni, who is always quiet and shy around males, has lost her father through death, we could make it a point to be more patient and understanding rather than pushy and demanding when it came to her relationship with boys. And if we know that 15-year-old Susan, who is forever pushing herself on boys, is from a divorced home, we could make an effort to help her understand that being available and clingy are behaviors more likely to drive the more desirable males away than to attract them to her.

In a study involving over 1,000 adolescents, Burchinal's (1964) data showed that youths from divorced homes do not fall into a class by themselves. Rather, they are as heterogeneous, with their share of good adjustment and poor adjustment, as young people who do not come from broken families. Goode (1966) a sociologist, who has studied family disorganization, points to a potent source of trouble:

> . . . a family in which there is continued marital conflict, or separation, is more likely to produce children with problems of personal adjustment than a family in which there is divorce or death. . . . [The] choice usually has to be between a continuing conflict or divorce. And the evidence suggests that it is the *conflict of divorce,* not the divorce itself, that has an impact on the children.

Whether it is prolonged conflict within an intact family or the protracted conflict of a messy, painful divorce, parents have the final word on how those things work out. Which brings us to an important point.

For Better or Worse, Parents Shape Divorce Outcomes

During the process of working on the fears and doubts that had shackled her since childhood, a 33-year-old woman with whom I was consulting had these reflections about what she lived with following her parents' divorce:

> My parents were divorced when I was eight. I knew they were unhappy and fought a lot and so I wasn't really surprised, I guess. My mother was really mad at my dad. Sometimes she would cry; other times she would say what an S. O. B. he was. At first I didn't know what to think, but, you know, pretty soon I started to think he was an S. O. B., too. I didn't see him very often, but when I did I had a hard time trusting him. I think I thought he might do to me what he did to my mother [a long pause here]—whatever that was. I'm not sure exactly why, but I just have always had the feeling that I wouldn't want to trust *any* man too much. And that's what I want to change. It gets so damn lonely at times.

From the time she was eight years old, this woman had learned from her mother that her father was no good. An eight year old is impressionable; she tends to believe what she hears and accept what she sees. Although she loved her father, her mother's persistence eventually nurtured the deep-seated attitude that her father could not be trusted, and from this, grew the more general and pervasive attitude that *men in general should not be trusted.* A little girl grows up being able to trust a man in a close, intimate relationship by first being able to trust her father or father figure. The same is true for a boy; he learns to trust a woman in a close, intimate relationship by first being able to trust his mother or mother figure. Among other reasons, this is why children from broken homes need to be free to love both of their parents, unencumbered by negative editorial remarks from either one about the other. Wise parents—married or unmarried—will look for the positive aspects in each other and comment on those. Children have always been pretty good at finding parental flaws all by themselves.

Reflecting back over almost 20 years of research related to divorce and its effects, Wallerstein (1989) observed:

> All our evidence shows that children exposed to open conflict, where parents terrorize or strike one another, turn out less well-adjusted than do children from divorced families. And although we lack systematic studies comparing children in divorced families from those in unhappy intact families, I am convinced that it is not useful to provide children with a model of adult behavior that avoids problem-solving and that stresses martyrdom, violence or apathy. A divorce undertaken thoughtfully and realistically can teach children how to confront serious life problems with compassion, wisdom, and appropriate action. (p. 41)

Tensions, insecurities, lack of proper and available models for identification, hostilities, guilt feelings—all these can follow in the wake of broken family units. To understand and identify the precise impact of death, separation, or divorce on any child, one needs to know how much love and understanding will continue afterward and how much real concern and affection remains for the child. In other words, do children see the "brokenness" of the home as punishment and rejection, or has the situation been handled with the sort of maturity and understanding that allows the children to retain their love and confidence in their parents? A basic condition for healthy self-concept development for children from broken homes lies in the fact that they are loved and *know* it—not the overindulging, overprotecting love of guilty parents trying to undo what they've done, but rather a love that allows the children to grow up without feeling upset and guilty about something they had no control over in the first place. *Ceasing to be a husband or a wife through separation or divorce does not mean that one has to stop being a responsible parent.*

Whatever their family background and genetic heritage, our hope is that all children have a chance to develop as positive a sense of themselves as possible. Before discussing more specifically how children can be helped to do this, let's first get a picture in our minds of the behavioral differences between high and low self-esteem children.

BEHAVIORAL DIFFERENCES BETWEEN CHILDREN WITH HIGH AND LOW SELF-ESTEEM

Consider Joey, age 12 and in the sixth grade. When asked to describe his behavior and performance in school, the teacher responds with the following description:

> Joey is a bright intelligent boy who seems to like himself and others. He is a friendly boy, someone other kids enjoy working with in the classroom or playing with on the playground. He participates actively in class activities and doesn't seem fearful of expressing his opinion. He has a positive attitude about

most things and likes learning new things. He's not the kind of boy who gets easily upset when things don't go well, like when he didn't do so well on a recent spelling test. His parents have told me that they expect him to work hard in school and he really tries to do that.

Now consider Jimmy, age 10 and in the fifth grade. Asked to describe his behavior and performance in school, his teacher gives the following description:

As measured by our intelligence tests, Jimmy is a bright boy. He is also a quiet, cautious boy. Although he's not unfriendly, he doesn't seem to have a lot of friends, primarily, I think, because he seems to have trouble liking himself. For example, he frequently says things like "Billy is smarter than I am" or "I'm too slow to play kickball." He doesn't take part in class activities, and when he does, you can see that he is afraid of saying or doing the wrong thing. I'm working hard to encourage him toward a more positive attitude about himself, but he seems to resist it. I told him recently that I thought his work really improved in math, and he could only say, "Well, I'm not very good in math." His parents have told me that although they don't push Jimmy, they have told him he would have to work very hard in school if he expected to do as well as his oldest brother.

Joey and Jimmy represent very real examples of the startling differences in self-esteem that separate children (and adults) at every age. Although some of these differences may be the result of genetic differences, they are also emotional and motivational. Joey is obviously a bright, outgoing, confident child, able to take risks and emotionally resilient enough to bounce back when things don't go smoothly. Jimmy, on the other hand, seems as filled with self-doubt as Joey is with self-confidence. His self-esteem is low, and as a result, he sees himself surrounded by children who are more able and capable. Joey looks for mountains to climb; Jimmy looks for places to hide.

Although, as measured by intelligence tests, both boys are "intelligent," one is living up to his potential, and the other is not. One boy is basically optimistic and outgoing; the other basically pessimistic and inward. Joey has high self-esteem, and Jimmy has low self-esteem. What does research teach us about how to encourage the development of high self-esteem in children?

TOWARD RAISING CHILDREN WITH HIGH SELF-ESTEEM

As discussed in Chapter 1, self-esteem refers to an individual's personal judgment of worthiness or unworthiness, approval or disapproval, which is expressed in the attitudes one has about oneself. If we could devise the best of all worlds, we would like the children in our charge, either at home or at school, to have as much positive self-regard as possible, to have enough positive self-esteem to function adequately as a contributing member of society. As adults who raise, teach, or counsel young people, what can we do to enhance this possibility?

Avoiding an Unhealthy Shame-Based Environment

Shame is one of our most difficult human emotions. As we learn more about this emotional state, it is emerging as a "master emotion" that influences all other feelings. You will recall from our discussion of Erikson's eight psychosocial stages of development in Chapter 1 that the second stage, occurring approximately between 18 months and three years of age, is a time when children develop a balance between a basic sense of autonomy or basic feelings of shame and doubt. Hopefully, it will be the kind of balance that tilts to the side of autonomy. It is an important balance, representing as it does an emotional foundation that enables children either to reach out into their world in venturesome and exploratory ways to develop their autonomy or to feel cautious and hesitant, forever fearful of doing or saying the wrong thing. It is not difficult to see why children who are subjected to heavy dosages of shame in their early years may find it difficult later on to move up the psychosocial continuum and develop the positive ego qualities associated with initiative, industry, identity, intimacy, generativity, and integrity.

Gershen Kaufman (1989) suggested that shame is the affect of inferiority, which is not only felt as an inner torment, but felt as an exposure of a most diminishing sort. In Kaufman's words:

> In the midst of shame, the attention turns inward, thereby generating the torment of self-consciousness. Sudden, unexpected exposure coupled with binding inner scrutiny characterize the essential nature of the affect of shame. . . . we feel fundamentally deficient as individuals, diseased, defective. . . . we become *self-conscious,* as if the self suddenly were impaled under a magnifying glass. . . . to live with shame is to experience the very essence or heart of the self as wanting. (pp. 18–23)

Shame is by no means an entirely negative emotion. John Bradshaw (1988), for example, observed that "Healthy shame keeps us grounded. . . . It is the emotional energy which signals us that we are not God—that we have made and will make mistakes, that we need help. Healthy shame gives us permission to be human" (p. 4).

Basically, shame is what we feel when we have done something wrong or have in some manner goofed up and others know it or soon find out about it. If it is a minor event, we may feel somewhat self-conscious and embarrassed, but the feeling passes and we go on, as in instances where we stumble over our words or our feet in a public place.

I think a key to understanding the dynamics of the kind of shame that is toxic and debilitating is in Kaufman's statement that "To live with shame is to experience the very essence or heart of the self as wanting." A shamed person is a wanting person, an individual who not only feels in some way flawed in character or deed, but who is exposed and then ridiculed or punished. Children raised in shame-based environments are frequently found "wanting" and are often humiliated, many times publicly, for their mistakes and errors.

I recently witnessed, for example, a little boy, maybe five or six, get spanked by his mother in the grocery store for moving a box of cereal from one shelf to another. She reminded him that he was a "bad, bad boy." Although the spanking was not all that severe, the shame that little boy felt ran deep. His eyes met mine as I walked down the aisle immediately after this public miniflogging, and he promptly dropped both his eyes and head and followed mother in slumped humiliation. That one incident will surely not turn him into a shame-filled person, but if he goes through hundreds of experiences of that sort during the next 10 years of his life, it is not hard to see why this five-year-old boy may grow up to be a somewhat inhibited, fearful, shame-controlled individual.

Repeated parent (and other adult) messages along the lines of "shame on you," "you should be ashamed of yourself," "you're embarrassing me," or other disparaging, put-down remarks are clear communications to children that they are in some way, deficient or flawed. Sadly, some parents learn too late that when they castigate they should castigate the fault, not the child; that when they reproach a fault, it can be reformed, but when they attack a personality, it may end up deformed.

Appropriate Levels of Demand and Responsiveness

Anyone who lives with or works with young people soon learns that there are times when certain demands must be made of them and that there are other times when we must be responsive to their needs. There are different ways for going about those things, and some are definitely better than others for the adults and children involved.

Consider first of all what Baumrind (1989) termed as "demandingness," which refers to the manner in which adults get children to do the things they want them to do. A method for doing this guaranteed to cause trouble—in the long run, if not the short run—is for the adult to be coercive, to make threats, to use power without reason. The problem with coerciveness is that it focuses the child's attention on the adult's power rather than on the possible harmful consequences of the child's behavior, thus irking the child and provoking oppositional behavior. Most healthy people—including children—resist being told what to do by someone who threatens them with the use of power but are quite willing to cooperate with the voice of reason. There is a vast difference between the child confronted with, "Alright Jason, you better clean your room or you're going to be spanked," and the child confronted with, "Jeffrey, I'm not at all pleased about your room not being picked up. What's going on here?" Jason may clean his room but feel angry and powerless. Jeffrey may not only clean his room but be more open to examining his own irresponsibility. Adults may coerce children to do what they want them to do for a certain length of time, but eventually this will fail. Ultimately, power runs out. It is not easy to demand that a 16 or 18 year old clean his or her room or be in at a certain time. As children grow older, it becomes increasingly more difficult to demand that they do this or that because one of the ways—and perhaps for some the only way—they can feel a sense of personal power is to resist the demander.

On the other hand, demandingness that is associated with direct confrontation, high maturity expectations, and firm control are techniques used by parents of competent children (Baumrind, 1971, 1989). Basically, we're talking here about the kind of demands that combine the power of reason with adult firmness and explicit expectations for mature behavior. Staub's (1975) research, for example, points clearly to the idea that when adults insist that children assume certain responsibilities and carry through with them, children end up behaving in more responsible, prosocial ways. And when they behave in ways like that, there are more opportunities to develop positive self-esteem because they have done something (washed the dishes, raked the leaves, finished a homework assignment, etc.) and finished it.

"Responsiveness" refers quite literally to the quality and quantity of the adults' way of responding to the needs of children. An adults' responsiveness to a child involves a consideration of qualities such as involvement, warmth, and approval. Research in this area suggests that it is the balance of these qualities in adults' interactions with children that can significantly influence children's feelings of personal competency and self-esteem (Baumrind, 1989; Parpel and Maccoby, 1985).

In order for parents and other adults to make a difference in children's lives, they must be involved with them in active, interactive ways. And they must demonstrate a certain amount of warmth and approval in order to encourage the kind of emotional closeness that allows relationships to develop. However, if a parent is *too* involved and excessively nurturing, it is possible that a child may feel stifled and overprotected, which can be roadblocks to developing a healthy sense of independence. It is difficult for children to explore either their environments or their possibilities while leashed to overly solicitous, overprotecting adults. The challenge of childhood is to grow up *and* move away, a task made more difficult when dependency is encouraged.

The approval we're talking about here does not just refer to unconditional approval, the kind of approval one may experience regardless of what one does. Rather than living in worlds of unconditional approval, competent, high self-esteem children are much more likely to also experience dosages of conditional approval. When children experience excessive amounts of unconditional approval for their behaviors and accomplishments, they are led to conclude that the environment is not particularly responsive to their behavior, which could have the effect of making them feel relatively powerless, even incompetent. Approval too easily won doesn't mean much. It is when we have done something to deserve it that it means the most.

It is the balance among and between the qualities of involvement, warmth, and approval that can affect, for better or worse, children's feelings of competence and self-esteem. The most emotionally impoverished children may not always be those who have received too little adult attention—experience may

*Good parents are responsive to children's needs but do not give
in easily to unreasonable demands.*

Reprinted by permission of Universal Press Syndicate.

teach them to look after themselves—but those who have been given too much
and, thus, fail to learn to stand on their own two feet.

What steps can parents and other adults take to help children to develop
positive self-esteem and encourage their growth into emotionally mature
adults? Let's turn our attention to this.

Child-Rearing Practices of Parents of High Self-Esteem Children

As discussed in Chapter 1, self-esteem refers to our personal evaluation of
worthiness or unworthiness, approval or disapproval, which is expressed in the

attitudes we have about ourselves. If we could construct the best of all worlds, we would like the children in our charge, at home and school, to have as much positive self-regard as possible, to have high self-esteem. Some parents seem naturally good at fostering this outcome. What is it they do, and what can we learn from them?

Stanley Coopersmith's (1967) research provides some important clues. We will first look briefly at how the research was conducted and then examine what the results suggest. To begin with, Coopersmith devised a 50-item self-esteem inventory, which he administered to 1,748 fifth- and sixth-grade children attending public schools in central Connecticut. From this pool, a small sample of 85 subjects was selected whose members could be clearly classified as high, medium, or low in self-esteem. The children chosen for these three special study groups were white, middle class, male, and free from any obvious emotional disorders. (On the average, boys and girls did not differ in the initial large sample. Boys only were studied because of the desire to eliminate sources of variance that might be associated with gender. In a study of this magnitude, it is wise to narrow it as much as possible.) The mother of each boy was interviewed for about two and one-half hours, and each mother was asked to fill out an 80-item questionnaire focusing on parental attitudes and practices. In addition, the children themselves were questioned for information on these issues. It was an exhaustive and carefully done study, major reasons why its findings are both informative and instructive. There is nothing, by the way, in the child-rearing literature to suggest that the results of this and similar studies are not equally applicable to girls.

To understand how the parents of high, medium, and low self-esteem children differed in their child-rearing practices and attitudes, Coopersmith's study focused on six different but overlapping aspects of parenting: (1) acceptance of the child and affection shown toward him; (2) kind and amount of punishment used; (3) consistency with which rules were enforced; (4) extent to which the child was listened to and consulted when rules were being set and enforced; (5) level of achievement demands placed on the child; and (6) extent to which the child was allowed to be independent (in contrast to being held in and overprotected).

When the data from mothers and children were analyzed, some clear relationships between parental child-rearing patterns and the self-esteem of their sons emerged. *Parents of boys with high self-esteem were more likely to have the following characteristics:*

1. *They were accepting, affectionate, and involved.* They openly and frequently displayed affection to their children, took an interest in their children's activities, and were acquainted with their children's friends. It is particularly significant, I think, that they considered their children's problems—even minor ones—important and meaningful, something worth their concern.

2. *They were strict, were firm, and consistently enforced family rules.*
Significantly more mothers of high self-esteem boys (85%) regarded discipline as very important as compared to mothers of low self-esteem boys (67%). In addition, a greater number of mothers of high self-esteem children believed that it was more important for children to meet high standards than simply to enjoy themselves. They enforced rules carefully and consistently, established many rules for a wide range of behaviors, and were firm and decisive in telling children what they could or could not do.

3. *They favored noncoercive forms of discipline.* They used very little in the way of physical punishment or threats to withdraw love. Rather, they used management methods: denial of privileges or temporary isolation. There was the important addition of explaining to the child why certain behaviors were good or bad. Mothers of children with medium self-esteem were more likely to use corporal punishment or withdrawal of love; this tendency was even more marked among mothers of children with low self-esteem.

4. *They favored a more democratic family atmosphere.* Although strict and firm, parents of high self-esteem children proved to be neither dogmatic nor dictatorial. For example, they tended to agree with both the following statements: "There is no reason why parents should have their own way all the time, any more than children should have their own way all the time." "Children should have a say in the making of family plans." Parents of low self-esteem children were far less inclined to agree with ideas of that sort. When it comes to attitudes about children's involvement in family matters, you can see the differences between the parents of high self-esteem children and other parents in Figure 5-3.

Table 5–3   SOME CHARACTERISTICS OF PARENTS OF CHILDREN WHO ARE HIGH, MEDIUM, OR LOW IN SELF-ESTEEM

Statements the Parents Were Given	Percent of Parents Who Agreed with the Statement Whose Child Had		
	Low Self-Esteem	*Medium Self-Esteem*	*High Self-Esteem*
"The child should not question the thinking of the parents."	50%	25%	19%
"A child has a right to his own point of view and ought to be allowed to express it."	68%	100%	90%
"Children should have a say in the making of family plans."	41%	68%	77%

Adapted from: S. Coopersmith, *The Antecedents of Self-Esteem,* San Francisco, W. H. Freeman, 1967.

All in all, parents of high self-esteem children tend to be characterized by a broad set of attitudes reflected in relationship practices that are essentially democratic in spirit and expression. These parents love their children, are firm and strict, have high expectations, and may consistently enforce family rules. Yet they rarely punish their children and, in fact, often let them have their own way. In many ways, their style of parenting closely resembles the authoritative approach, described earlier in this chapter. In the final analysis, strict but loving parents are more likely to raise high self-esteem children than parents who are permissive but loving. How can we explain this?

That Special Mix for Positive Self-Esteem: Love, Firmness, and High Expectations

These are key ingredients: Love and acceptance say, "I care about you and want the best for you." Firmness and consistency say, "These are the rules, and these are the consequences for breaking them, something you can count on that helps to make the world a predictable place in which to live." Expectations say, "You can do it; I believe in you."

Why firmness and clearly defined limits are associated with high self-esteem can be explained in several ways. First, establishing a limit—"Yes, you can ride your bike up to Tom's, but stay off the street" or "Yes, you can go out tonight, but remember to be home by ten o'clock"—is an expression of *caring,* particularly if the parent is viewed as warm and understanding to begin with. If, on the other hand, the parent is cold, distant, inconsistent, uncaring, or some combination of these behaviors, parental limits are more likely to be seen as unfair ("All the other kids are going"), arbitrary ("Well, you let me do it yesterday"), or punitive ("You never let me do anything"). When children are loved and accepted and know it, they are much more likely to interpret the limits and discipline they are subjected to as expressions of caring. On the other hand, children who are *not* accepted usually interpret parental restrictions exactly for what they are, namely, expressions of rejection and hostility. This is significant, since high self-esteem is deeply rooted in the experience of *being* esteemed (valued, prized) by others.

Second, clearly defined limits not only give children a basis for evaluating how well or poorly they're doing but also serve to define their social world in terms of what is safe and what is hazardous, what they can and cannot do. For example, if a child is supposed to stay off the street and does it, he *knows* he behaved correctly. If he's supposed to be home by ten o'clock and is, he *knows* he successfully lived up to an expectation. In other words, the existence of limits can give children the feeling that a definition of their social environment is possible, that the world does impose restrictions and make demands, and that they can learn to handle these in everyday living. Parents who are less certain and more permissive about their standards are likely to have children who are not only more dependent on their parents (not knowing exactly what's expected, they may linger around longer waiting to be told) but also more compliant with their peers. Another consideration is that if children have no limits to live up to, they are apt to feel that everything they do is all right, which in the long run robs them of important practice in dealing with situations and circumstances when everything is *not* all right.

Parents who *expect* their children to live up to the standards they established are more likely to facilitate growth than are parents who do *not* have these expectancies. Expectations perform an important function. They not only represent a belief in children's adequacy but also relay the message that the children have the ability to do what is required of them. When set at reasonable levels, expectations represent a very strong vote of confidence. Self-esteem grows out of successfully doing those things we weren't too sure of being able to do in the first place, and if we have someone who believes in us, "expects that we can," then taking that first step is at least a bit easier.

Another important finding of the Coopersmith study was that although all parents wanted their children to be self-confident, some behaved as if they wanted this characteristic to exist *only after the children grew up and left home.* In the meantime, they behaved in ways that fostered dependency and low self-esteem. For example, how often have you heard parents make remarks such as these to their children: "You're so clumsy, you must have two left feet." "No, no, not that way; why are you so stupid?"

Self-esteem is a pervasive characteristic. Children and adolescents with higher levels of self-esteem are apt to have parents who give them lots of attention and affection as well as clear expectations, firm rules, and just punishments. This is exactly the sort of atmosphere that enables the youths in such homes to work hard and aspire to do their best, both necessary prerequisites for maintaining a healthy level of positive self-esteem.

ADULT-CHILD RELATIONSHIPS ARE TWO-WAY STREETS

We have been discussing Coopersmith's findings as if parental practices were directly responsible for producing high self-esteem children, but as mentioned earlier, relationships work both ways. For example, mothers of high self-esteem boys reported that they had good rapport with their sons; the boys were the kind who were relatively easy to live with, self-confident, and competent in school and in their social relationships. They sound like the kind of children who are easy for parents to love, accept, and respect. Perhaps parents of children like this seldom use coercive, severe methods of punishment because they don't need to. Thus, it is not possible to say with certainty whether the parents' love, firmness, and high expectations led these boys to their high self-esteem or whether the boys' competence, cooperativeness, and positive attitude toward their parents enabled the parents to be loving, firm, and more democratic than autocratic. The influences no doubt run both ways in an ongoing stream of mutually reinforcing interactions.

Parents are enormously influential in shaping their children. At the same time, children, by virtue of their behavior and attitudes, can unconsciously influence their parents' manner and style of parenting. I would think that if parents could be helped to understand that responding reactively to children's negative behavior and attitudes only tends to make a bad situation worse, they might work harder at keeping their relationship positive.

However a positive parent-child relationship starts, a major point is this: high self-esteem children are likely to have established a good relationship with

When all else fails, a little creative parenting can help.
Reprinted by permission of Universal Press Syndicate.

their parents—a relationship supported by firm guidelines for living, strengthened by acceptance, nurtured by love, and nourished by attitudes of mutual trust.

IN PERSPECTIVE

Raising a child from its 5- or 6-pound beginning of total helplessness to a self-sustaining, contributing member of society is an enormous challenge. Each of us arrived in this world, not as an empty book waiting to be filled in by others, but as the beginnings of a manuscript already containing sketches of at least the broad outline of genetic possibilities and predispositions for our lives. For better or worse, the extent to which those possibilities are realized depends on many factors, not the least of which is the environment in which we have grown and the choices we have made.

Like sponges, we soaked up the main elements of the environment in which we were immersed—not just the positive elements that sustain healthy attitudes but also the toxic substances that spawn negative attitudes and breed seeds of self-doubt. No single day, or hour, or experience with our parents made a difference in our lives. Rather, it was the cumulation of many hours, days, and experiences strung together over many years that has shaped and formed the essence of our self-other attitudes. Whether parents are aware of it or not, through the way they manage their lives on a daily basis, they teach their children how to blend the basic ingredients for living—how to be close, how to deal with failure and anxiety, how to cope with emotional and physical pain, how to make friends and to *be* a friend, how to resolve conflicts and make decisions, how to love and be loved. Some personalities are shaped by what they admire; others are disfigured by what they despise; this is why providing children models they can look up to is so important to their development.

Some parents—the wise ones—recognize that they begin to lose their children almost as soon as they get them. They have what you might call a "readiness to be forgotten" and are willing participants in their children's growth toward independence. They recognize that it is their task to help their children develop into the best kind of human beings they are capable of becoming; they also know that this will be their whole reward. Wise parents know that children, as they mature, must first fall *out* of love with their own parents—and feel free to do so—before they can fall *in* love with another person and become parents themselves.

Some parents—perhaps those who are possessive and overprotecting—assume that a child "belongs" to them, like a thing. But children are not things and can never be possessions. Children treated as possessions are robbed of many experiences, not the least of which is being valued for their humanness, for their capacity to make their own choices and to learn from their own failures.

Although there is no one best way for raising children, there are some better ways. For example, healthy, balanced children who value themselves and others are likely to come from homes in which the parents respect and care for the children, each other, and themselves; where there are firm rules that are consistently enforced; and where there are high standards for behavior and performance that children are *expected* to live up to.

Children raised permissively by parents who make few demands are given a great deal of freedom but little in the way of challenge or guidance. Later, these children may have trouble finding their strengths because they've not had to look for them in the first place. Children raised autocratically by parents who make too many demands and offer too few options may have the security of knowing the direction they are to take, but the price they pay is subtracted from their growth and development as autonomous human beings.

As with all things in life, there is a balance between too much of this and too little of that, between too much freedom and too much control, between too much love and too little, between expectations that are too low and those that are too high, between too few demands and too many, between engulfment and abandonment. There are many general guidelines, but there is no simple one that fits all children in the same way. Some children need more of one thing and less of another. It depends on the child, the adult, and the interactive mix between the two.

Adults are fond of repeating the truism that children must learn to "grow up." I wonder if it isn't equally valid to suggest that parents, and adults generally, must learn to "grow down" to the child they once were, to the tastes and smells and point of view of those early years to understand the children they are raising, teaching, and guiding.

Basically, there are two things parents can give their children: roots and wings. Roots give children a sense of security and belongingness, while wings allow them to soar to the limits of their possibilities. There is a delicate balance between keeping children around too long and letting go too soon. Wise parents know that if the roots run too deep it is difficult for children to be free, and if children try their wings too soon and without guidance, crash landings are inevitable.

The most fortunate youths are not those who "have it all" and who have to do little to get what they want, but, rather, they are the ones who are expected to work hard to achieve their goals, and in so doing, end up with greater respect for themselves, their efforts, and for those that pointed them in the right direction.

QUESTIONS FOR STUDY, REVIEW, AND REFLECTION

1. How would you describe the changes in child-rearing practices that have occurred since the early 1800s?

2. What are the primary influences on parents' child-rearing methods? Can you explain why a child's temperament may affect the way a parent raises that child? From what you know about yourself as a child, how would you say you influenced your own parents' parenting practices?

3. If you were asked by a group of curious parents to explain the relative contributions of nature and nurture to a child's development, how would you respond?

4. Why is the study of fraternal and identical twins so important to our understanding of genetic and environmental influences on behavior? Can you explain why research involving identical twins is particularly revealing when sorting out the impact of genes and environment on children's development?

5. How would you describe the basic child-rearing styles associated with authoritative, authoritarian, and permissive modes of parenting? What behaviors are associated with children raised in each mode? Which style tends to fit your own parents? How would you describe its effect on you?

6. Can you identify the three basic kinds of attachment to parents that have been observed in children's behavior? What relationships have been found between children's early attachment patterns and their subsequent love relationships?

7. How is identification with parents different from attachment to parents? Is it possible to have one without the other? Why are parental characteristics such as power, availability, and warmth so important to the identification process?

8. If you were asked whether children from divorced families were destined to have troubled lives, how would you respond? What does research suggest about the possible behavioral differences between girls who came from homes where the father is lost through divorce compared to those where the father is lost through death?

9. What is it about a shame-based home environment that is so deleterious to healthy self-concept development?

10. You are asked to make a presentation to a group of parents and teachers on the topic: "Strategies for Helping Children Develop High Self-Esteem." What ideas would you want to be sure to include in your presentation?

REFERENCES _____

Ainsworth, M. D. "Attachment: Retrospect and Prospect," in C. M. Parkes and J. Stevenson-Hinde (Eds.), *The Place of Attachment in Human Behavior*. New York: Basic Books, 1982.

Ainsworth, M. D., Blehar, M., Waters, E., and Wall, S. *Patterns of Attachment*. Hillsdale, N. J.: Erlbaum, 1978.

Aries, P. *Centuries of Childhood*. R. Baldick trans. New York: Knopf, 1962.

Baldwin, A. L. "The Effect of Home Environment and Nursery School Behavior." *Child Development*, 1949, *20:* 49–62.

Baumrind, D. "Child Care Practices Anteceding Three Patterns of Preschool Behavior." *Genetic Psychology Monographs,* 1967, *75:* 43–88.

Baumrind, D. "Authoritarian vs. Authoritative Control." *Adolescence,* 1968, *3:* 256–261.

Baumrind, D. "Current Practices of Parental Authority." *Developmental Psychology Monographs,* 1971, *4:* No. 1, part 2.

Baumrind, D. "New Directions in Socialization Research." *American Psychologist,* 1980, *35:* 639–652.

Baumrind, D. "Rearing Competent Children," in W. Damon (Ed.), *Child Development Today and Tomorrow.* San Francisco: Jossey-Bass, 1989.

Blackwelder, D. E., and Passman, R. H. "Grandmothers' and Mothers' Disciplining in Three-Generational Families: The Role of Social Responsibility in Rewarding and Punishing Grandchildren." *Journal of Personality and Social Psychology,* 1986, *50:* 80–86.

Bouchard, T. J., Jr. "Twins Reared Apart and Together: What They Tell Us About Human Diversity," in S. Fox (Ed.), *The Chemical and Biological Bases of Individuality.* New York: Plenum, 1984.

Bouchard, T. J., Jr., and McGue, M. "Familial Studies of Intelligence: A Review." *Science,* 1981, *212:* 1055–1059.

Bradshaw, J. *Healing the Shame That Binds You.* Deerfield Beach, Fla.: Health Communications, 1988.

Bowlby, J. *Attachment and Loss,* Vol. 3. New York: Basic Books, 1980.

Burchinal, L. G. "Characteristics of Adolescents from Unbroken, Broken, and Reconstituted Families." *Journal of Marriage and Family,* February, 1964, 44–51.

Buss, D. M. "Predicting Parent-Child Interactions from Children's Activity Level." *Developmental Psychology,* 1981, *17:* 59–65.

Coleman, D. "Major Personality Study Finds That Traits Are Mostly Inherited." *New York Times,* December 2, 1986, pp. c1, c2.

Coopersmith, S. *The Antecedents of Self-Esteem.* San Francisco: W. H. Freeman, 1967.

Damon, W. *Social and Personality Development: Infancy Through Adolescence.* New York: Norton, 1983, pp. 153–168.

Ellis, M. V., and Robbins, E. S. "In Celebration of Nature: A Dialogue with Jerome Kagan." *Journal of Counseling and Development,* 1990, *68:* 623–627.

Falconer, D. W. *Introduction to Quantitative Genetics,* 3rd ed. New York: Wiley, 1990.

Fisher, S. *The Female Orgasm: Psychology, Physiology, Fantasy.* New York: Basic Books, 1972.

Fisher, S., and Fisher, R. L. *What We Really Know About Child Rearing: Science in Support of Effective Parenting.* New York: Basic Books, 1976.

Goode, W. J. "Family Disorganization," in R. K. Merton and R. A. Nisbet (Eds.), *Contemporary Social Problems.* New York: Harcourt, Brace, and World, 1966.

Halleck, S. "Hypotheses of Student Unrest," in D. Hamachek (Ed.), *Human Dynamics in Psychology and Education,* 2nd ed. Boston: Allyn and Bacon, 1972.

Harris, I. D. *Normal Children and Their Mothers.* New York: Free, 1959.

Hazan, N. L., and Durrett, M. E. "Relationships of Security of Attachment to Exploration and Mapping Abilities in 2-Year-Olds." *Developmental Psychology,* 1982, *18:* 751–759.

Hazan, C., and Shaver, P. "Romantic Love Conceptualized as an Attachment Process." *Journal of Personality and Social Psychology,* 1987, *52:* 511–524.

Hess, R. D. "Social Class and Ethnic Influences Upon Socialization," in P. H. Mussen (Ed.), *Carmichael's Manual of Child Psychology,* Vol. 2. New York: Wiley, 1970.

Hess, R. D., and Camera, K. A. "Post-Divorce Relationships as Mediating Factors in the Consequences of Divorce for Children." *Journal of Social Issues,* 1979, *35:* 79–96.

Hetherington, E. M. "A Developmental Study of the Effects of Sex of the Dominant Parent on Sex-Role Preference, Identification, and Imitation in Children." *Journal of Personality and Social Psychology,* 1965a, *2:* 188–194.

Hetherington, E. M. "A Developmental Study of the Effects of Sex of the Dominant Parent on Sex-Role Preference, Identification, and Imitation in Children." *Journal of Personality and Social Psychology,* 1965b, *2:* 188–194.

Hetherington, E. M. "The Effects of Father-Absence on Personality Development in Adolescent Daughters." *Developmental Psychology,* 1972, *7:* 313–336.

Hetherington, E. M., Cox, M., and Cox, R. "Effects of Divorce on Parents and Children," in M. Lamb (Ed.), *Nontraditional Families.* Hillsdale, N. J.: Erlbaum, 1982.

Holden, C. "Genes and Behavior: A Twin Legacy." *Psychology Today,* September, 1987, pp. 18–19.

Jensen, L. C., and Kingston, M. *Parenting.* New York: Holt, Rinehart and Winston, 1986.

Kaufman, G. *The Psychology of Shame.* New York: Springer, 1989.

Klein, M., and Stern, L. "Low Birth Weight and the Battered Child Syndrome." *American Journal of Diseases of Children,* 1971, *122:* 171–178.

Kohn, M. L. "Social Class and Parent-Child Relationships: An Interpretation." *American Journal of Sociology,* 1963, *68:* 471–480.

Kohn, M. L. *Class and Conformity,* 2nd ed. Chicago: University of Chicago Press, 1977.

Korner, A. F. "Conceptual Issues in Infancy Research," in J. D. Osofsky (Ed.), *Handbook of Infant Development.* New York: Wiley, 1979.

Leo, J. "Exploring the Traits of Twins." *Time,* January 12, 1987, p. 63.

Londerville, S., and Main, M. "Security of Attachment and Compliance in Maternal Training Methods in the Second Year of Life." *Developmental Psychology,* 1981: *17:* 289–299.

Lynn, D. B. *Daughters and Parents: Past, Present, and Future.* Monterey, Calif.: Brooks/Cole, 1979.

Maccoby, E. E. *Social Development: Psychological Growth and Parent-Child Relationship.* New York: Harcourt, Brace, Jovanovich, 1980.

Mantell, D. B. "Guess Who Had the Authoritarian Parents?" *Psychology Today,* September, 1974, pp. 56–62.

Matas, L., Arend, R. A., and Stroufe, L. A. "Continuity of Adaptation in the Second Year: The Relationship Between Quality of Attachment and Later Competence." *Child Development,* 1978, *49:* 547–556.

Moulton, R. W., Liberty, P. G., Jr., Burnstein, E., and Altacher, N. "Patterning of Parental Affection and Disciplinary Dominance as a Determinant of Guilt and Sex-Typing." *Journal of Personality and Social Psychology,* 1966, *4:* 456–463.

Mussen, P., and Rutherford, E. "Parent-Child Relations and Parental Personality in Relation to Young Children's Sex-Role Preferences." *Child Development,* 1963, *34:* 589–607.

Parpel, M., and Maccoby, E. E. "Maternal Involvement and Subsequent Child Compliance." *Child Development,* 1985, *56:* 1326–1334.

Parke, R. D. *Fathers.* Cambridge, Mass.: Harvard University Press, 1981.

Pastor, D. L. "The Quality of Mother-Infant Attachment in Its Relationship to Toddlers' Initial Sociability with Peers." *Developmental Psychology,* 1981, *17:* 326–385.

Plomin, R. "Environment and Genes: Determinants of Behavior." *American Psychologist,* 1989, *44:* 105–111.

Ribble, M. A. *The Rights of Infants.* New York: Columbia University Press, 1943.

Rousseau, J. J. *Emile, or on Education.* London: Dent, 1974. (Originally published 1762.)

Rubin, J., Provenzano, F., and Luria, Z. "The Eye of the Beholder: Parents' Views on Sex of Newborns." *Journal of Orthopsychiatry,* 1974, *44:* 512–519.

Scarr, S. "What's a Parent to Do?" *Psychology Today,* May, 1984, pp. 58–63.

Schaffer, H. R., and Emerson, P. E. "The Development of Social Attachments in Infancy." *Monographs of the Society for Research in Child Development,* 1964, 29, (3).

Sears, P. S. "Child-Rearing Factors Related to Playing of Sex-Typed Roles." *American Psychologist,* 1953, *8:* 431. (Abstract.)

Sears, R. R., Maccoby, E. E., and Levin, H. *Patterns of Child-Rearing.* Evanston, Ill.: Row, Peterson, 1957.

Segel, N. L. "The Importance of Twin Studies for Individual Differences Research." *Journal of Counseling and Development,* July/August 1990, *68:* 612–622.

Siegel, A. E., and Kohn, L. G. "Permissiveness, Permission, and Aggression: The Effects of Adult Presence or Absence on Aggression in Children's Play." *Child Development,* 1959, *36:* 131–141.

Spock, B. M. *Baby and Child Care.* New York: Pocket Books, 1947.

Spock, B. M. *Baby and Child Care: Revised and Enlarged.* New York: Pocket Books, 1957.

Spock, B. M. "Don't Blame Me!" *Look Magazine.* January 26, 1971.

Sports Illustrated. December, 1975, p. 52.

Staub, E. "To Rear a Prosocial Child: Reasoning, Learning by Doing, and Learning by Teaching Others," in D. DePalma and J. Foley (Eds.), *Moral Development: Current Theory and Research.* Hillsdale, N. J.: Erlbaum, 1975.

Sunley, R. "Early Nineteenth Century American Literature on Child Rearing," in M. Mead and M. Wolfstein (Eds.), *Childhood in Contemporary Cultures.* Chicago: University of Chicago Press, 1955.

Tellegen, A., Lykken, D. T., Bouchard, T. J., Wilcox, K. J., Segal, N. L., and Rich, S. "Personality Similarity in Twins Reared Apart and Together." *Journal of Personality and Social Psychology,* 1988, *54:* 1031–1039.

Thomas, A., and Chess, S. *Temperament and Development.* New York: Brunner/Mazel, 1977.

U. S. Census Bureau, Population Division, Current Reports, Series P-20, No. 423, Washington, D. C.: U. S. Government Printing Office, March, 1988.

Wallerstein, J. S. "Effects of Divorce." *New York Times Magazine,* January 22, 1989.

Wallerstein, J. S., and Blakeslee, S. *Second Chances: Men, Women, and Children a Decade After Divorce.* New York: Ticknor and Fields, 1989.

Watson, J. B. *Psychological Care of Infant and Child.* New York: Norton, 1928.

Weiss, R. S. "Growing Up a Little Faster: The Experience of Growing Up in a Single-Parent Household." *Journal of Social Issues,* 1979, *35:* 97–111.

Willerman, L. "Effects of Families on Intellectual Development." *American Psychologist,* 1979, *34:* 923–929.

Wolfstein, M. "The Emergence of Fun Morality." *Journal of Social Issues,* 1951, *7:* 15–25.

Zussman, J. S. *Situational Determinants of Parental Behavior,* Doctoral Thesis, Department of Psychology, Stanford University, 1977.

Chapter 6

Self-Concept as Related to Academic Performance, Teachers' Expectations, and Teaching Practices

PROLOGUE

If we were to stand outside a school at the beginning of a day and watch the children as they enter, we would, of course, see youngsters of various sizes and shapes, and we would see that they carried books, school supplies, lunch bags, and other paraphernalia necessary for daily survival. We would see all the things that they had on the outside for us to observe. What we wouldn't see are the pictures they carried of themselves on the inside, pictures of themselves as students with particular strengths and shortcomings.

Here comes Christine, a happy, lively fourth-grader who usually does well in school and looks forward to each school day. The positive picture she carries around of herself was reinforced by her mother as she left for school: "Have a good day in school today, Chris. I know you'll do as well as you can." Christine has a spelling test coming up in the morning, a test she feels she'll do quite well on because she studied the words last night and believes in herself.

And here comes Christopher, a somewhat somber-looking lad shuffling along in no apparent hurry to get to his fifth-grade class. Christopher's picture of himself is colored with negative feelings, a hue that was reinforced by the last words he heard as he left for school: "Christopher, for heaven's sake, pay attention today. Don't do something stupid like you usually do." Christopher has an arithmetic test facing him in the

262

afternoon, and he feels pretty sure he won't do well on it, unless he's very lucky.

The private picture that Christine and Christopher each carry around with them is essentially a composite blend of their innate abilities, personal experiences, and the feedback they've received from significant others. Each of these three components is important in its own way, and each has the potential for being more or less potent than the other two. If, for example, Christine has just average innate abilities but receives consistently supportive, encouraging feedback from her significant others, this may help develop in her the kind of confidence in herself that enables her to take risks, to try to do things that are at the limits of her ability. This, in turn, makes it possible for her to have more success experiences, which increases the positive feedback she receives, which encourages her to take more risks, and a positive cycle is perpetuated. If, on the other hand, Christopher has above-average ability but hears primarily negative feedback about his efforts from his significant others (he could always do better), this may cause him to fall below his possibilities because of his anxiety about letting others down. This, in turn, interferes with his ability to think clearly, which gets in the way of doing as well as he might otherwise do, which leads to more negative feedback, and a negative cycle is perpetuated.

Christine and Christopher's "private pictures"—which are called "self-concept"—are the emotional undercurrents that shape the direction of their attitudes toward themselves and school. This is important to be aware of because self-concept dynamics and learning go hand in hand. If Christopher, who we know has an above-average IQ, says, "I just know I'm going to have trouble on that arithmetic test—I'm just not good at numbers," chances are that Christopher will have a tough time with arithmetic. If Christine, who we know has an IQ in the average range, says, "I'm looking forward to math—I feel I can do pretty well in that subject," chances are equally good that Christine will, all things being equal, do pretty well in math. Classroom observations and research are helping us understand that how people perform in school—or anywhere else for that matter—depends not only on what they are actually capable of doing but also on what they believe they are capable of doing.

The self is made up of two basic components—concepts and feelings. We know we have particular qualities, but equally important, we have certain feelings about those qualities. For example, we may know that our measured IQ is, say, 120, but unless we have the self-confidence and necessary belief in ourselves to do the things that are possible within our abilities, our 120 IQ is a practically useless possession. What we have by way of personal attributes is far less important than how we feel about those attributes.

Is a student's school self-concept a single global attribute, or is it specific to subject matter areas? What is the relationship between self-concept and school achievement? How do children acquire a particular mind set about their ability to do academic work? What is the effect of school failure on one's self-concept and self-esteem? How are self-concept and level of self-esteem related? Which comes first, a positive self-concept or high achievement? How does the psychology of teachers' expectations work? It is to these and related issues that we will address ourselves in this chapter.

Let's turn our attention first to a way we can conceptualize self-concept as it is related to academic matters.

SELF-CONCEPT AS RELATED TO SCHOOLING: ITS HIERARCHICAL AND MULTIDIMENSIONAL STRUCTURE

Although it would simplify matters to be able to think about self-concept as a single global intrapsychic construct that governed all aspects of one's school-related behaviors, it turns out to be a bit more complicated than that. Fortunately, however, not much more. As a result of a series of studies and analyses by Marsh and Shavelson (1985) and Marsh (1990a, 1990b), four components of one's school self-concept have been identified: (1) general self-concept, (2) nonacademic self-concept, (3) academic English self-concept, and (4) academic mathematics self-concept. General self-concept refers to our overall integration of the various components of the self; it helps determine the course of our more general everyday behavior. For students—and perhaps for others, too—general self-concept is organized along nonacademic and academic lines, while academic self-concept is associated with English and math.

Figure 6-1 provides a visual conceptualization of how self-concept and its various facets are configured. You can see that one's nonacademic self-concept includes components such as physical ability and appearance, and peer and parent relationships, while academic English self-concept includes components such as parent relationships, reading, and general school performance. The fourth facet, academic mathematics self-concept, represents the components of parent relationships, general school performance, and mathematics. The hierarchical configuration in Figure 6-1 gives you an idea of how the various components and facets of self-concept are related to each other. For example, English self-concept and nonacademic self-concept are positively correlated with each other, as are mathematics self-concept and nonacademic self-concept. This suggests that as one's self-concept goes up or down in one of these areas, it is likely to go up or down in the other as well. Note, however, that there is no line connecting English self-concept to math self-concept, which suggests that these two facets of self-concept are nearly uncorrelated. What this means is that a person could have a rather low self-concept when it comes to mathematics ability but still have a fairly high self-concept in areas involving English skills. Or, a student could have a fairly low self-concept when it came to mathematics and English skills but still have a positive general self-concept

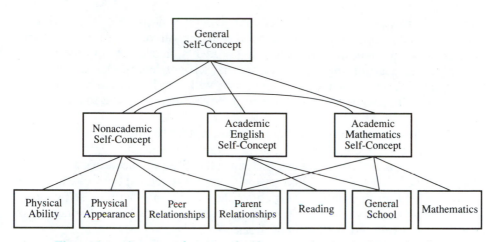

Figure 6-1 *Conceptualization of self-concept showing its hierarchical and multifaceted organization.*

Adapted from: H. W. Marsh, "A Multidimensional, Hierarchical Model of Self-Concept: Theoretical and Empirical Justification," *Educational Psychology Review,* 1990, 2: 90.

because his or her nonacademic self-concept was high enough to compensate for the math and English deficiencies. This might be the case for a student who had a low self-concept when it came to math or English but whose nonacademic self-concept was especially high in the areas of physical ability and peer relationships. A gifted athlete, for example, might have a positive general self-concept even though his or her self-concept in mathematics or English was low.

What affects one area of a person's self-concept may or may not affect other areas. Self-concept is not made up of just one thing but is constructed from various skills, deficits, strengths, and experiences, which as a package comprise our more global perceptions (general self-concept) of who we are and what we can do. Because one's general self-concept is constructed from so many factors, measures of general self-concept tend not to be very good predictors of achievement in specific school subjects (Marsh, Byrne, and Shavelson, 1988; Shavelson and Marsh, 1986).

An example may make this clearer. If we were to measure, say, a man's general physical strength and agility and find that he was above average in those areas, this may allow us to make some general predictions about his athletic prowess. However, we would be pressing our luck if we tried to predict the *particular* athletic event(s) he would be best at. In order to do this, we would need at least two additional pieces of information: (1) his own assessment of ability in specific areas, and (2) more specific measures of his skills in those areas. Knowing only that a man is above average in physical strength tells us nothing about how the strength can or will be used, nor does it say anything about the events that have contributed to its development. In a similar fashion, the same is true in predicting a student's achievement in specific content areas when only information on that student's general self-concept is available. If we know that a student has, for example, a high positive general self-concept, this tells us only that, in relation to other students, it is at the very least above average. It tells us nothing about whether that self-concept is related to particular academic and nonacademic talents, nor will it tell us anything about the experiences (academic and nonacademic) that have contributed to its development.

By conceptualizing one's school self-concept as having various facets and arranged in a hierarchical manner, as in Figure 6-1, you can begin to see how various people and experiences can influence the different facets of self-concept. As pointed out in Marsh's (1990a) review of literature related to this idea, we are more likely to get a reliable reading about the relationship between self-concept and achievement by paying attention to students' specific self-concepts in specific academic and nonacademic areas.

Having looked at a way for conceptualizing self-concept in relation to academic matters, let's turn our attention to a closer look at the nature of the relationship between self-concept and achievement.

THE RELATIONSHIP BETWEEN SELF-CONCEPT AND ACADEMIC PERFORMANCE

The idea that there is a relationship between self-concept and school performance is not a new one. Over 45 years ago, Prescott Lecky (1945) was one of the first to point out that low academic achievement might be related to a student's self-perception of being unable to learn academic material. Noticing that some children made about the same number of spelling errors per page no matter how difficult or easy the material, it occurred to Lecky that the children might be responding more in terms of how they thought they could spell than in terms of their actual spelling abilities. He arranged to have a group of these children spend some time with a counselor who helped them explore their feelings about their spelling abilities. As a consequence of these discussions, and despite the fact that these children had no additional work in spelling, there was a notable improvement in their spelling. As they moved from believing they were poor spellers to believing they were at least better spellers than they thought they were, their performance changed in the direction of being consistent with those new perceptions.

Lecky's pioneering research, although simplistic and uncontrolled by today's standards, opened the door to a mind-boggling possibility: How students feel about their abilities may, for better or for worse, consciously or unconsciously, affect their academic performance. Thus, the idea was planted that suggested that academic achievement may not be simply an expression of students' intelligence, but of students' *perceptions* of their intelligence, which when positive helps them feel confident and able, but when negative makes them feel hesitant and uncertain.

Consider the following interview I had with a tenth-grade male high school student (Jerry), who at the time was trying to solve some problems he was having at school. (He had an IQ of 127 and scored at the 11th-grade level on a Math Achievement Test.) It captures the flavor, I think, of how one's self-perceptions of ability can affect one's performance.

DH:	You seem to be having a lot of problems in math this year.
Jerry:	Yeah . . . I don't know, I just don't do well on tests.
DH:	That may be, but yet I notice you do well on other tests in other courses.
Jerry:	Well, math is different.
DH:	How is it different?
Jerry:	Well, I don't know—I just don't think I'm very good at it.
DH:	And yet on the math achievement test you got a high enough score to put you among the 11th graders.
Jerry:	I must've been lucky the day I took it.
DH:	Do you suppose you study as hard as you can in order to prepare for your math tests?
Jerry:	Well, probably not—at least not like I do for my tests in other classes.
DH:	Wonder why you don't.
Jerry:	The way I look at it, it wouldn't do any good anyway— I'd still only get maybe a C or C+.

You can see from Jerry's responses that his perceptions of his math abilities were affecting not only his feelings about math but also important aspects of his math behavior, for example, his decision about how much time to study.

Once a student's self-perception of ability has evolved in a certain direction, the tendency seems to be to make choices that work to reinforce the validity of that self-concept. In Jerry's case, for example, choosing to put less time into math reduced his chances of improving his performance, thereby perpetuating a somewhat shaky self-image concerning math ability. Inasmuch as self-concept reflects our private integration of feelings and ideas we have developed about our abilities, talents, potentials, and actual behavior, it is not surprising that the feelings and ideas we have about ourselves as learners may be directly or indirectly related to our *performance* as learners.

Numerous reviews of self-concept research conducted over the past 25 years or so point to a consistent finding: There is a small-to-moderate positive correlation between students' academic achievement and their self-concept of ability (Bloom, 1976; Byrne, 1984; Hamachek, 1990; Hansford and Hattie, 1982; Marsh, 1990a; Skaalvik and Hagtvet, 1990; Wylie, 1979). Hansford and Hattie's review is particularly significant because of the sheer weight of the 128 studies they included in their meta-analysis, which involved a total sample of 202,823 persons, producing a data base of 1,136 correlations between self-ratings and performance measures. A range in the relationship of −.77 to .96 was reported with an average correlation of .21. This is by no means a large correlation, but the fact that it remains positive in the face of so many different variables across so many studies (e.g., differences in grade level of subjects, socioeconomic status, ethnicity, ability of subjects, type of performance and achievement measures) suggests that the relationship between self-concept and academic achievement, though small, is real, not an artifact of measurement tools or research design.

Self-concept and school achievement seem to be most highly correlated between about seven and 15 years of age. For example, Williams (1973) found a high correlation between the two at the first-grade level; Piers and Harris (1964) noted a similarly high correlation at the sixth-grade level; and Rubin (1978), with a sample of nine to 15 year olds, reported that the correlation between self-esteem and achievement increases in strength over this time. However, O'Malley and Bachman's (1979) analysis of a nationwide sample of 3,183 male and female high school seniors found that *educational success becomes less central to self-esteem during late high school years and the years that follow.*

The research related to self-concept and achievement serves to underscore two ongoing themes: (1) How students perform in school is affected by how they *think* they can perform; and (2) the direction of their thinking—positive or negative—begins early in their school careers. O'Malley and Bachman's findings suggest strongly that by the time students are juniors and seniors their sources of self-esteem are far less connected to school performance. The implication here is a powerful one: A student's concept of self has been influenced about as much, for better or worse, by school experiences as it can be influenced by about the middle of high school, which suggests that it is most malleable during the first ten years or so of schooling. The years that really make a difference are the early years, when the effects of success and especially failure can have an enormous impact on a growing child's fragile identity and vulnerable psyche. Which leads us to an important consideration.

THE IMPORTANCE OF SUCCESS IN ELEMENTARY SCHOOL

The years from ages five to 12—from kindergarten through sixth grade—are crucial years in children's development. It is during this time frame that children test themselves, expand their range further from home, and are exposed to increasingly more complicated challenges. Learning, which during their preschool years was random and informal, now becomes more systematic and organized. Not only are there more experiences in which to take part, but there are increased demands to *remember* those experiences, which can range all the way from learning the alphabet to learning to read, add, subtract, spell, and write coherent sentences. What happens in these early years to children is central to all their subsequent schooling, not just in terms of basic knowledge but in terms of basic attitudes about themselves. These are years when the footings of children's self-concepts are either firmly established in experiences of success, accomplishment, and pride in themselves or planted in shifting sands of self-doubt, failure, and feelings of worthlessness. There are at least three good reasons for these possible outcomes.

1. *Elementary-school-aged children's self-esteem is incomplete and impressionable.* Children at this age are in the early phases of forming their concept of self. This does not mean that they have no sense of identity whatsoever, but it does suggest that *their sense of who they are and what they can do is incompletely formed.* Characteristically, elementary-school-aged youngsters are malleable and impressionable. They are ready not only to please adults but to *believe* them as well. Indeed, what adults say about them or how they evaluate either their person or performance is incorporated more readily, more easily, and more uncritically than at any other developmental stage. The feedback children receive from peers and adults—particularly significant adults like parents and teachers—is more likely to have a greater impact because a child this age is still developing and is incomplete, is more open to input, and, thus, more susceptible to influence.

2. *Elementary-school-aged children have immature defenses—they are vulnerable.* Youth this age are not well defended psychologically. In the absence of a consolidated and reasonably well-integrated self-image, they are less likely to use active and assertive mechanisms such as denial or projection in order to protect themselves from ego-damaging experiences and more likely to use the passive and more primitive mechanism of regression, which allows them to stay at a safer and more dependent level of development. (Indeed, whether in children or adults, regressive behavior is not an uncommon phenomenon following failure experiences.) In order to use a defense mechanism, one first of all has to have a reasonably well-defined self to begin with. Elementary-school-aged children are not totally incapable of compensating for their failure by displacing their anger or projecting blame for poor work on the teacher. It is a matter of degree. If a second grader fails a spelling test, he is more likely to "believe" that mark (that is, incorporate it, internalize it) than is a 12th-grader with a positive view of herself, and a history of doing well in school, who fails a geometry test. The 12th-grader can blame her performance on a fluke,

deny its importance, rationalize her lack of study, or project it on her teacher. As long as her performance is inconsistent with her concept of self, she can defend herself against the loss of self-esteem. The second grader, on the other hand, does not yet have a well-defined self with which he can or has to be consistent. Hence, whether it is a failure or success experience, elementary-school-aged children can offer far less resistance to its impact and will be much less critical recipients of its place in their evolving sense of self.

3. *Elementary-school-aged children are still in the "industry versus inferiority" stage.* As noted in greater detail in Chapter 1, the six- to 12-year-old age group represents a growth phase that Erikson (1980)

Some students seem to have more trouble being successful in school than others.

Reprinted by permission of Universal Press Syndicate.

has referred to as the "industry versus inferiority" stage. This is a natural time in the children's growth and development when they learn to be either industrious, productive, and autonomous, or feel inferior, withdrawn, and dependent. The major danger of this period is the development of a sense of inadequacy and inferiority in children who do not experience enough successes.

Our hope is that all children going to school would experience enough success to maintain an interest in school and, thereby, continue to learn and improve themselves. But this doesn't always happen. Then what?

Dropping Out: A Possible Consequence of Low Self-Esteem and Too Much Failure

Usually, when we discover that we're not very good at something, we either reduce the time we put into it or cease doing it altogether. To continue is too painful because it reminds us of a failing or shortcoming we would just as soon forget. Most of us can live with our various shortcomings if we can periodically experience at least some success in areas that are more central to our self-esteem. For example, doing reasonably well in school or work, which may be more central to our feelings of self-worth, makes it possible for us to do other things less well—e.g., sing, dance, play tennis, golf—without losing our self-esteem. It is, likely, however, that people who do those things for a living might experience dips in self-esteem if they suddenly find themselves not singing, or dancing, or playing tennis, or golfing as well as they had. For them, those activities *would* be more central to their feelings of self-worth. If their skills decreased significantly enough, they very likely would stop doing what they were doing and go on to something more rewarding.

Basically, this is exactly what happens to the millions of dropouts who, because of their many failures and commensurate feelings of low self-worth, terminate their education. Schooling *is* central to their lives. When that is not going well, there is nothing that can be put in its place. It is not particularly surprising that the results of a nine-year study of more than 1,600 males from 10th grade onward showed that the average level of self-esteem of those who eventually dropped out was consistently lower than that of all other students (Bachman, O'Malley, and Johnson, 1978). And perhaps it is also not surprising to find, as Bachman and O'Malley (1977) did in a four-year study, that dropouts' self-esteem got *higher* once they were out of school. Like any of us who experience too much failure in what we're doing, leaving it and going on to something else usually helps us feel better. It is sad but true that some students must leave school to improve their sense of self-worth.

Not all dropouts, of course, leave school because of failure to do well. Some leave because they are bored, angry, beset with personal problems, or have low intelligence, or some combination of these factors. As pointed out by Fine and Rosenberg (1983), about one-fifth of all dropouts can be classified as gifted.

Most, however, leave to escape the painful cumulative effects of repeated failure experiences (Eckstrom, et al., 1987; Kagan, 1990).

The breadth and depth of failures felt by many of those who drop out covers a wide range of experiences and goes back deep in time. Consider some of the evidence:

1. Eckstrom and his colleagues (1987) found, in their review of data from a national longitudinal dropout study, that one-third of those who dropped out said they did so because they did not like school because of negative experiences, and another one-third specifically cited poor grades as their reason for leaving.

2. In an earlier investigation of the long-term effects of early school failure, Dillon (1949) found that out of 2,000 children who began first grade at the same time in the same school system, 643 dropped out before completing high school. All but five of these dropouts— 638, or 99 percent—had been retained in the first grade. As a combined total, these 643 students failed a total of more than 1,800 grades during their first six years of school. This averages out that each dropout failed every other year for six years!

3. Over 74 percent of the dropouts in one school system repeated at least one grade as compared to only 18 percent among students who graduated from high school (Hall, 1964).

4. More than 1,200 students in sixth and seventh grades from 14 representative schools in a North Carolina study were investigated to differentiate between repeaters and nonrepeaters (Godfrey, 1971). Results showed that those who had been retained were reading at a 6.8 grade level; those repeating one grade scored a 5.2 level. On mathematics achievement, nonrepeaters averaged in the 27th percentile; and those repeating were in the tenth percentile; and those repeating two or more grades dropped to the fifth percentile. Failing was also found to have a strong influence on a student's feeling of self-worth. For example, on all the subscales of the *Tennessee Self-Concept Scale,* students who repeated grades scored lower than those who had not. Students repeating two or more grades scored far below the mean subscale.

Achievement Potentials and Self-Concept Directions Are Formed Early

The dropout problem is one of enormous proportions. Over four million young people between the ages of 16 and 24 drop out of school, which is 13 percent of this age group. In large urban areas, this number jumps to somewhere between 40 and 60 percent (Hahn, 1987). The numbers are staggering, not to mention the economic and social problems created by incompletely educated young men and women trying to make it in an increasingly more knowledge-oriented, technology-based world.

Leaving school early is one very explicit and dramatic consequence of failures that occur too early and too frequently. What we haven't mentioned are those hundreds of thousands of children who are victimized by excessive early school failures but who do not choose so dramatic an exit. Rather, they persist through school, suffering quietly and inwardly, and eventually graduate into a competitive society that demands not only a reasonable level of competence in some kind of work but also a certain degree of confidence in one's ability to do it. Although we can take collective pride in the fact that our nation has the highest stay-in-school rate in the world, the reality is that thousands of young people graduate after 13 years of school feeling somewhat helpless, hopeless, and defeated. Feelings like these, whether among those who drop out because they can't tolerate more failure or among those who stay in school and suffer through it, start during the elementary years.

For example, although studies indicate that approximately 70 percent of all dropouts complete at least a ninth-grade education, there is increasing evidence that negative attitudes about school and thoughts of leaving it begin early in a child's school experiences. In an intensive study of 45 girls and 60 boys who were about to drop out of school, Lichter (1982) found that the reason was not the result of any specific learning failure but rather a broad educational disability that, for boys in particular, started in elementary school. Experiences of success or failure during this time in their lives can apparently have a significant impact on the self-perceptions of elementary age youths.

Findings of longitudinal research indicate that something like a critical period for the formation of abilities and attitudes for school learning occurs, or is set or stabilized, sometime between the ages of five and nine. For example, Bloom's (1964) analysis suggests that adolescent or adult intelligence is about 50 percent stabilized or predictable by the first grade, whereas adolescent *achievement* in school is predictable to the same extent only at age nine or at about the end of grade three. This means that factors that contribute to school achievement other than intelligence are to a considerable extent stabilized during the first three grades. In large measure, these factors are sheer skill factors, which are cumulative in nature. That is, if children have more skills in the first grade, they accumulate further skills in the second, and more in the third, and so on. However, as noted by Kolberg, LaCrosse, and Ricks (1972), "In large part . . . this stabilization of school achievement is based on the stabilization of factors of interest in learning, attention, and *sense of competence.*"

What all this research points to is the early establishment of a positive or negative attitudinal set that can influence, for better or worse, subsequent school achievement. Children's feelings about their ability to do schoolwork (their sense of competence) are rooted in their early school experiences, and these determine, to a great extent, both the intensity and direction of their emerging self-conceptions of ability. Which brings us to an important consideration.

Four Reasons Why Early School Successes Are Important

It is clear that early school experiences have lasting effects. The earlier they occur and the more similar they are, the more likely they will be incorporated as part of children's concept of academic ability and sense of personal worth. Thus, experiencing as much success as possible in the elementary years is important for at least four basic reasons: (1) Subsequent success is not only easier to build onto early success, but it also seems more possible to the student; (2) early success gives children not only a sense of competence and accomplishment, but also a precedent with which they can strive to be consistent; (3) early school success makes any later school failures more bearable because they are more likely to be cushioned by previous successes and a developed sense of personal competency; and (4) early school successes help students develop the kind of positive mental image of themselves with which they can strive to be consistent.

This last point is particularly important because it underscores what seems to be generally true about human behavior: People tend to behave in reasonably consistent and stable ways, which basically means that once an image of ourselves is fixed in our minds, we tend to behave (and achieve) in a manner more or less in line with that image.

SELF-IMAGE CONSISTENCY AND ITS RELATIONSHIP TO SCHOOL PERFORMANCE

We each have a mental picture of the kind of person we are. It may not be entirely conscious, but it is there, a kind of emotional blueprint consisting of an interfacing of ideas, values, attitudes, and outlooks that have been shaped by our past experiences, our successes and failures, our humiliations, our triumphs, and the way other people responded to us, particularly during our formative years. It is a blueprint that allows us to construct a consolidated framework of beliefs about ourselves. We then go about the business of living and performing in a manner that is more or less consistent with that framework.

The adolescent boy, for example, who carries around a dismal mental picture of himself as a student can find all sorts of excuses to avoid studying, participating in class, or doing homework. Frequently, he ends up with the low grade he thought he would get in the first place. This supports the picture he has of himself, which, in turn, reinforces his feelings that he's not very able, and so he concludes, "Why study anyway?" (For some students, there is a certain risk involved in studying. If, for example, I am a low self-esteem person concerned about the possibility of not doing well, I may be reluctant to study for fear that I *still won't do well,* which means I could be left with no excuse to explain it away.)

It seldom occurs to certain students that their academic trouble lies in their own evaluations of themselves. If you tell struggling students that they only "think" they cannot grasp algebra, or English, or reading, or whatever, they may very well give that "Who are you trying to kid?" look. In their own way, they may have tried again and again, but still their report cards tell the story. A request (more often a demand or admonishment) destined to fall on deaf ears is the one parents and teachers frequently make of some students to "study harder." This is fine if those are the students who already have a high self-concept and high need for achievement, because they are likely to respond to the challenge in order to produce at a level consistent with their self-image. However, for students whose self-picture is that of being poor students, the impact is lost. As a low-concept, low-achieving ninth-grade girl once told me, "Study? Ha! Why should I study to fail?" This young lady was not aware that her frustrations with failure had already set the wheels in motion for her to behave in ways that were consistent with a failure self-image. Again, we need to remind ourselves that this consistency is not always voluntary or deliberate, but compulsive, and generally unconsciously motivated.

It is important to keep the self-consistency idea in mind because it will help us understand better the relationship between school performance and self-concept. *Once students "lock in" on a perception of what they are and are not able to do, it is difficult to shake them from it, particularly if the perception has time to root itself into a firmly established belief.* The findings from a study done by Lepper, Ross, and Lau (1986) with 52 male and female high school students illustrates this principle. The format of the study was set up (rigged, actually) in such a way so that about half of the students were successful solving a set of math problems while the other half failed. The important aspect of this study is that those students who failed persisted in viewing themselves negatively even when it was made clear to them that their failures were due to clearly inferior instruction. Although the investigators expected failing students, in particular, to grasp at any reasonable explanation for their seemingly poor performance, they did not do so. The researchers concluded their report with an ominous warning:

> . . . the practical implications of the present studies seem relatively clear. Overcoming the pernicious effects of early school failures on students' self-perceptions and attitudes may indeed prove a difficult assignment. Simply demonstrating to a child, even in a clear and concrete fashion, that his or her poor performance may well have been the consequence of an inept or biased teacher, a substandard school, or even prior social, cultural, or economic disadvantages may have little impact on his or her feelings of personal competence or potential. If the student's beliefs are translated, as well, into a selective avoidance of related subjects or tasks in the future—as in the present experiment where failure subjects showed less optimism and enthusiasm about the inclusion of related materials in the curriculum—opportunities for subsequent enlightenment may be precluded, and negative views about one's abilities may become self-fulfilling. (p. 490)

In any discussions involving self-concept and academic achievement, the old chicken or the egg question inevitably comes up . . .

WHICH COMES FIRST—A POSITIVE SELF-CONCEPT OR HIGH ACHIEVEMENT?

Although one might argue that students would first have to do well in school in order to possess a positive self-image about their academic abilities, it could also be argued that a positive self-image must precede doing well in school. There is ammunition for both sides.

On the Side of Self-Concept Preceding Achievement

Consider first some of the evidence on the side of those who argue that a positive self-concept precedes doing well in school. For example, in an early study by Wattenberg and Clifford (1964) evidence was found suggesting that a negative self-image may affect a skill as basic as reading before children even enter first grade. In a sample that included 128 kindergarten students in two schools, they measured intelligence, self-concept, ego strength, and reading ability of all the students when they were in kindergarten and then again when they finished second grade. It was found that measures of self-concept and ego strength made at the beginning of kindergarten were more predictive of reading ability two and one-half years later than were measures of intelligence. In other words, the self-attitudes of kindergarten students were a more accurate indication of their potential reading skills than were intelligence test scores. However, we cannot assume from this finding that there is no relationship between mental ability and reading achievement. All we can safely conclude is that a measure of kindergarten students' self-concept and ego strength may be a good predictor of how they might fare in their reading skills by the third grade. Also, a five year old's verbal skills are usually not sufficiently developed to be measured with great accuracy, which may be one reason why Wattenberg and Clifford found a low relationship between intelligence and later reading achievement.

A study a year later by Lamy (1965), investigating the relationship between kindergarten children's perceptions of themselves and their subsequent reading in the first grade, demonstrated similar results. Her findings led her to suggest that not only do children's self-perceptions give as good a prediction of later reading achievement as intelligence test scores, but that children's self-concepts may be causal factors in their subsequent reading achievement.

Other evidence for the idea that a positive self-concept precedes high achievement was revealed in a study involving 53 children in two elementary classrooms. A major finding was that students who started with high self-concepts not only spent more time working on school-related tasks than low self-concept students, but they were also more likely to be among those who *improved* their self-images by getting things done, something referred to as a "positive feedback loop" (Shiffler, Lynch-Sauer, and Nadelman, 1977).

There is also evidence showing that doing well academically is preceded by a high self-concept for high school students, as well. For example, Felson's

(1984) analysis of self-concept and school achievement data collected during the tenth, 11th, and 12th grades for 2,213 high school males showed a consistent positive relationship between self-concept of ability and grade point average in the 11th and 12th grades. In other words, those students who perceived themselves as capable were more likely to be among those with a higher grade point average, an outcome due, in part, to what Felson saw as differences in effort. In his words, "Students who believe they are smart apparently work harder than students with less favorable self-appraisals and this effort results in higher grades" (p. 950).

Let us be clear in understanding that a positive or negative self-concept does not *cause* high or low achievement. What we can say is that one's self-concept can affect achievement. This effect can work in one of two ways, depending on the nature of one's self-concept. First, the more ability students attribute to themselves, the greater their estimation of the probability of success if they work hard. To put it differently, students whose self-concept of ability is high may expect greater payoffs from their efforts and work harder to obtain them. Second, students with low self-appraisals are more likely to expect low achievement (if not failure) and, as a result, be less inclined to work hard because to do so and fail could be a severe blow to their already shaky self-esteem. (Have you ever experienced a time in your life, for example, when you felt a great eagerness to prepare for something that you just *knew* you probably wouldn't do well in?)

On the Side of Achievement Preceding Self-Concept

On the other side of the argument, Kifer's (1975) longitudinal study of students from grades two through eight, which investigated how school achievement performance and personality characteristics, including self-concept, are related over time and over a series of tasks, revealed that successful achievement precedes a positive self-concept. On the basis of his findings, Kifer argues that success and failure of and by themselves are not sufficient to explain changes in self-concept. Rather, it is the *pattern* and *consistency* of success and failure and the *accumulation* of those experiences that affect an individual's self-concept. He found, for example, that the relationship between self-concept and achievement became stronger and more robust as success or failure became prolonged and as a consistent pattern of accomplishments or lack of accomplishments emerged.

Other studies, such as Bridgeman and Shipman's (1978) longitudinal investigation of 404 children from the time they were in preschool through third grade and Calsyn and Kenny's (1977) analysis of a five-year investigation of 556 high school students, found that a student's academic self-concept was more likely to be influenced by academic achievement than the other way around, a finding also supported by Kelly and Jordan's (1990) study of 197 male and female eighth-grade students. Bachman and O'Malley (1986) came to a similar conclusion in their longitudinal investigation of relationships between academic achievement and self-esteem of over 2,000 males followed up from about age 15 to 23. In their words, ". . . it is the actual abilities, not the self-concepts that make the difference" (p. 45). In response to the important question of which pathway actual abilities take to shape self-concepts, Bachman and O'Malley offer the following response:

> Our findings clearly show that one pathway is via classroom grades. But the findings also show that even more of an impact of actual ability on self-concepts occurs independent of grades (such as) personal communications from teachers (e.g., "You are much brighter than these grades reflect"), comments from parents (perhaps along similar lines), information from other significant adults, and in many cases direct knowledge about performance on standardized tests of ability. (p. 45)

This, then, is a sampling of the evidence that each side offers when debating the question of which comes first, a positive self-concept or high achievement. One of the reasons for why the answer to this question is equivocal has to do with differences in the methodologies used by researchers in this area. A second reason has to do with the fact that relationships between self-concept and academic achievement can vary with age, self-concept definition, and measure of academic performance.

On the Side of Both Sides

Does this mean that because no consistent causal relationship is found between self-concept and academic achievement that the self-concept idea has no validity? Not at all. Even though it is not possible to specify which came first, good schoolwork or high self-regard, it does not seem unreasonable to suggest that *each is mutually reinforcing to the other to the extent that a positive (or negative) change in one facilitates a commensurate change in the other.* If, for example, Diane, a low self-esteem fifth-grade student begins school with negative expectations for her chances of success but ends up experiencing small triumphs here and there and a few large successes now and then, chances are fairly good that she will begin to feel more confident in her abilities. In this case, achievement leads to a more positive self-concept. Have you ever had the experience of taking a difficult course in which you did not expect to fare well (your self-concept was shaky), but you ended up with a high grade? Chances are that your high grade enhanced your self-concept in that area, particularly if you were able to attribute your success to your own effort and knowledge, rather than to luck and good fortune.

As an example the other way, consider Dan, a high self-esteem tenth-grade student who takes a geometry course taught by a teacher with a reputation for being tough and demanding. Although some students wilt in the face of the pressures they feel, Dan remains firm in his conviction that he can handle the materials. A below-average grade on the first exam only firms his resolve to do better on subsequent tests. So he studies even harder and receives progressively better scores on other exams. Because his self-concept of his ability to do math is fairly high to begin with, his initial brush with low achievement does not depress his efforts but motivates him to work harder. In this case, a positive self-concept preceded high achievement and was a source of internal motivation to try harder even in the face of a below-average performance. Of course, if Dan were to experience enough sub-par performances, then we might expect that his own estimate of ability would begin to decline. I have seen nothing in the research literature to suggest that a high self-concept person is forever immunized to the effects of failure when failure is excessive and consistent.

As a general rule, however, a low self-concept person will tend to give up more easily following failure experiences. A higher self-concept individual, on the other hand, will tend to put more effort into improving what needs to be improved when things don't go well.

Fortunately, the chicken or the egg question is more academic than practical. The important thing is that self-concept and achievement are interactive and reciprocal forces, each with the potential to affect the other in positive or negative ways.

When a low self-concept is the problem, there is a particular kind of psychological medicine that's almost guaranteed to help.

SUCCESS: ANTIDOTE FOR A NEGATIVE SELF-CONCEPT

Success, self-esteem, and a positive self-concept are very much related. Success, for most people, is an affirming, positive happening that feeds egos and fuels motivation. It helps people in two ways: (1) They can feel good about themselves (internal reward) because they have accomplished something successfully, and (2) it provides an opportunity for significant others to respond positively and favorably (external reward) to the person behind the accomplishment. Success has a decided influence on students' behavior and on how they feel about themselves. For example, in their study involving 450 high school students, Yarworth and Gauthier (1978) found that high self-concept students took more risks and, as a result, experienced more success, which helped enhance their positive feelings. Low self-concept students, on the other hand, were more wary about the possibilities of success and took fewer chances, thereby reducing their opportunities for success, thus reinforcing their negative mind set about themselves. You can see the reciprocal influence of self-concept and achievement at work.

In his investigation involving 197 college freshmen, Borislow (1962) found that even though certain students began their studies with what seemed to be a somewhat indifferent and unmotivated "I don't care if I do well or not" attitude, doing poorly still had a decidedly negative effect on their self-attitudes. A person may act as if failure doesn't really matter, but in the final analysis, it *does* matter. Losing or doing poorly may "build character" as coaches are fond of saying, but it doesn't build confidence. Just as success is likely to breed a feeling of success, so does failure breed a feeling of failure.

Dyson's (1967) study investigating the relationships between self-concept and ability grouping among seventh grade students illustrates the point about the power of success. Among other things, it was found that high-achieving (high success) students reported significantly higher self-concepts than did low-achieving (low success) students, regardless of the type of grouping procedures utilized in the academic program. Noteworthy in Dyson's final observation:

> If there is one particularly significant result growing out of this research, it is that "Nothing succeeds like success." This is not a new understanding, as the old cliche indicates. The work reported here does, however, re-emphasize the importance of success in the learning situation as a contribution to positive psychological growth and it indicates that this feeling of success is probably more crucial in its effect on the student's self-concept than how an individual is grouped for instruction. (p. 404)

When considering the relationships between self-concept and achievement, an important principle stands out.

A POSITIVE SELF-CONCEPT IS IMPORTANT BUT NOT ENOUGH

In a huge research effort designed to investigate the relationship between self-concept of ability and academic performance of over 1,000 male and female students from the time they started seventh grade and completed tenth grade, Brookover and his associates (1962, 1965, 1967) found that self-concept was a significant factor in achievement at each grade level studied. In the final phase of this study, the following important observation was made:

> The correlation between self-concept of ability and grade point average ranges from .48 to .63 over the six years. It falls below .50 only among boys in the 12th grade. . . . In addition, the higher correlation between perceived evaluations and self-concepts tends to support the theory that perceived evaluations are a necessary and sufficient condition for [the growth of a positive or high] self-concept of ability, but [a positive] self-concept of ability is only a necessary, but not a sufficient condition for achievement. The latter is further supported by the analysis of the achievement of students with high and low self-concepts of ability. This revealed that although a significant proportion of students with high self-concepts of ability achieved at a relatively lower level, practically none of the students with lower [less positive] self-concepts of ability achieved at a high level. (pp. 142–143)

This research is important for two reasons. One, it underscored the influential impact that significant others—that is, emotionally important people like parents and teachers—can have in the self-concept of developing youths, a finding later supported by Bachman and O'Malley's (1986) large study of over 2,000 high-school-aged males, which was mentioned earlier. These findings remind us that children's self-concepts are molded, in part, during this long immersion in an interpersonal stream of reflected appraisals from people important to them. Second, this research supports the idea that it takes more than a positive self-concept to achieve and perform well academically; it also takes motivation, determination, and the help of emotionally supportive people, especially parents and teachers.

The bottom line is that *the possession of a high self-concept does not cause high academic achievement*; it does, however, play a vitally important supporting role. Remember, a person could have a positive self-concept that is sustained and nurtured by success in nonacademic pursuits—athletics, extracurricular activities, peer-group popularity, creative expression in the arts, and so. This same person might be just an average student academically but retain his or her high self-concept status because it is nurtured and reinforced in nonacademic areas. Here, we have an example of a person who has a high self-concept but who is doing only average work academically, which illustrates the idea that a high self-concept does not necessarily *cause* high achievement. When self-concept is thought of as being multidimensional and arranged hierarchically as in Figure 6-1, then it can be more readily seen how a student could be pretty good in one particular area but not so good in two or three or more areas and *still* have a rather high self-concept. Although it is possible to do average and even below-average work academically and still have a fairly high self-concept, it is far more difficult to have a low self-concept of ability and expect to do well academically.

How children and adolescents feel about themselves is very much affected by the kind of feedback they receive from parents and the nature of their relationship with them, an interpersonal dynamic we explore next.

STUDENTS' SELF-CONCEPT OF ABILITY: THE PART PARENTS PLAY

Parental judgments and evaluations about their children's academic abilities do not fall on deaf ears. Although many things said by parents go in one ear and out the other, these early *exiting* messages are usually related to particular things that children should *do*—pick up their rooms, do homework, rake the lawn, be in bed at a certain time, and so on. Messages related more to how children *are*—their behaviors, abilities, shortcomings, strengths, and so on— tend to be the ones that stick, particularly if repeated enough times.

Although children may act as though what their parents say about them is unimportant, particularly adolescents, parental feedback is bound to leave its mark if for no other reason than the sheer weight of it over many years. Parents or other primary caretakers are crucial people in children's lives; for example, Brookover and his colleagues (1962, 1965, 1967) found that almost all students in grades seven through 12 identified their parents as people who were "significant" to them. Furthermore, when asked to indicate who was concerned about how well they did in school, parents were again named by over 90 percent of the students. The perception of parental evaluations by students is, therefore, likely to have some kind of impact for better or worse on self-perceptions of most students, a possibility also discussed by Bachman and O'Malley (1986). The question is, how are these self-perceptions related to their feelings about their ability to do schoolwork, and how are these feelings picked up from their parents?

Consider the following interviews. The first is with a low-achieving, low self-concept, ninth-grade girl. As we enter the conversation, it has just moved into schoolwork and the parents' attitudes toward the girl's performance. Note the implicit and explicit ways in which her parents convinced her that she wasn't very good in math.

DH:	How does your mom feel about your schoolwork?
Girl:	It could be better, I guess; I don't know exactly—we don't discuss it much.
DH:	Do your parents say anything to you about your report card?
Girl:	Sometimes they do.
DH:	I noticed you did about C work last year.
Girl:	Yeah, mostly I do that and sometimes not that good. I used to do better.
DH:	Could you tell me more about that?
Girl:	Well, last year I got a B in social studies, and that's pretty good. Math got me though. I guess if I really tried—but I don't think I can because I've tried all I can. I'm telling you, it really gets me. My mother wasn't good in math either, but she's better now.
DH:	How do you know your mother used to be poor in it?
Girl:	She told me. *She says it's no wonder I'm not very good at it.*
DH:	What does she mean by that?
Girl:	Well, she says, well, I'm dumb—"I guess I've handed it to you" or something like that. I mean I'm real slow in math—it takes hours to get something in my head. One time my father and I were working on a problem, and he lost his patience. He said I was so stupid that I should be in a special school. He was really mad.
DH:	How did that make you feel?

Girl:	Well, it hurt me; I was a little bit mad, but I got over it; *maybe I am stupid* . . .

What follows is an excerpt from another interview with a different ninth-grade 14-year-old girl, who was also a low-achieving, low self-concept student. The conversation was about school, grades, and feelings about ability to succeed in different subjects. As it happens, the subject here, as in the previous illustration, is math. Once again, note the nature of the parental feedback that is gnawing away at this girl's self-confidence.

DH:	I see you've been having some trouble with math.
Girl:	Well, I don't know. My mother wasn't too good at it; my dad wasn't—I don't know; I'm just not very good at it.
DH:	How do you know that your mom and dad had trouble with math?
Girl:	Well, my mom told me the first time I got a D, and I brought it home, and I said, "I got a D in math," and she says, *"I'm not surprised because I wasn't great in it."* And my dad, he isn't the best in it either. He said he didn't always do the best in the subject.
DH:	How did that make you feel when you found they didn't do well in math?
Girl:	Well, I don't know. My brother, he must be pretty good at it because he's an engineer. He's pretty good; *I guess I was the one that got it.* Anyway, boys are better than girls in math anyway. I don't know why.
DH:	"You were the one that got it." What does that mean?
Girl:	I don't know, I guess my mom and dad passed it on to me. Maybe not, but *they aren't surprised that I do poorly in it.*

Although the parents of these two girls no doubt did not deliberately set out to harm their daughters, it is not difficult to see how parents may negatively influence children's feelings by telling them they're stupid or by inferring that they inherited "bad" genes. How students feel about their ability to do schoolwork depends, in part, on how they perceive the evaluations of those who are important to them.

It sometimes happens that some students do poorly in school, not because of low self-esteem or a negative self-concept, but because they get parental attention for their failures, but little for their successes. Roth and Meyersburg (1963) explain the dynamics of that kind of underachievement in the following way:

> The psychogenesis involves a series of very subtle devaluations of the child, stemming from the parent-child relationship. In our experience, the most frequent pattern is that of the parent who pays no attention at all to the accomplishments or failures of the child. (These students frequently exclaim, "What's the use; nobody gives a damn," in reference to their current college failure.) The life space of the child and the life space of the parent are in different realms, a state of affairs which constitutes a parental rejection. The only way a child can bring the life spaces together albeit momentarily, is through the production of a crisis, occasionally necessitating outsiders such as police, teacher, principal, or a counselor.
>
> Next in frequency is the parent who attends only to the child's failures and rarely to his successes. The latter are taken for granted, but the failures are punished. Thus, the contact between parent and child is through failure. If the child succeeds, he is alone, but if he fails, he is part of the concern of his parents.
>
> Both of these early experiences lead to three devastating, incipient pathological processes: The first of these is a process of self-denigration. In order for the child to maintain some kind of identity with the parent he must learn to see himself as a failure. He must hold back his productivity and blame himself for his lacks. Hostility, he is taught, is received by him and never expressed toward others. When he does experience resentments he directs them against himself and thus supports his own constructs about himself as being worth little. (p. 370)

Other students tend to do poorly in school because their parents' relationship with them is tied pretty much to the idea of doing well in school and getting good grades and that is *all* it is tied to. Whatever emotional warmth and support there may be is buried under an avalanche of admonishments to study, work hard, and get good grades. This, of course, frequently leads to a certain amount of anger at the parents and anxiety about failing, which makes it even more difficult to do well. As a high-ability but low-achieving 11th-grade boy said to me (referring to his parents), "They're always bugging me to do well in school, get good grades, make the honor roll. Hell, that's practically the only time they talk to me, when it has something to do with school or grades. If there was no school, they probably wouldn't talk to me at all." What this boy wanted, which is no different from what any of us wants, was to be treated and cared for as a person, not as an achievement machine. Sometimes, the only way children or adolescents can get back at parents is to *withhold* their success. After all, what do growing children have to offer their parents *except* their success? One has to wonder how many school failures can be traced to that conscious or unconscious motivation.

Before children begin their formal schooling, they are in the custody of their parents or parent surrogates for five or six years. In that period of time, an overall blueprint for subsequent self-concept development has been drawn.

Realistic feedback from parents is not always welcome but it is necessary.
Reprinted by permission of Universal Press Syndicate.

The details of that blueprint will be sketched in during the next ten years or so of the child's life. Parental input through feedback and evaluation, parental caring or lack of it, and parental acceptance or rejection contribute importantly to the finished draft.

In the final analysis, parents who are firm but caring, who are demanding but fair, and who have high but reachable expectations are the ones most likely to raise children who think well of themselves and who strive to do well in school.

A teacher's expectations, like those of parents, are powerful shapers of a student's self-concept of ability, an idea we turn to next.

TEACHERS' EXPECTATIONS: HOW DO THEY WORK?

Predicting rain or sunny skies doesn't affect tomorrow's weather, but a Harris poll predicting victory or defeat for a certain political candidate can have a definite effect on the outcome. Betting on the flip of a coin doesn't change the odds, but letting an athlete know you've bet on him or her can considerably affect the performance. When Roger Bannister began training for the four-minute mile, almost no one believed the barrier could be broken. Bannister himself wasn't sure, but he has said many times, "I knew my trainer believed in me and I couldn't let him down." Thus, in 1954, he became the first person in the world to break the four-minute barrier with a 3' 59.4'' mile, something that today is done routinely by top-flight runners in competition. Charles E. Wilcox, former General Motors president, was fond of saying that one of the differences between good bosses and poor bosses is that "good bosses make their workers feel that they have more ability than they think they have so that they consistently do better work than they thought they could." Hundreds of years ago, Goethe observed, "Treat people as if they were what they ought to be and you help them to become what they are capable of being."

One person's expectancy of another person's behavior somehow becomes realized—not always, but enough so that increasing attention in recent years has been given to the idea of how self-fulfilling prophecies work in the classroom. Eliza Doolittle, who was changed from an awkward Cockney flower girl into an elegant lady in George Bernard Shaw's famous play *Pygmalion,* described the process involved quite simply: ". . . the difference between a lady and a flower girl is not how she behaves, but how she is treated." Although it does not work quite so simply in the classroom, there is increasing evidence to suggest that perhaps one difference between poor students and good students is not how they behave, but how they are treated. Like Eliza, students in school—whether in first grade or the 12th—have a tendency to perform as they are expected to perform.

Perhaps the expectation idea can be conveyed more clearly via an analogy. Imagine the following scenario: Jason and Jane, being good hypnotic subjects (trusting, reasonably intelligent, able to be influenced), are put into a hypnotic trance. Jason is asked to place his arm into a pan of circulating ice water, and Jane's arm is tourniqueted above the elbow, cutting off the blood supply to the forearm. The hypnotist suggests to each of them that they will feel no pain, and they are asked to report their physical sensations. Ordinarily, a person in a normal waking state would feel and report excruciating pain after about 30 seconds. Jason and Jane report that they feel nothing, or if they do, it is described as a mere "tingling sensation." What's going on here?

What's going on is a striking example of how the mind can influence behavior. By accepting (believing) the hypnotist's suggestion that there would be no pain, Jason and Jane subjectively reinterpreted the sensation of pain and behaved accordingly, even though objective measures such as blood pressure and heart rate were very high, indicating extreme physiological stress. Reports of experiments of this sort have been reported many times with similar results (Hilgard and Hilgard, 1975).

Now imagine this scenario: Billy and Betty, being good elementary school students (trusting, reasonably intelligent, able to be influenced), are placed in the third grade. Billy is asked to do some arithmetic problems, and Betty is asked to spell some new words. The teacher, perhaps trying to be honest and, thereby, helpful, suggests to each of them they will no doubt have trouble with these tasks because "Billy, you always have difficulty with numbers" and "Betty, your older sister had problems with spelling, so this may be hard for you." After a time, they are asked to demonstrate the extent of their learning on a test. Ordinarily, most third-grade students—those who have reasonable levels of self-worth and self-confidence—would do fairly well, their efforts reflecting a positive mind set. Billy and Betty, however, do not do well at all. As Billy said, "I can't seem to do good work with numbers." And Betty concludes, "I guess I'm like everyone else in my family when it comes to spelling."

Billy and Betty's experience is not exactly the same as Jason and Jane's but there is one dominant similarity: Both pairs were strongly influenced by the expectations of another person. And both pairs behaved in a manner consistent with what they perceived those expectations to be. I have used hypnosis as an example because it is a phenomenon with which we are all familiar. One person deliberately and willfully attempts to influence the behavior of another person through the power of suggestion. It is intentional, person to person, and overt—impossible to miss. Hypnosis by no means works equally well for all people, but when it does work, it is a dramatic example of how one's behavior can be altered when the point of view of another person has been internalized.

What happens to the Billys and Bettys in our homes and schools is not so dramatic because the internalization of adult perceptions and expectations about how they should behave and feel about themselves is the by-product of day-to-day interactions spread out over weeks, months, and even years. Billy and Betty's self-concepts about their arithmetic or spelling ability were not shaped by a teacher's single statement, but rather, by many similar statements over time. Each of us is immersed in a continual stream of reflected appraisals in which we see images of ourselves mirrored in the input and feedback of people in our social world. In a way, each of us is exposed to ongoing "suggestions" about how we are to behave, think, and dress: "suggestions" about the limits and nature of our abilities and even "suggestions" about our potential as persons. Not all of us are equally suggestible, but I think it is safe to say that we all are suggestible to some degree. (The fact that advertising is so enormously successful is testimony enough for this statement.)

In a sense, this portion of the chapter is about the power of suggestion—not the explicit suggestions of hypnotist to subject, but the implicit, indirect, and sometimes very direct suggestions of adult to child, of teacher to student. How students perform in school is closely related to how they *think* they can perform, and how they think about it is related, to some extent at least, to others' suggestions (expectations, perceptions) about what they are capable of doing.

A teacher's expectations for how any given student will perform academically is an essentially private prediction about the potential of that student. Although these expectations are not necessarily conscious, they nonetheless can act as powerful mediators between how students feel about themselves and how they perform academically. Before a student ever enters a classroom, he or she has been subjected to a myriad of inputs that have shaped his or her

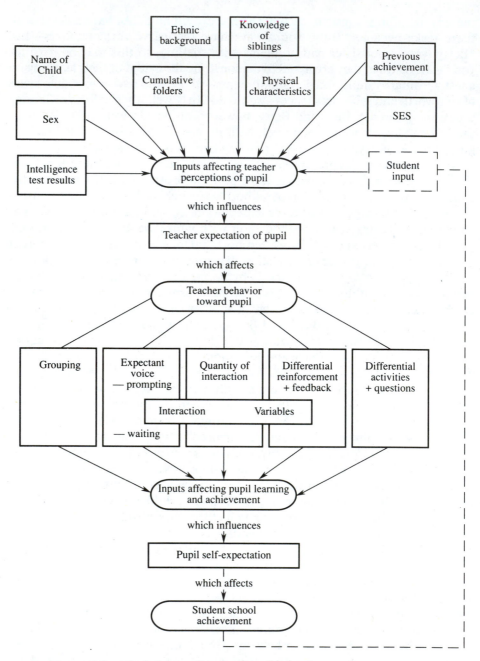

Figure 6-2   *The behavioral cycle of pupil behavior, teacher expectations, and student achievement.*

Adapted from: C. Braun, "Teacher Expectation: Sociopsychological Dynamics," *Review of Educational Research,* 1976, *46*: 185–213. Copyright © 1976, American Research Association, Washington, D. C.

self-concept, behavior, and attitudes in certain directions. Acting on the information that is before them, real or imagined (perhaps a bit of both), teachers develop certain expectations for how well or how poorly certain students will do in their classrooms. It is a continuous cycle of inputs and outputs (see Figure 6-2). Notice the many input variables that influence who a student is as a total person. These variables influence a teacher's expectations, which, in turn, influence how a teacher interacts with any given student, which affects how the student responds to the teacher—and the cycle begins.

Expectations Can Turn into Self-Fulfilling Prophecies

Johnny Carson made a joke on the "Tonight" show several years ago about supplies of toilet paper being tight. There really was no shortage—until Carson's joke. In a matter of days, toilet paper became a rare commodity. Americans, believing Carson was serious, bought every roll of toilet paper they could get their hands on. Soon, lots of people had several month's supply of toilet paper—but stores had virtually none.

Embedded in this Carson caper is a natural example of a *self-fulfilling prophecy,* as defined many years ago by Robert Merton (1948), who was the first to use the term. A self-fulfilling prophecy begins with a false belief (expectations) which, in turn, causes one to behave in a way that makes the belief come true. Thus, an erroneous belief (there would be a shortage of toilet paper) led to behavior (panic buying) that caused the expectation to be realized.

Although merely wishing for something is not likely to make it come true, our expectations do influence the way we behave, and the way we behave affects how other people respond. In fact, the expectations we have about people can cause us to interact with them in a way that causes them to respond just as we thought they would. This justifies our original expectations (predictions) and thus is born a self-fulfilling prophecy.

Consider an example of how this might work in everyday behavior. Suppose you were considering taking a course from an instructor of whom you knew nothing about and wanted to talk to him about course requirements. Before doing so, you ask a friend about him, and you are told, "Mr. Wilson is a terrific person. He knows his stuff; he has a sense of humor; he's a warm sort of person; and he's easy to talk to—someone you'll like." After hearing this, how do you think you would respond to Mr. Wilson when meeting him for the first time? However, suppose your friend had said, "You're thinking of taking a course with Wilson? Well, I'd be careful if I were you. It's hard to feel comfortable with him. He seems so . . . well, cold and abrupt. I never had the feeling that he enjoyed talking to people." If you heard this, how do you suppose you would react to Mr. Wilson?

If you are like most people, your response to Mr. Wilson would be quite different depending on which of these contrasting characterizations you had heard. If you had heard the first description, you would probably look forward to your visit with him; you might tell him that you had heard he was a fine instructor and someone with whom students liked to talk. You might further say that you were looking forward to taking his course and ask if he could tell you a bit about it. If, on the other hand, you had heard the second description, you might approach your appointment with apprehension and hesitancy. You might look somewhat more serious and guarded and present yourself in a more formal, businesslike manner.

Now, put yourself in Mr. Wilson's shoes. He knows nothing about you as a person and reacts solely on the basis of his impressions of you during that initial meeting. Consider for a moment how he might respond to the person you present yourself as being in the two approaches just described. Learning in the first instance that you heard he was a fine instructor, that students liked him, and that you were looking forward to taking his class, he probably would feel good about himself and you. Your behavior might help him feel comfortable with you and perhaps even more willing to spend a little extra time answering your questions. What you see in his behavior would tend to confirm what you thought about him in the first place.

If you approached Mr. Wilson somewhat nervously and formally, as in the second instance, no doubt he would respond in kind. If he were not already a somewhat nervous and formal person, he might soon become one. Sensing your cautious mood, he might feel that you really didn't want to spend a lot of time with him and even that you didn't like him. In light of your behavior, he might conclude that attempts at small talk would be risky, so he would give you the information you wanted, you would be on your way, and you would think to yourself, "My friend was right—he *is* cold; he really *doesn't* enjoy talking to people."

Thus, a self-fulfilling prophecy is an outgrowth of the behavior produced by the expectation. This behavior has an effect on other people, which increases the likelihood that they will act in expected ways.

How Expectations Become Self-Fulfilling in the Classroom

When thinking about how expectations work in a classroom setting, we need to remember that it is the constant interplay between expectations and behavior that finally converts an erroneous expectation into a self-fulfilling prophecy. Although every self-fulfilling prophecy begins with an expectation, it is the behavior that this expectation produces, not the expectation itself, that causes the self-fulfilling prophecy. Brophy and Good (1974) have suggested a five-step model to help us understand how teachers' expectations may become self-fulfilling prophecies:

1. Early in the school year, teachers form differential expectations of their students, which are shaped by their knowledge from school records and personal observations. Some of these expectations are appropriate, others not so. Sometimes these initial impressions are

relatively rigid and resistant to change even in the face of contradictory evidence. Expectations of this sort are called *sustaining expectations,* which are used in reference to situations in which teachers do not recognize student potential and hence do not respond in ways that help these students grow (Cooper and Good, 1983).

2. Student are treated in accordance with the teachers' expectations for them.

3. Other things being equal, student response to teacher behavior will be reciprocal (teacher warmth will lead to student warmth; teacher coldness or hostility will lead to student withdrawal or hostility, and so on).

4. If the teacher treatment is consistent over time, and if students do not resist its impact, it may begin to affect their self-concepts, aspirations, motivation, and interpersonal relationships.

5. Students' behavior will generally complement and reinforce teachers' expectations, which encourages them to act on their original expectations more forcefully, and which causes students to conform to these expectations more than they might have otherwise.

As you see, the process is cyclical. It begins with an expectation that may or may not be accurate; the teacher responds to the expectation; the student responds in kind to the teacher; the teacher's expectation is reinforced; the teacher behaves with greater conviction; the student, if susceptible to the teacher's input, performs in a manner that validates the teacher's original expectation. Thus, the cycle is completed.

According to Good and Brophy (1987), these self-fulfilling prophecy effects of teacher expectations can occur only if all elements of the model are present. For example, a teacher may have certain expectations but not communicate them consistently. Or the teacher's expectations may change. Another reason why a teacher's expectations may not become self-fulfilling is that students may put up a steady resistance to their effects. I have heard many accounts from students who said they were subjected to teachers' negative expectations, but who refused to bend. As one senior-year college student expressed it: "I had a math teacher who told me more times than I can count that I was one of his 'slower' students and that I may want to consider going to a trade school to learn a specific skill rather than to college, which was my dream. On more than one occasion I remember thinking, 'you're wrong and I'll show you.' "

The Effect of Teachers' Expectations on Students' Achievements

Rosenthal and Jacobson created a national stir with the book *Pygmalion in the Classroom* (1968), which reported the first major research showing that a teacher's positive expectations can affect students' actual school performance.

Their research focused on each of six grades—one through six—in a particular school where children in each classroom performed at above-average, average, and below-average levels of scholastic achievement. In each of these classes, an average of 20 percent of the children were identified to the teachers as having scores on the *Test for Intellectual Blooming,* which suggested that they would show unusual academic gains during the year. Actually, the children had been picked at random from the total population of children taking the same test. Eight months after the experimental conditions were instituted, all children were retested with the same IQ test. The results?

For the school as a whole, those children from whom the teachers had been led to expect greater intellectual gain showed significantly greater gain in IQ scores than did other children in school. In fact, the lower the grade level, the greater the IQ gain. Apparently, *teachers interacted with the "brighter" children more positively and more favorably, and the children responded in kind by showing greater gains in IQ.* One reason why there was more chance in the lower grades may be because younger children are generally more malleable, less fixed, and more capable of change. A second possibility is that younger, "newer" elementary school children do not have firmly established reputations which can be passed on from one teacher to the next. It may be that as students move from one grade to the next, their reputations—for better or worse—precede them, which colors both teachers' perceptions of, and expectations for, their behavior and academic performance. Thus, new students may show more expectancy effects because they have not been stereotyped by reputations passed on from teacher to teacher, which is in fact what Raudenbush (1984) found in his review of 18 experiments on induced teacher expectations. Effects were stronger in grades one and two than in grades three through six. Then they became strong again at grade seven, the first year of junior high for most students.

It is important to note that the kind of expectations reported by Rosenthal and Jacobson (1968) and reviewed by Raudenbush (1984) were what are called "induced expectations." That is, they were expectations created or "induced" in the minds of teachers by leading them to believe that certain students with whom they would work had unusually high learning potential, when in fact, those students had been selected randomly. Believing these students to have unusual potential, teachers presumably communicated their positive expectations in a variety of ways, which helped these students increase their achievement levels. Other studies have arrived at similar results (Babad, Inbar, and Rosenthal, 1982; Guttman and Bar-tel, 1982). What happens, however, when teachers form their *own* expectations based on their *own* experiences?

Seaver (1973) investigated this question by studying teachers' "natural expectancies," which involved analyzing the performance of 27 elementary-school-aged students who had older siblings precede them in school by no more than three grade levels and who, in addition, had the same teachers the younger siblings currently had. Seaver reasoned that teachers who had taught a student's older brother or sister would have a built-in expectancy for the younger child, high if the older child did well and low if he or she did poorly. In addition, the school environment provided a natural control group of students whose older siblings had different teachers. Teacher expectancies did, indeed, make a difference. When the older sibling's performance had been low, the expectancy group scored lower than did the controls on seven of the eight tests. The findings point to what we may always have suspected: The reputation that older siblings in a family establish in school gets passed on to their brothers and sisters, and teachers tend to expect—and therefore get—from the younger members of the family what they had learned to expect from the older ones.

Additional support for the power of natural expectancies comes from an investigation by Palardy (1969), who found that if first-grade teachers believed boys would achieve as well as girls in reading, the boys did, in fact, perform better than boys with teachers who believed girls were better readers. Another study along this vein found that elementary level teachers have a tendency to overestimate the IQs of girls and underestimate the IQs of boys (Doyle, Hancock, and Kifer, 1971). The revealing aspect of this is that even though there was no *actual* IQ difference between boys and girls, the girls showed higher reading achievement. Not only that, *but within both sexes, the children whose IQs had been overestimated by teachers showed higher reading achievement.* Remember, actual IQ is not the important factor here. What seems to make a difference is the teacher's *perceptions or beliefs* about a particular student's IQ, which, in turn, sets in motion certain expectancies.

This discussion leads to an important question . . .

Do Teachers' Expectations Really Make a Difference?

Although Rosenthal's original expectancy research has been criticized by some researchers (Elahoff and Snow, 1970; Gephart, 1970; Wineburg, 1987) for shortcomings in design and methodology, none of these criticisms denied the possibility that teachers' expectation may be an important variable in students' learning. Not all research supports the expectancy phenomenon, but much of it does. For example, Rosenthal (1973) reviewed 242 studies and found 84 of them reported that teachers' expectations made a significant difference in how subjects performed in various situations. Eighty-four may not seem like a large number of supporting studies. However, if we apply the rules of statistical significance, we would expect that in only about 5 percent of those 242 studies (about 12) would teachers' expectations have made a difference as predicted by chance alone. The fact that differences were found in 84, seven times more than chance would dictate, suggests that expectations do, indeed, affect performance in certain circumstances. Several large-scale reviews of expectancy research tend to confirm this conclusion (Cooper and Good, 1983; Dusek, 1985; Good and Brophy, 1982).

When used positively by aware teachers, expectations can perform another function that we haven't mentioned yet. Positive, reasonable, and fair expectations can play a part in stretching students beyond the safety of their own choices.

I say "safety" of their own choices because evidence indicates that when people do only what they choose to do, they may feel less successful and competent, even if they succeed, than those who accomplish a task that they did not choose and that represents another person's expectations.

Luginbuhl (1972) noted, for example, that if people succeed at a problem that they chose from a number of problems, their feeling of success may be blunted by the knowledge that *they influenced the situation to make success more possible.* It may not be wise for a teacher to permit students to have their own way (e.g., choose the number or kinds of books to read or the kinds of paper to write, etc.) *all the time.* Living up to a teacher's expectations (e.g., writing a report on an assigned topic, getting it done and in on time) can be another way students can feel successful and, thereby, add to their feelings of competence and self-esteem.

Clearly defined teachers' expectations can serve as an important framework for student self-evaluation. For example, if an elementary school child is supposed to keep quiet when someone is talking and does, he *knows* he is successful. If a high school student knows she is expected to participate and does, she *knows* she tried her best. If she is supposed to have a book report in by Friday noon and does, she knows she successfully lived up to an expectation. In other words, the existence of teachers' expectations can leave students with the feeling that a definition of their school environment is possible and that the world does impose restrictions and make demands that they can learn to handle on an everyday basis.

Expectations perform another important function. They not only represent a belief in students' adequacy, but they also relay the message that they have the ability to do what is required of them. When set at reasonable levels, expectations represent a vote of confidence. Do teachers' expectations make a difference? On the basis of the evidence, I think they definitely do. There is no magic in this. Students will not do better or work as hard as they are able just because the teacher "expects" or "believes" that they can do good work. A teacher's expectations or beliefs in a student's adequacy probably would not make a whit of difference unless those beliefs were explicitly expressed in the teacher's behavior that was supportive, encouraging, and functionally helpful. All in all, it appears that teachers see what they expect to see, and the pupil sees what the teacher sees.

For many students, teachers' expectations seem to make a difference in how they perform in school, which leads us to ask . . .

How Are Positive Expectations Communicated?

The actual mechanics by which teacher expectations are communicated are complex. The words spoken are important, to be sure. But so, too, are the subtle nuances built into the interactions that go on between teacher and student—for example, tone of voice, facial expression, posture, and other kinds of body English. Chaiken, Sigler, and Derlega (1974) zeroed in on nonverbal cues of that sort to study how teachers' expectations are actually transmitted. They found that teachers anticipating superior performance from their students engaged in more positive nonverbal behaviors—among them smiling, leaning forward toward the student, making eye contact, and nodding affirmatively—than teachers with either no expectations or with low expectations for performance. Thus, even when teachers do not tell students outright what the world anticipates from them, the message is still there in subtle but potent ways.

In an effort to explain how positive expectations are communicated, Rosenthal (1973) proposed a "four-factor theory" of the influences that are likely to encourage students to do well. As Rosenthal sees it, when teachers have positive expectations they tend to

1. Give more positive feedback to those students about their performance (feedback factor).

2. Give their special students more opportunities to respond to questions (output factor).

3. Create a warmer social-emotional mood for their "special students" (climate factor).

4. Teach more material and more difficult material to their special students (input factor).

You may find it useful to think of the acronym *FOCI* as an aid to remembering how positive expectations are communicated.

F—eedback. (Give more positive feedback.)

O—utput. (Give more opportunities for students to demonstrate learning.)

C—limate. (Create a warm, invitational classroom.)

I—nput. (Give students more material to think about and learn.)

All these factors interact together in such a way as to create a more positive and facilitating learning environment for students for whom teachers have high, positive expectations. It is easy to see why some students may flourish, and others not.

How Are Negative Expectations Communicated?

The transmission of low expectations is a subtle packaging of words, gestures, and decisions that, when received by certain students on a daily basis, have the cumulative effect of influencing their work in a downward direction. Teachers are frequently *unaware* of the things they do or say that may communicate low or high expectations. Inasmuch as this is usually—but not always—a communication that is done outside of awareness, there is practically no opportunity for modifying negative messages. Hence, there is an advantage to developing a conscious awareness of the sorts of teacher behaviors that may convey negative or positive expectations to students.

Good and Brophy's (1987) review of a large body of research related to teachers' expectations revealed that there is an almost endless list of ways that, directly or indirectly, teachers can communicate the idea that students are not very capable. Consider, for example, the following 15 actions that teachers may do unwittingly that communicate negative expectations to low achievers:

1. Waiting less time for lows to answer questions.

2. Giving lows the answers or calling on someone else rather than helping them over the rough spots (thus, lows have fewer chances to be successful).

3. Rewarding inappropriate behavior or incorrect answers by lows (which may make them feel embarrassed rather than helped).

4. Criticizing lows more often for failure.

5. Praising lows less frequently for success.

6. Failing to give feedback to the public responses of lows.

7. Paying less attention to lows and interacting with them less frequently.

8. Calling on lows less often to respond to questions, even when they volunteer, or asking them easier questions. (Success is too obvious and contrived, and lows know it.)

9. Seating the lows farther away from the teacher (possible nonverbal message: "You're not important").

10. Demanding less work, effort, and appropriate responses from lows. (Possible inference by lows: "I really must be dumb.")

11. Interacting with lows more privately than publicly, and monitoring their activities more closely. (This may underscore fears lows could have about *really* needing help, if it takes that much special attention.)

12. Giving lows, but not the highs, the benefit of the doubt in borderline cases when grading or giving assignments.

13. Briefer and less-informative feedback to questions of lows.

14. Less friendly interaction with lows, including less smiling and other nonverbal indicators of support and responsiveness.

15. Less acceptance of lows' ideas.

Note that practically all of these differential treatments have direct effect on students' opportunity and motivation to learn. The fact that teachers criticize lows more often for failure and praise them less often when successful is almost bound to have a negative effect on their motivations. If lows are provided with less information and given less feedback than the highs receive, this makes it even more difficult for the lows to progress. It can be a vicious cycle.

Good and Brophy (1987) suggest that we keep the following cautions in mind when thinking about how teachers may communicate low expectations:

1. There are vast differences among teachers in how much they dispense differential treatment to students for whom they have different expectations.

2. Where there are treatment differences, these are sometimes caused more by the student than by the teacher. For example, if lows choose not to be involved, it will be difficult for teachers to respond to them as often, and if their contributions are of lesser quality, the teacher may find it difficult to use their ideas as frequently as they do the highs.

3. Some forms of what appears to be differential treatment may actually represent sound individualized instruction. For example, since lows do require more structuring of their activities and closer monitoring of their work, it could be argued that it makes good instructional sense to have more frequent private conversations with them or ask them easier questions. We should not assume that the expressions of differential treatment described above are necessarily harmful or inappropriate.

What we observe in any given moment of a classroom's life is not enough to allow us to know whether what we saw is healthy or unhealthy, excellent teaching or poor teaching. No single interaction or classroom event dooms students to failure or propels them to success. It is the cumulative total of many similar events and interactions that can make a difference to a student, for better or worse. Being called on less often than others in a particular day probably doesn't make that much difference to any student; not being called on for days or even weeks on end probably will. Getting an earful of criticism in a particular class now and then is not likely to permanently destroy any student's motivation for learning; hearing criticism after criticism in many classes very likely could. It is the effect over time that takes the greatest toll.

A Note of Caution About Expectations

There is nothing mystical about how a teacher's expectations work and the influence these expectations can have on student behavior and performance. If students strive to live up to teachers' expectations, it will not only be because the expectations are reasonable, but also because of the existence of an inter-personal relationship in which teachers are viewed as persons who are basically trustworthy, friendly, warm, and sure of themselves. Students, particularly at the elementary school level, are anxious to please and will work hard to meet expectations when they like the teacher and when they are sure the teacher likes them.

Expectations are powerful, self-perpetuating attitudes for students, as well as teachers, because expectations guide both perceptions and behavior. When we expect that something will happen in a certain way, the likelihood of that "something" happening is far greater than if we didn't have those expectations. For example, if Steve anticipates teaching to be a drag, and somewhat boring, and if Stephanie looks forward to teaching because it is a challenge and seems exciting, is it difficult to predict which of the two will find the most reward in their work?

If, at the beginning of a new school year, one of Patrick's ninth-grade teachers is told that Patrick is "difficult to manage" because he is "so restless" and if another is given information suggesting that Patrick will "be a chal-lenge" because he is "so intellectually curious," is it difficult to predict which teacher will see a problem and which teacher will see potential? Thus, expecta-tions not only cause us to notice some things and fail to notice others, but they also affect the way we *interpret* what we notice, something we need to be conscious of in our interactions with others.

BEHAVIORAL DIFFERENCES BETWEEN HIGH AND LOW SELF-CONCEPT STUDENTS

Table 6-1 represents an effort to identify some of the primary behaviors that tend to distinguish between high and low self-concepts of ability in students. The following sources were particularly helpful in identifying differentiating behaviors (Byrne, 1986; Chiu, 1987; Coopersmith, 1967; Hogan and Weiss, 1974; Hoge and Luce, 1979; Marsh, 1984, 1990b; Maw and Maw, 1970). I am not suggesting that we will always find the high self-concept students on one side and the low self-concept students on the other, but overall, we are likely to find the higher self-concept students doing things that reflect their self-confidence and the lower self-concept students behaving in ways that reveal their self-doubts. High and low self-concept students are distinguished from each other as much by their differences in behavior as by their differences in motivation—highs being more motivated by their expectations of success and lows by their fear of failure.

STRATEGIES TEACHERS CAN USE TO ENHANCE SELF-CONCEPT AND SCHOOL ACHIEVEMENT

At every grade level, students come to school with preconceptions about them-selves and their abilities. Whereas successful students are typically characterized

Table 6–1 Ten Behaviors Commonly Associated with High and Low Self-Concepts of Ability in Students

Students with a High, Positive Self-Concept of Ability Tend to Be:	Students with a Low, Negative Self-Concept of Ability Tend to Be:
1. Intellectually active—do explore, probe, ask questions, get excited about learning new things.	1. Intellectually passive—do not ask many questions; seem unenthusiastic about learning new things.
2. Motivated to do as well as possible to get good grades; actively looking for ways to be successful.	2. Motivated to do as well as possible to avoid poor grades; actively looking for ways to avoid failing.
3. Involved in class discussions; not afraid to express themselves.	3. Quiet during class discussions; seem afraid to express their ideas.
4. Among those who, when given a choice, sit near the front of the room.	4. Among those who, when given a choice, sit near the back of a room.
5. Among those who attribute their successes to hard work, effort, ability on their part.	5. Among those who attribute their success to luck, fate, or some other outside source.
6. Among those who attribute their failures to a fluke, or unlucky break, or other outside sources.	6. Among those who attribute their failures to lack of ability, or lack of know-how, or low intelligence.
7. Among those who set realistic, reachable goals for themselves, making success more possible.	7. Among those who set unrealistic, unreachable goals for themselves, making success less possible.
8. Among those who are willing to ask for help; are able to admit not knowing without embarrassment.	8. Among those who are not willing to ask for help; seem to have problems admitting they do not know something.
9. Among those who do their work when it is to be done; assignments handed in on time.	9. Among those who procrastiante doing their school work; assignments frequently handed in late.
10. Among those who are able to take modest pride in their own abilities; are not pushy or overbearing.	10. Among those who may try to bluff others into believing that they know more than they really do; can be overbearing.

by self-confidence, self-acceptance, and feelings of adequacy and personal competence, less-successful students are recognized by their feeling of uncertainty, low self-regard, self-derogatory attitudes, and inferiority feelings. High self-concept students have the kinds of feelings about themselves and positive attitudes that we would like to see in all our students. But this is the real world we live in, and part of its reality is the fact that some students are very much down on themselves and their abilities. Are there specific things a teacher can do to help low self-concept students to feel better about themselves as part of an overall effort to raise achievement? Let's turn our attention now to some ideas for doing this.

Help Students Develop Specific Skills

We have already made the point that self-concept and achievement are interactive and reciprocal. When one goes up, it is likely the other will, too. This is no better illustrated than in Bachman and O'Malley's (1986) analysis of educational and psychological data collected on over 1,400 males five years after high school graduation. One of their clearest findings was that it was the actual abilities and skills of these young men rather than their self-concepts that had the biggest impact on their educational and occupational outcomes five years after graduation. This does not mean that their self-concepts of ability did not play an important part at earlier, more formative stages of their development. It does suggest, however, that having tangible and real skills and abilities are important working cogs in the psychological machinery which makes it possible for people to move onward and upward with their lives. A good way to promote this process is to . . .

Point Out Students' Talents and Abilities

In an effort to find out how teachers can influence students to feel either positive about their abilities and potentials or more negative, Staines (1958) set up a research format designed to answer the following questions:

1. What part do teachers play in the development of the child's self?
2. Can teachers change a student's self-picture?
3. If they can, what methods of teaching produce what kinds of self-picture?
4. Is it possible to distinguish between teachers in the frequency and kind of comment they make about a student's self?

The basic assumption of the study was that since teachers are an important aspect of students' emotional world, it is likely that they can have an important influence on students' self-concepts.

In order to test this assumption, two elementary classes were matched for age, intelligence, and socioeconomic class. In one class, Teacher A deliberately set out to assist students in viewing themselves as planning, purposeful, choosing, responsible, and accountable individuals. It was considered important that the students should test their purposes by carrying them through, see themselves as adequate and causal (i.e., persons who can *make* things happen), and, at the same time, differentiate between their strengths and weaknesses. In order to facilitate these goals, Teacher A made it a point to get to know each student and also to familiarize himself with the general area of self-concept dynamics and how these dynamics were related to behavior. In class, the teacher was likely to make comments such as the following, all designed to help students toward a more positive view of themselves, while at the same time assisting them to be realistic about their abilities:

1. "Randy, you're tall. Help me with this."
2. "Jayne, you know you're very good at solving addition problems."
3. "Good boy! Look at this, everyone!"
4. "Sally, you seem to do better in arithmetic than English."
5. "That's a good idea, Debbie; it helps us see how these two problems are related."
6. "I like the way you volunteered in class today, Dan; you really helped our discussion to move along."
7. "Jane, you have really good coordination. Have you thought of trying out for the kickball team?"
8. "You're a fine one, you are."

Note the emphasis on highlighting specific strengths, assets, and skills; on helping the students sort out his or her strengths and weaknesses; and, as in the last statement, on commenting on the student's worth as a total or "whole" person.

Teacher B was judged an equally effective teacher, but his techniques were more along the line of traditional teaching (more content oriented, telling, and

It takes so little for a teacher to make a big difference.
Reprinted by permission of UFS, INC.

testing) and not adapted to fit within a framework that explicitly considered strategies for self-concept enhancement.

When the 12-week experimental period was concluded, data from Teacher B's class indicated that traditional high-pressure teaching, with vigorous personal emphasis, with great stress on correctness and on the serious consequences of failure, and with the constant emphasis on passing examinations, leads to greater insecurity. Concerning achievement, the students of Teacher A reflected slightly higher average improvement than the students of Teacher B in standardized reading and number tests. If it is objected to that a teacher cannot spend time assisting students toward a more positive, healthy attitude for fear of shortchanging them in the way of content, here is some evidence to suggest that at least equally good academic results may be obtained while helping students see themselves in a more positive light. Feedback of this sort also gives students some external criteria from which to gauge how well they are doing and what needs to be improved.

Use Praise—But Do So Appropriately

When used wisely and appropriately, praise is a powerful motivator. A characteristic of effective praise is that it is personal and specific. An 11 year old (at the time) named Steve Kemp over 20 years ago asked his sixth-grade teacher to sign his autograph book. Steve was about to leave grammar school, and he wanted some memories and messages from his teachers and classmates at Buchanan School in Highland Park, California. The teacher wrote,

Steve— This has been some year for me, looking at your mischievous smile every morning. You are a person who has learned to use his talents of scholarship, leadership and sportsmanship. With these qualities I know you will lead a happy and successful life. You've been a good inspiration to many people. Never stop. Much luck in your new school with new-found friends and in your sports. I hope to read about you in the sports section of the paper in a few years. I'm very proud of you.

Steve Kemp did, indeed, end up on the sports pages, playing outfield in all-star fashion for three major-league baseball clubs. That must have been a very meaningful note to him because after all these years he still has it among his prized possessions.

A characteristic of *personalized* feedback is that it is specific to that person. Note, for example, that Mrs. Jamile remembered a "mischievous smile," not just any old smile. Note that she pointed to specific talents—scholarship, leadership, and sportsmanship—not just to talents generally. And note, too, her very specific reference to his athletic skills, something he had evidently clearly established at that young age. When feedback is specific, it is more believable, inasmuch as students *know* teachers are talking *about* them and *to* them and not everyone else in a more general way. Table 6-2 distinguishes between effective and ineffective praise.

In sum, it appears that the successful use of praise and criticism depends both on the needs and prior experiences of the students and on the teachers. Being ignored is less motivating than either praise or criticism; and as a general statement, praise that is not indiscriminately given helps most students feel more adequate and confident. Indeed, research shows that more learning goes on with praise than with criticism and that praise and criticism in one subject in the classroom may well transfer, in effects on academic performance, to other classroom behavior that is entirely distinct and independent (McMillan,

Table 6–2 DISTINCTIONS BETWEEN EFFECTIVE AND INEFFECTIVE PRAISE

Praise That Tends to Be More Effective in Increasing Motivation and Enhancing Self-Concept	Praise That Tends to Be Less Effective in Increasing Motivation and Enhancing Self-Concept
1. Is given contingently—i.e., is linked to a particular accomplishment or task completion (e.g., "Nice going, Janice, you did just as required by the assignment").	1. Is given randomly or indiscriminately —i.e., is not necessarily connected to a particular task completion or accomplishment; (e.g., "You always do good work, Janice").
2. Identifies the particulars of an accomplishment (e.g., "Well done, Randy, your spelling score improved by three points").	2. Tends to be restricted to global positive reactions (e.g., "Good job on the spelling test, class").
3. Reflects spontaneity, variety, and other signs of credibility; suggests clear attention to a student's accomplishment (e.g., teacher behaviors that are a mix of nonverbal approval behaviors—nods, smiles, touches—and verbal statements that give immediate attention to a student's performance).	3. Shows a bland uniformity that suggests a conditioned response made with minimal attention to the student's accomplishment (e.g., teacher uses pretty much the same words, phrases, or gestures to praise performance regardless of what it was or who did it).

(Continued)

Adapted from: J. Brophy, "Teacher Praise: A Functional Analysis," *Review of Educational Research*, 1981, *51:* 5–32. Copyright © 1981 by the American Educational Research Association. Adapted by permission of the publisher.

Table 6–2   *(Continued)*

Praise That Tends to Be More Effective in Increasing Motivation and Enhancing Self-Concept	Praise That Tends to Be Less Effective in Increasing Motivation and Enhancing Self-Concept
4. Rewards attainment of specified performance or effort creteria (e.g., "Excellent idea, Betty. I like the way you related it to our discussion").	4. Rewards mere participation, without consideration of performance processes or outcomes (e.g., "You really involved yourself in this discussion, Betty").
5. Gives information to students about their competence or the value of their accomplishemnts (e.g., "Your math skills have really improved, Debbie, and that will be very helpful to you in your next math class").	5. Either provides no information about competence at all or gives students information about their status (e.g., "You ranked about in the middle of the math test, Debbie").
6. Helps students to better appreciate both their thinking about problem solving and the work they put in on it (e.g., "I know you worked hard, Mary, and just look at the fine job that you ended up with").	6. Encourages students to compare themselves with others in a competitive way (e.g., "You didn't work as hard as Fran did, Mary, but I know you can do better if you do your homework like she does").
7. Uses student's prior performance as a measuring rod for describing present performance (e.g., "Good work, you've improved your score on each of the last two tests").	7. Uses the performance of peers as the measuring rod for describing student's present work (e.g., "Good work, you got ten right—that's only two less than Billy and Sharon got").
8. Is given in recognition of a noteworthy effort or success at difficult (for *this* student) tasks (i.e., makes a point to give something a little extra to a particular student when something especially difficult has been tried or completed).	8. Is given without regard to the effort expended on the meaning of one accomplishment (i.e., though a particularly difficult task has been accomplished, teacher treats it as an ordinary accomplishment).
9. Attributes success to effort and ability, implying that similar successes can be expected in the future (e.g., "Great job, Tom. Your hard work and good thinking really shows here, as I'm sure it will on your next assignment, too").	9. Attributes success to ability alone or to external factors such as an easy task or luck (e.g., "Great job, Tom. Your brains really show on this project," or "Great job, Tom, you really had luck on your side this time").
10. Encourages intrinsic attribution—students believe that they expend effort on the task becasue they enjoy the task or want to develop new task-related skills (i.e., the kind of praise that says, in effect, "You're successful because you have it in your power to learn and to be good at something").	10. Encourages extrinsic attribution—students believe that they expend effort on the task for external reasons —to please the teacher, come in first, win an award, etc. (i.e., the kind of praise that says, in effect, "You've done a good job when you please me or finish ahead of the others").

1976). We should not be surprised if the student harshly criticized in math class does less than his or her best in English.

There are at least five basic principles to keep in mind regarding the use of praise:

1. As a general rule, praise is a more powerful motivator than either criticism or reproof.

2. However, praise does not affect all students in the same way; for example, bright students with a high self-concept frequently work harder when their ideas are challenged and gently criticized. (They *want* to show you that they can do it.)

3. Praise is not just what is said but *how* it is said.

4. Effective praise tends to do at least three things. It (a) communicates how you feel about the performance, (b) communicates something about how well the student has done, and (c) encourages the student to evaluate his or her own performance. These are not necessarily communicated all at one time, but if they were, a praising remark might sound like this: "I feel really good about your performance (or effort) because you have made such a nice improvement over your last try. How do you feel about what you've accomplished?"

5. Honesty is important. Only praiseworthy performances or efforts should be praised.

Develop Positive Expectations—Believe Students Can Do It

The idea of positive expectations and believing in students is no better illustrated than in the results of a study reported by Pedersen, Faucher, and Eaton (1978) in the *Harvard Educational Review.* In the process of looking at the long-term outcomes of 59 adults who had all attended a single school in a poor neighborhood, one bit of information kept popping up; among the individuals being studied, those who had a particular first-grade teacher (called "Miss A" in the study) were more likely to show IQ increases during elementary school, got better grades, finished more years of schooling, and were more successful adults. Not a single one of Miss A's students whom Pedersen and his colleagues were able to find for an interview (44 others were interviewed who had other first-grade teachers) was in the lowest level of adult success defined in this study, despite the fact that most of the children in Miss A's classes came from poor families, many of which were minority families. Pedersen and his colleagues systematically ruled out other possible reasons for the success of Miss A's students. In race, religion, intelligence, and economic status, Miss A's pupils were similar to their schoolmates.

The reason for the difference was Miss A herself. She believed that all her students could learn, conveyed that message strongly to them, and got involved in the lives of her students in ways personally meaningful to them.

In the course of their research, Pedersen and his colleagues asked all the subjects to name as many of their elementary school teachers as they could. Everyone who had Miss A for first grade remembered her. Most of those who had other first-grade teachers could not remember their names. Four of the subjects said Miss A was their first-grade teacher when, in fact, records showed she wasn't. Pedersen ascribed it to "wishful thinking."

Although this is only one study, and with a small number of subjects, the results are consistent with other research. Teachers with good rapport and high but reasonable expectations can make a big difference for the better. As Pedersen and his colleagues said,

> If children are fortunate enough to begin their schooling with an optimistic teacher who expects them to do well and who teaches them the basic skills needed for further academic success, they are likely to perform better than those exposed to a teacher who conveys a discouraging, self-defeating outlook. (p. 29)

There is something else that teachers can do to enhance self-concept and achievement.

Take Advantage of the Psychological Content of the Curriculum

Nearly everything in a curriculum is charged with psychological and motivational possibilities when looked at for what it might do to help students find themselves, realize their potential, use their resources in productive ways, and enter into relationships that have a bearing on their ideas about school and attitudes toward themselves.

Sometimes, in the quest for "the right answers," teachers fall into the trap of asking only one kind of question: the convergent kind. Of course, there can be only one kind of answer to this sort of question, and it is usually a response that sorts through, synthesizes, and integrates answers from existing data. Divergent questions, however, invite a quite different type of thinking and responding. They demand answers that are original, novel, and creative. To ask a divergent question is to ask not only "What do you *know* about this?" but also "What do you *think* about this?"

Examples of both types of questions can be drawn from the classroom. If while teaching *Macbeth*, the teacher asks, "Who killed Duncan?" then clearly only convergent thinking is involved: Students either know the answer (from reading the play or Tom's notes), or they do not know. When the teacher asks, "Why did Macbeth kill Duncan?" the student's task is to gather appropriate data from the play and come up with a cogent answer. When the teacher asks, "What would you have done if you were Lady Macbeth?" students are invited to think divergently, to make up alternative plots for the play based on their own feelings. Finally, if the teacher asks, "Should Macbeth have gotten away with all the murders?" he or she is attempting to evoke some sort of moral judgment, which is an open invitation to all sorts of divergent possibilities.

Convergent, memory-type questions do have a place in the classroom, but we may seriously hinder motivation and learning if we encourage only convergent thinking. To take another example from the teaching of English, divergent questions and composition assignments about literature invite students to participate in the book, to become a character in it, to shape its plot to fit their own experience. The convergent question about the same book forces students to come to terms with the book as it is given, a collection of information to be analyzed in some logical way. If we remain aware of these distinctions, we can plan more purposefully, and we can also plan to make deliberate shifts from one kind of thinking to another.

Sometimes, in their anxiety to cover a certain unit of material in a given amount of time, to give students what they consider to be crucial information and knowledge, teachers teach in a "non-self-related" manner. Often, students dislike English or history or social studies or some other subject because it seems to have no personal meaning or relevance to their own lives. Indeed, many students see little relationship between what happens in school and what goes on outside of school. Can we make school more personally meaningful? Very probably so if we exploit the psychological as well as the academic content of a curriculum. Let's look at some examples.

Take history as a case in point. Wouldn't it be better to teach history in terms of people and their experiences rather than just events, institutions, and movements? We all know something about significant historical dates, but what do we know about the motivations of the people behind them? Or as another example, is it possible that high school students might get more out of Shakespeare's works by reading them not only as great literary masterpieces but also as unfolding dramas of human greed, love, and hate? How many students actually "see" *Julius Caesar* as an example of what untamed, selfish ambition can do to a person? How many contemporary people can you think of who reflect the personal qualities that led to Caesar's downfall? Could they be used as examples in class?

I know of a class of slow-learning ninth graders who not only read *Romeo and Juliet,* but also enjoyed it! A wise, sensitive teacher first exposed them to something they could understand—*West Side Story.* They listened to the music in class, and since the musical was being presented by a local theater group, most of the students made it a point to see it, particularly since the teacher strongly recommended it. True, the characters were Tony and Maria, not Romeo and Juliet; the scene was a fire escape, not a balcony; but the boy and girl were in love, there were two feuding families, and it did end tragically. Thus, through the simple process of exposing students to something they already knew about and liked, the teacher made a study of *Romeo and Juliet* not only possible, but also fun. What could easily have been a laborious, nonmeaningful English assignment was converted into an exciting adventure as the students puzzled through the similarities and differences between the two stories.

Biographies and autobiographies offer mirrors in which students can study, among other things, their own self-reflections. Drama and fiction are filled with conflicts such as occur in our daily lives; it only remains for the teacher to point these things out, to help students see the similarities to their lives, and to utilize the feelings that exist in all of us.

Physical education abounds in psychological possibilities. It can be more than basketball, swimming, and push-ups. It can be that part of a curriculum where students discover and accept their own bodies. They can be introduced to a human laboratory in which they see acts of meanness, cruelty, and hostility, on the one hand, or good sportsmanship and greatness in defeat, on the other. Moreover, they can learn to recognize the healthy as well as the morbid features of competition. Some students may discover that winning is not so impossible after all. Others may find that to do anything well, whether in the classroom or on the field, takes persistence, effort, hard work, and discipline. They may even discover that you don't have to win to be a winner. As the late Packer football coach, Vince Lombardi used to say, "Winning isn't everything, but *wanting* to win is." Indeed, if physical education is more than basketball, swimming, and the like, then students may carry over into life itself a constructive, positive attitude about the use and care of the body that could make possible a more healthy, vigorous, and physical existence.

Many events happen in a classroom that teachers could have no way of anticipating. Some will be rich with possibilities for real-life object lessons. These require some flexibility and creativity on the part of teachers. For example, I recall an incident involving a sixth-grade teacher who converted one girl's dismay, another boy's enthusiasm, and the entire class's anxiety into an exciting simulated courtroom trial. As the teacher walked along the side of the room during a lesson, she accidentally stepped on a cockroach. One of her 11-year-old students, sitting in an aisle seat, saw this happen and in dismay blurted out, "Ms. Criswell, you meanie, look at what you've done." Another student, also sitting in an aisle seat, immediately responded to the "accuser" by asserting that "all cockroaches should be killed anyway" and that what Ms. Criswell had done was not only right but her "duty." The rest of the class stirred somewhat restlessly, and a few of the children began to line themselves upon one side or the other. Within the span of 60 seconds or so, several important issues emerged.

One was the "moral" issue of whether the teacher did something that was good or bad. Another was the "legal" issue of whether the teacher did something that was right or wrong. The teacher was wise enough to know that a great deal of feeling was being expressed by her students. She suggested that the whole incident be explored from as many different points of view as possible and proposed a courtroom trial to settle the issue. The accusing student, naturally enough, was appointed prosecuting attorney. The child who originally defended the teacher was appointed the defense counsel. Ms. Criswell's lesson plan was abandoned for the remainder of the afternoon, and each of the "attorneys" talked to witnesses and gathered evidence for their side. Among the first things that occurred, by the way, was the the scraping of exhibit A off the bottom of Ms. Criswell's shoe. A portion of each morning for the next week was set aside for the children to plan the trial, and several students whose fathers were lawyers assumed the responsibility for seeing that the correct legal procedures were followed. A judge was chosen by a general class election. On the day of the "trial," a jury was picked from another sixth-grade class in the same school, and for the better part of one morning, the evidence for and against Ms. Criswell was weighed and debated.

When it was all over, the teacher was "acquitted." Actually, the outcome was not nearly so important as the process. The children were able to be personally involved with the concept of "justice," along with some of the social, legal, and moral implications associated with it. A short time later, the children visited a "real" judge and a "real" courtroom as part of the school's community awareness program. Referring to the judge's courtroom, one of the children was overheard saying to the judge, "We have one of these in our school."

IN PERSPECTIVE

School is the stage on which children and adolescents act out a significant portion of the unfolding drama of their developmental years. It houses an audience of viewers and critics who, on a daily basis, dispense praise or criticism according to their perceptions of each player's performance. Some students are applauded for their efforts and compete for more time on center stage and for more attention to their talents. Other students are politely but unenthusiastically acknowledged, and they keep hoping for better reviews. Some students are largely ignored and remain quietly in the wings hoping for a break in their luck. And still others, not a large number but significant nonetheless, are booed and hissed by an unappreciative audience and either hide in the wings hoping not to be noticed or leave the stage altogether.

Probably no 13-year span is more crucial in shaping attitudes about oneself—particularly feelings of adequacy and competency—than those that occur between the ages of five and 18 years. These are the years—the formative years—when growing children and developing adolescents internalize a self-image that says "I can" or one that says "I can't." The role of the school, teachers, and curriculum in developing and shaping that self-image is enormous. It apportions approval and disapproval, acceptance and rejection, on a colossal scale. School provides not only the stage on which much of the drama of a young person's formative years is played, but also the most scrutinizing audience in the world—peers and teachers. And it is here, onstage before their severest critics, that students are reminded again and again of either their failings and shortcomings or of their strengths and possibilities.

There is substantial evidence to link both students' school behavior and achievement to their feelings about themselves. As a general statement, high self-concept students do better in school than low self-concept students, although this is not always so. The possession of a high self-concept does not guarantee high academic achievement, but it does seem to be related to it. The attitudes students have about themselves and their ability to do schoolwork depends partly on how they were treated by people significant to them, their experiences with success and failure, and their perceptions of schools and teachers.

Each student brings to school a certain attitude about his or her ability to compete and succeed, whether in grade school or college. If the self-concept is learned as a function of experience—and evidence from all quarters suggests it is—then, whether students are aware of it or not, part of their accumulation of knowledge about themselves is acquired in the classroom. No matter what the grade level, teachers are a potent source of feedback. A child ridiculed at the blackboard by an insensitive teacher in front of all her peers may learn that it's better not to raise her hand, that maybe she's not as smart as the other kids. Or a shy, uncertain child appropriately praised in the presence of his classmates for doing a good job may learn that speaking out, that taking a risk now and then, is not so dangerous after all.

All in all, school must certainly rank as one of the most important experiences of children's lives. Depending on what happens there, students learn that they are able or unable, adequate or inadequate. As far as anyone knows, there is no gene for this or that kind of self-concept. Although it does seem to be true that each child comes into this world with what seems to be a constitutional predisposition to behave in one way or another, the way any given child feels about himself or herself is the result of a complex interplay among biology, psychology, and environment. Out of this emerges a concept of self that is learned. And what is learned can be taught. The question is not whether we approve of teaching for a positive sense of self in school settings but whether the effects of schooling are positive or negative.

Self-concept and school achievement are interrelated and interactive. Even though it is not possible to specify which comes first, good schoolwork or high self-regard, it does not seem unreasonable to suggest that each is mutually reinforcing to the other to the extent that a change in one facilitates a commensurate change in the other.

The change we would like to see is, of course, a positive one. This has a better chance of happening, and schooling, in general, has a greater chance of being a self-enhancing experience to the extent that we help students see not only their limitations, but also their strengths; that we acknowledge not only the product of their toil, but also the effort involved in achieving it; and that we establish reasonable, reachable expectations for performance so that some measure of success lies within a range of each student's ability.

Life may not always be fair, but school can be.

QUESTIONS FOR STUDY, REVIEW, AND REFLECTION

1. How would you explain the idea that self-concept, when thought about in relation to school, is hierarchical and multifaceted? If someone asked you what advantages there were to thinking about one's school self-concept in this way, how could you respond?

2. When you think about possible relationships between your own self-concept of ability and your achievement, do you see any

relationship between the two? Most people can remember three or four rather powerful early experiences—some good, some not so good—that had a big impact on their self-concept of ability. What were yours? How did they affect your self-esteem? What did you learn from them?

3. The question of which comes first—self-concept or achievement—is always an interesting one. In general, how would you say it worked in your case? If you were to give a presentation to a group of parents and teachers on this topic, what main ideas would you be sure to include?

4. How would you explain the finding that suggests that a positive self-concept is related to but does not guarantee high achievement?

5. Positive and negative expectations are something we have all experienced. Can you think of two or three instances of each kind in your school life? How was your performance affected by them?

6. Praise is a very effective means of reinforcing good work and encouraging more of the same. But sometimes, it causes students, and others, to feel uncomfortable. Why do you suppose this is so?

7. What are five or six basic differences between effective and ineffective praise?

8. Can you explain why a self-fulfilling prophecy begins with a false belief? What has to happen to make a self-fulfilling prophecy self-fulfilling?

REFERENCES

Babad, E. Y., Inbar, J., and Rosenthal, R. "Teachers' Judgment of Students' Potential as a Function of Teachers' Susceptibility to Biasing Information." *Journal of Personality and Social Psychology,* 1982, *42*: 541–547.

Bachman, J. G., and O'Malley, P. M. "Self-Esteem in Young Men: A Longitudinal Analysis of the Impact of Educational and Occupational Attainment." *Journal of Personality and Social Psychology,* 1977, *35*: 365–380.

Bachman, J. G., and O'Malley, P. M. "Self-Concepts, Self-Esteem, and Educational Experiences: The Frog Pond Revisited (Again)." *Journal of Personality and Social Psychology,* 1986, *50*: 35–46.

Bachman, J. G., O'Malley, P. M., and Johnson, J. *Adolescence to Adulthood: Changes and Stability in the Lives of Young Men.* Ann Arbor: University of Michigan, Institute for Social Research, 1978.

Bloom, B. S. *Stability and Change in Human Characteristics.* New York: Wiley, 1964.

Bloom, B. S. *Human Characteristics and School Learning.* New York: McGraw-Hill, 1976.

Borislow, B. "Self-Evaluation and Academic Achievement." *Journal of Counseling Psychology,* 1962, *9*: 246–254.

Bridgeman, B., and Shipman, V. C. "Preschool Measures of Self-Esteem and Achievement as Predictors of Third-Grade Achievement." *Journal of Educational Psychology,* 1978, *70*: 17–28.

Brookover, W. B., Paterson, A., and Thomas, S. *Self-Concept of Ability and School Achievement: I.* E. Lansing, Mich.: Educational Publication Services, 1962.

Brookover, W. B., LePere, J. M., Hamachek, D., Thomas, S., and Erickson, E. L. *Self-Concept of Ability and School Achievement: II.* E. Lansing, Mich.: Educational Publishing Services, 1965.

Brookover, W. B., Erickson, E. L., and Joiner, L. M. *Self-Concept of Ability and School Achievement: III.* E. Lansing, Mich.: Educational Publishing Services, 1967.

Brophy, J., and Good, T. *Teacher-Student Relationships: Causes and Consequences.* New York: Holt, Rinehart and Winston, 1974.

Byrne, B. M. "The General/Academic Self-Concept Homological Network: A Review of Construct Validation Research." *Review of Educational Research,* 1984, *54*: 427–456.

Byrne, B. M. "Self-Concept/Academic Achievement and Relations: An Investigation of Dimensionality, Stability, and Causality." *Canadian Journal of Behavioral Science,* 1986, *18*: 173–186.

Calsyn, R. L., and Kenny, D. A. "Self-Concept of Ability and Perceived Evaluation of Others: Cause or Effect of Achievement?" *Journal of Educational Psychology,* 1977, *69*: 135–145.

Chaiken, A., Sigler, E., and Derlega, V. "Non-Verbal Mediators of Teacher Expectancy Effects." *Journal of Personality and Social Psychology,* 1974, *30*: 144–149.

Chiu, L. H. "Development of the Self-Esteem Rating Scale for Children (revised)." *Measurement and Evaluation in Counseling and Development,* April 1987, pp. 36–41.

Cooper, H., and Good, T. *Pygmalion Grows Up: Studies in the Expectation Communication Process.* New York: Longman, 1983.

Coopersmith, S. *The Antecedents of Self-Esteem.* San Francisco: Freeman, 1967.

Dillon, H. A. *A Major Educational Problem.* New York: National Child Labor Committee, 1949, pp. 35–40.

Doyle, W. G., Hancock, G., and Kifer, E. "Teacher Perceptions: Do They Make a Difference?" Paper presented at the American Educational Research Association Annual Meeting, Chicago, April, 1971.

Dusek, J. (Ed.). *Teacher Expectancies.* Hillsdale, N. J.: Erlbaum, 1985.

Dyson, E. "A Study of Ability Grouping and Self-Concept." *Journal of Educational Research,* 1967, *60*: 403–405.

Eckstrom, R. B., Goertz, M. E., Pollack, J. M., and Rock, D. A. "Who Drops Out of School and Why?" Findings from a National Study. *Teachers College Record,* 1987, *87*: 356–373.

Elahoff, J. D., and Snow, R. E. *A Case Study in Statistical Reference: Reconsideration of the Rosenthal-Jacobson Data on Teacher Expectancy.* (Tech. rep. No. 15). Stanford, Calif.: Stanford Center for Research and Development in Teaching. Stanford University, 1970.

Erikson, E. H. *Identity and the Life Cycle.* New York: Norton, 1980.

Felson, R. B. "The Effects of Self-Appraisals of Ability on Academic Performance." *Journal of Personality and Social Psychology,* 1984, *47*: 944–952.

Fine, M., and Rosenberg, P. "Dropping Out of High School: The Ideology of School and Work." *Journal of Education,* 1983, *165*: 257–272.

Gephart, W. J. "Will the Real Pygmalion Please Stand Up?" *American Educational Research Journal,* 1970, *7*: 473–475.

Godfrey, E. *North Carolina Education.* October, 1971, *2*: 10–11, 29.

Good, T., and Brophy, J. *Looking in Classrooms,* 4th ed. New York: Harper and Row, 1987.

Guttman, J., and Bar-tel, D. "Stereotypic Perceptions of Teachers." *American Educational Research Journal,* 1982, *19*: 519–528.

Hahn, A. "Reaching Out to America's Dropouts: What to Do?" *Phi Delta Kappan,* December, 1987: 256–263.

Hall, J. *A Study of Dropouts.* Miami, Fla.: Dade County Schools, Dept. of Research and Information, 1964.

Hamachek, D. *Psychology in Teaching, Learning, and Growth,* 4th ed. Boston: Allyn and Bacon, 1990.

Hansford, B. C., and Hattie, J. A. "The Relationship Between Self and Achievement/Performance Measures." *Review of Education Research,* 1982, *52*: 123–142.

Hilgard, E. R., and Hilgard, J. R. *Hypnosis in the Relief of Pain.* Los Altos, Calif.: William Kaufman, 1975.

Hogan, R., and Weiss, D. S. "Personality Correlates of Superior Academic Achievement." *Journal of Counseling Psychology,* 1974, *21*: 144–149.

Hoge, R. D., and Luce, S. "Predicting Classroom Achievement from Classroom Behavior." *Review of Educational Research,* 1979, *49*: 479–496.

Kagan, D. M. "How Schools Alienate Students at Risk: A Model for Examining Proximal Classroom Variables." *Educational Psychologist,* 1990, *25*: 105–125.

Kelly, K. R., and Jordan, L. K. "Effects of Academic Achievement and Gender on Academic and Social Self-Concept: A Replication Study." *Journal of Counseling and Development,* 1990, *69*: 173–177.

Kifer, E. "Relationship Between Academic Achievement and Personality Characteristics: A Quasi-Longitudinal Study." *American Educational Research Journal,* 1975, *12*: 191–210.

Kolberg, L., LaCrosse, J., and Ricks, D. "The Predictability of Adult Mental Health from Childhood Behavior," in B. B. Wolman (Ed.), *Manual of Child Psychopathology.* New York: McGraw-Hill, 1972.

Lamy, M. W. "Relationship of Self-Perceptions of Early Primary Children to Achievement in Reading," in I. J. Gordon (Ed.), *Human Development: Readings in Research.* Glenview, Ill.: Scott, Foresman, 1965.

Lecky, P. *Self-Consistency—A Theory of Personality.* New York: Island Press, 1945.

Lepper, M. R., Ross, L., and Lau, R. R. "Persistence About Inaccurate Beliefs About the Self: Perseverance Effects in the Classroom." *Journal of Personality and Social Psychology,* 1986, *50*: 482–491.

Lichter, S. O. *The Dropouts.* New York: Free, 1962.

Luginbuhl, J. E. R. "Role of Choice and Outcome on Feelings of Success and Estimates of Ability." *Journal of Personality and Social Psychology,* 1972, *22*: 121–127.

Marsh, H. W. "Relations Among Dimensions of Self-Concept, and Academic Achievements." *Journal of Educational Psychology,* 1984, *76*: 1291–1308.

Marsh, H. W. "A Multidimensional, Hierarchical Model of Self-Concept: Theoretical and Empirical Justification." *Educational Psychology Review,* 1990a, *2*: 77–172.

Marsh, H. "The Influence of Internal and External Frames of Reference on the Formation of English and Math Self-Concepts." *Journal of Educational Psychology,* 1990b, *82*: 107–116.

Marsh, H. W., Byrne, B. M., and Shavelson, R. J. "A Multifaceted Academic Self-Concept: Its Hierarchical Structure and Its Relation to Academic Achievement." *Journal of Educational Psychology,* 1988, *80*: 366–380.

Marsh, H. W., and Shavelson, R. "Self-Concept: Its Multifaceted, Hierarchical Structure." *Educational Psychologist,* 1985, *20*: 107–123.

Maw, W. H., and Maw, E. H. "Self-Concepts of High- and Low-Curiosity Boys." *Child Development,* 1970, *70*: 169–175.

McMillan, J. H. "Factors Affecting the Development of Pupil Attitudes Toward School Subjects." *Psychology in the Schools,* 1976, *13*: 322–325.

Merton, R. K. "The Self-Fulfilling Prophecy." *Antioch Review,* 1948, *8*: 193–210.

O'Malley, P. M., and Bachman, J. G. "Self-Esteem and Education: Sex and Cohort Comparisons Among High School Seniors." *Journal of Personality and Social Psychology,* 1979, *37*: 1153–1159.

Palardy, M. J. "What Teachers Believe, What Children Achieve." *Elementary School Journal,* 1969, *69*: 370–374.

Pedersen, E., Faucher, T., and Eaton, W. W. "A New Perspective on the Effects of First-Grade Teachers on Children's Subsequent Adult Status." *Harvard Educational Review,* 1978, *48*: 1–31.

Piers, E. V., and Harris, D. B. "Age and Other Correlates of Self-Concept in Children." *Journal of Educational Psychology,* 1964, *55*: 91–95.

Raudenbush, S. "Magnitude of Teacher Expectancy Effects on Pupil IQ as a Function of the Credibility of Expectancy Induction: Synthesis of Finding from 18 Experiments." *Journal of Educational Psychology,* 1984, *76*: 85–97.

Rosenthal, R. "The Pygmalion Effect Lives." *Psychology Today,* September 1973, pp. 56–60.

Rosenthal, R., and Jacobson, L. *Pygmalion in the Classroom: Teacher Expectation and Pupil's Intellectual Development.* New York: Holt, Rinehart and Winston, 1968.

Roth, R. M., and Meyersburg, H. "The Non-Achievement Syndrome." *The Personnel and Guidance Journal,* 1963, *41*: 531–538.

Rubin, R. "Stability of Self-Esteem Ratings and Their Relation to Academic Achievement: A Longitudinal Study." *Psychology in the Schools,* 1978, *15*: 430–433.

Seaver, W. B. "Effects of Naturally Induced Teacher Expectancies." *Journal of Abnormal and Social Psychology,* 1973, *28*: 333–342.

Shavelson, R. J., and Marsh, H. W. "On the Structure of Self-Concept," in Schwarzer, R. (Ed.), *Anxiety and Cognitions.* Hillsdale, N. J.: Lawrence Erlbaum, 1986.

Shiffler, N., Lynch-Sauer, J., and Nadelman, L. "Relationship Between Self-Concept and Classroom Behavior in Two Informal Classrooms." *Journal of Educational Psychology,* 1977, *69*: 349–359.

Skaalvik, E. M., and Hagtvet, K. A. "Academic Achievement and Self-Concept: An Analysis of Causal Predominance in a Developmental Perspective." *Journal of Personality and Social Psychology,* 1990, *58*: 292–307.

Staines, J. W. "The Self-Picture as a Factor in the Classroom." *The British Journal of Educational Psychology,* 1958, *28*: 97–111.

Wattenberg, W. W., and Clifford, C. "Relation of Self-Concepts to Beginning Achievement in Reading." *Child Development,* 1964, *35*: 461–467.

Williams, J. H. "The Relationship of Self-Concept and Reading Achievement in First Grade Children." *Journal of Educational Research,* 1973, *66*: 378–389.

Wineburg, S. S. "The Self-Fulfillment of the Self-Fulfilling Prophecy." *Educational Researcher,* December 1987, pp. 28–37.

Wylie, R. *The Self-Concept,* Vol. 2. Lincoln: University of Nebraska Press, 1979.

Yarworth, J. S., and Gauthier, W. G. "Relationship of Student Self-Concept and Selected Personal Variables to Participation in School Activities." *Journal of Educational Psychology,* 1978, *70*: 335–344.

Chapter 7

Toward Developing and Maintaining a Positive Self-Concept

PROLOGUE

No doubt one of the oldest, and perhaps the most familiar, of all apho-risms in any language is the ancient injunction of Socrates: "Know thy-self." This is not an easy thing to do. Knowing oneself, deeply and fully, also means facing oneself, squarely and honestly. This means looking beyond and through the emotional costuming, the sham, and the pre-tense in order to see ourselves as we actually are. It means reconciling in a realistic way the discrepancies between our hopes and our accomplish-ments and making our peace with the differences that may exist be-tween our ambitions and our talents. It means accepting, in a deep and final way, a simple psychological truth: the self is not something we find, but something we create. Becoming an emotionally healthy, happy person, or a self-actualized, fully functioning individual, is not done by accident or coded in the genes. Rather, it is an emotional position built over time by blending reasonable, reachable goals with hard work, some sacrifice, and a willingness to take some risks now and then.

The voluminous literature concerning the self and self-concept leaves little doubt that mental health and personal adjustment depend deeply on each individual's basic feelings of personal adequacy. Just as it is possible to learn a healthy orientation to objective reality, so, too, it is possible to learn to think of ourselves in healthy ways. Feelings of per-sonal inadequacy, inferiority, and worthlessness tend to erode and weaken, sometimes to the point of collapse, the main pillars of one's self-structure. The growth of an adequate self-concept, free of neurotic

315

pride and unrealistic fears, is a critically important first step in creating a healthy self-image. To cope successfully with the reality of everyday living, we must have a firm grip on our own identity. Indeed, Socrates' admonition to "Know thyself" has been passed down through the ages as the criterion of wisdom and peace of mind until our present day, when it has emerged from a religious and philosophical notion into a slogan for better mental health.

I think it is sad but true that too few people take the time to realize and accept responsibility for the fact that where they are today is a direct consequence of decisions they have made in the past. And where they will be tomorrow will be a result of decisions they make today. It's not possible to let someone else do it for us unless we make the decision to allow that to happen. If we aren't in control of our lives, someone else is. This type of responsibility begins with taking the time to honestly and realistically understand who one is and what's important in one's life. We might be able to fool some of the people all of the time and others we can fool part of the time, but we can never fool ourselves.

Attaining a healthy self-image, with its concomitant feelings of adequacy, ability, personal worth, and confidence, is not some lofty goal beyond mortal reach, standing as a kind of poetic ideal. It is an attitude or cluster of attitudes that are learned and acquired, which means that sometimes "bad" (negative, destructive, self-defeating) attitudes must be replaced by healthier ones. Most people seem to want to move toward higher levels of physical and psychological health, although there are those occasional odd personalties who seem to get a perverse pleasure out of unhealth and suffering because it is the chief way of knowing they're alive. So busy are they contriving new defenses, inventing new excuses, enjoying their own self-pity, and blaming others that they seldom have any energy left for considering constructive avenues for living and looking ahead to better days. Personal growth slows considerably when one gets stuck at the level of blame. When this happens it's always the other person's fault, which means that change is not possible unless the other person changes. Knowing oneself is not likely to happen in any deep way when blame is present because one is forever looking "out there" for answers rather than "in here" where they are more likely to be found.

Knowing oneself involves a view of the self with at least three dimensions: looking behind to see what we were, looking at the moment to see what we are, and looking ahead to see what we can become. Along these lines, I've always liked an observation by Abraham Maslow (1962):

> *. . . from Freud we learned that the past exists* now *in the person. Now we must learn, from growth theory and self-actualization theory, that the future also* now *exists in the person in the form of ideals, hopes, goals, unrealized potential, mission, fate, destiny, etc. One for whom no future exists is reduced to the concrete, to helplessness, to emptiness. For him, time must be endlessly*

"filled." Striving, the usual organizer of most activity, when lost, leaves the person unorganized and unintegrated. (p. 48)

There is little question but that past experience can have a vast influence on current behavior. However, even though we cannot change what happened yesterday, we can change how we feel about it today. Although we cannot change past experiences, we can change our responses to those experiences, which is an important step toward becoming less of a reactor to life's happenings and more of an actor, one who acts to change things.

Two themes run as parallel undercurrents throughout this chapter. One is the idea that who we are and what we are becoming are very largely the outcomes of choices we have made. The second is the idea that, even though it is not possible to know ourselves totally, it is possible to know ourselves better, which gives us the distinct advantage of expanding our self-awareness and thereby increasing the choices we can make for our lives. In the pages ahead, we will examine some routes that one might take to understand oneself better, along with considering specific ideas for enhancing self-esteem. We begin with an important possibility, which is to move . . .

TOWARD DEVELOPING SELF-OTHER UNDERSTANDING

It is sometimes assumed that we get to know ourselves by learning about people in the abstract, that is, people as psychological, social, biological, economic, and religious beings. As a consequence, a person who is "psychologically knowledgeable" knows about a hypothetical being fabricated from theories, from research reporting how most people behave under certain conditions, and from other people's experiences but not very much about himself or herself. Indeed, it is possible to know a vast amount about psychology but very little about oneself. For example, I once worked with a highly educated woman (three degrees and over 25 credits in psychology), who although extremely conversant about how children's lives can be affected by their relationships to parents, was unable to see how her ongoing problems with her husband were related to the unresolved anger she felt toward her father. Although she knew how defense mechanisms such as denial, repression, displacement, and projection worked in the abstract, she was unaware of how her use of these very mechanisms enabled her to bring her unresolved feelings for her father into the marriage and to act as though it was her husband (who was a safer target) whom she was angry at and not her father. Hence, the problems. A psychologist I know has always had great trouble developing a close relationship with his son for the very reasons that his own father had such a poor relationship with him as a boy: difficulty being emotionally open and expressing warm feelings. Although this psychologist is able to lecture eloquently to students and parents about the importance of explicit love and open communication between parents and children, he seems to have a blind spot when it comes to applying that knowledge to his own life.

Although both the woman and the man in these examples know a considerable amount about psychology, their knowledge is not wisdom, nor have their intra- and interpersonal lives been particularly enriched because of it. Clearly, self-other understanding appears to be specific knowledge about how one's unique individuality interacts and grows in an interpersonal context. How, then, can we arrive at this kind of knowledge?

A maxim of Goethe may help here: "If you want to know yourself, observe what your neighbors are doing. If you want to understand others, probe within yourself." Most of us are inclined to do exactly the opposite. We observe the other person to understand him or her, and we probe within ourselves to understand ourselves better. Normally, we look at the other persons objectively; we behold their flaws, weaknesses, self-deceptions, and even their prejudices masquerading as principles.

When we probe within ourselves, however, we are not inclined to see the same personal distortions. What we "see" are our good intentions, our noblest ambitions, the fine deeds we have performed, and the sacrifices we have made. These self-serving perceptions may not be so much the result of trying to deceive ourselves and others as they are the outgrowth of trying to view a picture from inside the frame. We can no more see ourselves clearly from the inside out than we can see the dimensions of a forest while standing in the middle of it.

In the process of getting to know oneself better, introspection and self-examination are important parts of the process and good as far as each can go. There are, however, limits to how far we can go with these alone. We can meditate for hours or analyze ourselves for weeks and not progress an inch farther—any more than we can smell our own breath or laugh when we tickle ourselves no matter how hard we try.

Our self-reflection in the mirror does not tell us what we are like; only our reflection in other people. We are essentially social animals, and our personality resides in association, not in isolation. There is a certain paradoxical truth in the observation that we can get to know ourselves better through knowing others, and we can come to know others better through knowing ourselves. Let's turn our attention to those possible ways for doing this.

Cultivate the Capacity for Social Feeling or Empathy

Adler's (1964) concept of social feeling provides a useful conceptual tool for developing a healthy self-image. What does social feeling mean? Crandall (1980) suggested that it is the " . . . valuing of things other than the self . . . the capacity to transcend the limits of the self and to identify with the needs and concerns of others." The usefulness of this concept lies in the fact that it combines *social,* which is an objective reference to common experiences, with *feeling,* which is a subjective reference to private experiences. Their synthesis is one way of bridging the gap between "you" and "me."

Self-other understanding involves, strangely enough, self-transcendence, which calls for one to go beyond one's own private motives and thoughts in order to better understand and share another person's needs and goals. Thus, social

Developing a capacity for social interest can be expressed in many different ways.

Reprinted by permission of UFS, INC.

feeling is an attempt to understand oneself through the understanding of others. Fromm (1962), for example, observed, "I discover that I am everybody, and that I discover myself in discovering my fellow man, and vice versa." Self-other understanding, through the process of social feeling, means to see oneself (insight) by participating in and sharing mutual concerns with another, or more succinctly, being an "I" for a "thou," as Buber (1958) would say. It is a way of doing what Goethe suggested: If you wish to know yourself, watch what others are doing.

The fact is, we have a great deal in common, you and I. When I understand you better this may help me understand myself better, either because I see myself reflected clearly in the similarities of our behavior or because your behavior is so different from mine that I am able to see my own more clearly by contrast. Personal insights via this route are a common experience among people in counseling groups, which is an important reason why a positive group experience can help facilitate greater self-other understanding. Consider the following example:

> During a particular group session, an 18-year-old girl, the youngest of the nine people in the group, began to talk about her feelings toward her father. At one point she said: "I love him so much. And that's the part that hurts. I don't know whether he loves me or even really cares about me in any way. I think he loves me, but (she stopped here and cried quietly for a moment) you know, he has never said those words to me. Not ever. (And again she sobbed quietly.) I looked at the man sitting next to her, a gentleman in his mid-40s, and tears were streaming down his cheeks. He reached for her hand (the first time he had ever touched anyone in the group) and said to her in a gentle voice, "Your father could be me. My daughter could be you. I just never realized how important it could be until this moment to actually tell my daughter how I feel about her. Thank you for helping me to understand that." In an 18-year-old

girl's story, this man saw a buried part of himself clearly and for the first time. He resolved to change and to be more open about his feelings. As time went on, the girl grew to understand her father better through understanding this man, who was like him, and she was able to use that understanding in a positive way to feel closer to her father.

I think that the idea of social feeling, the capacity for empathy, is nicely revealed in the following story:

A little girl came home from a neighbor's house where her little friend had died.

"Why did you go?" questioned her father.

"To comfort her mother," said the child.

"What could you do to comfort her?"

"I climbed into her lap and cried with her."

Honesty and Self-Disclosure Open Interpersonal Doors

The kind of honesty we're talking about here is the honesty involved when I am able to reveal to you something about my own feelings and attitudes. Sometimes, however, honesty travels along a well-used one-way street rather than a two-lane highway. When people say to us, "I want to be perfectly honest with you," it often means that they want to be perfectly honest about *us,* rather than about *themselves.* Behaving in a reasonably honest and self-disclosing manner requires a certain amount of courage, the courage it takes to *be known,* to be perceived by others as we know ourselves to be. Jourard (1971), whose self-disclosure research unveiled new ways to understanding interpersonal relationships, was among the first to admit that self-disclosure could be risky business: ". . . you expose yourself not only to a lover's balm, but to a hater's bombs! When he knows you, he knows just where to plant them for maximum effect" (p. 5).

Honesty and self-disclosure go hand in hand. You can more easily accept in a nondefensive way my honest feedback—particularly if it is along more critical lines—if I am able to disclose my own faults and shortcomings. Also, if I am willing to disclose facets of myself to you, it is very likely that you will feel more open to revealing aspects of yourself to me. It has to do with trust. If you sense that I trust you with my disclosure, you may be willing to trust me with yours. Research has rather consistently shown the validity of this phenomenon: Self-disclosure begets self-disclosure (Hendrick, 1981; Tolstedt and Stokes, 1984).

Timing is an important consideration in whether or not self-disclosure works in a positive way (Archer and Burleson, 1980). The person who jumps in with great revelations very early in new relationships is apt to be viewed as immature, insecure, and somewhat dishonest. If an individual makes a highly personal remark to us early in a conversation, we may conclude that this remark has little to do with her feelings toward us and more to do, perhaps, with her insecurities or need for attention. For example, a man who, on a first date, launches into deep disclosures about his social and sexual inadequacies is not likely to win the affections of his new friend. (Unless, of course, she has a large need to mother someone, in which case they might make a perfect match.) On the other hand, if someone makes a disclosing comment after knowing us for a while, we are more likely to take the remark personally and infer that it has possible implications for developing a relationship. We are more likely to conclude that the disclosure was made because that person trusted us and not because he or she was simply looking for attention.

A major thesis in Jourard's work is the idea that maladjusted people are individuals who have not made themselves known to other human beings and, as a consequence, do not know themselves. In Jourard's (1963) words:

> When I say that self-disclosure is a means by which one achieves personality health, I mean something like the following: It is not until I am my real self and I act my real self that my real self is in a position to grow . . . . People's selves stop growing when they repress them . . . . Alienation from one's real self not only arrests one's growth as a person; it tends also to make a farce out of one's relationship with people. (pp. 497, 507)

That is, when we repress our inner feelings, we are not only withholding awareness of those feelings from someone else, but also withholding ourselves. *Thus, a way to understand ourselves is through the rich diversity of feedback about ourselves from others who see us in a variety of situations.* When the self we present is *consistently* a facade or a mere surface offering of the real person we know ourselves to be, we should not be surprised if we find ourselves wondering, "What do people really think of me?"

The gradations between communications that are least self-disclosing and least difficult to express to those that are most self-disclosing and most difficult to express can be seen in the following eight-step continuum:

Least Self-Disclosing   *Least Difficult to Express*

1. I tell you how Jack felt about Jill, neither person being present.
2. I tell you how Jill feels about Jack, neither person being present.
3. I tell you my past feelings about Jack, who is not present.
4. I tell you my present feelings about Jill, who is not present.
5. I tell you my past feelings about you.
6. I tell you my present feelings about you.
7. I tell you my past feelings about myself.
8. I tell you my present feelings about myself.

Most Self-Disclosing   *Most Difficult to Express*

A positive outcome of exposing and sharing feelings is usually greater inter-personal closeness (which, in fact, may explain why some people do not easily expose themselves at a feeling level—they are fearful of being too close to another person). If I am self-disclosing and honest with you about myself, this encourages you to be more self-disclosing and honest with me about yourself. If you are honest with me, I am freer to be more honest with you—and so the cycle goes. Consider an example:

Suppose a teacher (it could be a teacher at any level of education) has put in a relatively sleepless night and goes to class irritable, cranky, and short-tempered. She has two alternatives for handling her feelings. One, she can say nothing to the class and snap at innocent students all day as if they were the cause of her sleepless night. Or, two, she could frankly admit her irritable feelings and why they exist and thereby give her students a chance to respond to her honestly. Once they know that her irritability has a cause, they would have less need to be defensive and irritable themselves. Furthermore, once the students learn that their teacher has *feelings,* not all of which are pleasant or good, they are more apt to *admit feelings within themselves* that might otherwise have remained buried. If teachers are honest with their students and share with them some of their personal inner feelings, they can be much more assured that their students will give them honest feedback, good and bad, about the conduct of the course, its content, and them as teachers.

All in all, honesty and self-disclosure facilitate social feeling and healthy self-other understanding because they encourage greater freedom and open-ness of interpersonal exchange, the medium in which self-knowledge begins. There is a third thing that we can do, something that is very much associated with the practice of honesty and self-disclosure.

Foster the Art of Being a Good Listener

Probably no human behavior is simultaneously as easy to do and yet as difficult to accomplish as listening, at least good listening, the kind that goes beyond merely waiting for the other person to finish talking (during which time we are preparing what we are going to say), and which reflects an effort to see how the world is viewed by this person and to communicate this understanding.

Good listening responds to the feelings as well as to the *words* spoken. It implies no evaluation, no judgment, no agreement (or disagreement). It simply conveys an effort to understand what the person is feeling and trying to com-municate. It is the sort of listening that the psychoanalyst Reik (1948) referred to as "listening with the third ear" in a now-famous book of the same title. It is an effort to communicate to another person that we can accept, without judg-ing or criticizing, that the feelings and ideas communicated are valid for *him* or *her,* if not for us.

Good listening, although possible for any person, is not easy. For example, establish in any group discussion the ground rule that the members may not present their own views until they have first satisfied the one who has just spoken that they fully comprehend what he or she meant to communicate. That is, they must rephrase in their own words the essential meaning of the other person's message and obtain this person's agreement that this was indeed what was said. In doing this you may find out that (1) it is difficult to agree about what was said and what was heard ("listened" to); (2) we frequently are remiss in our good intentions to listen; (3) when we do listen carefully, we have a hard time remembering what it was that we were going to say, and when we do remember, we find it is a little off the subject; (4) much argument and irrational emotion is absent from such a discussion because we spend less time responding to what we *thought* we heard or *wanted* to hear and more time responding to what was *actually* said.

Good listening, or what we are calling "total" listening, goes beyond merely absorbing what another person is saying; it implies an active effort to understand what is being said from the other person's point of view. Although this is probably not possible or even necessary in all situations, it is a highly desirable process to exercise when (1) it is important to strengthen the personal or professional trust between ourselves and the other person and (2) the relationship is important enough for us to work on making it better.

One way to recognize good listening skills is by the number of times a person literally uses *understanding* responses, as opposed to *evaluative* or *interpretive* responses, in the course of the conversation. An understanding response has also been called a *reflective* response, that is, one that rephrases what the other person has said but in one's own words. "If I understand you correctly, you said . . ." or "In other words, you think that . . ." are common openers for a reflecting statement. It is an effort to hear from the outside in, with no effort to prejudge the offering. Rogers and Roethlisberger (1952) found that good listeners used many understanding responses.

Poor listeners, on the other hand, were found to use evaluative or interpretive responses more often. Both of these responses reflect an inclination to listen more from the inside out, suggesting a tendency to judge the offering before checking its meaning. An evaluative response weighs and measures; it assesses the goodness or rightness of what is said, as for example, "You shouldn't say things like that" or "I think that's wrong." An interpretive response tells the other person what the situation "really" means or how or why he feels the way he does, as, for example, "What your comment means is . . ." or "The underlying reason for your feeling is . . . ." Poor listeners are inclined to hear things from their own point of view—hence, their inclination to evaluate and interpret.

Do not misunderstand. There is a time and place for each of these response styles. However, when evaluative and interpretive responses are disproportionately high, particularly in interpersonal relationships, it is a possible sign that the other person is not listening and is also a signal to others to monitor carefully what they say. When communication starts to *shut* down, it usually breaks down. And when that occurs, so, too, does further growth in a particular relationship.

Good listeners tend to encourage dialogues. Poor listeners seem to get into many debates. This distinction is an important one, since in a debate we seek to change the other person's mind, something most people resist, whereas in a dialogue we are prepared to change our own.

Self-understanding is enhanced through understanding others. Understanding others is a function of one's capacity for social feeling. This capacity is both developed and encouraged by honest communication and "total" listening. Indeed, most of us know from personal experience that some of our most significant self-other discoveries have resulted from being in the company of persons characterized not only by their total honesty but also by their lack of preconceptions about how they expect us to behave, which has the effect of freeing us to be the person we really are.

I would like to conclude this section dealing with ideas for developing self-other understanding with a brief passage from Ben Franklin's autobiography. Franklin's wisdom and deep understanding of human nature shines through in this excerpt and reflects, I think, the basic themes we've looked at to this point: a capacity for social feeling, willingness to be honest and self-disclosing, and for sure, a talent for being a good listener. In Franklin's (1906) words:

> I made it a rule to forbear all direct contradiction to the sentiments of others, and all positive assertion of my own. I even forbid myself the use of every word or expression in the language that imported a fixed opinion, such as certainly, undoubtedly, etc., and I adopted, instead of them, I conceive, I apprehend, or I imagine a thing to be so, or it so appears to me at present.

> When another asserted something I thought an error, I denied myself the pleasure of contradicting him abruptly and of showing immediately some absurdity in his proposition; and in answering, I began by observing that in certain cases or circumstances his opinion would be right, but in the present case there appeared or seemed to me some difference, etc. I soon found the advantage of this change in my manner; the conversations I engaged in went on more pleasantly. The modest way in which I proposed my opinions procured them a readier reception and less contradiction; I had less mortification when I was found to be in the wrong, and I more easily prevailed with others to give up their mistakes and join with me when I happened to be in the right.

> And this mode, which I at first put on with some violence to natural inclination, became at length so easy, and so habitual to me, that perhaps for these fifty years past no one has ever heard a dogmatical expression escape me. And to this habit (after my character of integrity) I think it principally owing that I had early so much weight with my fellow-citizens when I proposed new institutions, or alterations in the old, and so much influence in public councils when I became a member; for I was but a bad speaker, never eloquent, subject to much hesitation in my choice of words, hardly correct in language, and yet I generally carried my points. (pp. 96–97)

Cultivating our capacity to empathize with others, being honest and more self-disclosing in our interpersonal relationships, and fostering the art of being good listeners are each ways of encouraging greater depths of self-other under-standing. The more we understand ourselves, the more we are able to under-stand others. The greater our insights into others, the deeper our insights into ourselves. It is a reciprocal process. As we move toward a more positive and accurate self-picture, we are also able to move toward greater self-acceptance, an idea we turn to next.

SELF-ACCEPTANCE: ITS PSYCHOLOGY AND EXPRESSION

In its broadest sense, *self-acceptance* is a term used when talking about the extent to which people are satisfied with who they are as individuals. In more technical terms, a person's degree of self-acceptance is the difference between his or her "actual" self and "ideal" self. Many self-concept studies, for example, in addition to asking subjects for *self-perceptions* also ask them to go through the same set of items again and indicate how they would like to be *ideally*. Since most of us would like to be "better" than we are, the *ideal* self is usually judged to be at least as good and almost always better than the perceived or "actual" self. The difference between the scores for the perceived self and ideal self is the *discrepancy* score, which is obtained by subtracting the score of the perceived "real" self from the score representing the perceived "ideal" self. The larger this discrepancy score the more dissatisfied with oneself and less self-accepting the person is presumed to be.

Psychological research designed to investigate the emotional consequences of such discrepancies has noted that people who are highly self-critical—that is, who reflect a significant discrepancy between the way they actually see themselves and the way they would like to be—tend to be less well adjusted than those who are at least moderately satisfied with themselves (Baumgardner, 1990; Gough, Fioravanti, and Lazzari, 1983). Evidence further suggests that people who tend to be highly self-critical are inclined to be not only more ambitious and driving, but also more insecure, more anxious, and somewhat more cynical and depressed than self-accepting people (Driscoll, 1981; Powers and Zuroff, 1988). Although they may be more anxious and driven, it is not clear whether those behaviors are the cause or the effect of greater insecurity and higher anxiety. Sometimes ambitious, driving people feel more insecure and anxious because they fear not reaching their goals, whereas other people allow their basic insecurities and anxieties to turn them into ambitious, driven personalities, forever needing to prove their worth.

The bottom line seems to be that self-accepting people usually have smaller self-ideal discrepancies than less self-accepting persons. They are generally more satisfied with themselves. You may wonder if it is ever appropriate to be *dissatisfied* with oneself. We might begin looking at this by considering a brief case excerpt. In an early session, a client of mine—a man in his mid-20s—asked what I have since come to discover is a kind of universal question of many people who are searching for a self-concept that "fits," one that best expresses the inner person they would like to be. As he expressed it:

> It seems that all my life I've heard two different kinds of messages—from my parents, friends, the church, even—but the messages seem to conflict. On the one hand, I've been told that I should accept myself as I am. That's fine, I would like to do that. But on the other hand, the advice I've heard seems to be that I should be dissatisfied with myself, almost as if who I am isn't quite good enough and that I should strive to be different. Which is right?

The trouble with what appears to be conflicting advice is that each side stresses one part of the truth at the expense of the other part. No reasonable person would advise that we accept the way we are if it meant persisting in self-defeating behaviors or if it appeared to be leading us to smugness and complacency. And we would probably not be advised to be satisfied with ourselves if we were behaving in a manner that short-circuited our best talents and fondest hopes.

"Becoming what you are" implies two things at once: accepting our basic strengths and limitations, while at the same time struggling to realize our outer limits and potentialities. A creative and developing life open to new possibilities usually results in a continued "tension" between these two.

The kind of self-acceptance that is probably the healthiest is the kind that says, in so many words, "This is what I was born with, this is how I look, and this is what I have. I will change what I can, accept that which I cannot, and do what I have to do to be the best that is within me."

The kind of "self-dissatisfaction" that probably will take us the furthest is aimed at the proper targets—not at the inner self or at those parts of us we cannot change, but rather at those modes of thinking, feeling, and behaving that interfere with our potential to become what we could be. Each of us stands as the final judge of what should be accepted or rejected within ourselves. No person can do this for us.

Basically, there are two pathways to self-acceptance. Let's briefly examine each of them.

Two Routes to Self-Acceptance: Indirect and Direct

Self-acceptance is something we all want and need, but the routes we choose to attain it can make a big difference in how we behave and how we feel about ourselves.

It is healthy and natural to want and need a certain amount of approval from others. When combined with a healthy level of *self*-approval, approval from others contributes to our confidence, adds a notch to our emotional stature, and buttresses our feelings of self-worth. However, when a person *lacks* self-approval, it is usually a sign that a personally acceptable self-concept has failed to develop. *When this happens, people learn to seek self-acceptance indirectly, which is basically a process of substituting the good opinion of others for their own lack of self-approval.* In this way, people become what social psychologists refer to as "other-directed" personalities.

Ultimately, however, the search for indirect self-acceptance is self-defeating. If our motivation is to present ourselves to others in an appealing way primarily as a means of commandeering their acceptance and gaining their good will, we risk giving up who we are in order to become what we think *they want us to be*. In this way, some people become chameleonlike in their relationships with other people. A young woman in one of my personal growth classes who had difficulties along this line, expressed the problem in the following way:

> I am so tired of waiting to see what others want and what others are thinking and how others will behave before I can ever do anything myself. I sometimes feel like I'm carrying a portable wardrobe around, with emotional changes I can hop into depending upon who my audience is. I'm so sick of doing this. There are times when it seems that I make so many changes in a day that I can't even recognize myself in the mirror. And the worst of it is that even when others do seem to accept me and like me, *I can't believe it.*

You may recognize the self-defeating aspects of this woman's behavior, reflected vividly in her comments. We can believe what *others say about us — particularly if it is positive — only when we believe that others see us for what we really are.* Ironically, the more successful we are in our quest for indirect self-acceptance, the more difficult it becomes to accept positive feedback. Privately, we know that we are getting it because we manipulated it rather than because we deserve it on merit. Critical and even negative feedback is easier for us to accept under these conditions because it is what we feel we should get in the first place.

Paradoxically, others may be quite aware and tolerant of certain characteristics that an individual is trying to hide. For example, a man who conceals the fact that he has had little formal schooling may never realize that many in his social world recognize that he is largely self-educated, admire and respect him for it, and make allowances for whatever gaps there may be in his academic background. However, as long as he is afraid of being himself and accepting his limited academic training, he will never be in a position to believe that he is acceptable to others. As observed by Putney and Putney (1964),

> Inevitably, the pursuit of indirect self-acceptance produces an exaggerated concern with outward appearance. It leads a man to feign a friendliness he does not feel, rather than to develop a capacity for warmth. It leads a woman to feel that her grooming, but not her self, is acceptable. It leads to anxious conformity and a tense struggle for recognition . . . . It leads to the fake, to a mode of existence that, like a Hollywood set, is only an elaborate front with nothing but a few props to shore it up. (p. 74)

There is another, but related, explanation for why indirect self-acceptance is self-defeating. When gaining others' approval is a primary concern, we may be so self-conscious about how we behave that we stumble over our best (more often our worst) efforts to appear as the likable or competent person we would like others to see. When people's focus of attention shifts away from what they are saying to whether it is being evaluated positively or negatively, the result is usually a state of heightened self-consciousness, an emotional condition almost guaranteed to produce two left feet, ten thumbs, and paralysis of the tongue. Can you remember a time when it was *very* important for you to make a good impression to a person or group, but your confidence about doing this was very low? How did it go? If you fumbled all over yourself, you acted like most people who, when overly concerned about winning others' approval, tend to make themselves so nervous that they end up behaving like the bungling fool they were afraid of behaving like in the first place.

You may begin to see a pattern emerging. When our self-acceptance is low, we tend to become increasingly dependent on others' good feelings about us as a substitute for our own lack of positive self-regard. As our dependency on their good will increases, so too does our self-consciousness around them, a state that causes us to behave nervously and unnaturally.

The behavior associated with *direct* self-acceptance grows from a quite different motivational base. The intent is not to win approval "out there" through deception and manipulation but to gain acceptance "in here" through genuine give and take and honest self-disclosure. People who seek self-acceptance directly do so by being the person *they* want to be rather than trying to live up to the image of what they assume *others* want them to be. People who seek self-acceptance directly do not seem so fearful of failure, which has the effect of freeing them to test their upper limits and develop their capacities as much as possible. Genuine self-acceptance is available to any person, but it is, I think, more attainable to those who have the courage to explore the areas where their self-doubts reside.

In the final analysis, direct self-acceptance seems to reflect the ability to accept ourselves, within the limits we've defined, for what we are without either apology or braggadocio. I am reminded of an anecdote involving the great former world's heavyweight boxing champion Joe Louis. On this particular occasion, he was with a small group of people waiting to be seated in a large but crowded restaurant. The headwaiter said that he might be able to get them a table near the back, away from the floorshow. One of the men in Louis' party said, "Joe, why don't you tell this guy who you are?" To which Joe unabashedly replied, "If you have to tell 'em who you are, you ain't." Joe Louis was champion of the best world of all—his own—which is what direct self-acceptance is all about.

Self-Acceptance and Acceptance of Others Go Together

In almost biblical tones, psychiatrist Harry Stack Sullivan (1947) observed, "It is not as ye judge that he shall be judged, but as you judge yourself so shall you judge others." The idea expressed in the biblical "Love thy neighbor as thyself" implies that respect for one's own integrity and uniqueness, love and understanding of one's own self, cannot be separated from respect and love and understanding for another individual. Perhaps another way of saying this is that we cannot give to another person what we do not already have on hand for ourselves.

As you might guess, people who tend toward the low side on self-acceptance also lean toward the low side on self-esteem. And, as Wills' (1981) and Wylie's (1974) reviews have shown, individuals who are low in self-esteem are likely to be among those who are high in prejudice. Perhaps in an effort to enhance their own image, low self-esteem, high-prejudice people knock certain groups. But do these people really pride themselves and their crowd on being better than the rest? Or do they lash out at everyone, indiscriminately, because their low sense of self-worth and self-acceptance warps their view of others?

In an effort to explore these questions, Jennifer Crocker and Ian Schwartz (1985) had 42 college students complete a self-esteem inventory. Then, students were divided into two groups, labeled "alphas" and "betas." All the students were asked to reveal their perceptions of the personality of each person in both groups, rating them on desirable (including trustworthy and sincere) and undesirable (including unfriendly and self-centered) characteristics.

What did these two groups have to say about each other? Although the students in each group had never met, their views of each other were colored by their self-esteem. For example, high self-esteem individuals rated both groups more favorably than did those whose self-esteem was low. Most revealing was the fact that those with feelings of low self-worth were not at all discriminating. While they showed strong prejudice toward those in the other group, they did not value members of their own group to any greater degree. Concluded Crocker and Schwartz: "Low self-esteem individuals seem to have a generally negative view of themselves, their own group, other groups, and perhaps the world" (p. 386). It is a striking commentary on how our feelings about ourselves can affect our feelings about others.

Psychological research has rather consistently shown that there is a moderate but significantly positive relationship between how people view themselves and how they feel about others (Crocker et. al., 1987; Epstein and Feist, 1988; Lewicki, 1983; Markus, Smith, and Moreland, 1985). There is good reason for this. If I think highly of myself, I am more likely to think highly of you. And if I think well of you, you are more apt to think highly of me in return, which has the pleasing effect of reinforcing my good feelings about myself and about you, a cyclical process that is bound to have a positive effect on my feelings of self-worth and you as a person.

Not all people feel a healthy sense of self-worth and self-acceptance. Certain roadblocks exist, something we turn our attention to next.

Self-Alienation: Roadblock to Self-Acceptance

Self-alienation is the other side of self-acceptance. Alienation results when people fail to acknowledge or accept certain aspects of themselves, which are then seen as foreign, or alien. People of this sort are usually aware of their alienated feelings, but they tend to disown their awareness by contending that they belong to someone else. Projection is the primary mechanism here, something we discussed in Chapter 1. When people do this, they quite literally project their alienated characteristics onto another person, thus enabling them to view those characteristics with indignation, even contempt.

Some people, for example, have great trouble expressing any feelings that are tinged with anger. It is not that they are not capable of feeling angry—they do—but they are so emotionally separated—alienated—from their anger that the only place they can see it is in another person's behavior. Sometimes people repress their feelings of anger and, thus, alienate themselves from those feelings because they believe that if the anger were expressed people might not like them. Fears of this sort can have roots deep in a person's history. How many times, for example, have you heard a parent say to a child who's just expressed anger, "Now, Chris, don't talk like that. That's not nice. What will people think?"

The point is, some people, since childhood, may have learned that to express angry feelings is wrong, or naughty, or even sinful and that if they cannot say something nice "then don't say anything at all." Consider the following case excerpt, which involves a middle-aged woman taught from an early age that angry feelings were bad feelings.

This woman talked a lot about the "many angry feelings" she saw in her husband. It was true, he did have his share of negative feelings and angry moments, but even his minor demonstrations of frustration and irritation were accusingly labeled as expressions of anger by his wife. Ironically enough, this label really did cause him to be angry, since he was beginning to feel more and more as if his wife saw him as a one-dimensional person, capable of only one kind of emotion. What his wife failed to see was her own accumulated store of repressed anger, part of which she felt toward her work situation, and part of which she harbored toward an emotionally abusive father, which she unconsciously expressed in disguised form. For example, she might vacuum outside their bedroom door at 7:00 A.M. on a Saturday morning when he was sleeping ("There was so much housework to do and it had to be done") or she might withdraw a huge amount of money from their joint savings account without discussing it with him and invest it ("I was only trying to make more money"). Not surprisingly, she had frequent catastrophic dreams in which people she knew would have an illness, be in an accident, or even die, all signs of the swirl of angry feelings boiling deep inside her searching for an outlet. By projecting her disowned anger on her husband, she was able to relieve safely some of the pressure of her repressed anger because, in her mind, it was his problem. She reinforced the denial process by reading countless books about how to achieve high self-esteem, how to experience "joy" in one's life, and how to "think positively." *As long as she remained alienated from an important aspect of herself, she was never able to accept herself fully; genuine self-acceptance means taking the good and the bad.* The books she read were as much an escape from her real feelings as they were a search for self-esteem and happiness.

As other examples, it is sometimes the case that people who are most threatened by—and thus alienated from—their own sexual stirrings are the first to criticize, moralize, and become self-righteously indignant when they perceive other people behaving in sexual ways. On the other hand, people who accept their *own* sexual feelings are usually more tolerant of sexual expression by others. It seems to be generally true that we tend to hate in others those things—and usually only those things—that we despise in ourselves.

The man who gives the appearance of being strong and self-sufficient while denying (and despising) his need to be dependent and weak now and then may feel a strong loathing for men who can be dependent when necessary or who allow themselves to be taken care of when they are weak. By loathing such men, he remains alienated from his own needs to be dependent now and then. The avid women's liberationist, who denies (and despises) her need to be emotionally close to a man (perhaps because of an unconscious fear of losing her identity), may look contemptuously at women who choose to be "only housewives and mothers." In this way, she is able to alienate her own longing for closeness by concentrating her energies on what she views as other women's misguided choices.

Self-alienated people unconsciously look for others on whom to dump their alienated feelings, thus protecting the sanitized image they have of themselves. Self-accepting people's self-images may not be as sanitary, but they are in better position to deal with the emotional debris in their lives because of what appears to be a greater willingness to own *all* aspects of their personalities, not just the good parts.

Self-Acceptance of an Inflated Kind: The Narcissistic Personality

Narcissistic people are not necessarily self-accepting. They are more accurately self-inflated people, who, as described by Millon (1981), ". . . overvalue their personal worth, direct their affections toward themselves rather than others, and expect others will not only recognize but cater to the high esteem in which [they] hold themselves" (p. 158). Coming from, as they frequently do, childhood backgrounds in which even minor achievements were responded to with an intense mixture of fervor and favor, narcissistic persons carry into adulthood a deluded sense of extraordinary self-worth. Narcissists tend to convey a calm and self-assured quality in their social behavior, which is viewed by some as a sign of confident equanimity. Others see these behaviors less favorably: as reflecting pretentiousness and a haughty, snobbish, and arrogant way of relating to people. This self-assuredness is viewed by most as unwarranted, smacking as it does of an air of superiority without the necessary substance to justify it. Narcissistic persons talk a great deal about themselves, usually a good clue about who and what is most important in their lives.

As described in the American Psychiatric Association's third edition of the *Diagnostic and Statistical Manual of Mental Disorders* (1980), the following characteristics tend to be associated in varying degrees with narcissistic personalities:

1. Grandiose sense of self-importance or uniqueness, e.g., exaggeration of achievements and talents, focus on the special nature of one's problems.

2. Preoccupation with fantasies of unlimited success, power, brilliance, beauty, or ideal love.

3. Exhibitionism: the person requires constant attention and admiration.

4. Cool indifference or marked feelings of rage, inferiority, shame, humiliation, or emptiness in response to criticism, indifference from others, or defeat. (p. 317)

Although narcissistic people are quite capable of conveying an image of buoyant self-confidence, they tend to find true self-acceptance difficult because their incessant self-reference turns away the very people whose good will they most need to help them feel worthwhile.

A barrier to self-acceptance on one extreme is the over-inflated image of the person who feels superior to others, while on the other end we find the under-inflated image of the person who feels everyone is better. Let's examine this other end.

Barrier to Self-Esteem: An Inferiority Complex

Whereas the narcissistic person overvalues the self, the inferiority-ridden person undervalues the self. Neither person is usually as well off or as bad off as he or she may think, but it is their beliefs about the matter, not necessarily the facts related to it, that sustain the self-perceptions. Essentially, people with an inferiority complex tend to have a persisting and morbid preoccupation with the belief that they are generally less able (or less good or talented or attractive) than most other people. Closely allied to, but not to be confused with, inferiority is the feeling or conviction of inadequacy. However, whereas inferiority implies unfavorable comparison with others, inadequacy suggests personal inability to meet the demands of the situation.

We might make note of the fact that *feelings* of inferiority cannot be taken as an index of *actual* inferiority. A feeling of inferiority is a purely subjective effect related to the self and is roughly equal to the felt difference between one's successes and failures. Objective facts seem to make little difference in determining whether a person feels inferior or not. The highest-ranking student or the best athlete or the beauty contest winner may each suffer from a deep-seated sense of inferiority. On the other hand, the lowest student, the poorest athlete, or the plainest woman may not feel inferior at all. What we do, what we have, and how we look is far less important than how we feel about those things and what we aspire to be. If an attractive woman aspires to be an excellent student but falls short of that goal, being attractive is not likely to compensate for her academic failure.

Whereas self-accepting people are more likely to define themselves in terms of their strengths and what they *can* do, low self-accepting people, especially those with an inferiority complex seem more likely to define themselves in terms of their weaknesses and what they *cannot* do. There are, of course, degrees of self-acceptance and degrees of inferiority. We are not likely to be all one way or the other.

Signs and Symptoms of Inferiority Feelings

There are at least nine symptoms of inferiority feelings:

1. *Sensitivity to criticism:* Inferiority-ridden persons do not like their weaknesses pointed out to them. Criticism, as viewed by them, is further proof of their inferiority and serves only to accentuate the pain associated with it. Research is quite clear in showing that persons with inferiority feelings want very much to avoid the negative implications of failure (Greenberg and Pyszczynski, 1985; Strube and Roemmele, 1985).

2. *Overresponsiveness to flattery:* Persons with inferiority feelings have a tendency to grab at straws, particularly those constructed from praise and flattery, because they help them stand more secure against feelings of uncertainty and insecurity. The other response to flattery or praise, of course, is red-skinned embarrassment: "How could anyone say anything good about me? Me, of all people!"

3. *Hypercritical attitude:* This is a frequent defense and serves the purpose of redirecting attention away from one's own limitations. Whereas overresponse to flattery is defensive in character, hypercriticism takes the offensive. For example, if I feel inferior about the quality of something I've done in relation to what you have done, and I aggressively criticize your effort, you may become so busy defending what you've done that you won't notice the flaws in *my* effort. In other words, being hypercritical creates the illusion of superiority and relies on this illusion to belie inferiority.

4. *Tendency toward blaming:* Whenever personal weaknesses and failures are projected onto others, it is relatively easy to find in them the cause of one's own failures, leading directly to the response of blaming. Indeed, some persons operate a kind of psychological "pulley system": They are able to feel normal or adequate only if they are pulling other people down and themselves up in the process.

5. *Feelings of being persecuted:* It is only a short step away from blaming others for our personal misfortunes to believing that they are actively seeking our downfall. For example, if you give me a failing mark in a course and I can believe that you did so because you don't like me or are against me, I am spared the pain of having to admit my own responsibility. In this way, not only do I blame you for my failure but also I assign you a motive for doing it—you are "out to get me."

6. *Negative feelings about competition:* Inferiority-ridden people are as anxious to win in competition as is anyone else but far less optimistic about being able to do so. People who feel inferior are usually among the first to complain about the breaks, their opponents' good luck, or favoritism. In some instances, their attitude toward competition is so extreme that they refuse to participate in any competitive situation and tend to shy away in a fearful and hesitant manner. I'm reminded of a sign that my high school football coach had tacked on the bulletin board in his office: "If you're afraid of competition, then learn to do something difficult."

7. *Tendency to be easily persuaded and influenced:* Social psychology research in this area has rather consistently shown that people who feel inferior and who have low self-esteem tend to be more conforming and more easily influenced than people with higher self-esteem (Hamachek, 1982). If I am not sure of my own opinions, one way to reduce the ambiguity and anxiety of my indecisiveness is to rely on your point of view. Not only will you tell me what to do but also I am absolved of responsibility if it is the *wrong* thing to do.

8. *Tendency toward seclusiveness, shyness, and timidity:* Inferiority feelings are usually accompanied by a certain degree of fear, particularly in situations involving other people (Shrauger, 1972). Inferior-feeling persons prefer the cloak of anonymity, feeling that if they are neither seen nor heard their shortcomings (real or imagined) will less likely be seen. Sometimes, students who feel less able than their peers sit near the back of the classroom because of the protection it offers. ("If I'm not so easily seen, perhaps I will not so easily be called on.")

9. *A neurotic need for perfectionism:* I think the dynamics involved here are well illustrated by a student in one of my graduate classes who once asked me, "When I finish my term paper, will you like it?" On another occasion, a client, working through a marital difficulty, wondered, "What if I try my very best and the marriage still doesn't work out? How do you think you'll feel about me?"

Built into these two simple and direct questions is one of the most important inner workings of neurotic perfectionists—the overwhelming need for approval from other persons because their own self-approval system is short-circuited by low self-esteem and commensurate feelings of inferiority.

Most of us have a certain perfectionistic strain, but whether or not one's perfectionism leans more to the neurotic side depends on whether it fits certain criteria. One of the most important differences between healthy and neurotic perfectionists is that the striving of the first group brings them a deep sense of satisfaction, whereas the efforts of neurotic perfectionists—even their best ones—never seem quite good enough, at least in their own eyes. Another important difference between neurotic and healthy perfectionists is that those on the neurotic side are motivated not so much by a desire for improvement as they are by a fear of failure and the criticism that may follow. Thus, where healthy perfectionists are inclined to focus on strengths and concentrate on how to do things right, those with a neurotic leaning tend to worry about their deficiencies and labor at how to avoid doing

Perfectionists have a hard time believing that they are not perfect.
Reprinted by permission of UFS, INC.

things wrong (Hamachek, 1978). For some, the fear of disapproval and rejection is an intense and life-controlling concern.

These nine symptoms are not mutually exclusive; they overlap in expression and character. For example, timidity leads to avoidance of competition and also to greater sensitivity to criticism. At the same time, sensitivity to criticism can lead to blaming others or overresponding to flattery. All these symptoms spring from a basic sense of inferiority, and any one of them can serve as the catalytic agent, triggering a chain reaction of defensive and generally self-defeating behaviors, which can stand in the way of healthy self-acceptance.

Some Positive Outcomes of Healthy Self-Acceptance

A dramatic illustration of the power of self-acceptance emerged as one of the major findings in Mahoney and Avener's (1977) study of elite male gymnasts. All were candidates for the U. S. Olympic team and were superb athletes. The researchers were interested in exploring the differences between those who made the team and those who did not. The decisive differences, they found, were not so much in physical skills—they were all fairly even in this regard— but in certain personality characteristics. For example, those who qualified for Olympic competition were *less perfectionistic and more self-accepting* than were those who did not qualify. Those who qualified tended to underemphasize the importance of past performance failures, while those who didn't make it were more likely to feel anxious and panicky during competition because of their mental images of self-doubt and possible defeat. Those who made the team were far less likely to have mental images of that kind. Rather, they were much more accepting of themselves, including their failures, which may have had the effect of helping them to view the Olympic trials as a chance to do their best rather than as an opportunity they might blow.

Self-accepting people seem to have a sense of perspective about themselves. They see not just their failures and flaws, but they are able to balance those with the recognition of their successes and strengths. Perhaps they are able to see the deep truth in the old adage, "When mistakes are made, even serious ones, there is always another chance. Failure is not the result of falling down, but staying down."

PRECURSORS TO SELF-ESTEEM: COURAGE AND WORK

"Courage is simply the willingness to be afraid and act anyway." I've always liked this saying because it embodies, I think, the very essence of what courage is all about. In his book *The Road Less Traveled* (1978), Peck defined courage as the ability to move against the resistance engendered by fear. Courage is not the absence of fear; rather, it is taking action in spite of fear, moving against the resistance associated with fear into the unknown and into the future. Similarly, work can be defined as what is necessary to move against the inertia of laziness. Work requires attention to that which needs to be done. Attention is an act of will, of work against the inertia of our own minds.

Peck used these two concepts in connection with the construction (and repair) of a loving relationship, something I am very much in accordance with, particularly when the two people involved agree that there is sufficient mutual trust and respect on which to build.

Courage and work are concepts rich in meaning and implication for the enhancement not just of a relationship, but also of self-concept. After all, what does it take to bolster self-esteem, to reinforce self-confidence, and to find creative means of self-expression if not the courage to override the fear of failure and the willingness to work toward the accomplishment of one's goals? We do not have to go far to find people who have exuded these qualities in their lives. Consider some examples:

1. Failed in business, 1832; defeated for legislature, 1832; again failed in business, 1833; elected to legislature, 1834; sweetheart died, 1835; had nervous breakdown, 1836; defeated for speaker, 1838; defeated for nomination to Congress, 1843; elected to Congress, 1846, lost renomination, 1848; rejected for land officer, 1849; defeated for Senate, 1854; defeated for nomination for vice-president, 1856; again defeated for Senate, 1858; but in 1860, Abraham Lincoln was elected president of the United States.

2. After nearly flunking out of military school, he fought with the Spanish in Cuba, then in India and the Sudan. As a high-ranking naval official, his first expedition was a disaster, and he was discredited and forced to resign. He was defeated twice at the polls and remained out of power for a full decade. After his greatest triumph, he was once more defeated at the polls. In 1951, he was again elected prime minister, and in 1953, Winston Churchill was knighted and received the Nobel Prize in literature for his writing and oratory.

3. Although born black at a time when civil rights barely existed, raised in impoverished conditions, and also totally blind, Ray Charles became a monumental success in the popular music field.

4. Although he was, by his own admission, a hopeless alcoholic, Bill Wilson pulled himself out the gutter and founded Alcoholics Anonymous.

5. Although blind and deaf from the age of two, she immersed herself in a totally dedicated effort to learn, and in 1904, she graduated from Radcliffe College with honors; from that point, Helen Keller devoted her life to writing and lecturing to raise funds for the training of the blind and for other social causes.

6. Although addicted to drugs and the victim of a cancer that resulted in a radical surgery, Betty Ford (wife of ex-President Gerald Ford) found the courage to fight back and to "go public" so that others might find the strength to do the same.

(There are no doubt many other examples of people who reflect the qualities we're talking about. Which ones come to mind for you?)

I suspect it would be easy enough to conclude that because each of these persons has done exceptional things, they must, therefore, be exceptional people. Perhaps they are; there is no way of proving that one way or the other. What is subject to proof, however, is the extraordinary courage they exhibited in the face of adversity and the willingness to work very hard to accomplish what they thought was important.

Success is a relative term. It means accomplishing this for one person and achieving that for another. The best practical definition I can think of is that success is that which enables us to get out of life what we want to get out of life. By whatever criteria success is measured, its psychology remains disarmingly simple: Unless there is the possibility of failure, there is little feeling of success. There are many exceptions, of course, not the least of which are the multitude of noncompetitive experiences we have during, say, friendly games or matches when the interactions are more important than the outcomes. But when it makes a difference in our feelings about ourselves, then it seems increasingly important that the success we want is neither guaranteed nor too easily won. For example, in his experimental investigation about the role of choice on feelings of success, Luginbuhl (1972) found that people who felt the *most* successful on the tasks they successfully accomplished were those who felt the greatest possibility of failing at those tasks. People who felt the *least* successful, even though they successfully completed the tasks before them, were those for whom the sense of possible failure was sharply reduced.

I think that many people are overwhelmed by the spectacle of superiority and wrongly imagine that the so-called "best" are endowed with vastly greater capacities than the rest. Actually, it is probably closer to the truth that the similarities among men and women are much closer than seems to be the case. In sports, for instance, the best batting or passing records are not a great deal higher than the average. In field or track, the differences between winners and losers are measured in fractions of an inch or hundredths of a second. The real difference between those at the top and those at the bottom (in whatever endeavor) may not be so much in raw ability—although when all other things are equal, that has to be considered—as in the willingness to combine the courage necessary for going after a goal and the work necessary to achieve it. The student who studies when others have stopped and the athlete who practices when others have gone are examples of work in action. If that student and that athlete make a decision to try to be the best or among the best at what they do, then they would be examples of courage in action.

Both courage and work are necessary to maintain and enhance self-esteem. Courage without the willingness to work may be easily reduced to a certain amount of horn tooting, a possibility that reminds me of some wry advice offered by Will Rogers: "Be careful of bragging. It isn't the whistle that pulls the train." And work without courage may result in any number of fitful starts and stops, possible signs that a person may be motivated more by a fear of doing poorly than by the hope of doing well. As long as one lacks the courage to face the fears—e.g., the fear of failing—one's behavior is usually marked by an ongoing series of delays and postponements. The tendency to procrastinate is high when courage is low.

Courage is required not only to move ahead in the face of our fears, but a certain amount of it is also necessary when looking at how our selective perceptions of ourselves and others may interfere with seeing ourselves clearly. Let's turn to how this process operates.

SELECTIVE PERCEPTION: HOW IT WORKS TO PROTECT SELF-ESTEEM

Selective perception is pretty much what the term implies. It is the process of selectively seeing, hearing, believing what we *want* to see and hear and believe. It is a complex perceptual process that works in the service of protecting our self-esteem and enhancing our self-concept. Standing, as many of us do, with one foot on our egos and the other on a moist banana peel, we tend to selectively interpret the world around us in such a way as to protect our own best interests.

A simple example of the conscious use of selective perception is probably evident during times when people put together vital information for job applications. Although we tend to include our significant achievements and lofty ambitions, how often do we mention a low grade we may have received or that at times we feel no ambition at all?

We find a more remarkable and surely more complex example of selective perception at work in John Dean's testimony during the famous Watergate hearings in the early 1970s. Dean, as one of President Nixon's inner circle of personal advisors, was privy to many of the secret (and recorded) conversations that went on in the president's office regarding the Watergate events after the break-in was discovered. In preparation for the congressional investigation into the Watergate affair, Dean submitted a 245-page account of the events and conversations that he was part of during the cover-up. Consider, for example, Dean's written account of a 50-minute meeting that involved himself, President Nixon, and Bob Haldeman on September 15, 1972 (Hearings, 1973):

> The President asked me to sit down. Both men appeared to be in very good spirits and my reception was very warm and cordial. The President then told me that Bob—referring to Haldeman—had kept him posted on my handling

of the Watergate case. The President told me I had done a good job and he appreciated how difficult a task it had been and the President was pleased that the case had stopped with Liddy. I responded that I could not take credit because others had done much more difficult things than I had done. . . . I told him that all I had been able to do was to contain the case and assist in keeping it out of the White House. I also told him there was a long way to go before this matter would end and that I certainly could make no assurances that the day would not come when this matter would start to unravel.

Dean gave practically the same version of this incident in his verbal account of this incident to the congressional committee. Is there any similarity between what Dean said and what actually happened? Very little, according to Neisser's (1981) analysis of what the secret tape recordings revealed and what John Dean said. In Neisser's words:

Comparison with the transcript shows that hardly a word of Dean's account is true. Nixon did not say any of the things attributed to him here: he didn't ask Dean to sit down, he didn't say Haldeman had kept him posted, he didn't say Dean had done a good job (at least not in that part of the conversation), he didn't say anything about Liddy or the indictments. Nor had Dean himself said the things he later describes himself as saying: that he couldn't take credit, that the matter might unravel some day, etc. (Indeed, he said just the opposite later on: "Nothing is going to come crashing down.") His account is plausible, but entirely incorrect. (p. 9)

Neisser concluded that Dean's testimony did not so much describe the meeting as it did his *fantasy* of it. He remembers the meeting as he *wanted* it to be, as it *should* have been. In John Dean's selective memory of that meeting, "Nixon *should* have been glad that the indictments stopped with Liddy, Haldeman *should* have told Nixon what a great job Dean was doing; and, most of all, praising him *should* have been the first order of business" (p. 10).

Neisser speculated that perhaps there is a bit of John Dean in all of us:

His ambition reorganized his recollections; even when he tries to tell the truth, he can't help but emphasize his own role in every event. A different man in the same position might have observed more dispassionately, reflected on his experiences more thoughtfully, and reported them more accurately. Unfortunately, such traits of character are rare. (p. 19)

We will never know whether John Dean knowingly twisted the truth or whether he deeply believed his own account and simply misled himself. Whether his self-serving account was knowing or not, his memory of the events he was part of reflects the inner workings of selective recall.

Because selection perception plays such an important part in helping people maintain a positive self-concept, let's turn our attention to some of the other ways that this process works.

What the "Facts" Are Depends on Who Interprets Them

"Facts" are highly susceptible to the personal meanings people assign to them. For example, let's say that in the face of a roaring fire, you rush into a burning house and manage to lead two previously trapped people to safety. What you have done is certainly an objective fact. But how shall we interpret it? Does it mean that you are a fearless, courageous person so unselfish as to take little note of your own welfare? Or does it mean that you are simply too stupid and blind to recognize obvious danger? The act is clear, but whether it reflects "courage" or "foolhardiness" is a matter of interpretation.

Whenever there is sufficient lack of clarity about what a "fact" or "set of facts" means there is always room for a person to salvage a certain amount of self-esteem. Consider, for example, the matter of grades. One study found that although most people agree that grades are a good indication of whether they are good students, they are not convinced that grades indicate whether they are "clear-thinking and clever" or "imaginative and original" (Rosenberg, 1967). In fact, it was found that nearly three-fourths of the students with D and F averages considered themselves very likely or fairly likely to be imaginative and original and to have good sense and sound judgment. This is not a denial of reality. D or F students *know* they have poor grades. There are, however, many expressions of intelligence, and there is nothing in their "objective" grades to compel them to believe that they are less "clear-thinking" or "clever" than students with higher grades.

Another factor that makes it easy (or at least easier) to interpret the "facts" to fit our personal needs and, thereby, to maintain our self-esteem is the nature of the language used to describe personal traits. For example, if one person says we are sensitive observers of human behavior and another says we are nosy busybodies, are they really describing anything different? If someone says we are ingenious and resourceful and another observes that we are cunning and cagey, is there really any dissimilarity between the two? Indeed, both you and your critic may agree that you are "too tough and aggressive," terms used by the critic to condemn qualities in which you may take the utmost pride. Even though you and your critic may agree on the evidence, you do not necessarily agree on its meaning.

The point is, there is scarcely any behavior that we cannot interpret as admirable in some way. In the seclusion of our mind's eye, generally free of the intrusion of alternative interpretations, we are free to review and weigh the evidence (the "facts") as our biases dictate, to shift our personal perceptions until a congenial one emerges, and eventually to choose the one that is self-enhancing.

Most of us, for example, become quite adept at describing the "facts" surrounding our motives and behavior in such a way as to make ourselves seem virtuous and even noble. On the other hand, the "facts" associated with the behavior and motives of those with whom we take exception are painted with a hue of a somewhat darker color. Consider some examples:

Gallup and Suarz (1985) observed that although pet owners and research scientists may engage in similar activities regarding animal care or research, each group describes these activities quite differently:

When pet owners do these things it's called	but when research scientists do these things it's called
Having pets neutered	Castration
Putting pets to sleep	Murder
Feeding pets once a day	Deprivation/starvation
Cosmetic alteration	Mutilation/torture
Boarding pets	Social isolation
Housebreaking/obedience training	Aversive conditioning
Pet control	Restraint/confinement
Keeping pets	Placing animals in captivity
Selective breeding	Genetic manipulation

Consider a few illustrations of how we may interpret the world to our best advantage.

> My personal remark was intended as a "good-natured jest," but your personal remark was "cutting and unkind."
>
> I have put on a few pounds; your waistline is expanding; she is getting as big as a house.
>
> I merely assert my point of view; you push yourself on others; he walks all over people.
>
> "Mere rhetoric" is what we probably would call "powerful oratory" if we agreed with the speaker.
>
> I am neat and orderly; you are compulsively clean; he is a fuss budget.
>
> I change my mind because I am flexible; you change yours because you are wishy-washy; she changes hers because she has no convictions.
>
> I am quiet because I learn best by listening; you are quiet because you're afraid to speak out; he is quiet because he has nothing to say.

Well, I think you get the idea.

We not only choose to see the facts that are most congenial to our point of view, but we are also free to choose the evidence that is most supportive of that point of view. The type of evidence relevant to a given situation is widely varied. For example, suppose a person had to make a judgment about whether or not he was a sociable person. What criteria should he use? Does he speak to strangers? Has he gone to parties with friends? Is he among the first to speak in a crowd? Does he have one close friend but many acquaintances? Does he smile when passing people in the street?

He is not obliged to consider *all* these criteria; he can choose one, any one he wants that *fits.* The quality, in this instance, of being sociable is so ambiguous that there is no way to prove him wrong. By his choice of criteria, he may be a very friendly person. By your choice, he may fall far short. What we see in ourselves, others, and the world around us is colored very much by what we *want* to see.

Selective interpretation of the "facts" then, is one way of maintaining and enhancing the image we have of ourselves. So, too, is our selection of personal standards.

Selection of Personal Standards Makes Success Possible

It is not simply how good we *think* we are with regard to some quality, but how good we *want to be* that counts. We have a wide range of options in setting standards for ourselves. For example, we can aspire to the very pinnacle of achievement, to a high level of performance, to a good level of performance, to moderate accomplishment, or even to modest success. We may aspire to be the superintendent of a school system or to be a competent teacher within that system. Some of us may aspire to love and care for "all humankind," whereas others are satisfied to love and care for just a few individuals we know well. There is obviously a wide choice available in personal standards of performance in the immense sweep of areas pertaining to the self.

We have already seen from our discussion in Chapter 1 that, as a general rule, people are apt to set higher standards in those areas in which they consider themselves to be good, competent, or above average. In Chapter 6, we noted that persons who had more failures than successes were unpredictable in setting personal standards; that is, they established standards for performance that were either too high or too low. On the whole, however, research suggests that most people tend to set goals that fall within a reasonable range of their potential accomplishments.

For example, in Rosenberg's (1957) study of college students' values and aspirations, they were asked, "What business or profession would you *most like* to go into?" and "What business or profession do you realistically think you are *most apt* to go into?" It was found that most students had scaled down their aspirations to correspond to what they considered their ability. In general, we tend to select goals (standards, levels of performance, aspirations) in accordance with our assessment of our abilities. This selectivity enables us to achieve our personal goals, to consider ourselves "good enough," and to maintain a favorable self-image.

It is a sociological fact that the occupational attainments of people of working-class families are usually lower than those of people raised in middle-class families. Does lower occupational "attainment" or "achievement" result in a lower self-esteem? Not necessarily, because the level of personal standards is a relative matter. For example, if a boy aspires to be a master plumber and becomes one, this can be as self-enhancing for him as the boy who aspires to be an engineer, and does so. If a girl aspires to be a medical secretary and does so, this is as boosting to her self-esteem as it is for the girl who aspires to be a medical doctor and achieves that goal. What is important is not so much the *kind* of goal one sets, but its achievement. Accomplishment of a personal goal, whether in a physical, intellectual, or social realm, can be a self-enhancing experience to the extent that it is personally meaningful and not too easily won.

Interpersonal Selectivity: The Friends We Choose

One of the most consistent findings in interpersonal communications research is that *people tend to relate best and most frequently with other people with whom they agree.* When given a choice, most people tend to associate with those who think well of them and to avoid those who dislike them, thereby biasing the communications about themselves in a favorable direction.

The outstanding case in point is *friendship,* which is, perhaps, the purest example of selectively choosing one's propaganda. Characteristically, not only do we like our friends, but also they like us. Indeed, it is possible that we may like them *because* they like us. And of course, friends are inclined to say friendly things, which increases the likelihood of hearing more of what we like to hear about ourselves. Friendship is at least to some extent a "mutual admiration unit," whereby each party helps to sustain the desired self-image of the other.

Indeed, one of the most important props of romantic love is the remarkable intensity of the mutual admiration. To discover that someone considers us the most wonderful girl in the world or the most talented boy is the kind of communication we very much like to hear.

What is true for friends and lovers is equally true of groups. The persistent search for social acceptance is a major enterprise of both young and old and is apparent in our active involvement in groups that accept and approve of us, thereby enhancing our self-esteem.

It is important to note, however, that interpersonal selectivity that is too cautious and defensive may serve to stunt personal growth. For example, the loner who has no friends or the anxious, insecure person who avoids people because he or she is fearful of negative feedback both limit the possibility of input that might, in fact, spur them to the kind of insights that help them to be more at peace with themselves. Inasmuch as the self grows best in an interpersonal stream of reflected appraisals, the opportunity for this kind of nurturance is severely curtailed when the selectivity is too guarded. *When we interact only with those who agree with us and seldom challenge us, we are seldom forced into the position of having to reevaluate ourselves and our positions on different issues.* Perhaps the best kind of friends are those who can, when it seems appropriate, challenge our most cherished beliefs without being threatened by the possibility of rejection. A true friend is not necessarily one who agrees with us, but one who will be honest with us.

Self-Esteem Protection Through Situational Selectivity

In a society as complex as ours, we are not always able to *create* the personal, social, and work experiences that are most congenial to our needs and wishes, but we are often able to *select* those experiences. The primary motivation behind this selectivity is, as always, the desire to maintain a positive self-image. For the most part, we tend to expose ourselves to experiences in which we have a fair chance of success rather than those in which we may be found wanting. This is not more true than in our choice of occupations. Research shows that given a choice, most people naturally gravitate toward the kind of work in which their skills and talents are most likely to find expression and be appreciated (McClelland, 1985).

Situational selectivity is reflected in many areas of everyday life. For example, people who tend to be more socially than intellectually inclined may choose a party for entertainment rather than a lecture. People who are long on insecurity and short on confidence may choose friends who are more nurturing than challenging. People who are good at golf but poor in tennis are more apt to choose the fairways for a social outing than the courts. An introverted person may collect stamps as a hobby; a more extroverted person may join a bowling team. Given a choice, most students tend to take courses in which they are strong and avoid those in which they are weak.

Insofar as possible, we tend to choose those situations and relationships that help us feel good about ourselves and avoid those that do not. However, if our feelings of accomplishment are too easily won, it could be detrimental to the development and enhancement of positive self-esteem. Success doesn't mean much if the possibility of failure is virtually absent. The willingness to take a risk now and then is usually a prerequisite for doing something difficult. Taking on and accomplishing those things we were not sure we could do in the first place is an excellent way to build a positive self-concept and to enhance self-esteem.

And so it goes—people's selective perception of the "facts," their selection of personal values, standards, experiences, occupations, friends, and so on are a pervasive and central outgrowth of their need to maintain and enhance a positive self-image. One way of doing this is through the process of selectivity; we "see" and "hear" much of what is happening around us, but we "miss" other happenings; we choose to participate in this activity or to be with that person, but we avoid others. Thus, people are highly motivated to select from available options on life's smorgasbord of choices those that are likely to buttress self-esteem and to enhance the self that they would both like to be and hope that others see.

Selectivity Has Certain Restrictions

The mechanism of selectivity is constantly working to help us protect our feelings of self-esteem and the way we see ourselves. We see, hear, and make choices that, insofar as possible, are designed to protect our self-interests. We might wonder, then, why all people do not have favorable self-attitudes, why some have serious doubts about themselves, and still others have doubts so serious that they are convinced they're worthless.

Part of this may have to do with the fact that certain conditions of human experience are characterized by a narrow range of alternatives, especially in interpersonal areas. For example, although we are relatively free to choose our friends, the same is not true of our parents, teachers, or classmates. If our parents reject us, if our teachers berate us, of if our classmates laugh at us, we are largely deprived of the option of avoiding their company or their criticism. Thus, it is not difficult to see why some children run away from home, drop out of school, or become socially isolated.

The self-attitudes that are the easiest to influence, modify, or change are the least structured, and it is precisely in childhood that the self-image is most unstructured and unformed. Until children reach the age of about 16, their range of interpersonal alternatives is somewhat restricted by virtue of being the offspring of a particular set of parents. They must abide by *their* rules, listen to *their* appraisals, and relate as they can to such friends as there are in *their* neighborhood. These are their parents' choices, not theirs. Of course, with no options there can be no selectivity. Hence, the selections parents make have a particularly powerful influence on a child's self-esteem. For better or for worse, children are stuck with their parents. If parents choose wisely and if they love their children, their offspring may have a substantial foundation for thinking well of themselves. If parents do not make wise selections—if they, say, live in a neighborhood where there are few children for their own to play with—their children may be slow in developing social confidence; if they indulge and overprotect them, children may be self-centered and insecure; if they disparage or reject them, children may feel insignificant and unworthy.

Rosenberg (1979) has noted that the relative absence of interpersonal options for growing children is no less serious than the restrictions on their situational selectivity. That is, children's environment is largely fixed. For example, a bright child with intellectual potential, in a family that does not particularly value thinking and ideas, cannot choose to move into a family happy to answer questions and encourage curiosity. Similarly, there is no guarantee that one's personal whims and interests will meet the norms of the neighborhood peer group. If children gain no recognition and applause for talents disdained by the group, they are powerless to select a different school or neighborhood. Of course, some do; they run away. Others may get in trouble because, unconsciously, they want to be sent away.

Once again, we can see the enormous impact childhood experiences and parents can have on children's later feelings about themselves. Despite the generality and power of the principle of selectivity, it is easy to see why many people *do* have low self-esteem. All in all, the evidence is consistent in suggesting that the vast majority of us *want* to have favorable opinions of ourselves and that the defense mechanisms described and discussed in Chapter 1, along with the various mechanisms of psychological selectivity, are some of the strategies we use, consciously and unconsciously, to maintain and enhance positive self-attitudes.

A word of caution about the business of selective perceptions. The point in discussing how selective perception works is to raise our awareness about how this complex and largely self-serving process operates in behalf of keeping our perceptions and interpretations in line with how *we* want things to be. It is helpful, I think, to be aware of what seems to be a natural tendency to view things one way—usually *our* way—in order to consciously control an inclination to have a somewhat myopic view of the world around us.

So far, we've been discussing how our selectively chosen perceptions—the way we *see* things and the way we interpret our world—can affect behavior and self-esteem. It is not just our perceptions that help or hinder us but our cognitions as well; that is, the way we mentally process our life experiences on a day-to-day basis.

CAUTION: FAULTY COGNITIONS MAY CAUSE TROUBLE

By definition, *cognition* refers to the act or process of knowing, including both awareness and judgment. More often than not, we hope, our cognitions are rational and sensible, thus enabling us to live and make decisions in emotionally healthy ways. But many times, our cognitive processing is irrational and nonsensible, and we may be totally unaware of it. The major purpose of this section is to identify certain thought patterns and forms of self-talk people use that have been found to be self-defeating and growth inhibiting. We will also consider ways to avoid these cognitive traps.

In recent years, considerable theorizing and research has been devoted to the way we think about ourselves and others, and how these thought processes can affect both the way we see ourselves and our interpersonal relationships. An area of psychology known as "cognitive psychology" has been the source of exciting new insights into the way the human mind processes knowledge. The term "cognitive restructuring" applies to a procedure that involves observing and changing thought processes that may lure people into unhealthy thinking and self-defeating behavior. At least three different approaches to cognitive restructuring have been described, including the "cognitive therapeutic approaches" of Aaron Beck (1976) and David Burns (1980, 1989), the "rational-emotive therapy" of Albert Ellis (1984), and the "self-instructional training" of Donald Meichenbaum (1977). The basic idea behind each of these approaches is that changing the way we think (cognitive restructuring) can help improve how we feel about ourselves. Cognitive psychologists suggest that we can work toward accomplishing this end by (1) detecting maladaptive thought patterns, (2) becoming aware of their damaging impact, and (3) replacing them with more accurate and emotionally healthy thought patterns.

The cognitive approach I have found particularly useful in identifying and understanding how we may allow certain cognitive processes to lead us astray is the one developed by Beck (1976) and Burns (1980, 1989). A strength of this approach is, I feel, in its careful descriptive analysis of the sort of erroneous mental processing that, if not recognized, can keep people from upscaling their self-esteem and mental health status. Let's take a look at some of the cognitive pitfalls into which we sometimes fall.

Ten Cognitive Traps That Block Self-Growth

Although there are no doubt many more "traps" that can catch us up than the ones described here, Burns (1989), who was able to build from Beck's (1976) earlier work dealing with the way people cognitively process the affective content of their lives, identified ten rather common cognitive traps associated with self-defeating thinking. Do you recognize any of these traps in your own life?

1. *All-or-Nothing thinking:* This is seen most often among people who live in a black-or-white world; there are few shades of gray and many absolutes. Life events tend to be perceived as all good or all bad. A graduate student in one of my courses, who was accustomed to receiving all A's, received a B+ from me and concluded that now he was a "total failure." There was no room for error in his system. It is this kind of thinking that serves as one of the bases for perfectionism of a neurotic kind. It causes people to fear any mistake or imperfection because they so quickly jump to the conclusion that they are complete losers, inadequate, and worthless.

2. *Overgeneralization:* Here there is the tendency to see a single event as an ongoing, never-ending pattern of defeat. The tendency is kept alive with words like "always" or "never" when thinking about the event. A young man, for example, might be refused a date by the girl of his dreams and conclude: "I *always* get turned down. I'll *never* get a chance to go out with someone like her." By overgeneralizing the consequences of a single or small number of experiences, a person may unwittingly plant the seed of a self-fulfilling prophecy that comes true because he or she behaves in such a way as to *make* it come true.

3. *Mental filtering:* The basic process involved here is that of picking out a single negative detail about a situation or oneself and dwelling on it exclusively, a process that effectively reduces the possibility of seeing any of the positives. A teacher, for example, might receive 25 positive student evaluations and only three that are somewhat negative but wind up so disturbed by the three negatives that neither solace nor satisfaction is derived from the heavy positive feedback.

4. *Discounting the positive:* Those who do this are skillful in discounting positive experiences. These are the kind of people who, even in the face of doing well on something, are apt to say, "Anyone could have

done it." A person like this, upon receiving a compliment about his or her performance or appearance, might think privately, "You're just saying this to be nice." Even when the feedback is all positive, this person manages to find a way to discount it.

5. *Jumping to conclusions:* In this instance, a person jumps to a negative conclusion that is not justified by the available facts. Two common variations of this are *mind reading* (we arbitrarily conclude that someone feels negatively about us) and *fortune telling* (we assume and predict that what is ahead for us will turn out badly). It is a basic form of cognitive processing used by people who expect—and prepare for—the worst.

6. *Magnification or minimization:* This is sometimes referred to as the "binocular trick" because those who do this are either blowing things out of proportion or shrinking them. Magnification commonly occurs when a person looks at his or her own shortcomings or errors and catastrophizes their importance: "My God, how terrible I am!" However, when considering strengths, this same person may look at them as though viewing them through the wrong end of the binoculars, thus diminishing their importance.

7. *Emotional reasoning:* In this case, a person takes his or her emotions as the truth. The process goes something like this: "I feel dumb; therefore, I *am* dumb" or "I feel overwhelmed; therefore, I just can't do this job." Because things *feel* so negative, this person assumes they truly are. Procrastinators subject themselves to this sort of feeling a lot. Because they tell themselves that they really feel lousy when they think about what needs to be done, doing it seems even more impossible. Thus, putting off what needs to be done continues, and a vicious cycle of emotional reasoning is reinforced.

8. *Should statements:* These are the kind of statements people make when trying to motivate themselves to behave in certain ways. "I should clean the house, wash the car, do my homework, etc." "I shouldn't eat those sweets, stay up late, spend this money, etc." There are many *should* and *ought to's* in the lives of some people. "Should" statements tend to generate essentially negative self-feelings because they are constant reminders of having fallen short of one's own standards, reminders that generate feelings of shame, guilt, and self-loathing.

9. *Labeling and mislabeling:* Personal labeling is an extreme form of overgeneralization that creates a negative self-image based on one's errors. Instead of saying, "I made a mistake," a person says, "I'm a failure." Sentences beginning with "I'm a . . ." are usually signals that a person is about to attach a negative label on himself or herself.

Saying to oneself, "I hit a bad serve" is vastly different than concluding, "I'm a lousy tennis player."

10. *Personalization:* This distortion is a seedbed for guilt. A person who does this assumes unrealistic responsibility for the behavior of others. For example, when students fail to complete their homework or to do as well as might be expected, a teacher in this mode might conclude, "There must be something wrong with my teaching." A doctor whose patient develops lung cancer because of excessive smoking inwardly says, "I must be a poor doctor. I couldn't get him to drop the cigarette habit." Personalization leads to guilt because those who do this feel they have failed in their responsibility. They tend to confuse *influence* with *control* over others. There is a vast difference between feeling that we can influence others to behave in certain ways and thinking that we can control their behavior.

Positive Self-Talk: A Way to Avoid the Traps

It has been said that there's nothing wrong with talking to yourself, but if you should ever start answering back, then it's time to be concerned. Actually, this is not true. Although going around talking to yourself in public may cause people to wonder about you, holding an internal dialogue is not only very useful, but quite normal.

In fact, the inner conversations we have with ourselves can have a powerful effect on our emotional well-being and motivation. Developing an awareness of precisely what we are saying to ourselves and about ourselves can help us understand why we react the way we do to various people and events in our lives.

We have to be cautious not to confuse positive self-talk with mindless positive thinking, Pollyannish affirmations, or, worse, self-delusion. For example, if I were to tell myself that I'm not much good at games like *Trivial Pursuit,* my self-talk would be negative but not necessarily flawed or unhealthy. The cold truth of the matter is, I have trouble quickly recalling specific facts, names, and dates, the very talent it takes to enjoy a game of this sort. On the other hand, if I say I don't know anything, then I would fall into the cognitive traps of all-or-nothing thinking and overgeneralization. If I went further with my self-admonishments, I could very well fall into the cognitive trap of magnification, which would exaggerate the importance of my deficiency, and this could lead me to the trap of a strong "should" statement: "I should know more answers quickly." This could easily trigger feelings of guilt because I don't know more answers, and this may take me directly to the self-deprecating cognitive trap of labeling: "I'm really stupid."

There is a very large difference between my initial inner statement; "I'm not much good at games like *Trivial Pursuit*" and the final statement, "I'm really stupid." When we say things like the first statement to ourselves (and perhaps to others), it not only reflects accurately and honestly a deficiency we see in ourselves, but it leaves the door open to seeing our strengths in other areas. It is, after all, games like *Trivial Pursuit* with which we have trouble, not *all* games. Thus, we face up to a particular shortcoming rather than condemn our entire intellectual system.

A guiding tenet of the cognitive point of view is the idea that beliefs and thoughts, as reflected and represented by our words and assumptions, can have an enormous impact on our emotions, behavior, and state of mind. So by directly assaulting self-hindering thoughts and word patterns, we stand a good chance of significantly improving our emotional well-being and overall functioning.

Examples of Positive Self-Talk in Action

The words we use in our everyday interactions are outer expressions of the inner person. The sentences we string together are not only the *result* of our cognitive processing, but they very likely contribute significantly to *causing* the processing to be the way it is in the first place. In many ways, the brain is like a computer that takes in, stores, and retrieves information. Each brain is "programmed" to process information—especially personal and interpersonal content—in a certain way. Whereas a computer is programmed with numbers, the human computer is programmed by an endless stream of highly emotionalized thoughts, words, and experiences.

When we were very young, the programming was done mostly by our primary caretakers and other significant people in our lives. As we grew older, we unconsciously and unwittingly contributed to the content of the attitudes and beliefs we developed about ourselves and others through our own choice of words. We "hear" the words we say or think more than we hear anyone else's. It seems logical that what we hear coming from ourselves not only reflects our beliefs, but reinforces existing beliefs and plays a part in creating new ones.

Let's consider, as examples, two common expressions of self-talk that can be seen in practically everyone's life and briefly examine how each can be expressed in ways that are positive or negative, self-confirming or self-disconfirming. The two expressions that we'll consider are those that reflect choice versus helplessness and control versus noncontrol.

CHOICE SELF-TALK VERSUS HELPLESSNESS SELF-TALK

This kind of self-talk is perhaps the commonest of all. Its origins no doubt go back deep in our lives when we were not only young, but small, a combination guaranteed to underscore a very real sense of helplessness, a feeling that was experienced as "I can't." If our early life experiences were such that there were many things that we couldn't do because of various rules, injunctions, and lack of opportunity to make choices, then the "I can't" feeling and language was probably reinforced and strengthened. (I can't eat the food I want; I can't wear my choice of clothes; I can't go to bed when I want; I can't choose my own hairstyle; I can't have my own friends, etc.) How often, for example, do you hear people (including yourself) say, "I can't" to a request to do this or that?

You may find it insightful to make a list of those things you are likely to say "I can't" to. An illustrative list might look like this:

I can't lose weight.

I can't speak in front of large groups.

I can't go to bed as early as I would like.

I can't stand country music.

I can't make friends.

I can't say no when asked to do something.

I can't hold my breath for five minutes.

When you look at the list, the only real "I can't" is the last one. No one can hold his or her breath for five minutes. But all the rest *are* possible. Consider your own list of "I can'ts." How many of those "can'ts" are actually "won'ts"? What does it feel like to change the "I won't" to "I choose not to"?

Choice self-talk says "I won't" or "I choose not to." Helplessness self-talk says "I can't," unless it is, of course, something that really *can't* be done because of some physical limitation. You might say, "But I can't stop so-and-so from criticizing me." That is true, you can't, but even when we cannot control the other person's behavior we can choose how we will *react* to that person. Thus, though we "can't" stop another person's criticism of us, we can choose our response to the criticism. In this way, we keep the choice of positive self-talk alive and well, which is where our power is, and downgrade negative helplessness self-talk, which reinforces a sense of powerlessness. Criticism is something with which we all live. The idea is to listen to it nondefensively (who knows, there *could* be something to it), recognizing that it simply represents another person's point of view and not an automatic truth about ourselves. Criticism belongs to the critic; it becomes ours only if we accept it.

CONTROL SELF-TALK VERSUS NONCONTROL SELF-TALK

Control self-talk is easy to recognize. It tends to be unrelentingly critical, judgmental, and severe. It is the kind of self-talk that underscores the things that we "should," "ought," or "must" do. We're not talking here about the basic "shoulds" that are part of every society's rules of conduct and behavior (e.g., people should not kill, should not cheat, should not steal, etc.), but the "shoulds" that we use in a controlling, judgmental manner about ourselves. For example, how often do you find yourself thinking or saying:

I *should* be a better player.

I *should* have remembered her birthday.

I *ought* to be neater.

I *must* get going on that job.

I *have* to start writing that paper.

Can you hear the judgmental, critical tone in those controlling self-talk statements? It's not difficult to see how a sense of low self-worth and a certain level of guilt are maintained by that kind of negative self-talk. Notice the difference, however, when words like "choose," "prefer," "desire," "would like to," "wish," or "want to" are used:

I *would like* to be a better player. (Translation: Improvement is a goal I can shoot for. This is something I *desire* to accomplish.)

I *wish* I had remembered her birthday. (Translation: I own up to the fact that I was responsible for forgetting, and I would have *preferred* not to have forgotten.)

I *prefer* to be neater. (Translation: It would be to my advantage to be neater and I *choose not* to appear sloppy.)

I *want* to get that job done. (Translation: It will be advantageous for me to complete this assignment soon.)

I *choose* to start writing that paper. (Translation: This is something I *want* to do and I *prefer* to do it sooner than later.)

Whereas phrases like "I should" or "I must" deemphasize one's feelings of personal control and self-responsibility, phrases like "I would like to" or "I prefer" stress one's personal control over important life matters.

From a more cosmic point of view, I suppose it could be argued that the words we use in our everyday interactions really don't matter that much, that what really matters are those significant life events that have a huge impact on us. Life experiences involving, say, our successes, failures, loss of loved ones, and so forth do make a difference because of their potent emotional significance. Events like these are life's macroevents; they are powerful and they grab our total attention. The words and phrases we use when thinking or talking about ourselves are small by comparison. They have to be included among the many microevents of our lives, those little things that occur so fleetingly that they occur practically unnoticed. And yet, the words we use and the thoughts we have fill our heads all day long, a process which, over time, subtly program our minds to think and feel in certain ways. How we feel about ourselves is affected, in part, by what we say and how we think about ourselves, and what we say and how we think about ourselves is affected by how we feel about ourselves. It is a reciprocal process.

Choice self-talk and noncontrol self-talk reflect thought patterns and verbal modes that can be helpful in directing us toward a greater sense of personal control over our lives. The goal of developing an enlarged sense of personal control is not some Zen-like possibility that has no practical application to day-to-day functioning. Research related to stress and stress management, for example, has clearly shown that the people who are most likely to deal with the stress in their lives in healthy and effective ways are those who realize that they, not others, are in control of their lives (Alfred and Smith, 1989; Kobasa, 1982). Feelings of being in control (as opposed to feeling helpless) ranks right up along side of feelings of commitment (as opposed to feeling alienated), and challenge (as opposed to feeling threatened) when it comes to identifying those who are emotionally healthy, stress-resistant individuals.

Positive self-talk can help a person feel more in charge of his or her own life and also more responsible about, and for, his or her own behavior, both of which are ways to enhance self-concept and reduce the chances of falling into the cognitive traps discussed earlier.

As we conclude this section, I'm reminded of a saying I came across some time ago in a now forgotten source:

> *There are only two things*
> *you "have" to do in life.*
> *You "have to" die,*
> *and you "have to" live*
> *until you die.*
> *What happens in between*
> *is up to you.*

BEHAVIORS AND ATTITUDES ASSOCIATED WITH PSYCHOLOGICAL HEALTH

What kinds of "behaviors" and attitudes are we likely to see in psychologically healthy, balanced people? This is one of the questions I am asked most frequently when talking to my students and others about self-concept issues related to emotional health and interpersonal effectiveness. It is an important question, one that comes up often because it is helpful to have examples of the sorts of attitudes and behavior that can be found on the side of psychological well-being. The behaviors and attitudes I'm about to suggest are surely not the only ones associated with psychological health, but they are ones that, based on my reading of psychological research and clinical observations, tend to be seen frequently in the lives of emotionally intact individuals.

People who have reasonably self-accepting attitudes underscored by a positive sense of self-worth present a behavioral picture quite different from those who feel inadequate and inferior. An awareness of how emotionally together people respond to life may be useful for establishing guidelines for new behaviors. Although there are certainly variations from one individual to another and for the same individual among situations, psychologically healthy people can be characterized in the following 12 ways:

1. They tend to be *doers* rather than simply *talkers,* something that is distinctive about them in the way they conduct themselves at work and in their private lives. They seem to recognize that an approach to life that says, "*I* must do something" will always accomplish more than one that says, "Something must be done."

2. They retain confidence in their ability to deal with problems, even in the face of failures and setbacks. They do not conclude, "Because I failed, I am a failure," but are more likely to say, "I failed; I will try again and work even harder." They are people whose lives reflect the idea that a person who tries to do something and fails is on much more solid emotional footing than one who tries to do nothing and succeeds.

3. They have certain values and principles they believe in strongly and are willing to defend even in the face of strong group opinion; however, they feel personally secure enough to modify them if new experience and evidence suggest that they are in error. Although they may have firm beliefs, they tend to be flexibly adaptive, capable of change in the face of new evidence.

4. They feel equal to others *as people*—not superior or inferior—regardless of the differences in specific abilities, family backgrounds, or attitudes of others toward them. They are able to say, "You are more skilled than I in a specific endeavor, but I am as much a person as you," which is different from thinking, "You are more skilled than I; therefore, you are a better person." They are able to see that another individual's skills or abilities neither devalue nor elevate their own status as individuals.

5. They are willing and able to assume ultimate responsibility for their own lives. They do not look around for others to blame. They realize that *who* they are, *what* they do, and *where* they are, in terms of physical location and psychological status, are very largely the consequences of *their own choices.* They accept the idea that short of someone pointing a gun at their heads, no one can "make" them do anything without their own consent.

6. They are able to accept the idea (and admit to others) that they are capable of feeling and expressing a broad array of impulses and desires, ranging from being very angry to being very loving, from being very sad to being very happy, from feeling deep resentment to feeling great acceptance. It does not follow, however, that they *act* on all their feelings and desires.

7. They have come to terms with the idea that most people are neither for them or against them, but rather, are thinking about themselves. And they make their peace with the reality that no matter how much they try to please, some people are never going to love them or even

like them—an insight that enables them to have a more realistic view of relationships.

8. They know how important it is to have meaning in their lives, which they recognize as achievable only when a commitment has been made to something larger than their own egos, whether to their work, to loved ones, to fellow humans, or to some moral or religious concept, or some combination of those possibilities. They seem to understand that happiness grows out of the *meaning* in one's life; meaning does not grow out of happiness.

9. When it comes to interpersonal relationships they recognize that it is very difficult to find happiness with another person if they do not first find it in themselves.

10. They are able to enjoy themselves in a wide variety of activities involving work, play, creative self-expression, companionship, or just loafing. They are, in a sense, "masters of living." In the words of an unknown author: "They draw no sharp distinction between their work and their play, their labour and their leisure, their mind and their body, their education and their recreation. They hardly know what they are doing and leave it to others to determine whether they are working or playing. To themselves they always seem to be doing both."

11. Samuel Johnson once observed, "It is not within our power to be fond, but it is within our power to be kind." Psychologically healthy people seem to make frequent use of this "power." It seems a natural by-product of liking themselves, looking for the best in others, and feeling that this world and this life, whatever the shortcomings, are really pretty good things after all.

12. It is characteristic of healthy people to take some risks now and then. They seem to recognize that to get what they want, to grow beyond where they are, requires reaching into the unknown and testing themselves in new ways. I think the idea here is best summed up by an unknown author in the following verse titled, simply . . .

Risks

To laugh is to risk appearing the fool.
To weep is to risk appearing sentimental.
To reach out to another is to risk involvement.
To expose feelings is to risk exposing your true self.
To place your ideas and dreams before a crowd is to risk their loss.
To love is to risk not being loved in return.
To live is to risk dying.
To try is to risk failure.
But risks must be taken because the greatest hazard in life is to risk nothing.

*The person who risks nothing does nothing, has nothing, and is
nothing.*
*He may avoid suffering and sorrow, but he cannot learn, feel, change,
grow, or live.*
Chained by his certitudes, he is a slave; he has forfeited his freedom.
Only a person who risks is free.

I do not mean to suggest that a person has to fit all 12 of these characterizations
in order to be a psychologically healthy person. As mentioned many times in
this volume, we humans are far too complex to be reduced to any particular
series of statements about our emotional health or lack of it. Rather, consider
these characterizations as a broad framework within which you may see a
reflection of your behavior and, in particular, aspects of yourself that you may
want to change or improve.

I think that there are many ways to capture the essence of what makes
psychologically healthy people healthy in the first place. Although we are not
likely to find all of these qualities in any given person, I suspect we may find
more operative expressions of them in emotionally healthy people.

Whatever path we choose to express our potential for a full and contribu-
tory life, it is usually true that the motivation for doing this is more lasting and
the feeling of self-satisfaction more attainable when we make improvement
rather than perfection our goal.

IN PERSPECTIVE

Psychologically healthy people tend to be upbeat, positive individuals who
manage to be that way without projecting unrealistic Pollyannish attitudes. On
the whole, they see themselves as more liked than disliked, able, and worthy.
Not only do they feel that they are people of value, but they also behave as
though they were. Indeed, it is in this factor of how people see themselves that
we are likely to find the most outstanding differences between high and low
self-images. It is not the people who feel that they are liked and wanted and
acceptable and able who fill our prisons and mental hospitals. Rather, it is
those who feel deeply inadequate, unliked, unwanted, unacceptable, and unable. It is more and more apparent that self-acceptance and personal happiness
have a lot to do with accepting others and enjoying what one is and what one
has, maintaining a balance between expectations and achievements.

Self and self-other understanding are not mystical ideals or unreachable
goals. Social feeling, empathic listening, honesty, and an understanding of
how we use our defense mechanisms are all ways to help develop greater
self-awareness and a more positive self-image.

A way almost guaranteed to bar greater self-acceptance and self-esteem is
to substitute the good opinion of others for one's own lack of self-approval. As
long as a person needs the approval of others for his or her own feelings of
self-worth, that person will usually lack the daring to explore beyond what
other people deem important.

At the extremes of the self-acceptance continuum are the narcissistic personality at one end and the inferiority-ridden person at the other. Whereas narcissistic people overvalue their worth with a deluded sense of self-importance, inferior-feeling people undervalue their worth with an exaggerated sense of personal failure. Unless they learn to view themselves and others' responses to them more realistically, positive self-esteem will remain an elusive quality.

The willingness to work, coupled with a certain amount of courage, may be a potent antidote to the debilitating effects of a negative self-image and low self-esteem. The willingness to work hard can help a person move against the inertia of laziness, and behaving courageously can help one face the fear of the unknown. Because enhancing self-esteem usually means successfully accomplishing those things we had some doubts about being able to do in the first place, the capacity for work and courage are essential for getting us started and keeping us going.

Self-esteem is a fragile and tender quality. Because it reflects how we feel about ourselves, we are ever watchful for ways to maintain and protect its delicate structure. One way for doing so is by using the principle of selectivity. Thus, people are able to choose *those* friends, pay attention to *those* facts, and interpret the world according to *those* values and standards that are most congenial to their own needs and point of view. In this way, people can to some extent see and hear what they *want* to see and hear. As long as they can interpret their experiences within the framework of their own selective perceptions, those experiences, whatever they may be, are subject to each individual's own personal filtration system. Thus, hateful people, whose sense of worth may be derived from being able to "spot" trouble, may look on the world and see malicious acts; loving people, whose personal esteem is nourished by private, charitable giving, may look on that same world and see benevolent deeds. And each group is correct in its perceptions. We do not just look at the world and perceive what is there; rather, it is what we add to or subtract from the world around us that determines what we "see."

We have a great tendency to view what we call "reality" through a lens of our own making and conditioning; our view of the world is a projection of the mental map we carry inside our heads. Some people are willing to modify the map when they see that it does not agree with the outside territory; others insist their map is correct, distorting the territory to make it fit. Choosing to interact with people who can be honest with us, who do not always tell us what we would like to hear, is a good way of allowing our perceptions of "reality" (which is usually our version of the truth) to be challenged now and then. Subjecting our mental maps to this kind of scrutiny from time to time, we may discover that the opinions we thought were holding were really holding *us,* in one fixed place.

Listening to our critics, although sometimes painful, can be educational and revealing, particularly if we're careful not to fall into the trap of all-or-nothing thinking, or over-generalizations, or magnification, or any of the other cognitive pitfalls that can lead us to negative, self-condemning conclusions. It is not just what other people say to us and about us that can encourage a negative self-concept, but it is also what we say and think about ourselves that can get us into self-image trouble. The human brain is like a computer in the sense that it can be "programmed" to function in very positive or quite negative ways. Avoiding the cognitive traps discussed in this chapter along with using more choice self-talk rather than control self-talk are useful ways to encourage the kind of positive mental processing seen among psychologically healthy people.

Our feelings about ourselves are *learned* responses. Sometimes bad feelings have to be unlearned and new feelings acquired. This is not always easy, but it is possible. Sometimes it means "taking stock" of oneself—a kind of personal inventory. Or it may mean baring oneself to another person—a friend or therapist—so that the possibility for honest evaluation and feedback is more probable. Certainly, it means changing those things that one can and accepting those one cannot.

If, as parents or as professional persons, we have a basic understanding of how a healthy self is developed and of the conditions and interpersonal relations that nurture it, we are in a position to move toward *creating* those conditions and interpersonal relationships most conducive to positive mental health.

Perhaps, rather than working so fervently on trying to change others, the best place to begin is with ourselves.

The idea here is conveyed nicely, I feel, in a fable I've always liked. It goes like this:

There was a very wise old person who lived in the hills. It was rumored that this wise person, who came to be called Wisdom, knew all there was to know about living and life. One day, a young boy and girl, who thought *they* knew it all, decided to show Wisdom up. They each found a small sparrow and, holding their birds lightly, carried them up the mountain to where Wisdom lived. It was their plan that, holding the sparrows behind their backs they would ask Wisdom a single question: Since you are supposed to be all-knowing, tell us whether the birds we are carrying are alive or dead. If Wisdom said, "dead," they would take the fluttering sparrows from behind their backs and show them to be alive. If he answered, "alive," they would crush the sparrows in their hands and then produce them dead. Laughing inwardly at their devious plan to outwit Wisdom, they asked the question. Wisdom sat quietly and looked deep into their eyes. Wisdom's face gathered a small smile and in a knowing and loving voice said to their youthful innocence: "The answer, my children, is in your hands."

QUESTIONS FOR STUDY, REVIEW, AND REFLECTION

1. Explain in your own words why and how "observing what our neighbors are doing" can be a useful way to understand oneself and enhance self-esteem. Give examples of how this process might work.

2. How would you explain the difference between direct and indirect self-acceptance? Give examples of how each works.

3. Why is it that people who tend to be low in self-acceptance also lean toward the low side when it comes to self-esteem? Can you explain why low self-esteem and high prejudice tend to go together?

4. If you see yourself as a person who rather consistently tries to please others and who more often than not puts others' needs and desires ahead of your own, but you do not like doing this so often, try this simple experiment: For two days, concentrate on doing the things that *you* feel are important rather than what you feel others want you to do. Then, ask yourself, "What have I learned?"

   If, however, you see yourself as a person who more often than not does what *you* want to do and who does not pay that much mind to what others want, try this experiment: For two consecutive days, put your own needs and point of view aside and pay attention to others. Then, ask yourself, "What have I learned?"

5. Explain why the "self-acceptance" of a narcissistic person is not particularly healthy.

6. What behavioral signs would you look for in order to determine whether or not a person was suffering from an inferiority complex? Can you explain why a person who has a sense of inferiority might display symptoms of neurotic perfectionism?

7. Think of two or three things (events, achievements, relationships, etc.) in your life that you really want but are fearful, for whatever reasons, of trying to get. If you were to muster up the necessary work and courage to try to get those things, what do you suppose would happen? What is the *worst* that could happen? What might you learn about yourself in the process?

8. How would you explain the psychodynamics of selective perception? That is, what is selective perception? How does it work? What is the basic purpose of this mechanism?

9. How does our selection of personal standards, interpersonal selectivity, and situational selectivity work to protect self-esteem? Give some examples of how, in each instance, you have used those processes in your own behalf. What restrictions are there on the selectivity of a person's choices in life?

10. If someone were to ask you how the "cognitive restructuring" ideas developed by cognitive psychologists help a person maintain a positive self-concept, how would you respond?

11. What is it about a "cognitive trap" that makes it a trap in the first place? If you had to develop three or four general principles that would help explain how and why "cognitive traps" are harmful to

people's self-esteem, what would they be? What cognitive traps have *you* fallen into most often?

12. Suppose you were to make a presentation on the following topic to a group of your peers: "Positive Self-Talk: How and Why it Can Contribute to Healthy Psychological Growth." What are the major ideas you would want to be sure to discuss in your presentation? What examples of negative and positive self-talk from your own life can you use to illustrate the points you want to make?

13. Twelve examples of psychologically healthy behavior were listed at the end of this chapter. As you think about what psychological health means to you, what would you add to that list (or delete from it)?

REFERENCES

Adler, A. *Social Interest: A Challenge to Mankind.* New York: Capricorn Books, 1964 (Originally published, 1938.)

Alfred, K. D., and Smith, T. W. "The Hardy Personality: Cognitive and Physiological Responses to Evaluative Threat." *Journal of Personality and Social Psychology,* 1989, *56:* 257–266.

Archer, R. L., and Burleson, J. A. "The Effects of Timing of Self-Disclosure on Attraction and Reciprocity." *Journal of Personality and Social Psychology,* 1980, *38:* 120–130.

Baumgardner, A. H. "To Know Oneself Is to Like Oneself: Self-Certainty and Self-Affect." *Journal of Personality and Social Psychology,* 1990, *58:* 1062–1072.

Beck, A. T. *Cognitive Therapy and the Emotional Disorders.* New York: International Universities Press, 1976.

Buber, M. *I and Thou.* New York: Charles Scribner's Sons, 1958.

Burns, D. D. *Feeling Good: The New Mood Therapy.* New York: W. Morrow, 1980.

Burns, D. D. *The Feeling Good Handbook.* New York: W. Morrow, 1989.

Crandall, J. E. "Adler's Concept of Social Interest: Theory, Measurement, and Implications for Adjustment." *Journal of Personality and Social Psychology,* 1980, *39:* 481–495.

Crocker, J., and Schwartz, I. "Prejudice and Ingroup Favoritism in a Minimal Group Situation: Effects of Self-Esteem." *Personality and Social Psychology Bulletin,* 1985, *11:* 379–386.

Crocker, J., Thompson, L. L., McGraw, K. M., and Ingerham, C. "Downward Comparison, Prejudice, and Evaluations of Others: Effects of Self-Esteem and Threat." *Journal of Personality and Social Psychology,* 1987, *52:* 907–916.

Diagnostic and Statistical Manual of Mental Disorders, 3rd ed. (DSM-III). American Psychiatric Association, Washington, D. C.: 1980.

Driscoll, R. "Self-Criticism: Analysis and Treatment." *Advances in Descriptive Psychology,* 1981, *I:* 321–355.

Ellis, A. "Rational-Emotive Therapy," in R. Corsini (Ed.). *Current Psychotherapies,* 2nd ed. Itasca, Ill.: F. E. Peacock, 1984.

Epstein, S., and Feist, G. J. "Relation Between Self- and Other-Acceptance and Its Moderation by Identification." *Journal of Personality and Social Psychology,* 1988, *54:* 309–315.

Franklin, B. *The Autobiography of Benjamin Franklin with Illustrations.* Boston: Houghton Mifflin, 1906.

Fromm, E. *Beyond the Chains of Illusion.* New York: Pocket Books, 1962.

Gallup, G. G., Jr., and Suarz, S. "Animal Research Versus the Care and Maintenance of Pets: The Names Have Been Changed, But the Results Remain the Same." *American Psychologist,* August, 1985, p. 968.

Gough, H., Fioravanti, M., and Lazzari, R. "Some Implications of Self Versus Ideal-Self Congruence on the Revised Adjective Check List." *Journal of Personality and Social Psychology,* 1983, *44:* 1214–1220.

Greenberg, J., and Pyszczynski, T. "Compensatory Self-Inflation: A Response to the Threat to Self-Regard of Public Failure." *Journal of Personality and Social Psychology,* 1985, *49:* 273–280.

Hamachek, D. "Psychodynamics of Normal and Neurotic Perfectionism." *Psychology: A Journal of Human Behavior,* 1978, *15:* 27–33.

Hamachek, D. *Encounters With Others; Interpersonal Relationships and You.* New York: Holt, Rinehart and Winston, 1982.

Hearings Before the Select Committee on Presidential Campaign Activities of the United States Senate, 93rd Congress, First Session, 1973, p. 957.

Hendrick, S. S. "Self-Disclosure and Marital Satisfaction." *Journal of Personality and Social Psychology,* 1981, *40:* 1150–1159.

Jourard, S. M. "Healthy Personality and Self-Disclosure." *Mental Hygiene,* 1963, *43:* 499–507.

Jourard, S. M. *The Transparent Self* (rev. ed.). New York: Van Nostrand Reinhold, 1971.

Kobasa, S. C. "The Hardy Personality: Toward a Social Psychology of Stress and Health," in G. Sanders and J. Suls (Eds.), *Social Psychology of Health and Illness.* Hillsdale, N. J.: Erlbaum, 1982.

Lewicki, P. "Self-Image Bias in Person Perception." *Journal of Personality and Social Psychology,* 1983, *45:* 384–393.

Luginbuhl, J. E. R. "Role of Choice and Outcome on Feelings of Success and Estimates of Ability." *Journal of Personality and Social Psychology,* 1972, *22:* 121–127.

Markus, H., Smith, J., and Moreland, R. L. "Role of the Self-Concept in the Perception of Others." *Journal of Personality and Social Psychology,* 1985, *49:* 1494–1512.

Maslow, A. H. "Some Basic Propositions of a Growth and Self-Actualization Psychology," in A. W. Combs (Ed.), *Perceiving, Behaving, Becoming.* Association for Supervision and Curriculum Development Yearbook, Washington, D. C.: National Education Association, 1962, p. 48.

McClelland, D. A. *Human Motivation.* Glenview, Ill.: Scott, Foresman, 1985.

Millon, T. *Disorders of Personality: DSM-III: Axis II.* New York: Wiley, 1981.

Mahoney, M. J., and Avener, M. "Psychology of the Elite Athlete: An Exploratory Study." *Cognitive Therapy and Research,* 1977, *I:* 135–141.

Meichenbaum, D. *Cognitive-Behavior Modification: An Integrative Approach.* New York: Plenum, 1977.

Neisser, U. "John Dean's Memory: A Case Study." *Cognition,* 1981, *9:* 1–22.

Peck, M. S. *The Road Less Traveled.* New York: Simon & Schuster, 1978.

Powers, T. A., and Zuroff, D. C. "Interpersonal Consequences of Overt Self-Criticism: A Comparison with Neutral and Self-Enhancing Presentations of Self." *Journal of Personality and Social Psychology,* 1988, *54:* 1054–1062.

Putney, S., and Putney, G. T. *The Adjusted American: Normal Neuroses in the Individual and Society.* New York: Harper & Row, 1964.

Reik, T. *Listening with the Third Ear.* New York: Grove Press, 1948.

Rogers, C. R., and Roethlisberger, F. J. "Barriers and Gateways to Communication." *Harvard Business Review,* July-August, 1952, pp. 28–35.

Rosenberg, M. *Occupations and Values.* New York: The Free Press, 1957.

Rosenberg, M. "Psychological Selectivity in Self-Esteem Formation," in C. W. Sherif and M. Sherif (Eds.), *Attitude, Ego-Involvement and Change.* New York: Wiley, 1967.

Rosenberg, M. *Concerning the Self.* New York: Basic Books, 1979.

Shrauger, J. S. "Self-Esteem and Reactions to being Observed by Others." *Journal of Personality and Social Psychology,* 1972, *23:* 192–200.

Strube, M. J., and Roemmele, L. A. "Self-Enhancement, Self-Assessment, and Self-Evaluative Task Choice." *Journal of Personality and Social Psychology,* 1985, *49:* 481–993.

Sullivan, H. S. *Conceptions of Modern Psychiatry.* Washington, D. C.: William Alanson White Psychiatric Foundation, 1947.

Tolstedt, B. E., and Stokes, J. P. "Self-Disclosure Intimacy, and the Depenetration Process." *Journal of Personality and Social Psychology,* 1984, *46:* 84–90.

Wills, T. A. "Downward Comparison Principles in Social Psychology." *Psychological Bulletin,* 1981, *90:* 245–271.

Wylie, R. *The Self Concept,* Vol. I (rev. ed.). Lincoln, Neb.: University of Nebraska Press, 1974.

Appendix

SELF-CONCEPT AND SELF-ESTEEM INVENTORIES

There are literally hundreds of inventories and tests of various types on the market that are designed to assess self-concept and self-esteem, either from one's own point of view or someone else's. This is a very brief sampling and description of some of the inventories that are available and where to send for review copies. The ones listed here happen to be ones with which I have some familiarity and I included them to give you an idea of their range. There are many others. (For extensive reviews and listings of various tests and inventories in all arenas of human behavior, including personality and self-concept, you will find the *Mental Measurement Yearbook,* published by the University of Nebraska Press, to be quite useful.)

Behavior Academic Self-Esteem (S. Coopersmith & R. Gilberts): This is an observational rating scale that assesses the academic self-esteem of children from preschool (age 4) through eighth grade. It can be filled out by a teacher, parent, or professional who has access to direct observation of the child. The scale assesses student initiative, social attention, success and failure, social attraction, and self-confidence.
Publisher: Consulting Psychological Press, P.O. Box 60070, Palo Alto, CA, 94306

Children's Self-Concept Scale (E. V. Piers & G. Harris): This is a simple rating scale of 80 items composed of statements to which children respond "Yes" or "No"—for example, "I am a happy person," "I am shy," "I am clever." It is a wide-ranging scale covering physical appearance, social behavior, academic status, depreciation, dissatisfaction and contentment with self, with statements divided equally between high and low reflections of self-concept. Widely used and easy to interpret, this scale provides quick insights into children's self-perceptions. It is appropriate for 8–16-year-olds.
Publisher: Western Psychological Services, 12031 Wilshire Blvd., Los Angeles, CA, 90025

Coopersmith Self-Esteem Inventories (S. Coopersmith): These inventories are designed to measure attitudes toward the self in social, academic, and personal contexts. Supported by research on thousands of subjects, they show

significant relationships to academic achievement and personal satisfaction in school and adult life. The school form is used for 8–15-year-olds and the adult form is used for those age 16 and above.
Publisher: Psychological Assessment Resources, Inc., P.O. Box 98, Odessa, FL, 33556

Inferred Self-Concept Scale (E. L. McDaniel): This paper-pencil inventory of 30 items contains statements that describe various behaviors. A teacher or counselor rates these behaviors on a 5-point scale based on observations of the child being evaluated. Assessment of self-concept is inferred from this behavior profile with the aid of standardized scoring and interpretation. The inventory should be administered by a teacher or counselor familiar with the child. It is appropriate for students in grades 1–6.
Publisher: Western Psychological Services, 12031 Wilshire Blvd., Los Angeles, CA, 90025

The Offer Self-Image Questionnaire for Adolescents (D. Offer): This brief self-report measure is designed to be used with teenagers 13–19 years old. The inventory is comprised of 11 scales organized into 5 categories: the psychological self, the sexual self, the social self, family relationships, and the coping self. Widely used with over 10,000 adolescents, this is an excellent and quick measure of adolescent self-concept.
Obtained through: Dr. Daniel Offer, Michael Reese Hospital and Medical Center, Lake Shore Dr. at 31st St., Chicago, IL, 60616

Personal Orientation Inventory (E. L. Shostrom): The purpose of this inventory is to measure values and behaviors important in the development of actualizing persons. It was designed with Maslow's theory of self-actualization in mind and assesses such qualities as spontaneity, self-regard, capacity for intimate contact, existentiality, and view of human kind. This inventory is widely used to measure one's potential for "self-actualization." It is appropriate for use in grades 10–12 and with adults.
Publisher: Educational and Industrial Testing Service, P.O. Box 7234, San Diego, CA, 92107

Primary Self-Concept Inventory (D. G. Muller & R. Leonetti): This is a paper-pencil verbal test of 20 items that evaluates social, personal, and intellectual self-concepts of preschool and early elementary school children. (Because of the difficulty of accurately assessing young children, this is one of the few inventories designed for this age group.)
Publisher: Teaching Resources Corporation, 50 Pond Park Road, Hingham, MA, 02043

A Self-Appraisal Scale for Teachers (H. Wilson): This inventory is designed to help teachers make a self-appraisal of classroom performance by using ratings in six areas: teacher as a person, teacher as a specialist and educator, teacher's relations with students, course content, classroom performance, and the way

teachers feel they are perceived by students. It is self-administered and, if taken honestly, a source of valuable feedback for a teacher.
Publisher: Administrative Research Associates, Inc., Irvine Town Center, Box 4211, Irvine, CA, 92644

Self-Perception Inventory (A. T. Soares & L. M. Soares): There are three forms of this inventory, each designed for a different group: a) student forms for grades 1–12, b) adult forms for high school students and adults, and c) teacher forms for teachers and student teachers. Each form is designed to assess how subjects see themselves, how they see others, and how others (classmates, teachers, parents, or supervising teachers, depending on the forms) see them. It provides a look at the self from a wide variety of perspectives and is easily administered, completed, and scored.
Obtained through: Soares Associates, 111 Teeter Rock Rd., Trumbull, CT, 06611

The Tennessee Self-Concept Scale (W. H. Fitts): This scale of 100 items consists of self-descriptive statements that people use to rate themselves in terms of a variety of identity issues, feelings, and behaviors. It is a widely used and popular inventory for those age 12 and above.
Publisher: Western Psychological Services, 12031 Wilshire Blvd., Los Angeles, CA, 90025

NAME INDEX

SUBJECT INDEX